SEA COBRA

SEA COBRA

ADMIRAL HALSEY'S TASK FORCE
AND THE GREAT PACIFIC TYPHOON

BUCKNER F. MELTON, JR.

THE LYONS PRESS
Guilford, Connecticut
An imprint of The Globe Pequot Press

The Lyons Press is an imprint of The Globe Pequot Press.

10 9 8 7 6 5 4 3 2 1

Printed in the United States of America

ISBN: 978-1-59228-978-3

Library of Congress Cataloging-in-Publication Data is available on file.

To the veterans of Typhoons Cobra and Viper,
living and dead,
and to all members of the United States Navy
this volume is respectfully dedicated.

Contents

In the six hundredth year of Noah's life, in the second month, the seventeenth day of the month, the same day were all the fountains of the great deep broken up, and the windows of heaven were opened.

—Genesis 7:11

The motion of the ship was extravagant. Her lurches had an appalling helplessness: she pitched as if taking a header into a void, and seemed to find a wall to hit every time. . . . The gale howled and scuffled about gigantically in the darkness, as though the entire world were one black gully. At certain moments the air streamed against the ship as if sucked through a tunnel with a concentrated solid force of impact that seemed to lift her clean out of the water and keep her up for an instant with only a quiver running through her from end to end. And then she would begin her tumbling again as if dropped back into a boiling cauldron.

—Joseph Conrad, "Typhoon"

The world's arena remains, to this hour, somewhat too big for the most ambitious human contrivances. The fact is, a typhoon, just one little racing whirlpool of air in one insignificant corner of ocean, can be too big.

—Herman Wouk, The Caine Mutiny

SEA COBRA

The Fleet

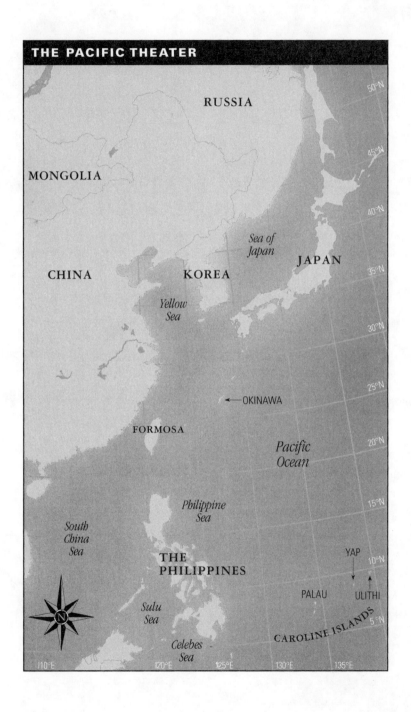

THE PACIFIC THEATER

RUSSIA

MONGOLIA

CHINA

KOREA

Sea of
Japan

JAPAN

Yellow
Sea

50°N

45°N

40°N

35°N

30°N

25°N

←— OKINAWA

FORMOSA

Pacific
Ocean

20°N

Philippine
Sea

15°N

South
China
Sea

THE
PHILIPPINES

YAP

10°N

PALAU

ULITHI

Sulu
Sea

CAROLINE ISLANDS

5°N

Celebes
Sea

N

110°E

120°E

125°E

130°E

135°E

A TROPICAL MIDNIGHT, FAR OUT IN THE PACIFIC.

The continents are far distant, so remote as to seem nonexistent. The great ocean depths, their swells rolling beneath an infinite sky, lie cradled in darkness. Only the stars prevent this world from being totally black — stars by the thousands, winking down on a seemingly endless ocean whose waters softly gurgle and sigh.

But destruction, not creation, moves upon the face of these waters. Massive, unseen, it moves steadily through the dusk, stirring up long, deep trails of phosphorescence as it passes, waiting for the dawn to come.

Gradually, as the hours pass, the dark begins to recede, and as it does, colossal gray shapes begin to emerge from the void, larger than any leviathan. A red-orange balloon soars slowly above the horizon, shimmers of heat preceding it and distorting the atmosphere, and grayness transmutes into brilliant, sunlit luster with bright-enough glints from the wave tops to sting the eye. At last the daylight reveals the otherness that has lain in the night waiting quietly. Not a single ship, not a few, not a dozen, but hundreds, gray and businesslike in the brilliance, but majestic for all of their drabness.

It is the core, the heart, of a naval armada — the most potent armada the world has ever seen, the greatest concentration of firepower in all of human history. It is sometimes called Murderers' Row, and by other nicknames too, though its official name is just as well known in the annals of war. It is Task Force 38, the main striking arm of the United States Navy's Third Fleet.

It had been years in the building. More than two decades earlier, the treaties signed at the Washington Naval Conference had emasculated the world's greatest navies in a futile effort at arms control. Throughout the 1920s and for most of the 1930s, America's navy languished. But as armed conflict smoldered in Asia and Europe, the United States bestirred itself, belatedly starting a naval buildup. For a year and a half after Pearl Harbor, the Pacific Fleet hung on grimly, only a shadow of what it had been before the attack, and only a shadow of what it needed to be. Then, by the summer of 1943, ship after ship began sliding down the ways from Bath, Maine, to Oakland, California, in ever-increasing numbers.

Now, here, a thousand miles south of Tokyo, the payoff cruised on glistening waters, available, ready, waiting. No fleet ever to put to sea had remotely equaled the striking power collected in this anonymous patch of ocean in September of 1944. A long heritage stood behind these hulls, a heritage of watery battles to determine the fate and very existence of empires. Many of the vessels were battleships: *Alabama*, *South Dakota*, *Iowa*, always named after states, direct descendants of the ships of the line that had ruled the seas since before the days of Trafalgar and Nelson. But Lord Nelson could not have begun to imagine a modern battleship's power. The ships of the *Iowa* class, three of which were with this task force, could throw shells weighing as much as automobiles at targets more than twenty miles distant, at well beyond the speed of sound. A full broadside of these shells could lay waste a plot of land the size of a football field, or obliterate an enemy warship as if it had never existed. The *Iowa*s, potent and fast, were at the pinnacle of battleship design, avenging angels of the vessels sunk at Pearl Harbor, and the ships of the *North Carolina* and *South Dakota* classes were nearly as lethal.

For all of their majesty, though, the battleships were no longer the stars they had been in earlier years. The war had shown that fighters and bombers launched from aircraft carriers could be weapons even more deadly than the huge rifled guns that battleships carried to sea, and they had ten times the range of those guns. It had been carrier-based planes, flying nearly two hundred miles, that had severely or mortally damaged eight out of eight battleships in the infamous December 7 attack. In the wake of that rout, stunned battleship men might have dazedly protested that the Pearl Harbor Raid proved nothing, that it hadn't been a fair fight, that the big-gun dreadnoughts were still viable weapons systems, but that excuse lasted barely three days. On the tenth of December, Japanese planes caught HMS *Prince of Wales* and *Repulse*, two veteran heavy hitters of the Royal Navy, in the open sea off Malaysia. The ships, at action stations and fully ready for combat, pumped massive amounts of antiaircraft (AA) fire into the sky, to the tune of sixty thousand rounds per minute by *Prince of Wales* alone. For all that, they lasted only three hours, not much longer than Pearl Harbor's sleeping battleships.[1] The day of airpower had indisputably come.

Thus it was carriers that formed the heart of Task Force (TF) 38. For the first year and a half of the war, America had never had more than two or three primitive flattops of prewar design to cover the whole Pacific, and sometimes only one. But then the *Essex*-class fleet carriers began to slide down the ways, arriving in Pearl in ever-greater numbers. Now there were eight of them in the task force, each one dwarfing anything Japan had ever produced. A single *Essex*-class ship had nearly three acres of flight deck space and room enough for almost a hundred planes. And the *Essex* ships weren't alone; they were accompanied by a half dozen lighter and smaller carriers of the *Independence* class, which could also deliver a serious punch. These classes of vessels, *Independence* and *Essex*, were the famous "fast carriers" that were making headlines back home in America while taking the war ever more deeply into what only recently had been Japanese waters.[2]

There were other ships, too, including heavy and light cruisers, which sacrificed the protection of armor for an extra measure of speed, the better to overtake enemy merchant ships and blast them with medium-caliber guns of six to eight inches. Such, at least, was the theory. But just as the use of battleships had changed in this war, so too had the employment of cruisers. The primary role of both was to protect the carriers rather than to seek out enemy battleships or merchant vessels. They did other things, too, of course, such as shore bombardment; but in Task Force 38, their first job was to guard the carriers.

The fleet submarines were also involved. Even more than the carriers, they were taking the fight to the enemy, sinking thousands of tons of merchant shipping each month, slowly robbing Japan of everything from fuel oil to food to munitions, all the things a nation needed to wage modern, industrial war.

But even the subs served the carriers; when the fighters and bombers and torpedo planes sortied, whether against Japanese warships or targets on land,
some inevitably didn't come back, either because of enemy action or of
something as mundane as an engine oil leak. Whenever that happened and
a plane had to ditch, a sub would be there on lifeguard duty, waiting, with
luck, to pick up the downed pilot. The planes were expendable; by 1944 the
United States was churning out upward of fifty thousand a year. Pilots were
more valuable, and, what was more, the knowledge that lifeguards were there
did a lot to boost the flyers' morale.

Then there were the tenders, the oilers, the munitions ships. There were
usually the amphibious warfare ships, landing ships of various sizes—LSTs,
LSDs, LCIs, and many others,—although for now these ships were elsewhere,
serving farther south with the U.S. Seventh Fleet. And, of course, there were
the destroyers, destroyers by the dozen, and destroyer escorts (DE) too.

"When I die," Lord Nelson once said while pursuing an enemy fleet, trying to find it with scout ships too few in number, "you will find this want of
frigates graven upon my heart."[3] He was referring to the Royal Navy's work-
horse. Smaller and faster than a ship of the line, a frigate was a jack of all
trades: commerce raider and cruiser, sometimes a transport or supply ship,
but always one with a mouthful of teeth. The frigate was too light to stand in
the line of battle and slug it out with the heaviest warships; still, she was heavily armed, and the navy never ran out of things for her to do. In many ways
the modern destroyer was the heir to frigate.[4]

While the largest American battleships displaced forty-five thousand tons
at full load, and the fleet carriers thirty-three thousand, destroyers weighed in
at something closer to two thousand. The *Essex*-class carrier had a complement
of three thousand men, an average destroyer less than a tenth as many. But destroyers had a certain panache that made up for their lack of size. They were
swift and highly maneuverable, usually scorning harbor tugs when it came to
mooring or putting to sea. They had versatile, capable weaponry. Their main
batteries, usually four or five guns of the five-inch variety, had a range of several miles; they also came well armed with light machine guns, "twenties" and
"forties," for antiaircraft work. They had batteries of torpedoes and depth
charges, which, together with the guns, made them a dangerous threat to everything from battleships to submarines, including lumbering merchantmen. And

they could move. The "fast carriers" and "fast battleships" of Third Fleet could, with good seas and a fair wind, travel at thirty knots or maybe a bit more, but a good modern destroyer running full-out could reach past the midthirties and turn sharply enough to run circles around the rest of the fleet.[5]

Of course, the destroyers were no luxury liners. Even the modern ones of the *Fletcher* and *Sumner* classes that were well represented in Task Force 38 were small and cramped. And because they were small, heavy weather could toss them around. But they tended to be seaworthy craft, especially if properly handled. And as the backbone of the fleet's antisubmarine screens, they played a vital role.

The destroyers, and the battleships and the carriers and all of the other ships here, had been designed to do a five-thousand-year-old job: to project military force across a body of water. In the earliest days of humanity, when the water was a river or lake, or perhaps a small sea, that water was at the outset a barrier, an obstacle. Then with the advance of technology and the advent of oars and sails, the barrier could become a highway, and a cheap one at that. But as commerce began to flow over the waters, it became a ripe target for pirates and foreign communities. To protect that commerce, navies were born. And navies, in turn, came to pose a threat to enemy shores.

Over the years, with the growth of ambition, people tackled larger and larger bodies of water, from the Nile to the Red Sea to the Mediterranean to the North Atlantic to beyond. The nations that developed the technology to let them harness the elements blossomed at last into empires, empires mightier than land-bound nations could build. The greatest ancient land power—Rome—became the ruler of the classical world not so much because of its power on land as because of its conquest of the Mediterranean. A thousand years after its fall, the Spanish and Dutch built imperial realms that spanned the world's oceans; then England emerged as the greatest sea power in history, using her naval and merchant fleets to assimilate a quarter of the globe's land, a quarter of its people, and all of its oceans.

But even England had never achieved what was happening in the Pacific in 1944. For decades, Japan and the United States had faced each other uneasily across the world's largest sea, a sea vast enough to swallow whole continents, a sea surrounded by some of the world's richest land and resources. As the twentieth century dawned, both of these nations were industrialized, expansionist, and aggressive in various ways. Japan had come late to the game, modernizing herself after the visit of Commodore Matthew C. Perry's American naval squadron in the mid-1800s. But she quickly made up for her rather slow start. Embracing industrialism, entering the international arena, launching rapid, devastating military offensives against China and Russia around the turn of the century, by the late 1920s she looked north to the desirable land of Manchuria and south to the oil fields of the Dutch East Indies.[6]

By then the United States, too, had long sensed the possibilities and wealth of the East. It had fought a lark of a war against a decaying Spain in 1898, taking the Philippines as an imperial prize, a stepping-stone to mainland East Asia. The Philippines figured large in what was to come. It was far from America's shores, hard to defend, and nearly at Japan's own doorstep. And Japan's ambitions were growing. The American presence on her side of the Pacific was a constant irritant, as was Americans' condescending treatment of Japan's citizens in its immigration laws and other such matters. Slowly the confrontation approached, at first hull down on a Pacific horizon, then steaming steadily closer.

In Japan's wars against China and Russia, she followed the same general strategy, leading off with sneak attacks against counterforce assets while in the middle of peace talks, using her technology smartly, seeking and securing quick gains against larger, more powerful enemies. Twice the strategy worked. Then, as the 1930s began, a new and militaristic outlook started to dominate the country. Prodded by economic depression, Japan grew openly expansionist and resentful of the American presence on the eastern Pacific Rim, and given the success of her strategy in the past, it was only natural for her to try the same gambit again, this time on a United States determined to check her aggression. In 1940 and 1941, the Roosevelt administration banned sales of American oil and scrap iron—two of modern war's main building blocks—to Nippon. In partial retaliation came the strike on Pearl Harbor.

The attack was not the first move in an attempted invasion of the United States. That was far beyond what Japan wanted or could have accomplished. The hit-and-run raid was merely designed to destroy the U.S. Pacific Fleet, America's only means of projecting its martial power into the western Pacific. The death of that fleet would give Japan time to expand—to "advance," so went the euphemism—into desirable areas, including the vital East Indian oil fields that would keep Japan's war machine running.

But the attack enraged America, bringing about a mobilization the likes of which had never been seen. The first year was hard, but by 1943 ships and men began to pour into the Pacific, a feat made all the more impressive by the fact that the country was also fighting—and indeed giving priority to—a major war in Europe, sending unprecedented resources there as well.

But while the European war, though massive, resembled World War I in significant ways, this new Pacific war was something very different from all earlier wars. It was a different war because the Pacific was a different place, a unique world in itself.

It was, and is, the largest body of water known to exist. Turn a tabletop globe to the proper angle, and you will be able to see almost nothing of any continent—not even Australia—but instead only water, the water of the Pacific, dotted with flyspecks of islands. At the equator a voyager can travel ten thousand miles, from the South American coast of Ecuador to the northernmost tip of New Guinea, without touching land. It is an ocean twice the size of the Atlantic: the North Pacific alone accounts for a sixth of the earth's surface area, and even there, the distances are astonishing.[7] The great circle route from San Francisco to Tokyo is all of five thousand miles, five thousand miles of cold, green-blue, stormy Pacific, greater than the distance between Key West and Anchorage.

But the Pacific is more than just large. It is remote. Remote, that is, from the oceangoing powers of Europe, whose inhabitants first ventured upon the deep to any great degree, changing it from impassable barrier to unequalled highway. China, with one of the Pacific's best frontages, developed deep-ocean sailing technology, too, by the late Middle Ages. China, like England and Spain and other countries of Western Europe, might conceivably have become a maritime nation. But the Chinese peoples were walled off from the rest of the world by mountains, deserts, and the nomadic tribes of the steppes that posed a perennial security risk. This made Chinese society insular, and it never developed a maritime mind-set, never launched itself into the ocean as Europe did early on. Thus, the distant Pacific had to await the coming of the West, and that took a long time to happen.

It began to occur, tentatively, in the sixteenth century, with the coming of the likes of Magellan and Drake, and things speeded up by the late eighteenth. By the time of the mid-nineteenth century, the Industrial Revolution had married itself to imperialism, finally extending Western influence in a major way to the world of the Pacific Rim. And one of the major players by then was the United States of America, a resource-rich country that, alone of all the countries of the Atlantic world, fronted on the Pacific as well. It was an American outward thrust, in fact, the arrival of Commodore Perry's squadron off Uraga, that provoked change in a Japan that had been insular, like China, up to that point. After that, the clock started ticking, counting down to Pearl Harbor. Once the showdown finally happened in 1941's last few weeks, it provoked a war in a theater unlike any other in history, a war of nearly impossible distances in an environment so sweeping, so inhospitable to men and machinery, that the latest technology of the mid-twentieth century was barely up to waging it.

Indeed, the technology *wasn't* up to waging it at first. The Pearl Harbor attack was an audacious throw of the dice, one that pushed Japan's war-making potential to its limits. It was an unprecedented projection of tactical airpower across wintry, treacherous seas, unbounded by any land other than tiny atolls, to a point three thousand miles from home waters. The attack, almost incredibly, succeeded in sinking a whole battleship fleet, a force of aging vessels designed to stop Japan's aggression in the western Pacific. As a result, for the next year or so, a patchwork of American vessels, and only a handful of capital ships, were forced to range over millions of square miles of Pacific, in environments ranging from the freezing subarctic to the blazingly tropical, to counter Japanese moves. And the conditions under which they steamed and fought were anything but ideal.

Modern navigational tools, such as gyroscopes and LORAN, were still very basic. Radar was still raw and new, entirely vacuum-tube based, as was radio, which sunspots, inversions, and corrosive salt water could easily frustrate. Encounters among enemy ships and fleets were often a game of blind-man's bluff in this, the world's largest arena. And even when contact occurred, landing effective punches was hard. The hits and misses of big-gun salvos were hard to spot in the dark. Excited pilots, plagued by adrenaline and sleep deprivation, misidentified types and numbers of enemy ships over and over again. Destroyers' torpedo launchers corroded quickly from salt spray. Once launched, even the best torpedoes could do nothing but run mindlessly straight, lacking the brains to see, turn, and follow a moving target, and all too often the defective American brands failed to explode even upon scoring a hit. Depth charge runs were usually based on a captain's best guess as to where an enemy submarine lurked; thus the need for a whole pattern of charges, rather than a single, precisely targeted explosive device. The whole Pacific war, in a way, resembled two large and powerful men hunting each other while locked in a huge, dark gymnasium, each holding a baseball bat and a flashlight. And a flashlight, if improperly used, would reveal more *to* the enemy than *about* him. Given these conditions, it is amazing that a decisive war could be fought in the Pacific.

Yet decisive it was. At a few crucial moments, a combination of skill, sheer guts, and the purest of luck or Providence combined to deal critical blows to Japan. The turning point came at the Battle of Midway, six months after Pearl Harbor; then followed a string of successes, interspersed with costly defeats, at Guadalcanal in the southwest Pacific, beginning a few months later. After that the main and sustained offensive, backed by the mightiest industrial system the world has ever known, began to take hold.

It was all a question of distance, distance along with mobility. The Japanese goal had been to keep America out of East Asia and the western Pacific. After Midway and Guadalcanal, that plan was doomed to failure. The American objective, on the other hand, was Japan's surrender and occupation. But given the reaches of the Pacific and the state of technology, that would be no easy task.

Japan was an island group, unapproachable except by water or air. In 1944 no armed force in the world would have been up to the task of making an intercontinental air assault from America to Asia. And an amphibious naval assault on Japan would be open to annihilation by a short-range air attack launched from Japan's Home Islands as the fleet neared Japanese shores. So the American approach across this largest of oceans had to be oblique. First, Japan's outlying naval and air bases, forming its defensive perimeter, had to be beaten down or taken out of the game by being cut off from supplies. This would allow American forces to build their own bases, thus extending their reach, and America's own airpower, ever closer to Japan's Home Islands. The next step, when closer in, would be to switch aim from the extremities to the

vitals, interdicting the Home Islands, cutting off the maritime transport of food
and fuel oil flowing into them across the water from the East Indies and mainland Asia. This would cripple Japan's war effort, and in the meantime the
United States would build even closer airbases, which would finally bring
Japan within range of America's newest long-range strategic bombers that
were beginning to come off the line in 1944. At last, with Japan sufficiently
weakened, the navy could commence tactical strikes directly against the Home
Islands, and then transport an army ashore to finish the war.[8]

To do all this, the United States relied on the newest, most critical, capital ship: the aircraft carrier, which could carry a bubble of American airpower
nearly anywhere in the Pacific. It was the carrier that provided the air umbrella that protected marines and army troops from the dangers of Japanese
airpower as their invasion flotillas approached enemy-held islands and archi-
pelagoes. It was the carrier that allowed battleships to get close enough to
shore to turn their awesome gunfire onto defended coastlines, softening up
the beaches for the marines. It was the carrier that controlled the skies long
enough for landing fields and naval bases to be built, that allowed submarines to fuel and arm safely in these forward bases before they began
hunting for merchant ships. In the sprawling, stormy, heaving Pacific, blood
warm and ice cold by turns, the carrier was the key to it all.

But the bubble of airpower that carriers provided was a very fragile thing,
because the carriers themselves were fragile. They could sink; island airfields
could not. They were large, at least as ships go, and not very maneuverable.
Carrier-based planes usually had shorter ranges than their land-based opposite numbers, so carriers had to move in uncomfortably close for the kill. If
found by enemy planes, or by silent and sometimes nearly undetectable submarines, a carrier could be taken out of action by a single bomb or torpedo
hit, for it lacked a battleship's armor. So a carrier desperately needed the
other ships of the fleet—cruisers, destroyers, even battleships—to protect it
from air, submarine, and surface assault. Thus it was that the carriers fought
not alone but in fleets and task forces, formidable combinations of well-de-
fended striking power. And in 1944 the most lethal such force anywhere in the
world was Fast Carrier Task Force 38, the nexus of the U.S. Third Fleet.

Of course, it wasn't all about ships. The ships were nothing without the
men. And there were plenty of men in Task Force 38. They were quite a

collection. Among them were grizzled admirals and whiskerless teens; African American and Filipino stewards; Irish Americans from Chicago, Louisiana Cajuns, Italian Americans with strong Brooklyn accents, and sailors descended from old Scots and British stock who spoke in southern drawls, Tennessee twangs, and classical tidewater tones. There were bosuns and old, bulky chiefs who could take these ships to pieces and put them back together again, whose seamanship was among the best in the world. There were officers wearing Annapolis rings who had sailed nearly every sea on the planet, and young ninety-day wonders who had never seen an ocean until a few months before after going through a three-month crash course to make them naval reservists. There were water tenders and firemen, quartermasters and ping jockeys, young hotshot pilots, and lithe airplane mechanics who could worm their way into crawl spaces with ease. There were pale technicians, in love with wiring and vacuum tubes, who reeked of stale cigarette smoke, with stations deep inside the bowels of the ships, staring at dim radar screens or listening to the zing and chatter of Fox, TBS (Talk Between Ships), and the other radio circuits.

They had come from all over America, from beside chill Boston Harbor; from the Iowa cornfields; from the deep Appalachians; from Wichita, Kansas; and Moultrie, Georgia; tens of thousands of them in Third Fleet alone. And for all of its size, Third Fleet was far from being the whole of the navy.

Most of these sailors supplied the brawn or some specialized knowledge needed to make the ships go. But the higher up the ladder of rank that one climbed, the more a man tended to earn his pay based on what he knew rather than by the physical things he did. Near the top of the pile were the flag officers and their staffs.

There was no shortage of brass in the Pacific of World War II. At one major meeting of both admirals and general officers, a sailor recalled counting 146 stars on various lapels.[9] Task Force 38 was no different, having its fair share of admirals. But all of them were subordinate to the fleet's commander, the man who called all the shots. Everyone in the fleet, even these admirals, merely had to be told what to do; the fleet commander was the one who did the telling. Third Fleet, in the final analysis, was his, a weapon he wielded as a medieval knight wielded a sword.

His name was William F. Halsey.

⚓

He was a few weeks short of his sixty-second birthday. Dapper, graying, he was a charming bantam of a man and a media darling. Few other men in World War II uniform fascinated or played to the public as much as Halsey did, and none of the others were sailors. Montgomery, Patton, and of course Douglas MacArthur were high-profile soldiers; the navy had Halsey. He didn't have much competition for all the attention. There was Admiral Ernest J. King, the navy's top officer, chief of naval operations and commander in chief of the U.S. Fleet—CNO and Cominch, respectively—but despite his great strategic ability, he had a desk job, and anyway he was too irascible for the press. (King was "the most even-tempered man in the navy," his daughter once said. "He is always in a rage."[10]) Then, of course, there was Chester A. Nimitz, the cool and utterly capable commander in chief of the Pacific Fleet (CincPac) and Pacific Ocean Areas (CincPoa). But Nimitz never sought the limelight, instead just getting on with the job. And as for Vice Admiral Raymond A. Spruance, who had won in masterly fashion one of the most critical battles America has ever fought, the Battle of Midway—well, nobody had ever heard of Raymond A. Spruance. Even after he won another great victory in the Philippine Sea, nearly eradicating Japanese naval airpower, he remained a quiet and almost totally unsung hero.

But Halsey was different from all of them. He wasn't quiet like Nimitz and Spruance, and he wasn't tied to a desk like Nimitz and King. People knew about him. One of his most famous and quotable lines came on the heels of the December 7 attack. As the carrier *Enterprise*, with Halsey aboard, steamed into smoking, oil- and debris-filled Pearl Harbor on the evening of the eighth, the pugnacious mariner surveyed the wreckage and carnage. "Before we're through with 'em," he growled, "the Japanese language will be spoken only in hell!"[11] And Halsey being Halsey, he meant it.

Thereafter the Halsey image gained ground. There seemed to be a blunt ferocity about him, a hard-drinking, hard-fighting, win-at-all-costs-with-no-quarter-given streak that ran straight through him, and a 1941 America needed that in its warriors. He provided it.

He was both colorful and approachable, which made him a favorite with the men who served under him. Ray Spruance they knew and respected, but

Spruance kept his distance. Halsey they liked. Everyone who met him, it seems, has a favorite story or two about him. Walt Barry, a wounded sailor flying home from the western Pacific, found himself on a PBY Catalina with Halsey, who walked back to where Barry was resting and visited with him for a time. The twenty-four-year-old Barry had found the officers on his destroyer irritating because they never told the crew anything, but Halsey was different. Don Beaty, a young Georgia marine, was once in a makeshift bar in New Caledonia watching a crap game in the corner of the room when Halsey and his people came in. The admiral, too, spied the game, and he went over and began raking the players over the coals for gambling in defiance of regulations. Then, finishing his tirade, he smiled and pulled a twenty-dollar bill from his wallet. "Shoot twenty!" he exclaimed, joining the game.[12]

When on his Third Fleet flagship, the grand *Iowa*-class battlewagon *New Jersey*, Halsey was even more familiar with the men, some of whom he saw regularly during his daily routine. Several gunners were once airing out their blues, uniforms designed for colder climes than that of the central Pacific, when Halsey strode by, his marine orderly in tow. "What's this?" he exclaimed.

"Well, Admiral," Blackie Leonard, a young Louisianan, piped up unabashedly, in his marked Cajun accent, "we're hopin' one day we'll be goin' home."

Halsey took the hint. "We're gonna be going home," he assured the sailors in Leonard's gun tub. "We're gonna get this damn thing over with!"[13]

It was these men, too, who could see the real Halsey, and one day another sailor saw the more ruthless side. In the fall of 1944, after one of her consorts had sunk a Japanese warship, *New Jersey* was on her way to rescue American sailors and found herself steaming through the patch of sea where the ship had gone down. True to the spirit of Nippon's military code of behavior, Bushido, the Japanese survivors, swimming and floating on boxes, were resisting rescue attempts, yelling in rage at their enemies.

Robert Harp, a twenty-three-year-old farm boy from Morgan County, Illinois, was on the bridge at the time at the helm of a ship that had a population close to that of his hometown of Jacksonville. "What do we do with 'em?" he heard the officer of the deck (OOD) ask Halsey. "Should we go around 'em?"

"Hell, no! We didn't put them there," Halsey snapped, somewhat inaccurately. "Keep on going!"

Then Halsey walked out on deck, flanked by marine guards, with a megaphone in his hand. Anthony Iacono, a gun striker, was sitting near his gun shack when Halsey appeared next to him. Iacono and everyone nearby bolted to their feet.

"At ease," Halsey said, waving his hand casually at the men. The admiral then watched for a while as *New Jersey*'s whaleboats struggled to pick up survivors who didn't seem to want to be rescued. Finally he put his megaphone to his mouth and shouted a brusque order to *New Jersey*'s crew. "Accommodate 'em!" he barked.

At first Iacono didn't understand. Then, as the whaleboats returned to the ship and the destroyers rolled depth charges among the Japanese sailors, he did.[14]

Even by the war's opening months, Halsey was a national figure. The image portrayed by the radio and the press was that of a simple, straight-shooting warrior, and that image remains to this day. But as the anecdotes of those around him reveal, the real Halsey was somewhat more complex, even a little self-contradictory at times. Here was a man who could utter public and heartfelt thanks to God in his announcements to the fleet but who could swear with a sailor's tongue.[15] He was said to be a kind and generous man, but there was a ruthlessness about him. By the end of the war he denounced the Japanese as "lousy yellow rat monkey bastards" as if no single noun or adjective could hold all the hatred he felt for them. His "accommodation" of the defiant swimmers was no anomaly; a few days before the surrender, when Japan's desire for peace had already grown clear, Halsey heard a radioed rumor that his enemy was about to throw in the towel. His task force was headed away from the Japanese Home Islands at that moment in order to refit. But as soon as he read the message, Halsey fired a question at his chief of staff. "Have we got enough fuel," he snapped, "to turn around and hit the bastards once more before they quit?"[16]

There were other contradictions as well. He was approachable by the lowliest sailor, but even his highest and most trusted aides sometimes feared to bother or wake him.[17] He never liked or answered to the nickname "Bull"—it was the media's invention—but MacArthur called him that to his face, and Halsey seemed not to mind.[18] He smoked and drank mightily, and he generally distrusted men who didn't, but he was great friends with the puritanical Ray Spruance. He had been a destroyer man for nearly thirty years, but in the mid-1930s he left that background behind forever for the very different world of naval aviation. Yet he made his Third Fleet headquarters in still another world where he had spent almost no time, aboard battleships, first *New Jersey* and later *Missouri*. And though one of the things he sought most of all was to command a major fleet action, he never got the chance, or rather, he got it and threw it away, in one of the most controversial episodes of the whole Pacific war. But that controversy still lay a few weeks in the future as of that fine September morning in 1944, and it would only be the latest in a run of bad luck for Halsey.

A New Jersey native and 1904 Naval Academy graduate, Halsey had built a solid reputation by 1941. He had had command of the Pacific Battle Force's aircraft assets back then, and he'd then gone on to command the Southwest Pacific Area, including part of the Solomons, under Nimitz. During all of this time he had missed tangling with the Japanese at Pearl Harbor almost by chance, returning to Oahu aboard *Enterprise* from a Wake Island mission as the Japanese fleet began to withdraw. A reciprocal radio bearing mistakenly placed the enemy strike force 180 degrees in the wrong direction, and Halsey, looking for battle, dashed off away from the Japanese rather than toward them. In the end it was a good thing. *Enterprise* would have been outcarriered six ships to one if she and the Japanese force had managed to find each other on December 7 or 8. Six months later, when a major fleet battle arose the following May, Halsey had come down with a pestiferous skin disease that wrecked his health and took him out of action. Thus it was a very junior Ray Spruance, a mere rear admiral, who commanded the Midway task force and won a smashing victory.[19] Halsey probably found no consolation in the fact that he himself had been the one to recommend that Spruance be his replacement.

Later, in the Southwest Pacific, Halsey did a fine job of rebuilding sagging morale and holding the line at Guadalcanal. His was a famous name in the navy, and his very presence was a huge boost. "I'll never forget it!" one officer wrote of his reaction to hearing the news that Halsey had taken command of the area. "One minute we were too limp with malaria to crawl out of our foxholes; the next we were running around whooping like kids."[20]

For the next year and a half Halsey fought like a demon, a demon on a shoestring budget, spending his few ships slowly and painfully to push the Japanese off Guadalcanal, from which they could have threatened the safety of New Guinea and the fragile, crucial American line of communication with Australia. He did it, too. By February 1943, Guadalcanal was indisputably in American hands, though not without the fighting of a good many battles. So many vessels went down off the island that sailors labeled the waters "Ironbottom Sound," and compasses went wild as surviving ships steamed over thousands of tons of sunken metal. But amid all of this combat, Halsey himself never got to take part in a fleet action, never got to play the prima donna role of Officer in Tactical Command, the mystical abbreviation of OTC, in combat with an enemy naval force.[21]

His bad luck held throughout the first half of 1944. By then the massive Third Fleet had come into being—except that it wasn't called Third Fleet. The Fast Carrier Task Force and the units that gave it support were collectively designated Third Fleet only when Halsey commanded it.[22]

But Halsey alternated command with Ray Spruance, which allowed one admiral and his staff to fight while the other planned, a system likened to keeping the horses and changing the drivers.[23]

When Spruance was holding the reins, the organization's name was Fifth Fleet, and Task Force 38 became Task Force 58. Among other things, this system prompted the Japanese to believe that there were two Fast Carrier Task Forces abroad.

In June it was Spruance, not Halsey, who commanded the fleet, and so, as had happened at Midway two years before, it was Spruance who got to fight a key battle. That month, Fifth Fleet had to cover the capture of the Mariana Islands—the amphibious invaders setting out from Pearl Harbor, four thousand miles away, and from Guadalcanal, fifteen hundred miles closer. And the Japanese were ready and waiting.

To a degree, it was a mirror image of Midway. An attacking fleet launched an invasion in the central Pacific in June from far-distant bases, with the enemy having a fleet stationed close by the target islands. But this time, Spruance was the attacker and not the defender.[24]

He had orders to use his airpower to cover the American landings on Tinian, Guam, and Saipan.[25] Meanwhile, a Japanese fleet of nine carriers set out to sink Spruance's fleet. But because of Spruance's victory two years before at Midway, Japan had few good naval aviators left.

On the morning of June 19, four waves of Japanese carrier-based attack planes came quavering out of the western ocean, headed straight for Fifth Fleet. It was a slaughter. None got a hit on a single American carrier, while Spruance's pilots swatted down planes by the hundreds, losing barely three dozen of their own. Soon this battle of the Philippine Sea became known colloquially as the Marianas Turkey Shoot. Before it took place, Japanese carrier-based airpower, though consisting of a lot of ships, planes, and inferior pilots, was weak; afterward it was nearly nonexistent. Spruance had done it again. And Halsey had missed it again.

Halsey was probably disappointed, as others definitely were. Spruance had won a stunning victory. But although he had destroyed the planes and the pilots, he had not sunk the enemy carriers. Many flag officers, some of them aviators whom Nimitz had passed up for Fifth Fleet command in favor of nonaviator Spruance, found fault in the fact that those ships had gotten away. For them, one of the greatest triumphs in all of American naval history apparently wasn't great enough, and more than one man, no doubt, imagined that it would have been greater if only he'd been in Spruance's place.

Halsey was probably one of these officers, but whatever complaints he had with what Spruance had done, he kept them to himself. Still, given his makeup, Halsey would almost certainly have gone sprinting off after the enemy carriers, and he probably would have nailed them. But Spruance had had his orders, and he had followed them. Fifth Fleet's mission had been to run defense, to protect the American landings, not to chase the retiring enemy carrier force. Halsey probably understood that.

A few months later, Halsey's orders would read differently from Spruance's, and these orders would, at long last, give him a chance to fight a major fleet engagement at the head of Task Force 38.

Slowly, relentlessly, came the march across the Pacific. It came from two directions, in fact. From the east, from Pearl Harbor, the navy steamed, marines hopping from island to island, the Marshalls, the Gilberts, the Carolines. Meanwhile, up from the south came the army and air corps, with the aid of the navy. Nimitz may have commanded the central Pacific, but the southwest Pacific was General Douglas MacArthur's.

MacArthur was America's most seasoned and senior officer. Although a few others, such as Nimitz and King, now matched him in rank, he had earned his first star long before they, all the way back in the First World War. A West Pointer, the son of a Congressional Medal of Honor recipient, MacArthur—himself a Medal of Honor holder—was also a consummate showman, one with more than a touch of genuine megalomania. During the Second World War, a woman once asked Dwight D. Eisenhower if he had ever met MacArthur. "Not only have I met him, ma'am," replied Ike, a former chief of staff to MacArthur, "I studied dramatics under him for five years in Washington and four years in the Philippines."[26]

But for all of his preoccupation with himself and his image, MacArthur was an outstanding tactician and strategist, and also one of those rare army officers with an intuitive understanding of sea power and navies.[27] A veteran of World War I's Western Front, MacArthur could see, and appreciate, that the Pacific campaign was a different kind of war from that of the Somme and Verdun. It was a war of vast space and extraordinary mobility, a mobility both allowed and required by the ocean's all-encompassing presence. So he used that ocean to move his armies, staging no fewer than eighty-seven amphibious landings. Of these, eighty-seven succeeded. While it is true that he could choose to hit weak spots, unlike Nimitz's marines in the central Pacific, and that the Japanese had a huge perimeter they had to defend and were thus spread thinly, it was still an impressive record. Generals, admirals, statesmen, and theorists all conceded that he was among the best. MacArthur, one of them noted, "took more territory, with less loss of life, than any military commander since Darius the Great."[28]

By the middle of 1944, MacArthur had long known that some of that territory was going to include the Philippines, the American colony that the Japanese had taken from him in the opening months of the war. For him it wasn't merely a matter of strategy; it was also a matter of honor and image. Two years earlier, sealed off on Corregidor, besieged by Japanese forces, he had watched as the United States turned its energies elsewhere, to the Filipinos' justifiable fury. Philippine President Manuel Quezon's reaction was typical. Hearing a war address by Franklin D. Roosevelt in which the president didn't even mention the islands, Quezon simply exploded. "Come, listen to this scoundrel! *Que demonio!*" he shouted. "How typical of America to writhe in anguish at the fate of a distant cousin, Europe, while a daughter, the Philippines, is being raped in the back room!"[29]

MacArthur, watching his own troops dwindle and drop, completely agreed. He fully expected to die with his men. He would have preferred it, in fact, but Roosevelt and the War Department sent orders for him to get out while he could and head to Australia to assume command there at the Australians' request. Even then, however, MacArthur was planning his reconquest. Shortly before boarding the battered PT boat that would evacuate him, he took General Jonathan M. Wainwright aside for a talk. Wainwright would take command of America's Philippine forces as soon as MacArthur departed. "If I get through to Australia," MacArthur assured him, "I'll come back as soon as I can with as much as I can." Then his boat started its struggle through debris-ridden Manila Bay in the dark while the guns boomed above him, beginning a cat and mouse game with the roving Japanese warships and the heaving and choppy ocean.

Later, in Adelaide, MacArthur made his most famous statement of all. "The President of the United States ordered me to break through the Japanese lines," he explained, as much to Filipinos as to anyone, "for the purpose of organizing the American offensive against Japan, a primary object of which is the relief of the Philippines." Then he uttered the magic phrase. "I came through and I shall return."[30]

The return was delayed. MacArthur found that he had no weapons and troops with which he could fight. Wainwright was unable to hold, starved as he was of men and supplies. In May came the surrender, followed by the notorious Death March. But MacArthur never forgot, and he never let Washington do so.

Two years later, American power in the Pacific was nearing flood tide. Having taken key points in the Gilberts and Marshalls, the navy, in the personae of Admirals Nimitz and King, wanted to strike Formosa, and then island-hop up the Ryukyu chain to Okinawa and the Japanese Home Islands themselves, choking them off and winning the war unconditionally, all while neatly bypassing the Philippines.

For MacArthur that was unthinkable for a lot of different reasons. For one thing, Formosa was held by some of Japan's best soldiers, and taking it would be a hard, bloody business. For another, while MacArthur understood the ways and uses of sea power, he was still an army officer, and like any general he saw conquest in the taking and holding of land, not in blockade and interdiction. Reconquest of the Philippines meant invading it and throwing the Japanese back into the ocean, not in winning a capitulation later on in Tokyo. He had promised to return, and by that he damn well meant returning to the Philippines at the head of an army, not in safety after the war.

Roosevelt, sensing an army-navy deadlock in the making, traveled to Pearl Harbor in July to meet with MacArthur and Nimitz. It was a high-profile, election-year summit. One night after dinner the president took the two men into a room, one wall of which bore a large map of the Pacific. "Well, Douglas," asked Roosevelt—he was one of the few men alive who could get away with calling MacArthur "Douglas"—"where do we go from here?"

The answer was instant and obvious. "Mindanao, Mr. President," the general replied, "then Leyte—and then Luzon." A trinity of Philippine islands. "Promises must be kept."[31]

MacArthur didn't let it rest there. Later that night he spoke to the president in private. Ignoring the line between military and political subjects, he warned Roosevelt that if he chose the navy plan, "I daresay that the American people would be so aroused that they would register most complete resentment against you at the polls this fall."

It was nearly too much for a weary Franklin D. Roosevelt. "Give me an aspirin before I go to bed," he told his doctor before retiring that night. "In fact, give me another aspirin to take in the morning. In all my life nobody has ever talked to me the way MacArthur did."[32]

But MacArthur had made his point, and by the end of the Pearl Harbor conference, Roosevelt had made his decision. "Well, Douglas, you win!" he is supposed to have told a downcast MacArthur, who thought he had lost. "But I'm going to have a hell of a time over this with that old bear, Ernie King!" he added, knowing that the prickly admiral would resent Roosevelt's choice of the army strategy.[33]

The objective had been chosen. Now came the preparing.

To bring maximum firepower to bear on the Philippines, as well as to give both theater commanders a role, the plan the Joint Chiefs of Staff approved involved the forces of both MacArthur and Nimitz.[34] MacArthur already had a fleet working for him—"MacArthur's Navy," the Seventh Fleet under Admiral Thomas Kinkaid—and to this Nimitz would add the Third Fleet and Admiral Halsey. But unlike Kinkaid, Halsey would report to Nimitz and King, not to MacArthur. As a result, no one short of the White House and the Joint Chiefs would be in overall command of the American forces, and they were in Washington, a half world away from the scene of the fighting.

The target would be the Philippine island of Leyte, where MacArthur would make a massive amphibious landing and from which he would stage a drive on the larger island of Luzon, on which sat Manila with its fine harbor. Third Fleet's job would be to give him air cover and beat off any attempt by the Imperial Japanese Navy to stop the American landing. Nimitz crafted Halsey's orders with care. Third Fleet was to "cover and support forces of the Southwest Pacific"—that is, MacArthur's army and navy—"in order to assist in the seizure and occupation of objectives in the central Philippines."

But Nimitz recalled what Spruance had done, and failed to do, in the Philippine Sea the previous June. Spruance had followed orders to guard the amphibious landing, and in doing so he'd refused to be distracted into pursuing and sinking the Japanese carriers, the carriers Spruance's critics claimed he could and should have wiped out. Neither Nimitz nor King had joined the chorus of the critics. But Nimitz, or at least one of his staff, added a single sentence to CincPac's orders to Halsey, almost, it seems, as an afterthought. "In case opportunity for destruction of major portion of the enemy fleet offer or can be created," it read, "such destruction becomes the primary task."[35]

Thus it happened that not only did American forces in the approaching campaign lack a single commander, a substantial part of those forces, because of that single sentence, also lacked a single objective. Was Third Fleet suppose to stick close to MacArthur, or to find and destroy the enemy fleet? Still, the sentence offered the possibility of a major fleet action, the sort of action that Third Fleet's commander had always wanted to fight. It was precisely the sentence that Halsey had wanted to see in his orders.

Unfortunately for Halsey, it was the sentence the Imperial Japanese Navy wanted to see in his orders as well.

The Japanese were getting desperate. Their defensive perimeter was collapsing, their supplies were running low, a sizable part of their navy was gone, and many of their most experienced warriors were now dead. They feared a strike on the Philippines as the beginning of the end, a prelude to a choke hold that would stop the flow of war materiel up from southeast Asia and extend American strategic airpower over Japan itself. To counter such an American move, they had devised a plan: Operation Victory One (Sho Ichi Go). Because most of Japan's fangs had been drawn, the plan was largely, though by no means completely, one of deception.

On learning of an impending attack on the Philippines, Japan would send her surface combat forces toward the scene of the American landings in two separate prongs, trying to catch the Americans between the pincers of battleship guns. But the Japanese knew that the Americans had battleships, too, and carriers, and lots of them. So, to draw off the American capital ships, Japan would send a third force in from the north—the carriers that Spruance had failed to destroy. They were toothless by now, with few planes and fewer experienced pilots, but perhaps the enemy wouldn't know that. As the American task force struck out north after the impotent carriers, the Japanese surfaceaction pincers would close in from the west on the American beachhead and the helpless amphibious ships. A major victory there could keep Japan's tenuous lifelines to southeast Asia alive. It might also give the Roosevelt administration a black eye just weeks before a presidential election, and could even encourage America to negotiate a peace settlement that might favor Japan. Anything would be better than unconditional surrender.

Such, at least, was the plan. And Halsey's orders, with their single aggressive sentence, unwittingly played right into it.[36]

The kickoff came on October 18, as the shore bombardment began.[37] Japanese commanders soon knew that the objective was Leyte, and orders went out to execute Sho Ichi Go.

Halsey was already spoiling for a fight with the Japanese navy. "My goal is the same as yours," he had written to Nimitz soon after reading his orders, "to completely annihilate the Jap fleet if the opportunity offers."[38]

There was only one problem. That *wasn't* Nimitz's goal, at least not the main one, and certainly not the only one. One of Third Fleet's inescapable missions was to protect the American landings. Already Halsey was showing that he didn't quite grasp this critical fact, and he would keep on showing it.

The Japanese fleet, if it came, might come from one of several directions. One was Surigao Strait, to Leyte's south, through which Magellan had long ago sailed on his voyage of discovery. Another was San Bernardino Strait, north of Leyte. These led west into cramped Philippine waters where it would be hard to maneuver a fleet or task force, but provided that the Japanese could get through, they could then steam into the gulf adjacent to Leyte and threaten the whole American operation.

Halsey was ready and waiting to take the initiative. As the amphibious landings proceeded, he radioed Admiral Kinkaid and asked if the two straits were clear of mines. He was planning to steam through them as soon as he knew that the Japanese fleet lay beyond.

Nimitz, several thousand miles away at Pearl Harbor, heard Halsey's question. Normally CincPac did not intervene in distant battles, in the decision making of the commander on the scene. But this time he did. Nimitz quickly sent a dispatch reminding Halsey that Third Fleet's main job wasn't to go chasing off after the Japanese fleet; it was to cover MacArthur. To make himself clear, Nimitz put some teeth in his wording. "Movement of major units of the Third Fleet through Surigao and San Bernardino Straits," he told Halsey, "will not be initiated without orders from CincPac."[39]

Halsey had guessed right. The Japanese fleet was coming, in two great groups, up from Lingga Roads near Singapore and down from the Japanese Home Islands, two potent surface-action forces that included both *Yamato* and *Musashi*, the largest and most powerful battleships that have ever been built, larger than even the *Iowa*s. One force, a meld of two smaller units, was shaping a course for Surigao Strait to the south. The other, deadlier force, built around both of the superdreadnoughts, was heading for San Bernardino Strait in the north. The largest naval battle in the history of the world was about to begin. And a few miles off Leyte, Halsey and Third Fleet waited.

⚓

For all of the power on the sea and aloft in the air, the first licks in the battle for Leyte Gulf came from beneath the waves. On the twenty-third of October, torpedoes lanced out of the tubes of USS *Darter* and USS *Dace*, fleet subs cruising the South China Sea west of the Philippines. The silvery wakes drew pretty lines toward heavy cruisers *Takao* and *Atago*; a few moments later came the ugly cacophony of the warheads' explosions. Metal crumpled, armor gave way, water smashed into the ships' innards, and men began dying. They would soon have a great deal of company, for *Darter* had sounded the alarm, and the subs lashed out again before they were through, mauling the heavy cruiser *Maya*. Before long the first of the four great, discrete battles that formed the whole naval action at Leyte Gulf was going full tilt.[40]

That first battle was Halsey and Third Fleet versus the Japanese San Bernardino Force under Admiral Takeo Kurita. The radioed warnings of *Darter* had Halsey on the alert. At dawn on the twenty-fourth he'd had the task force launch search planes, which arced out over the Sibuyan Sea on the west side of Leyte. A few minutes after eight in the morning, a Helldiver pilot from the carrier *Intrepid* spotted Kurita's force. Counting the wakes and identifying the ships in the carpet spread out thousands of feet below him, he quickly reported the contact. "Five Fox Lucky," he called. "13DD, 4BB, 8CA off the southern tip of Mindoro, course 050, speed 10 to 12 knots. No train or transports."

The cryptic, economical wording spoke volumes. This was no convoy; it was a surface-action force of more than a dozen destroyers, more than a half dozen cruisers, and five battleships—one more than the pilot had spotted— all of them heading for San Bernardino Strait.[41]

Within ten minutes the information was in Halsey's hands. At last he was going to fight his major fleet battle. Just after 0830, he lifted his handset and sent the message he had long wanted to send. "Strike! Repeat, Strike!" he snapped to his ships and his men. "Good luck!"[42]

Less than two hours later, a great wave of attack planes and fighters came barreling in toward Admiral Kurita's fleet. Then came another. And another. The morning devolved into hell as Kurita watched the navy dive-bombers slicing down from high altitude to guide their iron bombs onto the decks of his ships. At the same time, American torpedo planes came skimming in low over the deep blue of the sea to release the fish that could hull and sink his vessels, no matter how tough they were. And other than pumping out antiaircraft fire as fast as he could, there was not a thing he could do to stop them, or even slow them down. This was a surface-action force, and he had no air cover to speak of.

Musashi, one of Kurita's two superdreadnoughts, became the attackers' prime target. Built in great secrecy and at enormous cost to the Japanese people, the ship had been designed to outclass the best battleships that America could send against her. Her main battery of nine eighteen-inch guns was the most powerful ever to go to sea. But her builders hadn't reckoned on the threat of carrier-based aircraft, which were now buzzing around her like a nest of enraged hornets around a lumbering bear. The ship had spent her entire life half starved of fuel and on the run from American airpower, and she had never seen battle until today. And the battle wasn't with ships but with small, flimsy aircraft that were beginning to sting her to death.

As *Musashi* began to slow, falling out of formation and trailing gobs of oil, the American pilots focused their attention on her, the way a wolf pack singles out a lone, faltering stag. Bomb after bomb angled in, starting to wreck her superstructure and cutting down scores of sailors. But the torpedoes were worse, blowing holes clean through her armor and flooding vital spaces.

To be sure, she was tough. Bombs sometimes simply bounced off her thick hide, doing nothing more than taking off some of her paint. Even after the second air strike had ended, *Musashi* was still in fair shape, having received enough bomb and torpedo hits to sink any other ship in the world. But *Musashi* couldn't take on all of Third Fleet, and a sizable amount of Halsey's resources were concentrating on the task of putting her on the bottom. By 1230 one of her engine rooms was on fire and one of her four propeller shafts damaged. Bodies and body parts began to pile up on the decks, which were literally awash in blood.

And still the attacks kept coming. In midafternoon, a bomb found the main bridge. As the explosion died out, a weak voice—the commanding officer's—emerged from the speaking tube. "Captain is wounded," it said. "Executive Officer, take command."

By then there wasn't much left to command. *Musashi* had a ten-degree list to port and her speed was dropping off rapidly. Finally, having been hit by nearly twenty bombs and as many torpedoes, not counting more than a

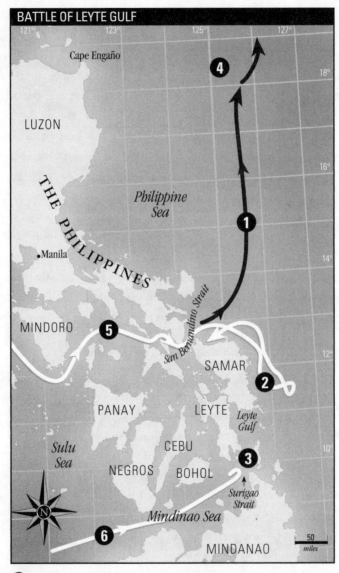

BATTLE OF LEYTE GULF

Cape Engaño

LUZON

Philippine Sea

THE PHILIPPINES

•Manila

MINDORO

San Bernardino Strait

SAMAR

PANAY   LEYTE   *Leyte Gulf*

Sulu Sea   CEBU

NEGROS   BOHOL

Surigao Strait

Mindinao Sea   MINDANAO

50 miles

1 Task Force 38 (Halsey/Mitscher)
2 Taffy 3 (C. Sprague)
3 Seventh Fleet battleships (Kinkaid)
4 Japanese Northern Force (Ozawa)
5 Japanese Center Force (Kurita)
6 Japanese Southern Force (Nishimura)

dozen more bomb hits close aboard, she went down by the bow. A tremendous explosion made the sea tremble a few moments after she sank. She took more than a thousand men with her, nearly half the number that had died at Pearl Harbor. And *Musashi* wasn't the only victim of the Americans' vengeance.[43]

Kurita was having a very bad day. He had already lost three heavy cruisers to the torpedoes of *Darter* and *Dace*; he'd had his flagship blown out from under him by *Darter*, in fact, and he'd had to swim for it before being pulled from the water by one of his destroyers. From *Musashi*'s twin, *Yamato*, he watched the unrelenting storm of torpedoes and bombs from the clouds of American warplanes. Some of his ships, including *Musashi*, had as many as 120 antiaircraft guns; they seemed to be making no difference at all. Again and again he screamed for air cover from land-based Japanese planes; it never arrived. *Yamato* began to take hits. Heavy cruiser *Myoko* received a severe torpedo strike and began to limp back the way she had come.[44] The battleships *Nagato* and *Haruna* came under attack, too, although they survived more or less intact, as did *Yamato*. Still, the pounding was dreadful and the attackers were nearly untouched. "The small number of enemy planes shot down is regrettable," one Japanese battleship division commander told his war diary with fatalistic understatement. "If we are attacked by planes as often as this, we will have expended ourselves before reaching the battle area."[45]

By "battle area," he meant the surface combat area, the American beachhead. Kurita's force was already in a battle area, a zone of combat between surface power and airpower, and airpower was winning. But it hadn't won yet. For all of the slaughter, Kurita still had an effective force, if he could hold it together. He had four nearly undamaged battleships and eight cruisers, along with an entourage of destroyers, enough to do someone serious harm if he could close to main battery range. To do that, however, he had to steam through the close waters of San Bernardino Strait, where he would be unable to maneuver at all in case of another attack from the air. If he kept to schedule, he would enter the strait in late afternoon, the skies filled with killing daylight. So in midafternoon he reversed course, heading back west, waiting for night and hoping that Japanese land-based planes would appear over him in the meantime. They never did.[46]

The American attacks had ended for the time being. After something like 260 sorties in a half dozen air strikes, the pilots, who had been at sea and fighting without respite for weeks, were worn down. And there was another problem. The Americans knew about Kurita's beleaguered force and about the smaller groups approaching from the south. But these were surface-action groups, and vulnerable to American aircraft. There was a missing piece to the puzzle, and it had Admiral Halsey and his people worried: where were the Japanese carriers?

They were out there somewhere. They had to be. This was a carrier war. And when they showed up, Halsey would probably hit them. He was, after all, an aviator, and he had heard what people had said about Spruance for failing to get the carriers earlier. But first he had to find them, although there was still the matter of Kurita's force, wounded but still dangerous.

To deal with Kurita, Halsey came up with a plan. It was just that, he later insisted—a plan. But given the plan's wording and the navy's tendency to confuse the imperative mode with the future tense, it sounded like a command to take action immediately. In case Kurita came through the strait, it read, the battleships of Task Force 38 would be detached. These battleships, said Halsey's dispatch, "will be formed as Task Force 34 under VADM Lee. Task Force 38 engage decisively at long ranges." To someone overhearing the message without being on the scene, it might very well sound as if Halsey had ordered Task Force 34 and its battle line to form right away. In fact, this is just what Kinkaid, and possibly Nimitz, *did* think. In their mind's eye, a battleship task force had come into being and was holding station at the mouth of the strait, waiting for Kurita to come through. But Halsey and his fleet knew better. This was only a plan. For now, Task Force 34 simply didn't exist. The battleships hovered docilely beside their carriers.[47]

Meanwhile, the search for the Japanese carriers continued. At midday, a flight of sixty enemy planes had come in from the open sea to the north. It was a smallish strike and the pilots weren't any good, but their planes had tail hooks. They had to be carrier-based. Within a few hours, American reconnaissance flights to the north at last found the missing carrier force, a group of six of the ships[48]—the ships that the Japanese had wanted Halsey to find all along, so that they could lure him away from Leyte and into the empty ocean. But by then it was too late in the day for an American air strike.

Now that he had the carriers in his sights, Halsey had three choices. He could stay off the strait and wait for Kurita to come on through. Or he could leave Vice Admiral Willis "Ching" Lee and Task Force 34 to guard the strait and take his carriers north to attack the Japanese flattops. Or he could go north with everything, leaving nothing to guard the strait, nothing to wait for Kurita.

There was no other option, no other decision to make. Halsey talked a while with his staff; then he chose. "We will run north at top speed," he ruled, "and put those carriers out for keeps." This meant he would run north with everything, including his battleships, and be in position to strike the enemy carriers at dawn.

As dusk stole over the ocean, Halsey walked into flag plot. "Here's where we're going," he said, pointing to the last known position of the enemy carrier force. "Mick," he told Rear Admiral Robert B. Carney, his chief of staff, "start them north."

As an exhausted Halsey headed off to bed, his communicators sent out a dispatch to Kinkaid and Nimitz. "Am proceeding north with three groups to attack enemy carrier force at dawn." To these two admirals, who believed that Task Force 34 had been formed, it sounded as if Halsey were taking three carrier groups north while leaving Lee and the battleships to watch over the strait. He wasn't.[49]

The task force turned north and began a long sprint into the deep ocean night, its radar stabbing the darkness for miles ahead, searching for ships that wouldn't show until some time the following morning. Aboard *New Jersey*, Halsey dropped off for a few hours' sleep. The following day, if all went well, he would destroy what was left of Japanese naval airpower and avoid the criticism that Spruance had drawn. But in making that choice, he had heard, without giving much thought to, two vital pieces of information. The first was that Kurita's battleship force, shadowed by reconnaissance planes, had been spotted reversing course again. It was now on a direct course for the entrance to San Bernardino Strait.

The other news was that the navigation lights in the strait had been turned on.

Kurita was coming through to attack, and no one was there to stop him. No one at all.[50]

Five thousand miles east at Pearl Harbor, in the dead of night at CincPac Headquarters, Nimitz and his staff waited for news. Spruance looked at the chart that was the focus of so much attention. As a sometime commander of the fleet that belonged to Halsey this night, he was putting himself, quite naturally, in his friend Halsey's shoes. "If I were there," he said, almost to himself, "I would keep my force right there." His hand reached out and touched the chart just off San Bernardino Strait, the exact spot Halsey was sprinting away from.[51]

Just a few hours later the southernmost Japanese force began to emerge from the other strait, Surigao, and promptly ceased to exist.

Kinkaid had a force waiting for it, a line of old battleships resurrected from the mud of Pearl Harbor. As the Japanese commander steamed on with do-or-die orders, the American battle line crossed his T, performing the classic naval maneuver that placed one line at a right angle to the other. This meant that all the broadsides of the top of the T could concentrate on the leading ship of the T's stem, while the other force could return fire with only a few bow guns. The Japanese themselves had crossed the Russian T in the Straits of Tsushima not forty years earlier. Now it was their turn to have their own T crossed. In the predawn hours of the twenty-fifth of October, Rear Admiral Jesse Olendorf and his battle line crossed the last T in history, wiping out the southern Japanese force. The Pearl Harbor battleships at last had their vengeance, finally taking part, in the twilight of their old age, the engagement that they had been designed and built decades before to fight. It was the final echo of the Age of Lepanto and the defeat of the Spanish Armada, the afterglow of the glory days of Trafalgar, the last fleet gunnery action the world is ever likely to see.

Despite the rain of destructive fire from Olendorf's battleships, the biggest events of the day would focus on Halsey, and on what he did and didn't do.

Kinkaid and Nimitz, still thinking that Task Force 34 was guarding San Bernardino, weren't all that worried about Kurita. But some of the people steaming north at full speed with Halsey knew better, and they were worried indeed. If Kurita emerged from an unguarded strait, he could run amok at the American beachhead. The Normandy landings succeeded; those at Leyte might fail. "Jim," one task group (TG) commander said to his chief of staff, "we're playing a helluva dirty trick on the transports in Leyte Gulf."[52]

He wasn't alone in taking this view. Rear Admiral Gerald F. Bogan, another of Halsey's task group commanders, felt so strongly about what was happening that he called Halsey on TBS to make sure he had heard the reports that Kurita was heading toward San Bernardino. Halsey was sleeping by then; a staff officer listened to Bogan instead. "Yes, yes, we have that information," the staffer replied in a bored voice, and Bogan gave up.[53]

Ching Lee, who would command the battle line of Task Force 34—if Halsey ever decided to form it—also tried to warn Halsey by radio that he might want to reconsider his actions. Again came that anonymous voice: "Roger," it answered blandly, terminating the discussion. That left one final hope.

Vice Admiral Marc A. Mitscher was a wizened aviator, a fifty-seven-year-old who, friends said, "did not look a day over eighty." But looks don't win or lose wars, and the fact was that Mitscher was America's finest carrier tactician, which was why he was in charge of Task Force 38.[54]

The problem was that during the Leyte campaign, Task Force 38 and Third Fleet were pretty much the same thing. Most other Third Fleet units had been reassigned, for the time being, to Seventh Fleet and Kinkaid. Halsey, moreover, was bypassing Mitscher and giving orders directly to his task force. So Mitscher, for all his ability, was just along for the ride this time out, ignored and countermanded by turns and not at all happy about it.

Arleigh Burke, Mitscher's chief of staff, was one of those who had the feeling that something was wrong that night. He and the operations officer, hoping that Mitscher might be the one to talk some sense into Halsey, woke their admiral to tell him about Kurita's new course. A bleary-eyed Mitscher listened to them from his bunk. "Admiral," the ops officer concluded, "we'd better tell Halsey to turn around."

"Does Admiral Halsey have that report?" Mitscher asked the two men.

"Yes, he does," the ops officer answered.

Mitscher thought for a moment, perhaps about his own superfluous role in the battle so far, perhaps about the complexities of commanding a force as large as this one. Then he explained to his officers that Halsey, who already had the information in question, was no doubt busily planning and executing an intricate operation and that he didn't need the distraction of unsolicited opinions. Mitscher then ended the interview pointedly. "If he wants my advice," he told the two officers, "he'll ask for it." With that, Mitscher rolled over and went back to sleep.[55]

Halsey slept, too. And just after midnight, Kurita emerged from the strait and set course for Leyte Gulf.

The first call for help came eight hours later.

South of San Bernardino Strait steamed three escort carrier units of Seventh Fleet. Code-named "Taffy 1," "Taffy 2," and "Taffy 3," these very light carriers were providing close-air support for the amphibious landings on Leyte. They were no fleet carriers. Having only small numbers of planes, and with no armor-piercing munitions on hand, they would be helpless in the face of a large surface force, a force such as Kurita's, which found them a little while after dawn.

Taffy 3 was the unit in the wrong place at the wrong time. Consisting of six escort carriers, three destroyers, and three even smaller destroyer escorts, it was small and frail compared to a fast carrier group. The unit commander, Rear Admiral Clifton "Ziggy" Sprague, was on his bridge that morning when he heard a report that a massive enemy surface force had been spotted closing on Taffy 3 at high speed.

"Air plot," called Sprague, "tell that pilot to check his identification." He'd had no word of a Japanese force in the immediate area.

A few moments later air plot replied. "The pilot insists that these ships are Japanese," the communicator told Sprague. "He says they have pagoda masts!"

By then Sprague could see antiaircraft bursts far out on the horizon, and he realized he was in serious trouble. He began to fire off orders. "Come to course zero-niner-zero," he snapped. "Flank speed. Launch all aircraft." That was nearly all he could do other than calling for help, and it wasn't too much. Kurita was nearly twice as fast, and Sprague's few aircraft would be nearly useless against Kurita's well-armored warships. An ugly and lopsided battle was about to begin.

For the next two hours, Taffy 3 put on a display of heroism rarely matched in the annals of war. As the carriers chased salvos and dove into squalls to evade the murderous hailstorm of shells, pip-squeak destroyers and destroyer escorts charged like rampaging lions into the jaws of the Japanese force to serve as shields, launching their handful of torpedoes and firing their light five-inch guns until their barrels were broiling. Aboard his flagship, Sprague handled himself as if this were some massive training exercise, laying a smoke screen and expertly maneuvering the unit to buy as much time as he could until he got some assistance. As Kurita smashed away at the puny destroyers and carriers, the American ships, shredded and burning, began to go down. There was nothing more Sprague could do but wait for help to arrive.[56]

By now Halsey's whole force was four hundred miles north of Taffy 3 and Kurita, engaging the largely impotent Japanese carriers. Against all odds the Japanese Northern Force had done its job of deception perfectly, luring Halsey out of Kurita's way. Now they were paying the price. In Halsey's flag plot it was a different story. Just after eight in the morning Halsey got the first message that Taffy 3 was under attack: "Enemy BB and cruiser reported firing on TU 77.4.3 from 15 miles astern." That double B meant a battleship. When he saw it, Halsey had to have known what had happened. He decided to let Kinkaid handle it; Kinkaid, after all, had battleships of his own, although Halsey didn't realize that those ships, having crossed the T of the southern Japanese force, were now low on armor-piercing ammunition.

But a few minutes later came another request for aid. "Urgently need fast BB Leyte Gulf at once," Kinkaid pleaded. By now, though, He was closing in on the carriers he'd been chasing all night, with air strikes already in progress, and he intended to get them, succeeding where Spruance had failed. Anyway, if he started immediately back toward Leyte Gulf, he would need at least a half day to get there. By then the battle would be long over.

An hour later came another desperate report from Kinkaid. "Our CVEs being attacked by 4 BBs, 8 cruisers, plus others. Request Lee cover Leyte at top speed. Request fast carriers make immediate strike."

Halsey, now getting angry, radioed Kinkaid his position so that Kinkaid could see for himself that Third Fleet was too far away to help. "Am now engaging enemy carrier force," he explained, as if to a child. "My position . . . Lat. 17°18'N, Long. 126°11' E."

Kinkaid either didn't get the message or didn't understand what it really meant. "Where is Lee? Send Lee," he radioed, this time not even encoding the message in order to send it off as fast as he could. If paper dispatches could transmit emotion, this one was a howl of pure anguish. But Halsey, determined to have his fleet action and be in on the kill, kept after the Japanese carriers.

Nimitz was listening in on all of this. Earlier in the day he'd realized that there was confusion about Task Force 34, about its location as well as its existence. "I'm very concerned," he'd told one of his staff, "because nothing I have seen indicates that Admiral Halsey has left San Bernardino Strait guarded against Japanese units coming through there and getting our ships off Leyte."

"That *is* an unclear point in the dispatches," the officer agreed, "and several other people are wondering the same thing."

As the day wore on and Kinkaid's calls for help began streaming in, Nimitz decided that Halsey *hadn't* left the strait guarded, that Task Force 34, if Halsey had even formed it, was up north with the carriers. Nimitz's assistant chief of staff finally made a suggestion. "Admiral," he queried, "couldn't you just ask Admiral Halsey the simple question: 'Where is Task Force 34?'"

As a rule Nimitz tried to stay out of the local commander's hair during a battle; in his view the man on the scene knew better what was happening and what to do about it than a distant onlooker. This time, however, he felt the need to say something. Halsey needed some prompting, and such a question would do it. "Go ahead and write it up," he told his assistant chief. "That's a good idea."

As Nimitz's biographer E. B. Potter explains, CincPac wasn't so much asking Halsey where Task Force 34 was as reminding him where it should be. Nimitz figured that Halsey would read between the short message's lines. But as luck or fate would have it, Halsey ended up reading much more than Nimitz ever intended.

The assistant chief of staff dictated the message, and the yeoman who took the dictation, hearing strong emphasis, likewise made the writing emphatic by repeating the crucial phrase: "Where is rpt where is Task Force 34?" Then came another development.

To hamper any code-breaking attempts, communicators began and ended each transmission with padding—nonsense phrases set off from the actual message by double letters. But the CincPac encoder this day picked an ending phrase that sounded as if it were part of the message, a phrase reminiscent of

one from Tennyson's "Charge of the Light Brigade." It was the ninetieth an-
niversary of that charge, exactly to the day: October 25, 1854.

When *New Jersey* received the message, the padding at the end confused
the communicators. Rather than tearing it off the slip then, they sent it along
to Halsey attached to the message itself.

What Nimitz had intended to send was a gentle prod: "Where is Task
Force 34?" But what Halsey read was the following:

WHERE IS RPT WHERE IS TASK FORCE 34 RR THE WORLD
WONDERS

By then Halsey was sleep deprived, under enormous stress because of
the air strikes he was conducting and the repeated pleas from Kinkaid, and
within thirty or forty miles of being in gunnery range of the carriers his air
strikes had wounded. Within an hour or so, the battle he had waited to direct
for his whole career would be within view. Then he read Nimitz's message.
Thinking the padding was part of the message, seeing that Nimitz had sent
copies to King and Kinkaid, he felt, as he later said, "as if I had been struck
in the face." This was no gentle prod but a stinging, public rebuke. Even if he
deserved such a rebuke—and some believe that he did—that was not
Nimitz's usual way, and Halsey wasn't in any condition to take it. His hands
began trembling; then, as a filthy expression exploded out of his mouth, he
burst into tears and tore off his cap, slamming it onto the deck.

Admiral Carney sprang to his side, astonished at the display. "Stop it!" he
shouted at Halsey. "What the hell's the matter with you? Pull yourself together!"

But it was too late. Halsey didn't take orders from Thomas Kinkaid, but he
did have to answer to Nimitz and, given the message he thought Nimitz had
sent, he believed he had been told to get back to Leyte as fast as he could. So
that's just what he did. The situation became farcical, if it wasn't already. "I
turned my back on the opportunity I had dreamed of since my days as a cadet,"
Halsey wrote later. "For me, one of the biggest battles of the war was off, and
what has been called 'the Battle of Bull's Run' was on."[57]

As his carriers remained to finish off the motley collection of Japanese
carriers, Halsey took his battleships south to help out Taffy 3 and Kinkaid.
But then he had to slow to refuel his destroyers, made thirsty because of the

high-speed run to the north, and by then Taffy 3 was beyond help anyway.

Sprague and his men had fought with their backs to the wall. In the end, though, it wasn't Kinkaid, and certainly not Halsey, who saved part of Taffy 3—it was Kurita. Attacking the little carriers in haphazard fashion, afraid that Halsey or some other force would soon fall upon him, the Japanese admiral, exhausted and worn down by the previous days' battles, threw away one of the greatest opportunities his navy had had in the whole of the war. Rather than press on to the American beachhead, he broke off the attack and retired the way he had come, toward San Bernardino Strait, leaving five Taffy 3 ships sunk, several others mutilated, and hundreds of men dead in his wake. The landings would go unmolested; Japan's last major chance to influence American strategy was gone.

Shortly before midnight, Kurita's force withdrew through the strait. An hour or two later Halsey arrived with *New Jersey*, *Iowa*, and a few screening ships. Leaving the rest of the surface-action force behind to refuel, he had sprinted ahead to the strait to try to stop Kurita and to win another chance at directing a battle up close and in person. He failed on both counts. He found only a lone destroyer, an undignified and unsuitable target for battleships. He let his own destroyers and cruisers finish her off. "I was able to watch the action from *New Jersey*'s bridge," he wrote, "the first and only surface action I saw during my entire career." One can't help hearing the bitterness.[58]

The battle continued the following day, with continued air strikes against Kurita's retreating force, costing it another cruiser or two. But it was warfare at a remove and not as gratifying to Halsey as a close-quarters gunnery duel to the death would have been. And many of Kurita's ships got clean away, just as the carriers had gotten away from Spruance the previous spring. Worn down and without sources of fuel, they were as weak now as the carriers had been after Spruance had destroyed the carriers' planes, but the United States Navy couldn't be certain of that. All it knew was that Kurita had what the theorists call a fleet-in-being, a collection of warships that pose a threat by the fact of their very existence.

The fog of war can be thick, and it was extremely thick at Leyte. In size and scope, it was the greatest battle in history, yet it was strangely indecisive. It might well be called "the battle of missed opportunities." Through lack of resolve on the one hand and too much resolve on the other, nothing conclusive took place. Despite the lack of coordination and central command in the American force, the Japanese failed to disrupt the American reconquest of the Philippines, but the United States failed to wipe out what was left of the Japanese fleet. Afterward, that fleet was still out there somewhere, perhaps with one final battle left in it.

Halsey intended to fight that battle. He had fumbled at Leyte by failing to guard San Bernardino, though he never let on that he had. "I made a mistake in that battle," he told Admiral King when the two met a few months later. But the mistake he claimed wasn't the one at the strait. His mistake, Halsey told King, was "to turn south when the Japs were right under my guns" after receiving Nimitz's message. He held to this view for the rest of his life.[59]

The whole thing had been frustrating for Halsey, and he had to have been aware of the criticism that had already started. Just as bad, the prospect of directing a major, decisive fleet action from a ringside seat had eluded him. He'd missed his chance yet again. He wanted another, not only for the fight itself, but to efface the things that people were starting to say about him. If a chance didn't come up, he would make one.

But before he could create a chance such as that, he would have a different kind of battle to fight, and he would have to fight three of them, with three different enemies. In the end the outcome would call his very career into question. One of the enemies would continue to be the Japanese, though they would wield new and deadly weapons. Another would be Halsey's friend, General Douglas MacArthur.

The third was the sea herself.

PART TWO

The Beast

THE PACIFIC WAS A ROTTEN PLACE TO FIGHT A WAR. Most of the reason was distance; between them, MacArthur and Nimitz were responsible for a campaign that ranged over millions of square miles. Simply moving armies and fleets across such vast areas, let alone combating the enemy, was a tremendously complicated affair. And the Pacific's size was a source of still other complexities.

The battlefield spread over sixty degrees of latitude, from the Aleutians down past the equator and well into Australian waters. Between the Pacific Fleet's home in Pearl Harbor and the borders of China lay nearly ninety degrees of longitude out of a planetary total of three hundred and sixty. Within these far-flung boundaries, a voyager can find a matchless variety of climate as well as terrain, everything from tundra and permafrost to snake-infested tropical jungle to rain forest to sun-baked desert; everything from volcanic and earthquake-ridden island chains to impassable swampland and high, frosty mountains; and, nearly always, the ocean, whether choppy, or heaving, or windless and stifling. Even the seasons double-teamed the combatants: in the Pacific Theater, spanning two hemispheres, it was always simultaneously summer and winter, or autumn and spring.

Some of it could savor of tropical paradise, in the manner represented after the war in the work of James Michener and the *South Pacific* of Rodgers and Hammerstein, with their imagined world of lush music and sarong-clad

Polynesian beauties available to welcome American warriors. Stereotype and fable have their origins in some truth, after all. One of the most famous tales of the Pacific region is that of the British ship *Bounty* and her seduction by the ways of Tahiti. Bali Ha'i may have been real; during the battle to capture Truk in the opening weeks of 1944, Ray Spruance in *New Jersey* steamed in leisurely fashion close to the island's lagoon. Truk consisted of soaring green hills that were the tops of a submerged mountain range, and Spruance's chief of staff suspected that the admiral was indulging himself in some sightseeing. But Spruance had strategic reasons for showing the flag so insolently at Truk. It was a Japanese Gibraltar, and the American navy's presence there was a sure way to tell Nippon that the eastern empire was losing the war.[60]

And Hollywood and Broadway exaggerate, or get things flat wrong. The Gilberts, the Marshalls, the Carolines, and the Solomons are peopled not by Polynesians but by Micronesians and Melanesians, whose idea of feminine beauty is more akin to the Venus of Willendorf than to Fletcher Christian's Maimiti, Charles Nordhoff and James Norton Hall's Tehani, or James Michener's Liat. The scenery there was usually duller, with drab, sandy atolls that rose just a few feet above sea level, or islands with impenetrable carpets of jungle. Not until a soldier ventured ashore did the dullness turn deadly as combat ensued. As for the sailors, there was always sea and more sea, endless, interminable, all encompassing.[61]

The sea, though, was dangerous too. Always in motion, it could wreak the greatest destruction of all. Here lived demons that could alter the mood of the waters, changing them from placid to stormy—and beyond stormy into pure nightmare.

⚓

It was born in the ocean's far places, in abandoned reaches of the Pacific, unknown and invisible. Even if human eyes had been there to witness its beginning, they wouldn't have recognized it. There was nothing to see, almost nothing to feel. It started its brief, tempestuous life as nothing more than a murmur, a subtle stirring of atmosphere as gentle as the sigh of a lover.

To say it began with the wind is simplistic, even if true. Wind, they say, is air in motion. But all air is in motion, gentle or violent. The movements make the earth livable, distributing heat and humidity that would otherwise settle over the Planet in relative evenness. Early on, humanity sensed the importance of wind. *Ru, ruach, pneuma, animus* — Arabic, Hebrew, Greek, Latin, all of these words relating to wind, air, or breath have an unbreakable connection to the concept of soul, even divinity. The thing now rustling to life on the ocean was a creature of wind, but many things are creatures of wind. This one was different.

The winds — any winds — blow because the earth is curved and turns on its axis. If the planet were as flat as medieval sailors are supposed to have believed, the sun would strike all areas evenly, thus heating them evenly. But this isn't so. The sun heats the surface more at the equator and less at the poles, where its light shines less directly. As the solar rays hit the surface they warm it, especially in the tropics, and it reradiates the heat in the form of infrared waves, which then warm the atmosphere. As the air heats it expands, losing density, and thus it rises away from the warmth of the surface. Other cooler air from close to the poles rushes in to fill the partial vacuum that the rising warm air has created, making a vacuum of its own into which still other air moves. This other air is formerly tropical air, now high off the surface and losing its heat, sinking back toward the earth, beginning the process all over again. And so the wind blows.

Meanwhile the earth turns on its axis, imparting a spin to the wind, and that axis is tilted, so the sun's rays shift their angles with the change of the seasons, adding to the number of variables. The wind's twist is an intricate one. Someone standing a foot from the North or South Pole has a twenty-four-hour day, taking the full twenty-four hours to rotate the few feet around that pole. Meanwhile, in this same twenty-four hours, a Singaporean standing astride the equator dashes a distance of twenty-five thousand miles. The air masses above these places behave the same way, moving faster at the equator and much slower close to the poles, and as the air masses interact with each other, their wind patterns reflect the differing speeds.[62]

The result of all of these constants and variables is a complex system of winds that spans the whole planet — howling here, very calm there — generally predictable patterns that allow for widespread and unpredictable variations. We know the seasons when certain kinds of storms tend to occur; we can even know from statistics and history roughly how many of those storms are likely to happen in a given storm season. The exact number of storms, their

location and strength and timing—and their ferocity—we know less about.
The one thing we know for certain is that nature abhors a vacuum, and so do
the winds. As heated air rises away from the earth, other air will always move
in to fill the relative void. Low and high air pressure are facts of life in the atmosphere. But some low-pressure systems are different from others. Not all
low-pressure systems turn deadly.

The word *typhoon* is both strange and mysterious. *Hurricane*, too, is a strange
one, but we at least know where it comes from. It is not a European but a
tropical word; it is a derivation of *hurican*, or *hurakán*, the name given by the
now-extinct Taino people of the Bahamas and Greater Antilles to the Carib
god of evil.[63]

The origin of *typhoon* is much murkier. Perhaps it comes from the Can-
tonese phrase *t'ai fung*, which means "great wind." Or it could have its origins in *tufan*, the Arabic word for smoke. Its roots might even be found in
Greek: in that tongue *typhon* means "monster," and Aristotle once used it to
describe a type of cloud.[64]

Whatever the two words' exact meanings, hurricanes and typhoons are
related. In fact, they are the same thing, differing only in where they live and
die. Hurricanes appear in the Atlantic and the eastern Pacific. West of 180 degrees longitude lies the realm of the Pacific typhoons. Other names can be
found: Australians sometimes use the phrase willy-willy, and the Filipinos call
the storms *baguios*.[65] But all are the same, a phenomenon known as a tropical cyclone.

Cyclone, like hurricane, is a word of known meaning, quite clearly origi-
nating in Greek: κυκλωνis, or *kyklon*, means "to coil," as in the coiling of a
snake, a perfect description of the pattern of typhoon and hurricane winds.
The name was suggested by British scientist Henry Piddington in the mid-
nineteenth century, and it quickly caught on. For the key to the tropical cyclone's destructive potential lies in its whirling, concentric winds.[66]

These winds flow in a highly predictable fashion, blowing strongly counterclockwise in a Northern Hemisphere storm and vice versa south of the
equator, a line never crossed by hurricanes and typhoons. This pattern is just

another result of the laws that govern the earth's winds in general. A single, huge air mass stretching from the North Pole to the equator would move more slowly in the north, just as the polar citizen would move more slowly than the Singaporean. This would impart a vast counterclockwise movement to the whole mass. Tropical cyclones are far smaller than that, but the principle is the same.

In fact, tropical cyclones are just that: not equatorial, not polar, but tropical, at least in their origin, though they may stray far from the tropics before they blow themselves out. They need warmth to form, which excludes the high latitudes, and a stronger wind pattern than is found in the doldrums of the equatorial region. Their breeding grounds are well known, though the storms can travel thousands of miles from them once they are full grown. And one of the world's most cyclone-rich hothouses lay just a few hundred miles east of the Philippines, where Third Fleet was operating in 1944's autumn.

The invisible thing that lay on the water was growing. A sailor on a ship that chanced to voyage through this lone spot of ocean might have noted a falling barometer, no more than 29.6 inches of pressure at any rate—normal sea-level pressure is 29.92—and perhaps some heavy showers or even storms to the east. He would also find, if he bothered to check, that the water temperature was somewhat higher than seventy-eight degrees. These barometric and temperature readings would have shown him that two of the basic building blocks—low pressure and heat—were in place.[67]

Other things would be harder for him to know with just his barometer and a thermometer. Though he could see, with the former, evidence of falling air pressure, he might not realize that this was due to an easterly wave, a low-pressure zone where the trade winds converged, concentrating their force. Nor might he realize, without some meteorological training, that the zone where Northern and Southern Hemisphere winds converged had crept somewhat northward that month, and that it was now lying almost directly overhead. If he had known all of these things, and if he had added the fact that he was in a latitude where most tropical cyclones take shape, he might have grown dimly aware of what was stirring to life all around him.

The northward march of the intertropical conversion zone, as modern scientists call it, is key. It is a routine and somewhat predictable thing, floating over the equator only approximately, straying north or south with the seasons. If it moves over warm seas and a low-pressure area caused by an easterly wave, winds flowing from west and east can begin to circle each other like sharks, the way water whirlpools as it flows down a drain, the atmospheric low at the winds' center drawing them in.

But all this starts slowly. So far, nothing would seem very out of the ordinary to any seasoned mariner, especially in the days before satellite imagery and computer models that could be digitally flashed to a ship in an instant. Atmospheric disturbances can take place over very large areas, so the observations at a single location—such as on a lone ship—can only tell a voyager so much. A falling glass and a bit of heavy weather spotted on the horizon are hardly uncommon at sea. The storms to the east would seem to be nothing unusual, just another of the countless, so-called tropical disturbances that happen in any given year. Perhaps the first sure sign to our lone observer would be the telltale circular winds. They would have been gentle at first. He might not even know that they were counterclockwise, lacking the aggregate information from others nearby that alone could give a snapshot of what was happening. But perhaps he would realize that the wind was blowing over his ship in an odd way. It might still be rather soft . . . but it wouldn't be coming from the normal direction for this latitude. This might trigger his first premonitions of trouble.

He would be right. This odd counterclockwise wind was a milepost in the life of the creature that now stirred somewhere east or southeast of Guam. It had leapt the first hurdle on the way to achieving its destiny; the product of several, unrelated variables, it had knitted them all together, becoming a tropical depression—a discernible cyclone.

Hurricanes and typhoons are massive heat pumps. Simply put, they concentrate heat. Heat is energy, and energy can be destructive. Tropical cyclonic disturbances are so supremely destructive because they are so good at sucking in heat.

Tropical waters, bombarded as they are by the sun, are the world's richest heat source, or rather, heat storehouse. They radiate energy into the lower atmosphere, and because of the heat, the water also evaporates quickly, carrying humidity and still more energy into the air.[68]

A low-pressure area over these waters, such as the one now forming off Guam, draws this hot, moist air inward, while the planet's rotation and the prevailing wind directions conspire to give it a spinning route. As this air whirls closer and closer to the heart of the cyclone, the heat concentrations increase; by the time they come to the center, the warm air is rising, ultimately climbing tens of thousands of feet into the atmosphere.

High over the roiling clouds, an opposite force is at work: an anticyclone, an air mass with a warm, high-pressure center fed by the rising air from below, which by now has rained itself dry. Just as the air near the surface whirled inward to the low-pressure core, bringing its heat along with it, now, far above, it spins back out from the high-pressure zone that sits directly over the low. As the high flings the heat hundreds of miles outward, it makes room for more air to rise up from the storm core in a continuous cycle. The tropical ocean keeps making the air humid and hot; the hurricane or typhoon keeps sucking this air into its center and then blowing it up to the top of the sky, where, its energy spent, it flies far away. The process's only real limit is how much heat the cyclone can get.[69]

The bigger a cyclone is, the more heat is available to it, for it has more ocean, more surface area, from which it can draw. If it moves over land, which holds its warmth to itself, the storm can't find enough heat; if it stalls over one stretch of ocean too long, it exhausts the energy there and then starts to weaken. But if it keeps moving over tropical waters, it thrives, its intensity building as it seizes more heat. Then, when it does strike land, it strikes with a fury unmatched by anything else on earth, whether of natural or of human invention.

Water is heavy, but the air holds a great deal of water, even in low-humidity regions. The column of air that reaches from the top of a person's head to the top of the troposphere has enough water in it, on average, to make a half inch of rain, if the right conditions of pressure, temperature, and atmospheric impurities help it precipitate.[70] And the amount of precipitation that large storms produce is staggering. The massive North American winter storm of 1993 coated the ground with more than fifty billion tons of water, sleet, and snow, as much water as flows through the Mississippi River in a month and a half. In the 1996 blizzard, a hundred million tons of snow fell on New York City alone.[71] There is power, nearly incomprehensible power, in all of this water—and in some storms more than others.

A tropical cyclone is smaller in area than a winter storm of that kind, and its winds are usually lower than those of tornadoes. But it is far, far bigger than any tornado, and its winds are much more powerful than anything else, including winter storms. It is this unique combination of size and wind strength that allows the tropical cyclone to rank incontestably above any other weather phenomenon when it comes to sheer destructiveness.[72] Not even human-made forces can hope to match it. One of the early Bikini atomic bomb tests blew ten million tons of water into the atmosphere; compare that to one Caribbean hurricane that dropped 250 times more water than that onto Puerto Rico alone.[73]

Water is dozens of times denser than air. Precipitate a lot of it and then hurl it at buildings or people or ships at high speeds, and its ability to destroy can be truly terrible. But the A-bomb comparison doesn't end with the water. A-bombs produce heat, and lots of it, but the heat energy of just an average hurricane or typhoon far eclipses that of any *hydrogen* bomb. Hurricane Georges, which ripped through the Caribbean in 1998, released enough heat energy to have supplied the electrical needs of the entire United States for a decade, enough energy to equal a million Hiroshima-size weapons. Given an average cyclone with an average week or two life span, and the energy release is equal to a half dozen Hiroshimas every single second.[74]

The real-world effects of this force are often fatal and sometimes catastrophic. As many as nine thousand people died in the Galveston, Texas, hurricane of 1900, and the town was torn to pieces. Hurricane Flora took seven thousand lives in Haiti and Cuba in 1963. The Barbados storm of 1780 achieved a death toll of twenty-two thousand, and the Great Bengal Cyclone of 1737 is supposed to have killed three hundred thousand.[75] This last figure is probably an overestimate, but the typhoon was certainly capable of killing that many, as one of its cousins showed two and a half centuries later. In 1970 a typhoon hit the Ganges Delta at midnight, the densely populated islands there lacking any way of evacuation. Within a few days, according to some estimates, a million people were dead.[76]

Nonhuman damage from tropical cyclones reaches a similar, nearly in-credible scale, the storms cutting swaths of devastation forty or fifty miles wide, in much the same pattern that General William T. Sherman's army used while rampaging through Georgia and South Carolina. Striking just below Miami in 1992, Hurricane Andrew leveled an area as large as Chicago, wiping out thirty billion dollars of property; three years earlier, Hurricane Hugo, like Sherman, hit the Carolinas and Georgia, costing eight billion dollars or so. And Andrew and Hugo were merely Category 4 storms. Even the infamous Katrina, which burst New Orlean's levees and eradicated much of the city as well as devastat-ing the rest of the Gulf Coast in August 2005, came ashore in Louisiana only as a Category 4 hurricane. The most destructive is a Category 5.[77]

Almost nothing can stand in a tropical cyclone's path. When Category 5 Hurricane Mitch hit Guanaja off the northern coast of Honduras in October 1998, the few residents left on the island retreated to concrete bunkers de-signed for just such an event. Even so, as the fury struck and then raged for an astonishing sixty hours, they were unsure if the walls would hold up.[78] Hearing of a typhoon's approach toward Guam in 1962, some marines there secured their equipment in a Quonset hut, locking the building down tightly. After the typhoon had passed, the hut and everything in it had vanished com-pletely. Only the concrete slab remained.[79] When tropical cyclones hit, stout trees bend and then snap like twigs if they aren't uprooted completely, weather instruments are torn to pieces, and people who jump into the air are blown for a dozen feet before touching the ground again. Items can be carried aloft and travel for hundreds of miles before landing; one hurricane to hit the Carolinas brought debris all the way from Haiti. Dorothy's trip in her house from Kansas to Oz is one of the story's most believable details, even though it is about a tornado and even though the house would have been smashed into splinters before completing its journey.

The tropical depression was strengthening now, becoming self-sustaining as it began the heat-pump action. The winds, feeling the pull of the core of low pressure, were soaking up loads of warm water from the surface layer of the Pacific before starting their long path inward. As they whirled toward the core, a law of physics stepped in; the closer to the center they came, the smaller their spiral wound, like the inner grooves of a phonograph record as compared to the long outer ones. And as the winds' force was compressed into that shorter circular path, the law of angular momentum commanded them to speed up. The closer to the center they came, the faster and harder they blew, just as a spinning ice skater spins faster as she pulls her arms close to her body.[80] By the time the winds were as far in as they could go, they were a howling, shrieking mass, even though this was still a mere depression. Its sustained winds had reached something like thirty-three knots, or a touch under forty miles per hour. This was the steady wind speed, not the speed of brief, faster gusts. At thirty-three knots, the wind exerted a pressure of ten pounds per square foot on anything, or anyone, who faced it. As the depression grew in size and intensity, the wind speed picked up, and its force grew exponentially.[81]

Now, at the center of the disturbance, an eye was beginning to form, the telltale cyclone eye, a deceptively calm area where the pressure was the lowest of all, the warm core at the heart of the engine. The depression was becoming a tropical storm, and its winds were growing fearsome, especially at the eye wall, swirling as fast as sixty knots, nearly eighty miles an hour.[82]

No one who has seen an eye wall or has survived the feat of coming through one into the terrifying calm of the eye is likely to forget it. A survivor of Hurricane Mitch found, to his horror, that he could actually see the wind, not the rain that it drove but the very air itself, rippling in densely packed waves. Later, as he and others stood in the eye, ears popping from the extraordinarily low pressure, they looked out to sea and saw the eye wall slowly approaching. Gray, solid, featureless, occasionally shifting and bulging, it had the appearance and apparent solidity of concrete, a wall of concrete that reached higher than their own eyes could reach, perhaps as high as eight or ten miles. That was what they had just passed through, and what they would have to pass through again as the hurricane kept on its way.[83]

Joseph Conrad, too, described such a nightmarish place, and his description, perhaps, is the best.

> Through a jagged aperture in the dome of clouds the light of a few stars
> fell upon black sea, rising and falling confusedly. Sometimes the head

of a watery cone would topple on board and mingle with the rolling flurry of foam on the swamped deck; and the *Nan-Shan* wallowed heavily at the bottom of a circular cistern of clouds. The ring of dense vapors, gyrating madly round the calm of the center, encompassed the ship like a motionless and unbroken wall of an aspect inconceivably sinister. Within, the sea, as if agitated by an internal commotion, leaped in peaked mounds that jostled each other, slapping heavily against her sides; and a low moaning sound, the infinite plaint of the storm's fury, came from beyond the limits of the menacing calm.[84]

As the eye's conditions reveal, a cyclone commands not only the wind but the ocean, and the newly hatched tropical storm moving slowly past Guam was no exception. The wind spawns waves—high columns of water that break into foamy, cascading torrents—and lower, longer swells, which in time might grow into tall breaking waves. They rush far ahead of the cyclone's path, forerunners that warn of what lies below the horizon. A bright, sunny day becomes sinister when a beachcomber realizes not only that the breeze, though no stronger than usual on such a fine day, is blowing in the wrong direction for that spot of coastline, but that the booming surf is eerily loud.

If a tropical cyclone's wind pressure is destructive, then the force of its waters is murderous. A cubic yard of water weighs three-fourths of a ton, and large waves consist of untold thousands of cubic yards of water.[85] A strong hurricane or typhoon can generate monstrous waves that travel as much as fifty miles an hour. Close to the storm's center, these waves come in a fast, endless procession. The result can be almost mind shattering.

In the eye, the waters back up, forced inwards by the concentric winds. Even the extremely low pressure helps some, sucking the water level up, as if through a straw, by at least a few feet. Then, when a cyclone hits land, the water rises up not merely in waves but in a massive storm surge, as shallow coastal bottoms help it pile up still further. It is this storm surge, a high wall of pent-up water that hurtles onto and over the coast, that is the cyclone's deadliest weapon against land. It accounts for 90 percent of the loss of life in hurricanes and typhoons.[86] And even though the air of an eye may be calm, the sea there, as Conrad points out in his passage, can seemingly go insane.

This is one of the worst parts of all. A tropical cyclone may lay waste the land, but the storm surge can only reach so far from the coast; on shore, in most places at least, there is still something to cling to. The open ocean, however, does not hold out the hope that land offers typhoon and hurricane victims. "There is much difference in being involved in a cyclone on shore and at sea," one typhoon survivor described near the close of the nineteenth century. "In one case you have only the wind and rain to combat; in the other, you have not only these but a quivering ship and unstable deck to work your salvation on."[87] And on the enraged seas in the eye of a tropical cyclone, things are about as bad as can be. The waves there come smashing together in fantastic, furious ways that make the place a deathtrap for vessels. Raphael Semmes, captain of the Confederate Navy's famed *Alabama*, rode his ship through hours of a hurricane's nightmare, at last bursting suddenly into the false serenity of the airs of the eye. "The scene was the most remarkable I had ever witnessed," he wrote afterward.

> The aspect of the heavens was appalling. The clouds were writhing and twisting, like so many huge serpents engaged in combat, and hung so low, in the thin air of the vortex, as almost to touch our mastheads. The best description I can give of the sea, is that of a number of huge watery cones — or the waves seemed now in the diminished pressure of the atmosphere in the vortex to *jut up into the sky*, and assume a conical shape — that were dancing an infernal reel, played by some necromancer. They were not running in any given direction, there being no longer any wind to drive them, but were jostling each other, like drunken men in a crowd, and threatening every moment, to topple, one upon the other.[88]

It is this kind of demon-stirred ocean that can bury ships alive in thousands of fathoms of water, sweep whole fleets from the surface. Before the Great Bengal Cyclone of 1737, twenty thousand vessels dotted Calcutta Harbor; afterward none remained.[89] The "Great Hurricane" of 1780 decimated naval and merchant shipping from Barbados to Martinique. ("Good God!" wrote a young Alexander Hamilton of a similar Caribbean storm not many years earlier. "What horror and destruction. It's impossible for me describe or you to form any idea of it. It seemed as if a total dissolution of nature was taking place.")[90] And the Bangladesh cyclone of 1970 had much the same effect. The vessels that lay in the Ganges Delta vanished into the maw of the storm and never emerged.

The United States Navy wasn't spared such a horror. It was no newcomer to the Pacific in 1944; its ships had sailed there for more than a century. And in 1889, at a crucial historical moment, an American force that was primed and ready for battle met a foe of wind and water instead, learning an expensive and valuable lesson.

It happened in the Samoan chain. Pago Pago, on Tutuila Island there, had one of the finest anchorages in the mid-Pacific, second only to Pearl Harbor and perhaps Manila Bay. A decade or so earlier, in 1878, the United States had signed a treaty with the Samoans that gave it the right to build a naval station there in furtherance of American interests.[91]

American treaty rights notwithstanding, England and Germany both had economic and strategic interests in the Samoan chain, too, and by March 1889 they had sent warships to Apia Harbor on nearby Upolu. So America sent three of its own men-of-war, *Trenton*, *Vandalia*, and *Nipsic*, to Apia, although they were of older design than their English and German counterparts. Tensions were running high by mid-month; but before any shooting could start, a typhoon sprang out of the remote heart of the South Pacific, sweeping over Upolu Island. After days of poor weather, the storm hit full-force on the fifteenth of March.[92] By the time evening fell, the cascading rains were pouring a flood down the river feeding into the wine ragged V of the harbor, stripping the mud and sand from the bottom and leaving nothing but hard, bare coral into which no anchor could bite.[93]

Germany's *Eber* was the first to go. A high wave threw her broadside onto the harbor's coral reef, smashing her to pieces and killing all but four of her total complement.[94] Another German ship, *Olga*, floundered into the middle of the tempestuous harbor, her anchors totally useless, and crashed into *Nipsic*. Two of *Nipsic*'s boats were sheared off; the main yard and chains were damaged, and the funnel was torn away near the main deck. As the stack fell, sparks flew, and wind poured down into the boilers, the blowback hurling flames out through the doors of the furnaces. The firemen scrambled to get out of the way, and steam started dropping off fast, starving *Nipsic* of power just when she needed it most. In desperation, *Nipsic*'s commanding officer decided to beach what was left of the ship while he could still do it. Slipping her port anchor cable, the fourteen, hundred, ton warship pivoted sharply on the remaining sheet chain, ripping it out of her innards and then sprinting high up onto a short stretch of beach.[95]

The carnage continued into the following day. Soon after dawn, a massive wave hit the German ship *Adler*, lifting her high and carrying her 150 yards onto a solid coral reef, where she toppled over onto her side.[96] *Vandalia* was likewise being carried inexorably toward the reef; shipping heavy seas, she started to wallow, and her boilers began drowning.[97]

The larger *Trenton* was in trouble as well. Rear Admiral Lewis A. Kimberly had expected a storm, but neither he nor anyone else had dreamed that things would get this bad. For most of the night his flagship had ridden quite well, seas smashing over her bow into high plumes of spray that landed far back on her decks. At one point a heavy sea stove in her starboard bridle point, killing a crewman and threatening to flood the whole gun deck.[98] By heroic efforts the crew sealed the hole; one sailor crawled crazily over the outside of the hull to help lock a capstan bar into place over the shattered port, while from inside the ship other crewmen stuffed hammocks and mattresses into it, holding them in with beams and tables.[99]

The seas grew still rougher. *Trenton*'s rudder post gave way, perhaps because she had sounded bottom, and as the rudder came free, the two helmsmen went flying over the crazily spinning wheel, smashing their legs as they landed. One wave picked up two other sailors and threw them a hundred feet down the main deck. And still the pounding continued.[100]

Calliope, the sole British vessel, was the most modern and powerful warship at Apia, though not the largest. Captain Henry C. Kane, watching the other ships skittering across the coral-bottomed harbor, decided that his would be better off taking her chances on the open sea. Calling for every ounce of steam the boilers could give, he began to dodge the out-of-control vessels and the barrier reefs, fighting a hundred-knot wind and a six-knot tide. Miraculously, *Calliope* managed to claw her way out of Apia and then to survive somehow on the churning deep. By nightfall the worst was over, and before long the weather cleared enough to allow *Calliope* to put back in to Apia.[101]

An amazing sight greeted the ship. *Calliope*'s captain and men found "the harbour perfectly clear, not a craft, from *Trenton* to a schooner, afloat in it." *Trenton* and *Vandalia* were both flooded, the latter sunk up to her netting, and *Trenton*, with her bottom pounded out by the coral, awash to her main deck. *Nipsic* was beached, *Adler* dead on the reef; *Olga* was high and dry. *Eber* had completely disintegrated. All of the anchor buoys were gone, and of the merchant ships and the many small craft that had lately plied the harbor, none was left floating. The American and German warships were scattered around like a giant's broken playthings, which is precisely what they were.[102]

The death toll was high: In addition to *Eber*'s seventy-six dead, there were twenty from *Adler*, seven from *Nipsic*, and one aboard *Trenton*. *Vandalia*'s losses were heavy. Forty-three of her people were killed, including her captain. As she had foundered, her crew and officers tried to swim to the shore or to nearby *Nipsic*, but the torrent that was sweeping downriver had washed most of them out to sea. A few bodies came back in on the waves not long after being drawn out, mutilated by the treatment they had received from water and coral.[103]

There were plenty of Americans who had no interest at all in Samoa or Pacific expansion, and Bismarck held a low opinion of colonies, thinking them, as he thought of the Balkans, "not worth the bones of a single Pomeranian grenadier." *Calliope*'s survival betokened the fact of Great Britain's unchallengeable navy; with ships and seamanship of that sort, she could do without Samoa if need be. Now, the typhoon had destroyed a collection of warships that were likely worth more than the commercial value of the whole Samoan chain. The disaster brought about a conference in Berlin, at which the three powers paved over their differences, for the time being, by establishing a joint protectorate over the islands.[104]

Meanwhile, in Apia Harbor, the corpses of *Trenton*, *Vandalia*, and *Adler* bore witness to the helplessness of modern steam navies in the face of a furious nature. And the United States Navy took note, and remembered.

This wasn't the first time—as it would not be the last—that weather had played a role in war, or at least in diplomacy. Heavy autumn rains, for example, turned

Agincourt into a field of mud and bogged down the French advance on the
English in 1415, and it was the winter as much as anything else that had
foiled Napoléon's campaign to conquer Russia.[105] But the snows of winter
and the rain and muddy roads of the spring are predictable, at least in general terms. For that matter, so are hurricanes and typhoons. Because of various factors, they are spawned in seven general regions of the tropics,
among them the North Atlantic, the eastern North Pacific, and the western
reaches of the South Pacific. The young storm building off Guam was in another of these regions, the western North Pacific, the place called "typhoon
alley" by some because it is the most fertile by far of the seven breeding
grounds. And though this area, like the South Pacific, had no true typhoon
season, the storms here tend to happen more often in some months than
others. In some of the other places, of course, tropical cyclones come on a
highly seasonal basis.

Even the storms' general movements can be known with the help of time
and statistics. Tropical cyclones are large, but they move within, and can even
be steered by, still larger air masses. Given the prevailing winds, hurricanes
and typhoons tend to move west and to curve slowly away from the equator.
In some cases the curvature can be so great that the storms eventually swing
back toward the east, in which case the movement is called "recurvature."
Modern meteorology divides cyclone tracks into a dozen or so categories
that bear names such as "textbooker," "sharpcrooker," "straightshooter," and
"longlooper." But much of this knowledge is the result of years of observation and computerized number crunching, and it often fails to help much
when it comes to predicting exactly when and where a particular cyclone will
form, how strong it will be, how fast it will move, and where it will go.[106]

The general information can be useful to an extent. Statistics tell us, for
instance, that the new tropical storm off Guam had beaten the odds in becoming a tropical storm at all, for 90 percent of all tropical disturbances
never make it to that robust stage, dying in or before the tropical depression phase. But this leaves crucial questions unanswered, and even this
level of statistical knowledge is fairly recent. A century or so ago, meteorological science lacked a great many tools. It had no radar, no satellites, no
good, high-speed way of gathering widespread real-time data or sounding
the upper atmosphere. Telegraph and manned balloons were something but

not much. An even greater handicap was meteorology's lack of a solid theory. The basic knowledge of a cyclone's whirlwind pattern, for instance, only dated from the 1820s. Given these shortcomings, weather prediction was dicey at best.[107] So when the theory and technology began to improve, it was a welcome development, especially for the military.

The United States Signal Service began collecting data on tropical cyclones in 1871, but in a rudimentary way; lacking radio, the system was useless when it came to weather conditions at sea.[108] During the Spanish-American War, the threat of Caribbean hurricanes worried the government more than Spanish forces in Cuba did. But though the first modern theoretical breakthroughs had just lately begun—ironically, with the research of a Cuban, the Jesuit priest Benito Viñes—meteorology still wasn't up to the challenge of modern forecasting.[109]

World War I started to alter that. The cataclysm changed not only warfare, not only society, but meteorology too. Weather had always played a key part in armed conflict, but now it assumed a special importance. The warring nations had developed a way to make the air itself a weapon, corrupting it with chlorine, phosgene, and mustard gas, which could drift down on enemy trenches and burn a soldier to death from the inside out. Imagine pouring bleach into a bowl of goldfish; the poor creatures have nowhere to hide, the poison becoming one with the very thing that keeps them alive.

The problem was that while the toxic gases could be dumped into the atmosphere, the wind's direction could not be controlled and the weapon could thus turn on its master. The only option was to predict what the air was going to do, and that required good forecasting. Aviators, too, called out for that capability; wind direction determined how much fuel they would need to get to and from combat or whether they would be able to fly at all.[110]

The turning point came from the neutral Norwegians. Starved by the U-boat attacks on commercial shipping as well as by bad harvests, cut off from weather reports from the British Isles to the west since those reports were now military secrets, Norway needed alternatives, and she found them right at home. By 1918, Norwegian meteorologist Vilhelm Bjerknes was building an all-star team that would rewrite meteorological theory.

Armed with new methods of observation, including airplanes and unmanned balloons, by the mid-1920s the Bjerknes crew had given not just

Norway but everyone else more accurate ways of weather prediction. One of their more famous inventions was the modern weather map with its corresponding ideas of warm and cold fronts. The term "front" came from the war's trenches, which the warring convergence lines on the weather maps strongly resembled. The trenches were all front—no flanks, no accessible rear—and, like the weather, they must simply be faced. In this way war mixed with weather the way mustard gas mixes with air.[111]

Gradually, after the war, the theories of the Bergen school began to trickle over the borders and flow to other continents. Most American meteorologists were slow to accept the new methods—they had their own systems, after all—but the Bergen way was more accurate, and that was what mattered with weather prediction. The United States Navy, with its new interest in aviation, was one of the first organizations to start making the switch, years before the federal Weather Bureau showed any interest, and other aviators around the country soon followed suit. Throughout the twenties and thirties, Bergen disciples multiplied in America, partly through serendipity. An early American convert, navy meteorologist Francis W. Reichelderfer, introduced a friend of his to young Bergen hotshot Carl-Gustav Rossby, who now lived and worked in the United States. Reichelderfer's friend was a balloonist and a former World War I pilot named Harry Guggenheim. Before long, Rossby had Guggenheim money behind him, and through Reichelderfer's and Rossby's efforts, Bergen-style programs began springing up all over the country in key places such as Harvard, the Massachusetts Institute of Technology (MIT), Chicago, and Annapolis.[112]

One of the Bergen system's basic requirements, and a requirement of any good forecasting system, was a lot of real-time data collected over a widespread geographical area. Air masses are large and can move very quickly; the only way to get an accurate picture of them is to look at several places at once and high in the sky as well as near the earth's surface. Lots of observations means lots of trained observers armed with modern equipment and access to a fast communications network. Telegraph had helped; radio helped even more, and soon there was a modern teletype circuit, along with weather flights and balloon readings. By the time World War II broke out, the navy, along with nearly everyone else, had completely bought in. During the war years, Bergen programs across the country—

from Harvard in Cambridge, Massachusetts, to Cal Tech and the University
of California—churned out seven thousand military meteorologists who
served in the armed forces, including the U.S. Pacific Fleet. Rossby's own
personal program at the University of Chicago accounted for more than 20
percent of them.[113]

But this was the biggest war in history, fought all over the globe, with air
and other weather-critical operations taking place everywhere. The Pacific was
a very large place, and even seven thousand weathermen weren't enough.

The beast was still growing in the heart of the sea, hidden, unsuspected, unseen, feeding on the heat of the waters as if were mother's milk. But it was
growing; the time for milk alone was soon past, and soon it would require
something else. Massive armies and fleets struggled and steamed and fought
not far away in global terms, at less than one or two thousand miles' distance.
They were within easy reach. And it was far bigger than all of them.

The winds grew stronger, much stronger now than before. A tropical
storm no longer, the cyclone had grown up. It was now a typhoon. And it was
moving toward the Philippines. Toward the patch of Pacific that Third Fleet
sailed.

More than six hundred years before, the first typhoon on record had
come to the aid of the Japanese people. In 1281, as the invading forces of
Kublai Khan arrived in Kyushu's Hakata Bay and prepared to conquer
Japan, this storm—one of history's best-known—attacked the Mongol forces,
destroying the fleet of more than four thousand vessels as only a typhoon
could have. A hundred thousand Mongols died, and it was said that one could
walk across Hakata Bay on the wrecks of the ships in the wake of the storm.
Japan had lain open to Kublai, but then the wind conquered the conqueror,
the wind the Japanese were convinced must have been sent by the gods, if, indeed, it weren't a god itself. This was the Divine Wind, the *Kamikaze*.[114]

Now, in the tropical autumn of 1944, Japan faced an equally serious
threat from the ocean, the greatest ocean-borne threat since the Mongols,
and just as a typhoon had come to their aid six centuries earlier, so a typhoon
was once again headed toward the invading fleet.

The Japanese, however, would not leave everything to the gods. Before this typhoon could strike, the enemy's fleet would feel the wrath of another kamikaze. And it, too, would come with the winds.

PART THREE

The Smart Bombs

THE CHERRY BLOSSOM IS A NEARLY MYSTICAL THING to the Japanese people. It buds and blooms on thousands of trees on the Home Islands each year from January to May, a cascading, pale pink procession rolling up from the south to the north, fleeting, beautiful, transient. After a few fragile, glorious days, a mere breath of breeze, fainter than that of a typhoon's birth, will scatter the fragrant petals. Other blossoms will come in time, but these are gone forever, gone in a silent, perfumed blizzard of flowers, sometimes mingled with the chilly white snowflakes of a late-winter storm, the seasons of beginning and ending merged into one.

The cherry blossom's short-lived beauty best reflects an idea that Motoori Norinaga, eighteenth-century man of letters, called *mono no aware*. Literally, the phrase means "the pathos of things," but it goes far deeper than that; it is the comprehension, the understanding, that all beauty is fleeting. This melancholy insight into life's deepest wellsprings colors the Japanese outlook on human nature, human existence, aesthetics, and death.

In the fall of 1944, a troubled Japanese warrior, sensing death on his own horizons, seized on the ancient symbol as a way of expressing his thoughts about what he and his men were facing.

Blossoming now,
Tomorrow scattered on the winds,
Such is the flower of life.
So delicate a perfume
Cannot last long.

The warrior's name was Takijiro Ōnishi. He was a vice admiral of the Imperial Japanese Navy, and now that Admiral Isoroku Yamamoto was dead, killed in an ambush by American planes, Ōnishi was the foremost Japanese authority on the use of naval airpower. As Japan's war ground on and the Americans moved inexorably closer, it was Ōnishi who began to press a concept euphemistically known as Tokubetsukōgeki, or more simply Tokkō—"special attack." And as the battle for the Philippines began, he created a new organization based on this principle: the Special Attack Corps, an entity better known as the kamikaze.[115]

On October 21 1944, as American warships approached Leyte, they were spotted by Japanese scouts. Quickly the scouts alerted the Shikishima unit of the Japanese Navy's 201st Air Group, which immediately went on alert.[116]

The new unit—in fact, it was only a day or two old—was based at Mabalacat, part of Manila's Clark Field complex. The jungle embraced the small field; the mango leaves audibly rustled even in a soft breeze. When American planes struck, the sounds of war would echo across the field as explosions and bullets tore up the ground and anything on it. For the moment there were no American planes overhead, but there were still sounds of war, though they were sounds of a very different sort from those of attacking aircraft.

The first sound was a soft gurgle of water as a navy pilot filled cups for his gathered comrades. The water was from a container recently brought by Admiral Ōnishi himself, and this ritual of sharing water from a sacred spring was part of a very old samurai tradition.

Then came the strains of a song, as the pilots began to join in the traditional hymn of the dead that was a favorite with the navy.

> *If I go away to sea*
> *I shall return a corpse awash.*
> *If duty calls me to the mountain,*
> *A verdant sward will be my pall;*
> *For the sake of the Emperor I will not die*
> *Peacefully at home.*

Next came a quick, quiet crumple of paper. As the pilots prepared to man their planes, their leader, Lieutenant Yukio Seki, handed a folded sheet to a friend who was staying behind. It contained a few strands of Seki's hair; this, too, was part of the ritual for those samurai who had a rendezvous with death. Seki had recently married, and the hair would go to his family and his young wife, Mariko.[117]

At last came the more familiar war sounds of engines turning over and catching, of planes creaking into takeoff position and beginning to roll down the strip, clawing their way into the sky.

Shikishima was one of four Shinpū, or kamikaze, units. Both of the latter words mean the same thing: "divine wind"; it is well known that the phrase refers to the typhoon that had destroyed Kublai Kahn's invasion fleet. Less well known is the fact that Ōnishi rendered the Kanji characters as "Shinpū," a more formal, elegant enunciation than the relatively coarse "kamikaze." But the Westerners didn't know that when they translated the phrase, and before long the units had universally become known, even in Japan, as the kamikazes.[118]

The units were born of a strange blend of indomitable spirit and desperation, impending death and immortality, human intelligence and brute force. The strategic crisis that Leyte brought to a head made kamikaze efforts necessary; the samurai code of Bushido made those efforts possible.

The Bushido concept of self-sacrifice ran deep in Japanese culture. The eighteenth-century book *Hagakure*, one of the best summations of "the way of the warrior," made this clear in its very first passage. "The Way of the Samurai is found in death," it lectured to the aspiring samurai. Voluntary death, especially in battle, was a living statement of *mono no aware*, a recognition that self-sacrifice would bring glory, rob the enemy of his ultimate triumph over the samurai's spirit, and, if carried out properly, deal the opponent a deadly blow. The kamikaze spirit reflected all of these things.[119]

The Japanese had a long tradition of military suicide, for lack of a better term, and the tradition had often been honored during the war years. Wounded soldiers and injured pilots of badly damaged planes had often flung themselves at the enemy; during the capture of Saipan the previous spring, not just soldiers but civilians had embraced death in a great many ways, everything from taking cyanide to throwing themselves off cliffs—and, yes, smashing their aircraft into approaching American warships.

But what was happening in the Philippines was different. The thing that made the kamikaze unique was that it involved a system, a formal organization in which admirals and generals asked their subordinates for a premeditated decision to die for strategic reasons. This was new in the war, perhaps in any war. Given the fact of Bushido, especially in the aristocratic navy, the high-ranking officers probably knew they could expect a lot of volunteers, moved by everything from honor to duty. Many of the commanders were torn about asking; yet they asked. They felt that they had to, because a crisis required it.

Airpower's primary mission is to drop munitions onto surface targets. All in all, this is a fairly simple process. But when the target is shooting back, this mission gets a lot harder. In order to survive and to maintain a good hit-kill probability, the attacking plane has got to be able to defend itself, and self-defense takes up a lot of resources. The resources can include defensive weaponry, maneuverability, or tactics, to name but a few. But all of this makes flying in combat harder, requiring greater skill of the pilot and aircrew.[120]

By late 1944 Japan's best naval pilots were already dead, wiped out in battles ranging from Midway to the Philippine Sea. The replacement pilots weren't nearly as good, having had less training and much less experience. Attack planes were getting scarce, too. Japanese fighter planes, for instance, the famed Zero, code-named "Zeke" by the Allies, were still available, but they weren't built for bombing. Available torpedo planes and dive-bombers were rare, and with the American cordon tightening and Japanese industry faltering, the planes lacked fuel and spare parts. There were still army pilots, but they, too, lacked the right skills and right planes for attacking warships.[121]

The problem was simply one of complexity. Flying a plane takes skill. Flying a plane in combat, and surviving, takes not only skill but experience. But flying by itself does nothing to bring force to bear on the enemy. To do that, someone on the plane must release munitions—bullets, rockets, bombs, or in more recent decades, missiles. These things require aiming. If the pilot must aim and release the munitions in addition to flying the plane and dodging enemy fire, as was the case with many torpedo planes and dive-bombers, his task becomes hugely difficult. And once the projectile—for instance, a bomb—is released, it becomes subject to the laws of gravity and the vagaries of aerodynamic drag, for which it can't correct and which the pilot might not have properly taken account of amid the chaos of combat. If the target is a ship, the fact that it moves, that it can maneuver out of the way of munitions, makes hitting it even more difficult.[122]

All of this meant that precision naval bombing was hard, even with training. The obstacles were well known by 1944: a plane attacking a ship was going to encounter so many rounds of antiaircraft fire for every second of its approach, and that was if the pilot had managed to get by the enemy fighter planes of the combat air patrol (CAP). Then, if the pilot managed to deliver the projectile, he still faced the task of escaping.

If, on the other hand, a maneuverable fighter plane filled with explosives barreled straight in and slammed full throttle into a ship without the pilot having to worry about aiming and releasing a bomb or torpedo, the attack — and the flying — were far simpler prospects. The aircraft was no longer the delivery system for a projectile that in the end was unguided; instead, the aircraft *was* the projectile, under powered, controlled flight until the moment of impact. And escape, of course, became a nonissue. A Tokkō pilot explained it to his mother and sisters in simple but accurate terms. "Listen carefully," he told them. "You have nothing but a stone in your hand. What is the best way to hit a tree? To throw it, and perhaps miss, or to place the stone on the tree yourself? Do you see?"[123]

It was quite logical, really. Industrialized warfare had allowed nations to churn out huge quantities of powerful weapons, but with a few experimental exceptions, all of them were "dumb," as a later era would put it. What technology so far hadn't been able to do was invent a weapon that could sense the target somehow and change course to ensure impact. Building explosive devices was easy, and had been for centuries; processing information was hard, and in the 1940s and for some time thereafter only human brains were up to the task. As scientist Arthur C. Clarke might have put it, production of organic brains by unskilled labor, rather than artificial intelligence by skilled labor, was the only option, given the limits of the decade's technology.[124]

A weapon, to be smart, would thus require a human brain guiding it all the way onto the target. In theory, at least, this would increase the attackers' hit-kill probability dramatically, compensating for their small numbers. This was the essence of the kamikaze idea.[125]

Surviving Tokkō veterans despise being compared to modern-day suicide bombers. The kamikazes were motivated not by hatred but by a need to defend their homeland and families. As one biographer recently wrote, the Tokkō pilots weren't like those of September 11; instead they were the counterparts to the New York City firemen who rushed into the burning World Trade Center towers, forfeiting their own lives in an effort to rescue the victims of the disaster.[126]

This didn't necessarily make their mission easy; sometimes there could be ambivalence, even a natural fear. When Yukio Seki was first told that he was a possible choice to lead the first Tokkō attack, he paused for a few moments, during which time his superior feared that he might refuse. Then Seki looked up. "You absolutely must let me do it," he said firmly.[127]

But later he voiced his concern over the whole Tokkō concept. "Japan must be in very bad shape if it has to kill an experienced pilot like me," he mused. "If they would let me, I could drop a five hundred kilogram bomb on the flight deck of a carrier without going in for body-crashing and still make my way back."[128]

Of course, by late 1944 Seki's chances of scoring dive-bombing hits were much lower than before, since Japan's planes were older and in poorer repair, and fighter support was thin. And Seki was a relative rarity. Most of the Tokkō pilots weren't professional aviators or career officers, but young men fresh from universities and educational draft exemptions, pressed quickly into service as Japan's manpower shrank. These raw young pilots got what literally amounted to crash training, packing in as many flight hours as they could with their tight fuel supplies in just a few months. During this time, in addition to having to master the basics of flight, they had to learn two different styles of attack. A low-level approach, much like that of a torpedo plane's run, was suitable when the American combat air patrol was distracted or elsewhere. The alternative was the high, steep, diving attack in the fashion of the conventional dive-bomber. Each pilot had to know both, for in the end the call was up to the individual depending on the conditions he found. This was a lot of skill to have to develop in only a few months' time.[129]

So it was that as the invaders approached Leyte, Japan's defense would soon rest in the hands of boys who had barely become pilots and men, flying their rickety planes out into the Pacific in search of targets. But for all of their weaknesses they had one massive advantage. Their planes were the world's first fully intelligent projectiles, the advance guard of precision-guided munitions. They were the twentieth century's first smart bombs.

The emaciated Japanese air forces on the Philippines could do little in the way of scouting or reconnaissance. Their planes lacked radar, and the target-acquisition sensors in the case of the Tokkō smart bombs were the eyes of the pilots. As a result, the first Tokkō units had to make several sorties during the first few days in futile searches for targets. But they finally found what they sought. At dawn on the twenty-fifth of October, as the Leyte Gulf battle was reaching its climax, two kamikaze units took off. At 0740 one of them encountered the escort carriers of Taffy 1. The other, Lieutenant Seki's Shikishima unit, sighted Admiral Clifton Sprague's beleaguered Taffy 3, barely an hour after it had fought off Kurita's massive surface force.

The attack began.

PC-1122 had just arrived in Leyte Gulf with the rest of MacArthur's navy, and on the twenty-first of October, George Culpepper was hungry for fresh food. Off the island of Panaon in the south of the gulf, he and the rest of the patrol craft's crew were trading anything the natives would take in exchange for local chickens, bananas, and mangoes. The sailors were even offering to trade their own underwear. Storage could be a bit of a problem, for at 284 tons, PC-1122 was roughly a fifth the size of a small, *Farragut*-class destroyer, but the men were making do.

Happy with the new diet, the crew was taking things easy that morning. The real fireworks hadn't begun, and most of the fleet was farther north. So when Culpepper saw the approaching Zero, he was slow to react, staring dumbly at the plane as it bore down on his vessel.

The fighter was skimming almost at wave-top level, but as it closed it pulled up sharply. Then, aiming at the patrol craft, the pilot began a steep dive. But he did not open fire, and neither did the Americans, who were too stunned to react. Culpepper watched as the Zero grew bigger and bigger, and then, suddenly, the pilot pulled out of his dive and flew away.

That broke the spell mesmerizing the crew, and a second later sailors were scrambling to man weapons and get under way. Chickens roosting in the engine room squawked and feathers went flying as the men rushed to get up steam, and soon PC-1122 was on the move.

Culpepper knew that Japanese planes sometimes made suicide dives, and for a few moments he'd believed that he was about to be on the receiving end of one of them, but he couldn't have known about the kamikazes, for Ōnishi had just formed the Shinpū unit a few days before. Later, when news of the kamikazes spread, Culpepper grew certain that he'd seen the very first one. In fact, he was sure that he and his shipmates had nearly become the first kamikaze victims, and that they'd been saved only by the pilot's last-minute realization that the patrol craft was too puny a target to waste himself on, a decision for which Culpepper was most grateful.[130]

That same morning, a plane—perhaps the same one that had buzzed Culpepper's vessel, but probably a different one—crashed into the cruiser HMAS *Australia*, killing dozens and doing serious damage. That it was a deliberate, self-immolating attack is fairly certain. But Tokkōtai records indicate that it wasn't attached to any of the official Shinpū units. Although Seki's initial group first sortied on October 21, it didn't find targets until a few mornings later.[131]

As fate would have it, the inaugural kamikaze targets were the poor Taffy units off Samar on October 25, the same morning as Admiral Kurita's attack.

The first victim was USS *Santee*, an escort carrier belonging to Thomas Sprague's Taffy 1. The time was 0730, and the ship had just finished launching planes that were racing to the aid of Clifton Sprague's beleaguered Taffy 3, already under Kurita's guns. As three dive-bombers suddenly dropped toward Taffy 1, a Tokkō plane dove out of the clouds, straight toward *Santee*. The cloud cover left the crew with little time to react; the attack was so sudden, in fact, that the ship's skipper didn't even have time to identify the attacker correctly, believing the Zeke to be a Tony fighter or perhaps even a Judy dive-bomber. General quarters sounded as the plane screamed downward, its guns blazing—and then it slammed squarely into *Santee*'s flight deck.[132]

The pilot missed the after elevator, perhaps because he closed his eyes at the last moment, but he still blasted a thirty-foot hole in the flight deck before landing in the hangar deck. The wreckage set fire to the gas tanks of the planes on the flight deck; below, the impact blew open a number of depth charges, which also began burning; life jackets and clothing were on fire as well; and the heat threatened to cook off eight thousand-pound bombs near the hangar deck flames.

For the next ten minutes, crew and officers battled the angry fires, somehow getting them under control before anything could explode. Then, just a few minutes later, a torpedo slammed into the ship, bringing more havoc along with it, but the crew kept its composure and got things locked down.[133] It was close; the first Tokkō pilot to find the mark had done a good job, and only luck had kept his success from being spectacular. It was early evidence that Ōnishi's idea might actually work.

Nobody on *Santee* knew that, of course. The Americans weren't yet aware of what they were about to go up against. But in a few minutes they began to get the idea, for the doomed pilot who'd struck *Santee* had not been alone. He was part of two groups of planes from the Asahi and Kikusui units, which had sortied from Davao, and even as he spent his life on *Santee*'s decks, his comrades were choosing their targets and starting their runs.[134]

The pilots ignored the ships of the screen, much as the lone Zero had ignored PC-1122 a few days before, and for a similar reason. They wanted the carriers, the heart of the navy's offensive ability, and they went for them. Thirty seconds after *Santee* was hit, another plane headed toward USS *Suwannee*, and still another aimed itself at *Petrof Bay*. Sailors were now firing everything from twenty-millimeter antiaircraft weapons to five-inch guns; a shell from one of the latter hit *Suwannee*'s attacker, which then rolled, trying but failing to hit the carrier *Sangamon*, and AA fire found the *Petrof Bay* plane, which splashed nearby.[135]

Suwannee's respite was brief. As her AA chewed up a circling Zeke, the wounded plane turned and dove on her, this one hit taking out her after elevator and killing and wounding dozens.[136]

This first kamikaze attack was impressive, with 50 percent of the new intelligent weapons finding their targets. That figure compares favorably to the laser-guided Paveway system's performance a quarter century later in Vietnam.[137] And the Tokkō pilots weren't through for the day. Even as the Asahi and Kikusui units went after Taffy 1, the Shikishima unit, led by Lieutenant Seki, was heading for Taffy 3 off Samar.

A few minutes before 1100, the escort carrier group, which Kurita's surface force had just finished mauling, sighted a flight of five Zekes a few thousand yards off. Kurita had been withdrawing for almost an hour, and the jeep carrier *Kitkun Bay* was busy recovering the planes that had followed him. As the Zekes came within range, *Kitkun Bay*'s AA opened up on them. One of the planes, crossing ahead of the carrier, climbed, turned, and dove on her—an attack profile remarkably like that of a modern Harpoon missile. The Zeke aimed straight for the bridge with all guns blazing, but the pilot miscalculated, hitting only the port catwalk. Shrapnel from his bomb riddled the ship, sparking fires. Twenty minutes later another plane came in from astern. Thousands of rounds of AA splattered out at it, blowing off both of its wings, and it hit the water a few yards off the port bow, parts of it crashing into the forecastle.[138]

Kitkun Bay's sister ship, *Kalinin Bay*, also took hits. *Kalinin Bay* was having a terrible time of it: targeted by enemy cruisers, she'd already taken more than a dozen eight-inch shells that morning, turning into a vast, steaming chunk of metallic Swiss cheese. Then a Zero came up fast from astern and disintegrated against the flight deck's port side, sparking fires and flash-burning gun crews. Then came another, this one from the ship's starboard quarter, diving down steeply onto the after port stack. By now the crew had had more than enough for one day, and when a third Tokkō Zeke headed their way, they let loose a blistering torrent of fire that brought the plane down close aboard.[139]

Taffy 3's other carriers, *Fanshaw Bay* and *White Plains*, were also desperately fighting off Seki's people. *White Plains*, especially, had a close call with a Zeke. "The plane's approach gave the impression that the pilot at the end of his shallow dive expected to land on the after end of the flight deck and crash forward the entire length of the ship," her captain reported a few days later. But the ship's AA was accurate and effective; at the last second the Zeke veered, missing the stack by inches. It exploded just before hitting the water, showering the flight deck and port catwalk with, as the skipper put it, "debris and fragments of metal and Jap."[140]

The most devastating attack—perhaps delivered by Lieutenant Seki himself—fell upon USS *St. Lo*.

The lone Zero that targeted the escort carrier, diving straight down, dodged the hail of antiaircraft fire, and as the *Santee* and *Suwannee* attackers had done, smashed through the flight deck and onto the hangar deck, sparking a massive fire. But while *Santee*'s explosives hadn't cooked off, *St. Lo*'s did. Torpedoes and bombs quickly blew, throwing massive pieces of the carrier hundreds of feet skyward. Within a few minutes the survivors were abandoning what was left of the ship, and a half hour after the Tokkō attack, *St. Lo*, still billowing clouds of black smoke, went under.[141]

More than a dozen kamikazes attacked the Taffies that morning, and nearly half of them scored hits despite the AA. They wounded four carriers and sank one outright. Grim as the Tokkō concept was, it seemed, that morning, to prove the power of cherry blossoms.

The kamikaze attacks of the twenty-fifth of October were the start of a campaign of destruction and terror that would continue until the end of the war, still nearly a year in the future. The emperor, when he learned of these first raids, was saddened by both the use and the deaths of the Tokkō pilots—"It is truly regrettable that it should be necessary to let them go to this extent" he said—but for Ōnishi the twenty-fifth proved the worth of the whole Tokkō concept. While he noted Hirohito's concern, he told his assembled men, Ōnishi also proclaimed, drawing his sword, that "His Majesty did not say stop the Tokkō attacks!"[142]

The carriers would always remain the prime targets, but getting through the screens and sometimes even finding a carrier led many pilots to crash into battleships, cruisers, or transports—anything, in fact, and especially the ubiquitous destroyers. Within a week of the first successful attacks, Tokkō pilots smashed into two merchant ships, a cruiser, and three more carriers, as well as five destroyers, one of which sank.[143]

It all came as a bad dream; after Ray Spruance had crushed Japan's naval airpower the previous summer, there had been the hope that the threat from the air would diminish. But the Philippines were large and unsinkable; the Tokkō pilots could sortie from any of dozens of airfields where camouflaged planes could lurk in the fringes of tropical jungle until pouncing.

In the wake of the initial attacks and Japan's official announcement, sailors quickly found out what was happening. Captain D. J. Sullivan of *White Plains*, not knowing what name to give the new weapons, referred to them as "devil divers"; many others simply called them suicide pilots or suidivers.[144] Whatever their name, they were bad news for the navy. Before the battle for the Philippines ended, they would sink sixteen ships and damage another eighty-seven. Later, during the Okinawa campaign, the numbers would climb drastically. But the navy's reaction was instant. In the wake of the first deadly, and demoralizing, attacks, it began to censor news stories, barring any word of the kamikazes from reaching American shores.[145]

But the sailors knew. The threat soon became constant, wracking the nerves of everyone from the lowliest seaman to Halsey himself. "I would be a damn fool to pretend that individual *Kamikazes* did not scare me," Halsey readily admitted after the war. "They scared me thoroughly and repeatedly."[146] Many, probably most, of his men felt the same way. The planes could come in at any time, from any quarter, sometimes below radar, sometimes getting in among returning American strike planes. The sporadic enemy raids could hold a ship's company at general quarters for hours, exhausting the tired men still further. The attacks sometimes seemed to be going on everywhere. Walt Barry, a sailor aboard the destroyer *Lyman K. Swenson*, found them especially frightening. His battle station, high up on the superstructure near the officers, gave him an excellent view of things, and he saw at least a couple of carriers take Tokkō hits. One of them may have been the *Essex*-class *Franklin*; in that attack, a week or so after *St. Lo*'s sinking, a suicide bomber crashed through her flight deck, killing and wounding more than a hundred sailors. But Barry couldn't be sure, for the officers never told him anything. All he could do was watch the carnage and hope his destroyer wouldn't be next.[147]

This campaign was a battle of wills between young men who were committed to dying and young men who were striving to live, and often the struggle was desperate. *The Sullivans*, a destroyer named for the five navy brothers who all died aboard the doomed USS *Juneau* on Guadalcanal's infamous Ironbottom Sound, was one of dozens of ships to find herself at the heart of this contest. One day, as a Tokkō plane dove on the *Essex*-class carrier *Hancock*, the destroyer's crew watched transfixed, cheering when the plane spun away from the flattop. The cheering stopped dead as the plane hit another destroyer, *Halsey Powell*, which staggered under the blow and then steamed drunkenly into *Hancock*'s path. The carrier backed down, hard; if she hit, she would cut the smaller vessel in half. She missed, luckily, but *Halsey Powell* was still in a bad way, and as the rest of the task force retired, *The Sullivans* drew the job of shepherding her wounded sister back to base.

Soon the two destroyers were alone on the ocean, but still within range of Japanese airfields. Lieutenant Junior Grade Robert McAlpine watched from near a portside twin forty-millimeter AA mount as a boat with the ship's medic journeyed over to *Halsey Powell* and then began the return trip. Then he looked up . . .

High in the clouds a lone plane was circling.

The task force had a CAP on the way to give the two vessels air cover, but it hadn't arrived yet. McAlpine knew what he was seeing, and instantly he let the bridge know, but the clouds were obscuring the plane, and the bridge was less certain. McAlpine didn't care. "Don't wait for the commence fire order," he told the gun crew. "When you see that plane, you start shooting!"

As the plane emerged from the clouds and began diving, the gun crew leapt to obey, but the weapon was trained out and secured, and as the crew struggled to get it online, it stubbornly refused to go into automatic.

Nearly mad with rage, McAlpine tore off his helmet and threw it at the rest of the gun crew, which helped nothing. The plane loomed closer; McAlpine, now helmetless, crouched under the phone box, the only cover there was.

As the kamikaze dropped like a stone, the skipper, Commander Ralph J. Baum, threw the ship to flank speed and into a hard circle. He'd been drilling the crew for such a moment as this. When Tokkō planes went after destroyers, they usually aimed for the bridge, so Baum had come up with a system to get everyone away from the area as fast as they could move. Now it wasn't a drill. "Clear the bridge!" he barked, but even as he spoke, his men were scrambling in every direction, some hurling themselves all the way down to the main deck.

Then the plane pulled out of its dive, the pilot clawing for altitude. Maybe he feared that he was going to miss and wanted to avoid wasting himself, or maybe the same instinct for self-preservation that washed over the crew of *The Sullivans* also affected him. Nobody would ever find out. He began to circle about seven miles out, at the limit of five-inch range. The destroyers opened fire, and that was enough to discourage him; he broke off and left the area.[148]

Other ships were less fortunate, and when Tokkō planes hit, they unleashed the horrors of war and of human nature as well. When the minelayer *Terror*, a large, easy target, took a hit, young officer David Mincey, spared death himself, saw it firsthand. The impact had disemboweled the pilot, and Mincey saw that he'd been worm-ridden, victim of a horrible diet that many

Japanese had at last been reduced to. Without ceremony or fanfare, the minelayer's crew dumped the remains over the side.[149]

On the twenty-ninth of October, *Intrepid* became the first fleet carrier to take a hit from a Tokkō plane. The damage wasn't severe—though "severe" is a relative term, and sixteen men were wounded or killed—but it demoralized the task force, and especially the crew of *Intrepid*, which bore the nicknames "Dry I" and "Decrepit" since a series of casualties seemed to keep her always under repair. "She could hardly poke her nose out of port without it getting rapped," Halsey once commented.[150]

The next day was *Franklin*'s turn. Also an *Essex*, *Franklin* suffered much greater damage. The plane with her name on it blew a forty-foot hole in her flight deck and took out three dozen planes and seventy sailors. *Belleau Wood*, one of the *Independence*-class light carriers, also got a mauling that day; she lost only a dozen planes but nearly a hundred crew, with another half hundred injured. For a time the two bleeding carriers steamed in tandem, columns of smoke streaming behind them, before they withdrew for repair. On this one day, the Tokkōtai had removed two major carriers from the Philippine chessboard.

Japan's new intelligent weapons couldn't give it command of the sea, or even the potency the island empire had had in the war's early days. Nothing Japan could do, in fact, would let it use the seas for invasion or conquest, even if it had still had any troops left with which to conquer something. A few months later, when Allied political leaders were signing the United Nations Charter in San Francisco, some of them genuinely feared that the Imperial Japanese Navy would carry out a strike on the city to disrupt the proceedings, and Roosevelt put Halsey in charge of a special defense force. The American navy knew that Japan was utterly incapable of any project of that sort. The Japanese fleet—or rather, its tattered remains—couldn't even wield local superiority around the islands of the western Pacific.[151]

But while the Tokkōtai couldn't give Japan command of the sea, they did threaten to deny that command to the Americans.

This sea denial, if Japan could bring it off, would have the effect of turning critical parts of the Pacific into a vast, watery no-man's-land, a desert across which nothing could safely move, on which no ship could live with impunity. The sea would remain a buffer around the Philippines, and ultimately

the Home Islands if it came to that. This strategy might only delay the inevitable, but it might just make the Americans tire of the war and offer
Japan some concessions.[152] That was Ōnishi's hope anyway, but Ōnishi un-
derestimated American resolve, fueled by outrage over Pearl Harbor and the
Bataan Death March.

There was another factor that Ōnishi couldn't control: the navy's mobility. The Tokkōtai, land-based, had limited range, as well as difficulty finding American units even in the relatively localized Philippine waters. And
to eliminate the Tokkō danger entirely, all Halsey had to do was withdraw
from the region. That was what Halsey wanted to do; almost before the
Battle of Leyte Gulf ended, he was spoiling to hit Formosa or Indochina or
ideally to realize, he wrote, "my long-cherished hope of making the first
carrier raid on Tokyo since Jimmy Doolittle's."[153] That raid, too, had been
Halsey's; but now, instead of a handful of overtaxed medium bombers, he
would bring the wrath of Murderers' Row, planes by the hundreds that
would return again and again to rain vengeance on Japan from the skies.
His mistake in sprinting north after Ozawa's carrier force, moreover, had
left him hungry for the showdown he'd missed, and probably for an opportunity to redeem himself, although he never admitted it then or afterward.
But the Philippines being the scene of the late unpleasantness, he would
only naturally want to move on.

But even if Third Fleet advanced to happier killing grounds, that
wouldn't do anything to help Kinkaid's Seventh Fleet, whose destiny was still
intertwined with MacArthur's, and MacArthur was deep into Leyte. And
after Leyte, MacArthur's forces would be invading Mindoro, the next stop on
the way to the main island of Luzon, the home of Manila.

Two days after the attack on *Intrepid*, and a day after *Belleau Wood* and
Franklin took hits, Japanese planes mauled the Seventh Fleet's ships. Tokkō
planes damaged two destroyers and sank a third, while conventional
bombers savaged two more "tin cans," the familiar phrase for the unarmored
warships.[154] The monsoons had begun lashing the Philippines, turning
prospective army airfields to mush. The army had one good field, Tacloban:
strained to the limits, it was drawing a lot of unwanted attention from Japanese planes. One night a raid caught more than two dozen fighters squatting
on the sea of mud and blew them away. Army air cover wasn't getting the job

done, and Kinkaid said so to both MacArthur and Halsey. Halsey knew what Kinkaid wanted: fast carrier air cover.[155]

If the Fast Carrier Task Force was going to have to stay in the Tokkōtai crosshairs, it had to develop some powerful countermeasures. The kamikaze campaign was less than a week old and already two Third Fleet carriers were out of action. If the Tokkō planes continued to be as effective as this, they would hamstring the fleet in a matter of weeks. Halsey's people had to do something, and fast. Already ideas were coming in from subordinate commands, especially Tokkō victims. "In future operations," *Santee*'s skipper advised on the fifth of November, "it will be increasingly important to avoid remaining in a single, fixed area."[156] That was true, but in supporting MacArthur's landing, the fleet at least had to remain in or near Philippine waters. Vice Admiral John S. "Slew" McCain, who relieved Marc Mitscher on the thirtieth of October, was also soon at work devising defenses. Halsey met nightly with a small group of staffers, which he called his "Dirty Trick Department," who had the job of inventing new ways to confound the enemy. Before long the countermeasures began taking shape, though they would take some weeks to perfect.[157]

As Halsey later described things, the defenses were layered, falling into three categories: short, medium, and long range. Short range was nothing more or less than a lot of AA gunnery practice. "Before the innovation of suicide attacks by the enemy destruction of 80 or 90 per cent of his attackers was considered an eminent success," McCain observed. "Now 100 per cent destruction of the attackers is necessary to preserve the safety of the task force."[158] A solid AA barrage was the final line of defense, the last chance to reach the 100 percent mark. Bigger innovations kicked in earlier, at medium range.

In addition to the wave-top approach and the high, dive-bombing style attack, Tokkō pilots learned the trick of tailing Halsey's own planes as they retired from air strikes. This gave them a target bearing and also faked out fleet radar, the attackers seeming to be part of the returning strike force. To weed these out, McCain started posting picket destroyers—"Tom Cats"—about sixty miles forward of the main task force on either side of the target-bearing line. These ships had the best radars, extending the eyes of the fleet. Returning American planes now had to orbit these pickets in specified patterns, establishing their identity, while the CAP over each picket sniffed out any infiltrators.[159]

The tactic worked, though destroyer men came to fear the sound of their call sign coming over the TBS assigning them to the duty; lone destroyers, even with CAPs overhead, soon became prime Tokkō meat. Many destroyers left for the duty never again to return.[160] Still, the Tom Cat system functioned well.

McCain and his people also came up with ways to defeat the other approaches. For the wave-top attackers, McCain created the Jack Patrols, a ring of low-flying fighters surrounding each task group screen at visual distance. At an altitude of no more than three thousand feet, they could pounce on any wave-hopping bandit. For the "dive-bombers" that dropped steeply down through fleet radar nulls, the only solution was to fly CAPs higher and farther out from the screen.[161]

To make all of these countermeasures more potent, Halsey took another step around the end of November. Until then TF 38 had consisted of four task groups, each with four or five *Essex*- and light *Independence*-class carriers. But before December arrived, *Princeton* had been sunk and *Intrepid* hit—again— and this time badly enough to win her a ticket back to Hawaii. A couple of other flattops had been detached as well, leaving Halsey with a reduced force of around fourteen *Essex*- and *Independence*-class carriers on his hands. Reshuffling them into three task groups, he eliminated the fourth altogether, which let him increase the density of the screen around each task group: the number of destroyers guarding each group thus rose from around fifteen to a little more than twenty. Cruiser and battleship numbers also increased by around 30 percent. Each screen now bristled with antiaircraft defenses.[162]

All of this was fine, but the countermeasure that was fated to have the most impact on Third Fleet for the rest of the year fell into the third category, the long-range.

Halsey rankled at the idea of hanging around the Philippines. The thought of his planes flying CAP over MacArthur's soldiers while his carriers sat waiting to be turned into spectacular funeral pyres was almost more than he could bear. Loitering over friendly troops, anyway, waiting for the Japanese pilots to come to him, wasn't his idea of fighting. His preference was simple and he stated it bluntly: "Crush enemy air power at its source."[163] MacArthur and Nimitz agreed with this point of Halsey's, at least, and throughout November TF 38 struck the airbases on Luzon that were feeding pilots and planes into the battle over Leyte. The strategy worked fairly well, but now and then Tokkō pilots got through. By late November the Japanese had read the pattern of Third Fleet communications and exploited them; on November 25 they used this intelligence to find and make Tokkō strikes on several carriers, including the repeat performance on *Intrepid*. But by then the battle for Leyte was at last winding down, and Third Fleet retired to Ulithi for rest, upkeep, and planning.

MacArthur was about to take his next step toward Manila and Luzon by landing on Mindoro, and the navy had to be ready to cover him. Halsey, Slew McCain, and their staffs got ready by perfecting the new arts of kamikaze suppression. Instead of regular air strikes, they would keep a fighter patrol over Japanese airfields around the clock. This "Big Blue Blanket," as someone named it, thrown over the Philippines by the ships and planes of Halsey's "Big Blue Fleet," would deal with any Japanese plane that tried to take off, burning it out of the sky in short order. Not even the tropical night would be safe; Halsey's fighters had radar. The fleet could only put up this kind of airpower by dumping most of its torpedo planes and dive-bombers, replacing them with Corsairs and Hellcats, but that was no problem since these fighters could also carry bomb loads when needed.[164]

The Big Blue Blanket, the ultimate, long-range, anti-kamikaze tactic, worked wonders, but it took a lot of effort. Planes had to be in the air constantly; that took huge quantities of aviation gasoline. The carriers, too, had to steam nearby, constantly launching and recovering aircraft, and the quantity of fuel oil they ran through was prodigious, to say nothing of supplies and provisions.

Ulithi lay a thousand miles across the Philippine Sea, too far away to support this kind of effort. The key to the operation, then, lay in underway refueling and replenishment. And on this process, the fate of the task force would soon hang.

It swirled both in and over the sea, an amalgam of water and air. The boundary between ocean and atmosphere grew ever fainter as the rain fell in torrents and the roaring winds tore spray and foam from the wave tops. The heaving, breaking swell grew steadily deeper and rougher; had a human been present,

he would no longer be able to see any horizon. Sea and sky were now indistinct, a gray, roaring cacophony of violence in motion.

Yet no observer inhabited this tormented stretch of ocean, and if he had, his impression of chaos would have been myopic. On a grand scale, the roiling streams of atmosphere spiraled elegantly, majestically inward, sternly obeying the laws of physics. It was large; it was horrifyingly beautiful; and it was now a full-fledged typhoon.

The official line that it had crossed from the status of tropical storm seems arbitrary to the modern mind, even a nautical one. A tropical cyclone becomes a typhoon or a hurricane when its sustained winds reach the puzzling speed of seventy-four knots. But a familiarity with the days of sail, and the work of Royal Navy captain-turned-hydrographer Sir Francis Beaufort explains things. Beaufort did not pull figures out of a hat; in devising his famous wind scale during the early 1800s, he researched the effect of winds upon ships' sails, working out the formulas meticulously. Force 0 he described simply as "calm"; Force 1 was "just sufficient to give steerageway." And so went the descriptions up to the final category, Force 12, which we take today as typhoon or hurricane strength. A Force 12 wind of seventy-four knots Beaufort described as "That which no canvas could withstand."[165]

In 1944, canvas was largely a thing of the past; ships had found a new means of propulsion. But in the face of the storm that was now winding its way across the Philippine Sea, this new source of power would prove to have one weakness . . .

Her name was *Cimarron*.

When designed during the slack years of the thirties, she was something new. The colliers of the preceding century were lumbering dinosaurs, and transferring coal between them and warships—usually when both were moored or at anchor—was a slow, laborious, and thoroughly messy affair. Bags of the stuff would be hoisted across from the collier and unceremoniously dumped on the weather deck of the warship to be shoveled by sailors down chutes that led to the bunkers, where other sailors would rake out the piles to distribute the coal evenly. When oil came along, fueling got easier. At least oil, unlike coal, was fluid, and it could be pumped here and there. Even so, early oilers were slow and primitive, and by the time Germany blitzed Poland, the newest one in American service was nearly twenty years old.[166]

Cimarron was the first of the new breed, which far-sighted planners had been demanding for years, given the distances of the Pacific and the needs of War Plan Orange, the longstanding U. S. Navy plan for a naval war to retake the Philippines and conquer Japan. Powered by turbines, bursting with five times the horsepower and thousands of miles more range than her World War I ancestors, she could make twice their speed, hitting nearly twenty knots, which would let her keep up with Pacific Fleet warships.

By 1944 *Cimarron* was a veteran. She had brought nearly half of the navy's oil to Pearl Harbor in the months before the December 7 attack; she had been with Doolittle, Halsey, and Mitscher near Tokyo the following April, at Midway with Spruance two months later, and then at Guadalcanal. During and after Leyte she was back in the states for a much-needed overhaul, but two dozen oilers of various classes, including some of her sisters, were with Third Fleet off the Philippines, forming the core of Task Group 30.[167]

When ships traded steam power for sail during the nineteenth century, they gained the power to move at will against current and wind. But what they traded away was a source of free energy. Instead of drawing it from the wind, they had to carry it along with them, and when they had used it up, they became useless, unable to move, fight, or do anything else.

Until steam came along, a ship's range was limitless, or practically so. Food and water were the two main restrictions, and a ship could find supplies of them in most harbors and ports or even along many coastlines. But a steam-driven ship could only go so far without refueling. It was tied to the land in a way that sailing ships weren't. Coal was high tech, and oil even more so, and supplies of them weren't available everywhere, which meant that the steamship had to stay close to friendly bases. This was one of the key points stressed by the great naval historian Alfred Thayer Mahan in the late 1800s. In fact, it was one of the reasons why America, largely at the instigation of Mahan's friend Theodore Roosevelt, grabbed the Philippines at the close of the century: to provide the United States Navy with a fleet base and refueling facilities in the western Pacific. The defense, or at least the recapture, of the Philippines thus became a centerpiece of War Plan Orange for the following forty years. In a sense, then, coal caused the Battle of Leyte Gulf and the subsequent campaign for the Philippine Islands.[168]

By the 1940s the fleet ran on oil, but the principle was exactly the same; not until nuclear power—still in its infancy in Chicago, Oak Ridge, and Los Alamos—would range again become practically limitless. Oil was easier than coal to transfer and store, and it provided more energy. But ships still drank an awful lot of it, and the ships were no longer alone. The planes that operated from the decks of the carriers also needed it. The internal combustion engine, which powered this great war, was insatiable. By the 1940s it had become the master of armies with their tanks and trucks, of navies, of the air forces, and of whole governments. It dictated grand strategy. It had forced Hitler's Wehrmacht toward the Caucasus in quest of oil; it had made the Japanese lash out at Pearl Harbor so they could safely take the Dutch East Indies oil fields with impunity. Herman Wouk's fictitious Victor Henry, a battleship division commander at Leyte, put it best as he watched destroyers fueling under way.

> A despairing vision came over Pug Henry as these dragging hours passed. It struck him that the whole war had been generated by this damned viscous black fluid. Hitler's tanks and planes, the Jap carriers that had hit Pearl Harbor, all the war machinery hurtling and clashing all over the earth, ran on this same stinking gunk. The Japs had gone to war to grab a supply of it. Not fifty years had passed since the first Texas oil field had come in, and the stuff had caused this world inferno. . . . Pug felt on this October twenty-fifth, during this endless, nerve-wracking refueling crawl toward Leyte Gulf at ten knots, that he belonged to a doomed species. God had weighed modern man in the balance with three gifts of buried treasure—coal, oil, uranium—and found him wanting. Coal had fueled Jutland and the German trains in the Great War, petroleum had turned loose air war and tank war, and the Oak Ridge stuff would probably end the whole horrible business. God had promised not to send another deluge; He had said nothing about preventing men from setting fire to their planet and themselves.[169]

Underway replenishment, as it came to be known, was indeed a slow and delicate process, but it was the trick that allowed Third Fleet to operate here, off the Philippines, a thousand miles from Ulithi, five thousand miles from Pearl, and still farther from the American West Coast. In 1944 the United States produced more oil than the rest of the world put together, but that oil had to get to the fleet. That was where the oilers came in.[170]

From the very beginnings of Orange, American strategists knew that they would have to fight in the western Pacific, at the end of a long line of supply, especially if the Philippines fell early (which, of course, they had). The latest generations of fast battleships and fleet carriers, unlike earlier warships, had the range to get to the region, but to stay there day in and day out they needed constant replenishment. They required food, ammunition, supplies, personnel, and above all they required fuel: aviation gasoline (or avgas), diesel, and thousands of barrels of Navy Special fuel oil, a heavy, undistilled by-product of crude that fed hundreds of navy boilers.

In the first year or two of the war, the oilers had simply added to task force ranges when conducting hit-and-run raids. But by 1944 the American fleets had moved on to massive offensive campaigns that kept them in the forward areas for weeks or even months at a time. Every mile west the task forces steamed added to the logistical problems, and smaller ships such as destroyers, with their far more limited ranges, made things even tougher.

By the time of the Leyte invasion, the navy had come up with an intricate ritual for getting oil to the warships. Commercial tankers would set out from the East Coast through Panama and direct from the West Coast, bypassing Pearl, lugging their cargoes to the forward naval bases such as Ulithi. There the fleet oilers would take on the fuel, and in an endless procession, like some huge bucket brigade, they would run it out to designated areas and wait for a fleet rendezvous. During the Leyte campaign, the At-Sea Logistics Group, with the designation Task Group 30.8, numbered more than a hundred ships of various sorts, including nearly three dozen oilers.[171]

At-sea refueling was and is a dangerous mating dance between mountainous steel vessels. During World War I a young Chester Nimitz, assigned to one of the navy's first two oilers, had helped write the book on the process, and though the following quarter century had seen many improvements, the basic operation was still the same.

In principle things were pretty straightforward. A ship needing fuel would approach an oiler broadside and take station to port or starboard, steaming in parallel less than two hundred feet away, and usually a lot closer. Often the gap was only forty feet. Both ships had to be under way to maintain steerage, and moving at precisely the same speed to hold station on each other. Even at a speed of just a few knots, a ship could close that gap in mere seconds, and a collision could be deadly. The two helmsmen had to be as coordinated as dance partners. Officially the navy recommended that the oiler tow its customer, but a good hand at the helm made this time-consuming technique unnecessary.

Once the ships were on station, the parade of lines would begin. The oiler would throw a heaving line and then would come messengers, hawsers, and a telephone line. Then the fuel hose, or perhaps two or three, would be passed aboard the warship. Four or six inches in diameter, the long rubber hose consisting of several sections would be hung from a saddle attached to a boom. Ideally, especially in colder weather, the ships would try to keep the hose out of the water, which would cool down the thick oil and make it flow sluggishly. But the opposite danger was just as bad, if not worse: too little slack and the hose would rupture, costing oil and time. And time was crucial. Refueling a destroyer took nearly an hour, and filling a capital ship could take three or four; feeding the bunkers of an entire task group could easily take all day. All the while, in a combat zone, the ships were vulnerable, fat submarine targets. Risk grew with time; but given collision dangers, risk grew with speed, too, and refueling was always a tightrope walk between the twin dangers.

To hasten the process, destroyers could fuel from the capital ships they escorted, and by 1944, to speed things up even more, an oiler would simultaneously fuel one ship to starboard and another to port. Carriers, with their starboard islands, would always fuel from an oiler's port side to ensure visibility. Often the oiler would find herself sandwiched between a battleship and a carrier, or now and then even two battleships, for hours at a time. That could be a source of white knuckles, since a slip would crush the oiler between armored hulls as if it were a greasy black egg.

But the navy was good at complexities, and on the whole the process worked smoothly. It had to, if the Fast Carrier Task Force were to keep up the pressure in the western Pacific. Already, by the end of November, Halsey's personal campaign was behind schedule, and although he was getting enough oil and provisions, his men were exhausted, having been at sea for nearly three months straight. Returning to Ulithi at the end of November, the fleet rested and repaired itself, though even there it wasn't safe from Tokkō attacks. Several days earlier, a *kaiten*—a one-man suicide submarine built out of one of Japan's fabled Long Lance torpedoes—got inside the atoll and blew a fleet oiler, the *Mississinewa*, into a towering fireball.[172] At any rate, the fleet couldn't rest long. MacArthur needed it to support him in his next campaign, which he was soon ready to launch: the invasion of Mindoro.

Mindoro: Literally the name means "gold mine." So named by the Spanish when they ruled the seas centuries earlier, the island failed to live up to its name, though its strategic position made it valuable to MacArthur. It lay just off Luzon, less than a hundred air miles from Manila. The Leyte airfields hadn't paid off, and they were too far south anyway. Fields on Mindoro would give the Americans control of the sky over Manila—if they could keep the kamikazes suppressed.[173]

Task Force 38 had the responsibility for everything north of Manila Bay. Halsey and his staff identified dozens of known or suspected Japanese airfields in that expanse. The plan was for the carriers to blast these fields with all the aerial firepower it had for three days running, December 14, 15, and 16. The attacks would eat up tons of ammunition along with maybe one hundred thousand barrels of fuel oil per day for the ships, let alone avgas for the planes. At the end of those three days, the task force would have to replenish. To do that Halsey would steam a few hundred miles to the east, out of the range of the Philippine airbases. There he would meet Task Group 30.8, refuel and rearm, and return on December 19 for three more days of attacks.[174]

The kickoff came on the eleventh as the force steamed from Ulithi. The following day it rendezvoused with the logistics group and topped off; beginning soon after dawn, the oilers pumped more than a quarter million barrels of Navy Special and nearly half a million gallons of avgas. This was just to brim the tanks, which were already nearly full, but even with careful choreography, the dance kept up until midday. Then the partners split up, the logistics task group heading to a prearranged area to loiter until needed by Halsey, and the Fast Carrier Task Force beginning a high-speed run-in toward the Philippine coast.[175]

A carrier tactic adopted during the 1930s, the high-speed run-in was designed to protect a thin-skinned flattop with cloaks of motion and darkness. The carrier and its entourage would sprint through the night toward the enemy target and launch a strike before daylight that would hit the target at dawn, achieving surprise at minimal risk to the flattop since it would effectively be in the combat zone for less time. In late 1944 surprise was fine, as always, though with reduced enemy capabilities it wasn't as necessary as a defensive measure, as long as the new kamikaze suppression tactics worked.[176]

As the thirteenth spun into the fourteenth and the task force moved through midnight into enemy waters, the tensions native to combat started to climb. With every mile the fleet gobbled, the chances of a contact—aerial, submarine, something—increased. "Ship is darkened in material condition Yoke, condition of readiness III," a reservist lieutenant tersely noted on the bridge of the carrier *Hancock*, referring to the status of both ship and crew. Then came the contact, two hours before dawn. "Bogie on the screen," he reported, "bearing 260° T, distance 47 miles"—almost directly ahead. The game had begun.[177]

It was an Emily, a Kawanishi patrol plane, possibly radar equipped. Carrier *Independence*, getting word of the contact, immediately launched two radar-equipped planes of its own, night fighters that could hunt in the darkness. Emilys were heavily armed, being something of a cross between an American Catalina and a Flying Fortress, but this one's teeth and claws were no use this time. Within thirty minutes of initial contact, the night fighters blasted it into the water. They apparently got the plane in time, for three hours later, when the first of the day's half dozen air strikes hit the Japanese airfields, they achieved total surprise.[178]

For the next three days the Big Blue Blanket spread over northern Luzon. By day the fleet sent in strike after strike; planes were always launching or landing from before dawn until the huge equatorial sun sank toward the horizon. After dark came the night fighters' turn as they relentlessly heckled the Luzon airfields.[179]

The prime targets were the enemy planes, some of which the Japanese had hauled as much as five miles from their airstrips. But the defender's efforts were worthless; American aircraft found them and destroyed or damaged most of them on the ground, despite the still heavy AA fire around the

Clark Field complex. The Americans, though, didn't stop with the planes. They hit trains, fuel dumps, and road traffic, and they also went after the ships in Manila Bay.[180]

The Big Blue Blanket was working like a charm. Of the nearly three hundred Japanese planes that the fleet destroyed outright from the fourteenth through the sixteenth, only a quarter were airborne. The rest blew up or burned on the ground. Navy pilots also damaged another 161 planes, and given Japan's faltering industrial plant, damaged was nearly as good as destroyed. On top of these figures, Halsey reckoned nearly three dozen Japanese ships sunk and that many more damaged. And neither Tokkō planes nor conventional pilots ever came close to laying a glove on the task force. Eleven bandits drove in toward the fleet on the morning of the sixteenth, but the CAP from *Hancock* and *Lexington* got them. That was the only air attack on the fleet during the whole three-day offensive.[181]

The weather cooperated as well. Except for an occasional squall, ceiling and visibility were unlimited and stayed that way; light, fluffy cumulus clouds with their cotton candy appearance floated tranquilly over the task force. The wind blew mostly from the southeast quarter, and rarely more than fifteen knots, a typical pattern for December. Swell was light, and the air temperature, both night and day, hovered around eighty degrees. The water temperature tended to be a few degrees higher, a ready heat reservoir. But nobody was worried about that.[182]

The only problem was that the task force couldn't keep up the pressure for long. The campaign simply ate fuel and ammunition too quickly. On the early evening of December 16, Halsey gave the order for the task force to retire east, where the logistics task group was waiting with full oil tanks and tons of supplies and provisions. "To you and your Force," Halsey signaled Slew McCain, "well done on a brilliantly planned and executed operation."[183]

As the tropical darkness fell, the carriers and their thirsty escorts steamed away from the Philippines, deeper into the Pacific, heading toward an incongruous spot of ocean with nondescript coordinates: 14°50' N, 129°57' E.[184] Most of the crews turned in for a well-earned night's sleep. Around them, as they lay oblivious, the swell began to increase.

PART FOUR

Deluge

PATROL BOMBERS WERE USEFUL AIRCRAFT, especially on the Pacific's vast wastes and the jungles of tropical islands. They could set down on water or land, and they had very good range, as much as two thousand miles. They drew many duties: cargo delivery, medical evacuation, scouting, search and rescue, and antisubmarine warfare. With all this on their plate, then, the flight crews of these aircraft tended to be busy people.

The crew of the PBM-3 now flying 550 miles west-northwest of Ulithi was a case in point. Their twin-engined Martin Mariner was less famous, though larger and more capable, than the PBY Catalina. Based on the seaplane tender *Chandeleur*, now swinging at anchor in Kossol Roads in the Palaus southeast of the Philippines, the Mariner was busy combing the ocean for threats to American forces, or anything else of interest. The work required a lot of one's eyes, whether glued to the horizon, the instrumentation, or the radar screen. The Pacific was a big place.

Like the other crews of navy squadron VPN-21, this one had standing orders to note weather coordinates hourly on long flights, and to turn in the data to the local weather office on returning to base. It was also to contact base while in flight if it ever noted definite signs of a tropical cyclone. But all this was an adjunct to other duties: few, if any, flights were devoted to weather data collection. Such things had a lower priority than the main business of spotting and defending against enemy threats.[185] Even the United

States, by 1944 an industrial and mechanical powerhouse, had production and manpower limits, and it had to devote its resources to the most important matters.

This meant that the large patch of the Philippine Sea through which the Fast Carrier Task Force and its replenishment ships now roamed was only partly patrolled, and those doing the patrolling had things on their minds besides weather. So it was largely happenstance that the Mariner, some time around the midnight that separated the sixteenth from the seventeenth of December, radioed *Chandeleur* with a report of some nasty conditions. There were clouds and a thunderstorm, and, most ominously, winds in excess of sixty-five knots—nearly, but not quite, typhoon strength. The location was roughly 13° N, 132° E, 250 miles to the southeast of Halsey's main forces.[186]

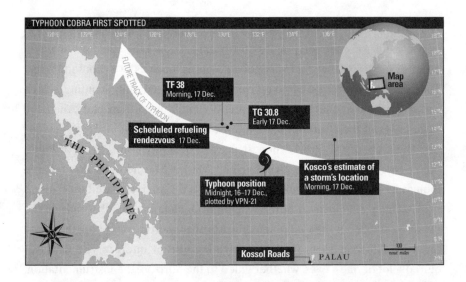

That report went only to the seaplane tender. Though a component of Task Group 30.5, and so part of Halsey's Third Fleet, the Mariners weren't in the habit of contacting TF 38 directly. There were proper channels for everything in order to make sure that the vast piles of messages were all routed correctly and in good time. The Mariner, having complied with its orders, flew on.

Shortly thereafter another VPN-21 Mariner radioed *Chandeleur* with a similar report. Something was definitely amiss in the weather department. Back on *Chandeleur*, Lieutenant Junior Grade Robert W. Young took notice.

Young, a reservist, was an aerologist—the naval term for what the civilian world called a meteorologist. Though young and not yet particularly experienced, he knew the dangers a tropical cyclone could pose.

Based on these two weather reports, Young wrote out a weather warning, addressing it to Halsey, Admiral Kinkaid of Seventh Fleet, and other task forces and groups, as well as the weather central at Pearl Harbor. "At 13° N and 132° E is definite storm center," he advised the commands. "Wind 60 knots."[187]

Later, on the seventeenth as part of his normal routine, Young would compile the squadron's hourly weather reports and pass them on to a broadcasting station on Saipan, which would transmit them on a preset schedule for all interested parties. Other than the extra warning he sent, that would be the extent of *Chandeleur*'s weather reporting for the next twenty-four hours.[188]

Carriers and battleships, especially those of the new World War II classes, had transoceanic range, or something close to it. Even the sweeping Pacific presented relatively few problems for capital ships, especially with the help of fleet oilers. The problem lay with the destroyers.

The "small boys" (as they were affectionately known), or "tin cans" (a shade more derogatory in nature), were very fast and highly maneuverable, all the better to intercept their archenemy, the submarine. Like the submarine, too, they had to make sacrifices for these special traits, and one of the trade-offs was fuel capacity. A modern battleship could gorge itself on well over a million gallons of oil at a single repast, while a destroyer could consume less than a fifth as much. The fleet had last feasted on December 13. During the following three days, ships had to make high-speed run-ins, steam in fuel-lavish antisubmarine screens, and dash off to serve as pickets and lifeguards. By dawn on the seventeenth, many of these small boys were nearing starvation levels. Some were down to as low as 15 percent of capacity: twenty-four more hours would drain them dry if they weren't very careful. Given that refueling even a single destroyer could take a couple of hours or more, many officers in the replenishment group were surprised, even shocked, to learn that the task force commanders had let margins get so dangerously thin.[189]

As the ships of TF 38 and TG 30.8 arrived on the large square of ocean that had been designated as the replenishment area, they began the intricately choreographed dance that most had performed dozens of times. The refueling group, which included a dozen fleet oilers, slowed from twelve to ten knots and dissolved itself into three units of four oilers each. As the skies grew steadily more laden with thick, heavy cumulus clouds, oilers and consorts positioned themselves in lines stretching for miles from north-northeast to south-southeast, slowing again to eight knots.[190]

The fleet, five hundred miles east of Luzon, was beyond the reach of the Tokkō planes; that was the whole point of steaming so far into the depths of the Philippine Sea to replenish. Still, the task force took the precaution of launching Jack Patrols along with the usual CAP, despite the roughness of the seas.[191] Submarines, on the other hand, were always a threat. Around the task units and groups the destroyers steamed in their usual screen, pinging with sonars and being constantly vigilant. As the fleet prepared to start fueling, USS *Aylwin*, steaming with Task Group 30.8, spotted something that may or may not have been a Japanese periscope; as a precaution she opened fire with twenty- and forty-millimeter and sank it. Meanwhile, preparations for fueling kept up along with other replenishment operations. Here, too, the destroyers were useful: *Hull* from the refueling group, and *Donaldson* and *Hobby* from one of the carrier groups, among others, set about receiving and distributing hundreds of bags of mail. *Buchanan*, one of *Hobby*'s squadron mates, drew the duty of ferrying replacement pilots to the carriers of her group; in other groups the same things were happening. Stores, ammunition, provisions, everything had its place in the dance, but the main thing, given the small boys' condition, was fuel.[192] Some larger ships needed it, too; light carriers took their place in line with the thirsty destroyers, preparing to take on Navy Special and, in their case, avgas. Other capital ships would themselves dispense fuel to destroyers as a means of making the fueling process go faster.[193]

The winds and seas had been edging up for some time. At midmorning, though, just as the first ships were beginning to come alongside, the seas grew still heavier. The sky was soon completely covered over with clouds; the seas, normally jewel-like in this part of the world, lay leaden hued under the blanket of gray. These were no typhoon conditions, or anything close to them. Still, they were a complication, and very ill timed.

The first signs of trouble was with flight operations, which, having little margin for error, were susceptible to any degraded weather. An hour and a half before noon, the fleet carrier *Yorktown*, busy launching patrols, had to throw herself into emergency maneuvers to avoid running down the cruiser *Boston*, which had had to begin zigzagging at nearly twice the task group's speed in order to hold her station relative to the formation guide ship.[194] Meanwhile, several miles to the east in Task Group 30.7, the main antisubmarine force, a torpedo plane was preparing to land on the escort carrier *Anzio* when the pilot was waved off. It came too late; the plane's tail hook caught one of the arresting cables just as the pilot gunned his engine to pull up and come around for another try. The plane tore itself loose from the cable and spun over the port side of the carrier and into the sea. As *Anzio* quickly stopped her screws lest they shred the downed men into hamburger, a destroyer sped over to pluck the three aviators, all relatively unhurt, out of the water.[195]

Still the operation went on. The ships due for refueling began to file into place, the officers conning them and the helmsmen steering them and struggling to hold station while the ritual of line passing took place. Even in the calmest of seas, two massive objects had to become motionless relative to one another while making their way through what Captain Nemo called a "mobile element." If the ships were too far apart, the hoses would separate; too close, and the ships would collide. On these seas, now stirring slowly to consternation, the process was far more difficult.

Before long, word of trouble began to flow from all the task groups. The first reports were of difficulty in steering and coming alongside. The remedy for that was simple, and soon task unit commanders had started instructing the vessels in need of fuel to increase their speed to ten knots. In normal conditions this would have interfered with the dance steps, but the dance floor—to stick with the analogy—was already slick and dangerous, throwing all the partners off kilter. Before noon, Slew McCain had ordered all his task groups to make ten knots to counteract the effect of the seas.[196]

It didn't work. Soon the TBS was alive with reports of parting lines. Grier Sims, an electrician's mate on the battleship *Iowa*, was at work keeping telephone communications working between his ship and the two destroyers, *Lewis Hancock* and *Brush*, that were alongside attempting to fuel. Sims had always admired the crews of oilers who were so expert at their jobs; he himself was an old hand at stringing the telephone wires, and his shipmates had often gone through the fueling routine. But today the sea was too rough, and Sims could only watch helplessly as his telephone line snapped off at the deck.[197]

More serious were parting fuel hoses. Normally a ship would take two aboard, one forward, one aft. *Stephen Potter*, trying to take on black oil, parted the forward hose; *Collett*, alongside a fast battleship, tore both of the hoses free. When the breakage took place on deck, the warm, viscous black gunk would spray everyone nearby until they could cut off the flow; the only cure for a coating of oil was a saltwater bath.[198]

The problem was soon an epidemic. In the next hour or two, *Lyman K. Swenson*, *Preston*, and *Thatcher* all reported broken fuel hoses. Fleet oiler *Nantahala* lost not one but a half dozen sets of sound-powered telephones and their cords as the lines gave way. Another oiler, *Manatee*, also reported both hoses on her starboard side mangled so badly that repair would take an hour. All over the fleet destroyers were breaking away from oilers and other sources of fuel, many of them having managed to gulp anywhere from five hundred to a few thousand gallons, far less than what they normally would have received.[199]

Human bodies took damage as well. Even aboard the gargantuan *Iowa*, the force of the weather was felt. While she was nursing *Brush* to starboard and *Lewis Hancock* to port, E. M. Sampson, a sailor on one of the fueling details, was trying to lash down one of the vital, troublesome hoses, when the sea burst over *Iowa*'s side, hurling him against a stanchion and smashing his toe. His shipmate F. W. Franklin was less fortunate; he caught the stanchion full on the nose. A coxswain, meanwhile, had been thrown against an electrical condenser, which mangled his leg.[200]

Things were worse aboard the auxiliaries and destroyers. Aboard the *Fletcher*-class *Owen*, for instance, a thunderous sea came showering over the forecastle as the ship pitched sharply upward, inundating the fueling detail; one unlucky sailor went flying, shredding his leg. *Caperton* took a similar headlong plunge while attempting to take aboard pilots from *Essex* via a carnival-like ride over the yawning space between ships on a bosun's chair, a contraption suspended by lines; in this case the victim suffered a broken leg.[201]

Aboard *Iowa*'s sister, the flagship *New Jersey*, Bill Halsey sat down to lunch sharply at noon in flag mess. All of the *Iowa*s had been designed with flag quarters; the staff living and working space was lavish for a modern warship, but cramped by most other standards. At a long mahogany table with a score of his officers, Halsey was sitting next to a partition that separated the eating and working space from his personal office and quarters. Among his fellow diners was an old acquaintance of his, a slightly stout moon-faced officer, George F. Kosco, who had just arrived several days earlier to serve as Third Fleet navigator and aerologist.

Kosco was no ninety-day wonder. Born in 1908, he had graduated from the Naval Academy twenty-two years later, and while at Annapolis he had gotten to know Halsey. Midshipman Kosco had been on the boxing team when Halsey had been its supervisor. Afterward, as Halsey had gone on to command an Atlantic destroyer squadron, Kosco began the usual grueling climb for young officers, serving first in a battleship, then in destroyers. He then got cruiser and even oiler experience, all of which would stand him in good stead in this new assignment.

In 1937, however, Kosco had begun work on a new subject, the rapidly developing field of aerology. First at Annapolis and various naval air stations, and then in the MIT program, Kosco spent three years learning the subject; in 1940, with war clouds looming on the horizon, he had earned his master's degree in the discipline.

Then came four years of duty as aerological officer for several ships and commands. During this time he had also spent three months in the West Indies concentrating on hurricane research. All in all, he had built a solid record, and with his qualifications he seemed a natural for this new posting with Halsey. Still, he was only in his midthirties, and he had less than five years of on-the-job weather experience when he arrived in Ulithi. With the wartime strain on aerological staffing, Halsey was perhaps lucky to have gotten someone as seasoned as that, and with some special cyclonic training to boot.[202]

New Jersey was steaming on a heading of 030 with the wind about ten points on her port bow. *Hunt*, too, was on her port, trying to take aboard oil; to her starboard, in the lee of her great bulk, Lieutenant Commander James Andrea jockeyed his destroyer, *USS Spence*, into position for fueling.

Oddly, though—a great many oddities occur in the chaotic weather surrounding a hurricane or typhoon—it was *Spence* that had more troubles. As *Hunt* commenced fueling, Andrea struggled to hold his ship, very low on fuel and high in the water, on station, but that was no concern of the insolent seas. Halsey, seated at the head of his table, was facing outboard, and through the open hatch he observed the continuing struggle put up by one of his ships and the weather, like some bizarre luncheon entertainment. High up in *New Jersey*, he couldn't see *Spence*'s hull because she was so close aboard, but he could see across to her superstructure. Then, as he watched, *Spence* took several sharp rolls. Yawing off to starboard, she recovered and then suddenly swung her bow to the port and made straight toward *New Jersey*.

Halsey, in the crosshairs of these two thousand tons of onrushing steel, involuntarily ducked, as most people would have. In an instant, however, it was over; *Spence* veered away. Still, it had been close, and the destroyer, still struggling mightily, had soon ruptured both of the fuel hoses, black oil spewing uncontrollably. She had taken in only six thousand gallons, a fraction of her total capacity.[203]

Vessels had been reporting trouble for hours. Halsey's ships were desperately low on fuel, and he had to see to them. But, as the fleet was soon to learn the hard way, reports were one thing; direct observation was another. Mick Carney, seated next to Halsey, mentioned the similar troubles of other destroyers, and, disturbed by what he had seen, the fleet commander abruptly called a weather conference to meet in twenty-five minutes' time.[204]

At once, Kosco bolted from the table and climbed to his miniscule office to collect the day's weather map, and then he went to flag plot, the fleet's nerve center, where he checked various reports that might help him develop the weather picture. As of yet, the report from *Chandeleur*'s patrol planes, now nearly twelve hours old, still hadn't arrived, and all other reports were sketchy. Kosco routinely had to rely on communications from other ships and the widely dispersed fleet weather centrals that collected and distributed aerological data around the Pacific, occasionally augmented by reports from partisans in the Philippines and decoded Japanese weather data. But without *Chandeleur*'s warning he had little information about the vacant swath of ocean that stretched to his east. His best estimate was that a storm center of some sort was brewing about four hundred miles in that direction.[205]

When the conference began a few minutes later, Kosco said as much. That was the bad news. The good—or at least better—news was that between the fleet and this storm center was a cold front, a weak one but still useful, running from northeast to southwest. It was far closer to the fleet than the hidden storm center; still, Kosco thought that it might shield the fleet from the storm. When the cyclonic heat engine hit the line of colder air drifting down from the Arctic, it would run out of fuel and disintegrate. The cold front would lay a blanket of cool air along the ocean's surface, and the cyclone would then expire. That was the theory, anyway. What the fleet needed was distance, for the cold front—the line of battle, as it were—was almost upon it. Halsey's ships had to get clear before the weather contest began.

Halsey had given orders to discontinue fueling before he had even left the dinner table. Now, at that same table, covered with green pool cloth beneath a profusion of weather maps, he queried Kosco and others about a desirable course. Kosco recommended steaming at a right angle to the cold front to put as much distance between it and the fleet as possible. This direction—northwest—would also take it more or less directly away from where he thought the storm center was. As Halsey listened Kosco gave the coordinates of a new suggested rendezvous for refueling: 17° N, 128° E, 140 miles to the northwest. It was closer to Luzon and its Tokkō pilots, but the fleet had countermeasures for that problem. It was an acceptable risk.[206]

Halsey agreed and gave the order: the fleet would meet there at 0700 the following morning. With that the conference broke up.

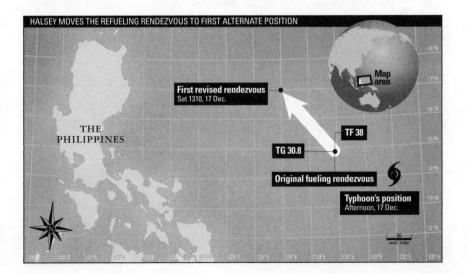

HALSEY MOVES THE REFUELING RENDEZVOUS TO FIRST ALTERNATE POSITION

Map area

First revised rendezvous
Set 1310, 17 Dec.

THE PHILIPPINES

TF 38

TG 30.8

Original fueling rendezvous

Typhoon's position
Afternoon, 17 Dec.

50
nautical miles

What Kosco still didn't know, and what *Chandeleur*'s report would have told him, was that he was definitely dealing with a typhoon, and, of far more crucial concern, it was swirling only two hundred miles to the east, not the four hundred miles his sketchy report had suggested. Kosco had hesitated to trust his own observations and measurements: calculations were more difficult on a moving weather station, and the whole point of reports was to expand one's vision. But the old barometric charts were still valid, and the glass, which Kosco had checked on his way to the conference, had dropped substantially in the preceding hour. Two measurements spaced an hour apart weren't much to base a forecast on. Nevertheless, the falling barometric pressure should perhaps have alerted the aerologist to the possibility that bad weather was closer than he thought, especially since he was essentially blind to the east, where there were no weather stations or ships.[207]

It was early afternoon. The fleet was beginning to disperse; TF 38 was to move to the rendezvous at a relatively high speed, the oilers and their consorts were to travel at their generally slower speed. Halsey's orders were not to cease fueling efforts immediately, but rather as soon as was practicable. This left some leeway for the critically low destroyers to keep trying to get oil enough to survive. Some of the small boys were already reporting fuel levels of less than 20 percent, and a few were even below 15 percent. At a standard speed of around fifteen knots, that added up to somewhere between twenty-four and forty-eight hours' steaming time, after which the ships would be dead in the water.[208]

Commanders were already taking measures to save the endangered warships. Some skippers were making plans for using the diesel fuel they had on hand for their emergency generators, mixing it with their remaining black oil and feeding it into the boilers. *Spence*, having failed in her efforts to fuel from *New Jersey*, fell into line to try to get oil from one of the tankers. As they began giving up on the general attempt to refuel in keeping with Halsey's instructions, individual task unit and group commanders ordered ships with critically low oil levels to stay with the replenishment group when TF 38 departed, which would allow them to keep trying to fuel.[209]

For some hours after the task force had dropped over the increasingly fuzzy horizon, the refueling task group kept at it, with little success. *Buchanan*, trying to fuel from the starboard of the oiler *Nantahala*, gave up in midafternoon. *Hickox*, to the starboard of *Atascosa*, temporarily quit about the same time. *Hickox* had barely 18 percent fuel remaining; without incident, she could last until the scheduled replenishment the following morning. But the wind was now a steady thirty knots, and the sea was heaving in a sickening fashion, now a Force 4. *Hickox* would need plenty of power to steam though it, and there was no guarantee that things would improve with the dawn. If they did not, then sometime the following day, *Hickox* and other destroyers might be hunks of dead metal bobbing as if they were corks.[210]

Aware that a crisis was a distinct possibility, Captain Jasper T. Acuff, who commanded the replenishment group, conferred with his screen commander, Preston V. Mercer, whose flag was aboard *Dewey*. *Dewey*'s captain, C. Raymond "Cal" Calhoun, was one of Mercer's most experienced skippers; *Dewey*, in fact, was his second destroyer command. An idea came to Mercer: let Calhoun try bringing his ship alongside to see if it could be done. This would also give Mercer the chance to see for himself what conditions were like.

With infinite care, Calhoun jockeyed his ship alongside an oiler. *Dewey* hung precariously for a time at the maximum reach of the hoses; then a swell hit, and the destroyer yawed wildly.

The helmsman spun the wheel, hard, and with full rudder *Dewey* clawed her way back to station, but Calhoun couldn't hold her. The swells were endless, inexorable; each time Calhoun bested one, another came at him hydralike. Then *Dewey* yawed once again. This time, silently praying, Calhoun managed to catch her when she was only five yards from the oiler. Again and again the two ships closed to barely a dozen feet.

After twenty minutes of this, Calhoun gave up, telling Mercer that it was impossible. Fuel hoses would never stay rigged in such weather; they would burst just like the others. Mercer agreed.[211]

With two hours of light remaining, *Atascosa* made a daring move. All fueling efforts so far had been by the standard alongside method, in which oiler and "customers" steamed in paralleling each other. But there was another way, the old over-the-stern method. Maybe it was the answer.

The navy had experimented with over-the-stern fueling exactly twenty years earlier, when it was working out the practical details of underway replenishment. In December 1924, steaming in line ahead rather than line

abreast, the oiler *Kanawha* had deployed a towline and fuel hose to the battleship *Arizona*, which had followed close behind her. During the next two
years the ships had successfully repeated their performance three times. But
compared to the volume of fuel that the alongside method could deliver,
over-the-stern was slow and anemic; the steam-driven tension engine that
controlled the towline, when combined with the demands of the oil pumps,
sucked too much power from the boilers to make the fuel transfer feasible.
While on paper the project continued for several more years, the brass had
been lukewarm about it, and the whole over-the-stern project ultimately got
the ax in 1931. Ever since then, the method had been as dead as *Arizona*, now
in her grave at Pearl Harbor's bottom.[212]

If *Atascosa* could resurrect the procedure on the fly, however, *Hickox*
might have a chance. A lot of fuel wasn't necessary; even a few thousand gallons would extend her life by a number of hours. By steaming behind the
oiler, she could avoid the dangers that Calhoun and *Dewey* had courted.

The oiler lacked the equipment and rigging for fueling a ship over the
stern, but that didn't stop her crew, who set about getting a hose off. Putting
the wind and seas on her stern, she waited as *Hickox* made the approach.

For nearly an hour the two ships struggled, slowing and then adding
steam, fighting the elements that seemed determined to frustrate them. At
last, with night coming on, *Hickox* gave up again. The effort had failed. In
resignation, the ships swung back to the base course that would take them to
the fleet rendezvous.[213]

Just as *Atascosa* and *Hickox* were preparing to start their unorthodox
mating dance, Acuff had received word that Halsey had changed the rendezvous to a new point farther south than the one he had set earlier in the
afternoon. When this final fueling attempt failed, Acuff grew worried, calling
up Captain Horace Butterfield on the jeep carrier *Nehenta Bay* to consult
with him. "What do you think about running out of it?" he asked Butterfield.[214]

The carrier skipper didn't think the new rendezvous would help the task
unit escape the storm. "My weatherman says that we may possibly run out of
it by morning," he told Acuff, "but we are going with it." Or rather, the storm
was going along more or less with the ships. That was no way for them to escape on this heading.

Then Acuff brought up what was obviously on his mind. "Do you think the old man was mistaken on his route?"

"That is the best way for him," Butterfield answered. "But we have come quite a ways with it. Big swells from the east make us move with it." Auxiliary vessels had neither the speed of destroyers nor the bulk and brute power of capital ships.

Acuff spoke again, with even greater foreboding. "I think we will come close to making rendezvous in the center of the storm."

"He probably thought center was more to the north, but it is actually more to east, I think," mused Butterfield in reply. "If he took report of the fleet broadcast from Pearl," the flattop commander grimly concluded, "he made an error."[215]

Dusk was beginning to fall, though in those tormented conditions there was no sunset, but instead a fading of gray skies into a murky indigo, and then sky and sea turned black. Red nightlights came on inside ships; in their combat information centers (CIC) the phosphorescent glow of the radar screens gave an eerie lighting to faces, like something of El Greco's. Below, in the fire rooms, oil gurgled steadily into the boilers.

Night had arrived. Desperate in its attempt to save fuel, the fleet ceased zigzagging.

The changes in the rendezvous orders were the result of a cat and mouse game Kosco had been playing with the typhoon for most of the afternoon, to no avail.

In the first place, Kosco wasn't sure that he was dealing with a typhoon. His weather reports, from weather centrals as distant and widely dispersed as Saipan, Kwajalein, and Pearl Harbor, were inconclusive; they were as blind as he was when it came to the swatch of the Philippine Sea where he intuited that something was brewing. He also began checking reports of other aerologists in the fleet, stationed for the most part aboard carriers, where flight operations demanded the best weather data. Few of his fellow forecasters believed that they were dealing with a typhoon; on that point most of the fleets aerologists agreed.[216]

Most, but not all. Much earlier in the day, before refueling began, *York-town*'s aerologist, sensing trouble ahead, emerged from his tiny office in the back of the carrier's island and confronted Captain T. S. Combs along with Rear Admiral Alfred E. Montgomery, the commander of Task Group 38.1. The weatherman, a lieutenant, was concerned that the replenishment couldn't wait. "I'm gonna suggest that you top off the destroyers," he told the senior officers emphatically, "because we're in for baaaad weather." They didn't take him seriously, and anyway the refueling would shortly begin. But as it turned out, "shortly" was not soon enough. A few hours later, with destroyers nearly colliding with oilers and carriers while trying to fuel, a quartermaster who'd seen the earlier exchange happened upon the lieutenant, seated in a rocking chair in his office, puffing on a pipe and rocking back and forth. "I told 'em so!" he puffed. "I told 'em so!"[217]

Lexington's aerographer also went so far as to approach Rear Admiral Gerald F. Bogan, the task group commander, to warn him that a tropical cyclone was building, showing him a map to help convince him. Bogan, having also gotten a sketchy report from the Pearl Harbor Fleet Weather Central, called up Halsey and recommended a turn south. Kosco began to consider it, but then another message came in.[218]

It was around two and a half hours after noon when Halsey received the message from USS *Chandeleur* that conveyed the storm warnings from the planes of VPN-21. This message, sent more than twelve hours earlier, was the first hard information from an outside source that Kosco had gotten, and that information was very bad news. Kosco had estimated the storm system to be perhaps 400 miles beyond the fleet, in the depths of the Pacific, but *Chandeleur*'s message put the storm at only around 125 miles to the east, and that position was now badly out of date. Typhoons can move at speeds ranging from a standstill to as much as fifty knots in some circumstances, and after twelve hours, the average error in plotting its position is more than fifty miles.[219]

On the other hand, Kosco knew that such storms usually moved west or northwest, at least until high pressure zones forced them to turn more sharply north, or even to double back to the northeast. He also knew that for all of the ugly weather about, the storm had not yet actually struck the fleet. *New Jersey*'s barometer, furthermore, was not particularly low, even after its sudden but brief drop around midday. So while potential danger was nearer than Kosco had thought, he was still not terribly worried. Perhaps he should have been. He was still playing blindman's bluff with something whose size and ferocity were beyond his ability to discern.[220]

Kosco did know one more thing, though; if this storm was moving on a typical northwest track, then Third Fleet, heading north toward its new fueling rendezvous, was steaming directly into it.[221]

Kosco talked things over with Halsey and other staffers. The weatherman now favored moving the fueling point southwest, moving at a right angle to the likely storm path. As later events would show, it was a good idea from an aerological perspective, but there was a major downside. The storm was crowding them toward Luzon. Too close and they would come within range of land-based Japanese airplanes. Postured for replenishment, the fleet would be vulnerable.

Kosco discounted the danger. If the weather kept the American pilots from flying, he argued, it would do the same to the Japanese. But even at that moment, the fleet was still conducting antisubmarine warfare flight operations despite the bad weather, and it if didn't degrade further, presumably the Tokkō planes could take to the air. More important, Halsey differed with Kosco; weather would be of little concern, he suggested, to a pilot who was heading out to die anyway.[222]

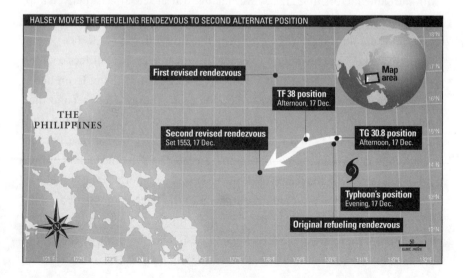

HALSEY MOVES THE REFUELING RENDEZVOUS TO SECOND ALTERNATE POSITION

THE PHILIPPINES

First revised rendezvous

TF 38 position
Afternoon, 17 Dec.

Second revised rendezvous
Set 1553, 17 Dec.

TG 30.8 position
Afternoon, 17 Dec.

Typhoon's position
Evening, 17 Dec.

Original refueling rendezvous

Map area

50
naut. miles

Eventually, though, Halsey agreed on a new refueling location, though it was due south of the fleet and not southwest. This, he and some other sailors hoped, would keep them clear of the track of—whatever it was.

As the word went out of the new rendezvous, task units and groups adjusted their readings, struggling through swells of increasing malevolence. Just as the replenishment group ceased zigzagging at dusk, so, too, did other commands turn to fuel-saving measures in preparation for the long night to come. Within minutes of putting TF 38 on its new base course to the rendezvous, McCain rescinded his order requiring his ships to be able to go to full boiler power on less than a half hour's notice. This would allow each vessel to take some boilers off the steam line and kill the hungry fires that burned in them, at least for a time.

No picket destroyers were posted, although the antisubmarine screen stayed in place around the precious carriers. In TG 38.5, Captain Ira H. Nunn directed that destroyers in his squadron running low on fuel do anything necessary with their boilers to get their fuel consumption down. In TG 38.3, the commander of Destroyer Squadron (DesRon) 50 ordered much the same thing. The captains of those ships would have to make some decisions concerning the trade-offs between economy and available power, but it couldn't be helped.[223]

In juggling these variables, the tin can skippers were dealing in microcosm with the same factors that Halsey was facing. War at sea, at least between opposing navies, is very much an exercise in maneuver, in moving one's forces in space and time in such a way as to bring maximum firepower to bear on an enemy, to strike more quickly, or to evade an attacker. Halsey's forces couldn't possibly damage the storm that was now moving toward them. Even had it been a more corporeal foe, it was releasing more energy every second than that of every scrap of weaponry Third Fleet possessed. All Halsey could do, if he didn't want to ride out the storm, was run. Maneuver, in that case, became a mathematical problem, an equation to translate the dynamic factors of time and speed into the static factor of position. It was a matter of range and bearing between two moving forces, the storm and the fleet, compounded by the different locations of various fleet components, the danger posed by the Tokkō planes to the west, the growing fuel crisis, and above all, by the lack of any hard information on the storm's location or track.[224] But as the typhoon

closed in on the fleet, variables began to gel and later solidify, and Halsey's options diminished. By the afternoon of the seventeenth, when he announced the
second change in the rendezvous to his ships, Halsey was already greatly constrained in his actions, though he perhaps didn't know it. A decisive sprint at a
right angle to the storm's track could still get the fleet clear; but as of that afternoon, that track, and the storm's location, were still unknown.

Kosco was trying. The miracle of modern technology had expanded his
vision far beyond the horizon, and he went over the reports from far-distant
stations again and again. He also gazed into the past, analyzing the historical
weather data on Philippine Sea typhoons of the previous fifty years. Most of
the December typhoons in the region, he established—in fact, three out of
four—tended to curve strongly north, or even recurve back to the northeast,
missing Luzon and points south completely. He rested a lot of his forecasting
on this important fact. But with this piercing vision, he may have lost sight of
the fact that one in four typhoons didn't curve, instead stabbing on westward
or slightly northwestward.[225]

Then there was the problem that would plague Kosco and the other fleet
aerologists for the next several days; seduced by reports from the radio, they
relied less heavily than their predecessors on their own direct observations.
Later—much later—the sailor and naval historian Samuel Eliot Morison
noted that if Kosco had used the sailor's rule of thumb, plotting the center of
the storm ten points to the right of the direction from which the wind was
blowing, he would have known the typhoon's position; *New Jersey*'s log and
subsequent data bear out that fact.[226]

The old sailor's manual known simply as *Bowditch* sets forth the wisdom
that the direction of the swells can reveal the same thing, and this, too, was
something for Kosco to fall back upon. But apparently he did neither, and as
night fell the storm kept its secrets.[227] Around the fleet, some mariners were
starting to worry, although others trusted Halsey implicitly. As *Dewey*
steamed into the darkness, Captain Calhoun, who tended to be one of the latter, evidently remembered the rule of thumb; even the most junior officers in
his wardroom, he told his squadron commander, Preston Mercer, knew that
they were facing not merely a storm but a typhoon, swirling to their southeast.

Mercer agreed. "I know," he replied, when Calhoun mentioned his worries. "I'm really tempted to call the fleet commander and tell him of my

concerns, but then I remember that he has a big staff, including an aerologist, and is getting analyses from Pearl Harbor." In light of all that, Mercer stated, "I can only conclude that it would be presumptuous of me to offer advice under those circumstances."[228]

Other commanders had similar thoughts. Captain George DeBaun of the carrier *Cowpens* sensed that heavy weather was coming, even though his own weatherman disagreed. Trusting his instincts, DeBaun ordered all of his department heads to begin securing the ship.[229]

Captain Michael H. Kernodle of the light carrier *San Jacinto* had worried since morning that he was in for bad weather; his own observations of both wind and sea, and his aerographer's warnings, clued him in as to what he was facing.[230] Captain Acuff, in command of the fueling group, called up the skipper of the jeep carrier *Nehenta Bay*, which had a weather forecaster on board; the aerologist liked the new southerly rendezvous and urged Acuff to get there quickly, but he warned the captain that it might not be far enough out of harm's way.[231] Meanwhile, Calhoun and other destroyer COs began rigging lifelines, stowing loose gear or lashing it down, and setting watertight conditions throughout their vessels. They also struck ready-room ammunition below, decreasing their ships' center of gravity to improve their riding characteristics.[232]

Carrier skippers did much the same thing, with some additions peculiar to their vessels. The airplanes aboard the flattops, even with no combat load, were quite heavy things for machines that spent time supported by nothing but air. The Grumman F6F Hellcat, the navy's most prolific fighter craft, weighed nearly ten tons, and the Curtiss SB2C Helldiver was heavier still. Aboard the light carrier *Cowpens*, DeBaun secured his planes and heavy equipment with both rope and wire; Captain Stuart H. "Slim" Ingersoll of the light carrier *Monterey* had each of his planes on the flight deck, and those below in the cavernous hanger deck, lashed down to the surface with as many as a dozen lines each, some of them stout manila and the others consisting of seven-eighths-inch wire cable.

The ritual was carried out on other flattops of whatever class. Captain G. C. Montgomery of the jeep carrier *Anzio* later verified that "an unusually large number of lines" held each of his planes to the deck. Crews sucked avgas from the planes' fuel tanks, or at least as much as they could, but given those tanks' design, they could never be totally empty unless the engine burned up the residual gallons that could not be pumped out. This spurred the crews to make sure the lines were secure, and while they were at it they lashed down tractors and jeeps just as tightly. Regular patrols began making rounds to check on the lashings' security.[233]

Many people were worried, then, about the threat from the weather. Surprisingly few, however, tried to share their worries with Halsey. Some, like Mercer, simply trusted the admiral; they also assumed he had access to the most and best weather data. Others saw the changes in the fueling rendezvous as evidence that Halsey was tracking the storm and reacting to it appropriately. The very fact that Halsey was there with them, experiencing the weather himself and ordering the fleet to break off fueling and get out of the way, showed that they didn't need to warn him. It crossed few people's minds, apparently, that Halsey didn't know where the storm was, or even what it was.[234]

There was one matter, though, that many commanders did feel the need to communicate. Bad weather, low fuel, even the changes in rendezvous were conspiring to make it hard, even impossible, for some of the slower or more widely scattered fleet movements to get to the latest refueling position by morning. In the hours after Halsey announced it, they radioed him back with the news. Two hours before midnight, when Halsey called another staff meeting, this was one of many things on his mind.[235]

The fact of the meeting was nothing out of the ordinary; Halsey usually finished up his day with a staff conference. This time, however, the weather, not the Japanese, was the center of all the attention. By now Halsey knew that he had to change the rendezvous for a third time if his ships were to get there on schedule; some of the vessels of the replenishment group, with their slower speed, wouldn't make it unless he changed the spot. South had seemed the best way to go, and Kosco still thought that was true. The new spot he suggested was to the north of the previous rendezvous, but still south of the one before that. In other words, this fourth proposed refueling location was on a line halfway between the second, most northerly and the third, most southerly ones. The very first rendezvous, from which the fleet had been driven nearly twelve hours before, was off to the southeast, in the general direction of the storm. But Kosco still, at the end of the day, was unsure of exactly where that storm lay.

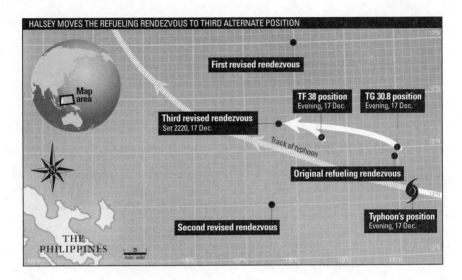

HALSEY MOVES THE REFUELING RENDEZVOUS TO THIRD ALTERNATE POSITION

First revised rendezvous

TF 38 position
Evening, 17 Dec.

TG 30.8 position
Evening, 17 Dec.

Third revised rendezvous
Set 2220, 17 Dec.

Track of typhoon

Map area

Original refueling rendezvous

Second revised rendezvous

Typhoon's position
Evening, 17 Dec.

THE PHILIPPINES

While at sea, neither Halsey nor his staff got much in the way of sleep. Halsey tried, but usually failed, to get five hours per night.[236] Given the circumstances, neither he nor Kosco got anywhere near that much during the evening to come. When the staff meeting ended, Kosco took a brief nap. Awakening at midnight, he found that *New Jersey* and her consorts were steaming southward, away from the latest fleet rendezvous; with their speed, they would reach it too early unless they opened the range some. Kosco liked the idea of continuing south, and a couple of hours later he dropped in on Halsey to tell him as much. After listening to what Kosco had to say, Halsey asked him a single question. "What do you think of a turn to the north?"[237]

Kosco didn't think much of it, and he said so. But there was nothing to be done for it; the fleet couldn't delay refueling much longer. The variables had now locked the fleet in, as surely as brick walls might have. And Halsey still had to consider his commitment to renew air strikes on December 19. If he detoured too far to the south in search of calm replenishment weather, he would spend too much time getting there and returning, putting the air strikes behind schedule. Kosco still hadn't committed himself to saying that the fleet was facing a typhoon; absent that danger, Halsey wanted to be ready to wade back into the fighting.[238]

If Halsey and Kosco had been more certain about what was happening, the latter's hunch about a course to the south would have seemed more imperative. Ideally a sailor should avoid a hurricane or typhoon completely; failing that, he should stay out of the storm's dangerous semicircle. In the Northern Hemisphere, tropical cyclones move generally to the west unless and until they recurve, and their winds move counterclockwise. This means that in the northern half of the cyclone, its forward momentum—anything from zero to fifty knots—augments its already formidable wind speeds, while in its southern half the effective speed of its winds, moving roughly eastward in that area, is reduced by the same amount.

Meteorologists and mariners thus call the northern semicircle "dangerous"—which it certainly is—and the southern one the "safe" or "navigable" semicircle—both of which are misnomers. The southern semicircle is safe only in comparison with the northern one; in absolute terms it can still be quite deadly. If the fleet had to do battle with a typhoon, though, it should make for the storm's southern half, which a southerly heading would help to achieve.[239]

But Halsey was oblivious to the weather. In the early hours of December 18, he even had to ask Kosco what it was like outside. Since Kosco hadn't warned him that they might be dealing with a typhoon, Halsey left the final rendezvous unchanged. Two hours after midnight, the fleet came around to the northwest.

That was the moment when the barometer began a precipitous drop.

The fall only went on for two or three hours, after which the pressure stabilized for a time, just as it had the previous afternoon and evening. The halting progression had lulled Kosco into thinking that he was seeing a normal daily fluctuation, even though the pressure was lower than it had been in days and the wind and seas were shouting warnings at him.

During the big drop between two and three in the morning, the exhausted aerologist was napping, trying to get in a few minutes of sleep before taking the watch at 0400. But the record shows all. At midnight the glass had stood at 29.78, considerably lower than average sea-level pressure, though not as low as it had been twelve hours before during all of the refueling trouble. By 0100 it had gone down to 29.76; in the next hour came a big drop, to 29.70. By 0300 it was at 29.65, bringing the decline since midnight to more than a tenth of an inch. That should have rung alarm bells. Throughout the rest of the fleet, many ships, though not all, saw similar or even greater drops, while some of them already had far lower readings as midnight came on.[240]

While Kosco lay trying to sleep, several miles away, in TG 30.8, the *Farragut*-class destroyer *Aylwin* also recorded a decrease in air pressure. Though it wasn't as great as that seen on *New Jersey*, *Aylwin*'s barometer was already several points lower; the small warship, a fraction of *New Jersey*'s size, lay closer to the typhoon, and she was already having to wrestle the elements more. Screening the precious fleet oilers, she was taking heavy seas several points on her starboard, making her roll in a sickening corkscrew fashion, while the wind blew from her starboard quarter.[241]

Commander Bill Rogers, *Aylwin*'s skipper, had been one of those who'd sensed bad weather coming. Early in the evening, he and several others had been in the wardroom when he got word from the radio messenger. "Captain," the man told him, "we have a new rendezvous for replenishment tomorrow, and an unimportant weather report."

The weather report *did* seem unimportant, mentioning only a mild disturbance somewhere nearby, but in conjunction with the rendezvous change it got Rogers thinking. "I'm probably wrong, but I'm afraid we may have rough weather tomorrow," he mused.

"Great!" shouted Seaman George Howes, who happened to be in the wardroom. "I've always wanted to see a typhoon."

That drew Chief Engineering Officer Lieutenant Elwood Rendahl's attention away from the book he was reading. "George, this steaming may be dull, but do not wish that on us," he warned. "These once were good destroyers, but with all the new guns and radars on board, we've got too much topside weight to want a typhoon. I for one do not want to see how far this ship will roll and not go over."

"That's exactly it," Rogers agreed. "We could have rough weather tomorrow and we've got too much topside weight." He set about correcting that problem as much as he could, and he took other precautions as well. "Guns," he told gunnery officer Erwin S. Jackson, "you won't need to do any shooting tomorrow with the Third Fleet all around us, so let's move all that ready service ammunition back to the magazines." Next he gave the generic command to the officer of the deck to rig for heavy weather. As the night deepened, the officers and the sailors in their departments began inspecting and securing the ship.[242]

Aylwin's voice call sign, the name ships used in radio communications, was Dracula; but unlike her namesake, she couldn't see in the dark. For that she relied on her SG radar, the premier microwave surface-search unit used by most of the ships in the fleet. *Aylwin*'s radar beam, like those from her squadron mates, stabbed into the thick, spray-filled blackness telling her where she was and how to keep her place in her task unit. But by the early hours of December 18, the radars' behavior was odd. In addition to showing a scattering of glowing pips, each of which represented a warship, the pale luminescence on several fleet radar screens was coalescing into odd, sweeping patterns of sea return, maybe sixty miles off in the Philippine Sea. The radar operators didn't know what these patterns were, nor did they care. Their job was to watch out for the ships. They had no way of knowing that they were seeing a typhoon coming at them.

Then at 0245, with no fanfare, one of *Aylwin*'s main turbogenerators packed in. The turbine was still driving the propeller shaft, but the electrical generator was dead. In an instant lights, instrumentation, gyrocompass, nearly everything needing electrical power was gone, including the radars the destroyer was using to feel her way through the night.

That wasn't all; with the loss of electrical power, the helmsman no longer had any control over the rudder. At once, *Aylwin* began drifting off station; no longer a guard against unlikely submarine threats, she was now a navigational menace herself.

The officer of the deck (OOD) was Lieutenant Junior Grade J. H. Wessells, Jr., a reservist with little experience steering twelve hundred tons of warship through pitch-black stormy waters while blind. Calling his skipper, Wessells snapped off a warning on the still-operational TBS. "*Aylwin* to TG 30.8," he spoke urgently into the handset. "We are broken down."

By now radarmen on nearby ships could probably see the pip that was *Aylwin* sliding out of position, even as Wessells sent out his alerts. Throughout the task group, conning officers prepared to maneuver their own ships to evade the destroyer if she went completely out of control.

Now another message from Wessells: "Have lost all power on genera-tors," the disembodied voice squawked through a dozen pilothouses, dis-torted by electronics and weather. "Am trying to come to base course."

That "trying" was not reassuring, especially with the task group com-mander aboard the stricken ship. "All ships take action," came word from *Nehenta Bay*, filling in for Acuff. "*Aylwin* has lost all power on generator, is trying to come to base course."

Bill Rogers, *Aylwin*'s skipper, quickly arrived and began conning the ship. With the wheel totally useless, he began firing off engine commands, using various combinations of speed on his starboard and port screws to bring *Aylwin* around to the right heading. Even in calm seas, the destroyer was more sluggish this way than when using her rudder, but in the rising swells she was even more piglike. Meanwhile, sailors were manning a hand-steering wheel for aft, in a compartment over the rudder. While this was a clumsier system for steering than the usual power-driven pilothouse wheel arrangement, it was better than steering with engines.

The power stayed out for ten minutes, while engineers brought a backup generator online, but in those conditions it likely seemed a lot longer. Then the power returned. The garish glow once again lit faces pressed to radar screens, and the gyrocompass began to spin up. The few minutes' slip had thrown *Aylwin* badly out of position, and for the next half hour she struggled to regain her station. She had gotten off lightly.[243]

Meanwhile, Kosco awoke on *New Jersey*, oblivious to the drama in the re-plenishment group. He climbed to the navigation deck, where for the first time he beheld the sharp drop the barometer had taken in the previous hour. Since the afternoon of the day before, the winds twisting around the fleet flagship had been in the mid- to high-twenty-knot range; now they were in the midthir-ties, and Kosco felt as if they were trying to tear him from the battleship's deck.

This was the moment when the awful word "typhoon" first crossed his mind. A tropical storm, maybe even just a depression, could have been re-sponsible for everything up to this point, but now, topside on a forty-five-thousand-ton armored ship that was itself beginning to roll, Kosco suspected that he was facing something much worse.

Kosco then went to flag plot to relieve the current watch officer, who told him that Halsey was up. "Maybe I had better go down and talk with

The Big Blue Fleet, December 1944. This is a small portion of just one of three task groups making up the Fast Carrier Task Force. (Photo courtesy of the Naval Historical Center)

Admiral William F. Halsey, December 1944. (Photo courtesy of the Naval Historical Center)

Halsey's fellow admirals (L-R): Raymond A. Spruance, Ernest J. King, and Chester A. Nimitz. (Photo courtesy of the Naval Historical Center)

Vice Admiral John S. McCain, Sr., commander of the Fast Carrier Task Force after Leyte Gulf. (Photo courtesy of the Naval Historical Center)

An early lesson in typhoons' fury: The wrecks of USS *Vandalia* and *Trenton* at Samoa, 1889. (Photo courtesy of the Naval Historical Center)

Farragut-class destroyers, 1930s. USS *Dewey* is on the left; Hull is second from the right; *Aylwin* is on the right. (Photo courtesy of the Naval Historical Center)

Underway replenishment: USS *Hull* prepares to refuel at sea, 1943. (Photo courtesy of the Naval Historical Center)

The *Fletcher*-class USS *Spence*, October 1944. Two months later she fell victim to Typhoon Cobra. (Photo courtesy of the Naval Historical Center)

Light carrier USS *Monterey* anchored at Ulithi less than a month before her battle with Cobra. (Photo courtesy of the Naval Historical Center)

Two storm-tossed flagships: Halsey's *New Jersey* (foreground) and Mc-
Cain's *Hancock* in rough weather a few weeks before Cobra. The typhoon would be far worse. (Photo courtesy of the Naval Historical Center)

Typhoon Cobra strikes; USS *Langley* heels over. (Photo courtesy of the
Naval Historical Center)

L ight cruiser *Santa Fe* takes a hard roll during Cobra. The destroyers' rolling was far worse. (Photo courtesy of the Naval Historical Center)

D estroyers in troughs during the typhoon. Breaking out could range from hard to impossible. (National Archives)

The aftermath: Wreckage on *Monterey*'s hangar deck after the typhoon. (Photo courtesy of the National Archives)

Survivors from the sunken destroyers on the deck of USS *Tabberer*. (Photo courtesy of the National Archives)

Reprise: Fleet carrier *Hornet* ships a massive wave over her bow during Typhoon Viper. Such a sight was commonplace during both typhoons. (Photo courtesy of the National Archives)

The results of the bow waves: Escort carrier *Windham Bay* after steaming through Viper. (Photo courtesy of the National Archives)

USS *Pittsburgh*, sans bow, after her duel with Viper. (Photo courtesy of the Naval Historical Center)

him," Kosco mused aloud. A few minutes later he did, warning the admiral that he thought the fleet's northwest course might take it into the storm.

"Get the chief of staff and operations officer," Halsey told Kosco. The aerologist went and found Mick Carney and Captain Ralph Wilson.

The four men then went to flag mess, where, sitting at the same table from which Halsey had seen the near collision a little more than twelve hours earlier, they dissected all the data they had. Kosco was still reluctant to use the word typhoon. Nevertheless, he had to face the possibility that whatever the storm was, the cold front hadn't bounced it off to the north. It still might be heading west or northwest, but he just didn't know its position. Even so, he thought north was the more dangerous direction, especially since the weather was getting worse with every mile the fleet traveled on the way to its rendezvous.

"What do you recommend?" Halsey asked Kosco point-blank. Kosco didn't hesitate; he suggested that "we turn immediately south."[244]

After that Kosco had to go on watch, but after a few minutes Halsey called him. "Get Task Force 38 on the TBS," he told the aerographer, "and ask him where he thinks the storm is."

Kosco put in the call. Soon he was talking with the crusty admiral. Mc-Cain's main concern wasn't with the storm itself; his first words to Kosco were that he feared he wouldn't be able to fuel his ships in this weather. It was apparently all the information that Kosco got from McCain, because he then went on to query Admiral Gerald F. Bogan, in command of TG 38.2.

Halsey, meanwhile, decided that he couldn't, or at least shouldn't, wait for the other estimates. Kosco was the fleet's top aerographer, so Halsey took him at his word. At 0500, two hours before the scheduled rendezvous, Halsey canceled it and ordered the fleet to turn to a heading of 180, directly south, and run for it. He set no new rendezvous, instead directing his vessels to "commence exercise when practicable." Halsey acknowledged as well that the fuel situation was grave. "Suggest leading destroyers take it over stern, if necessary," he added. That hadn't worked the previous afternoon, but anything was worth a try at this point.[245]

In flag plot aboard USS *Hancock*, Bill Hanger, communications officer, watched McCain struggle to give Halsey the information that he requested. Bogan had already done so; now Halsey's people plotted the data. They

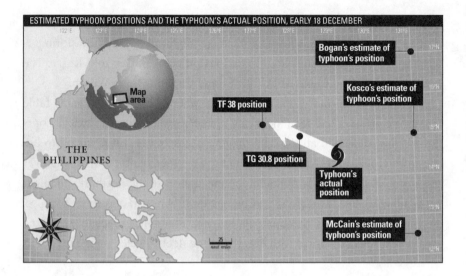

ESTIMATED TYPHOON POSITIONS AND THE TYPHOON'S ACTUAL POSITION, EARLY 18 DECEMBER

Bogan's estimate of typhoon's position

Kosco's estimate of typhoon's position

TF 38 position

THE PHILIPPINES

TG 30.8 position

Typhoon's actual position

McCain's estimate of typhoon's position

Map area

quickly saw that none of the estimates agreed. All placed the storm on a line running roughly northeast to southwest, perhaps a hundred miles east of the fleet; but the critical question went unanswered. Bogan's people placed the storm's center even farther north than Kosco had; McCain's located it much farther south than either of the other two estimates. If McCain's guess was right, the fleet was steaming into disaster.[246]

According to Joseph Conrad, who wrote so powerfully of the sea, a great storm has a "disintegrating power" that "isolates one from one's kind."[247] Halsey's ships, many of which were now unwittingly on an intercept heading with the typhoon, were scattered over hundreds of square miles of ocean. The cyclone's forces, arbitrary and wild, overtook each ship singly, at unique places and times. Meteorology works largely by statistics and averages; it couldn't allow its practitioners to read the discrete tales that each vessel was now to write. For now, at least, there was radar and radio contact throughout the task forces and groups that knit the ships together. Those would not begin to fail until later, as water invaded electronics and high winds gobbled up antennas and masts.

Throughout the night, on most ships, the glass stayed low and often continued to drop. Some ships, such as *Anzio*, saw the bottom begin to fall out as early as 0400, even as Halsey met with his staff. For others, including *New Jersey*, the big plunge came later, sometimes as late as noon. A lot depended on each ship's position.[248]

The same was true for the wind's direction as well as its force. Aboard the fleet flagship, Kosco himself first saw direct evidence of a typhoon only at ten in the morning, when the winds began backing around, starting to blow from the north, then from the west, instead of from the usual east. It was the counterclockwise, inward-sucking blast of a tropical cyclone, without any doubt. By then, though, other ships had long since seen the same thing. In the patch of ocean holding destroyer *Cushing*, the wind changed by nearly 180 degrees between five and six in the morning; then, between 0800 and 0900, it leapt from forty to sixty knots, lashing her starboard quarter.[249] Steaming in the very same task group, *McCord* had a different experience. Her OOD noted no such wild shifts in direction, but by 0200, about an hour before the force of the gales struck *Cushing*, the breeze, already considerable, began climbing drastically.[250] Secure in its strength, the typhoon was attacking the fleet piecemeal, as Kurita, with far less force, had done to Taffy 3 two months before. This time, however, the attacker had more than enough strength to defeat its opponent in detail.

Most of the fleet's sailors had no access to a barometer; they had to rely on other signals that things were getting rough. A lot of the signs dealt with food, both input and output. As the ships swung to the new fleet course of 180—directly south—the wind, for most vessels, began to strike from astern, or nearly so, making them hard to control, and the pitching and rolling, to say nothing of yawing, got more severe. This was no weather to allow a hot breakfast; cooking for hundreds, or in the case of the big vessels more than a thousand men, was simply impossible in such conditions. Cooks could offer nothing but sandwiches, and even those would slide off the tables if people didn't hang onto them, even aboard large, stable ships like *New Jersey*.

The sailors couldn't even eat their cold chow while sitting at tables, for the unsteady decks wouldn't hold the collapsible and removable furniture. Aboard *Nehenta Bay*, Storekeeper Second Class Delos W. Smith and his shipmates had learned this the hard way the evening before. While the sailors were eating, bracing themselves against the tables, the carrier took a hard roll, recovered, and then rolled in the other direction. The tables went down with a clatter, sliming the decks with dinner. Aboard the lurching fleet carrier *Yorktown,* sailors simply sat on deck from the outset to eat; the men would shift the food into their mouths and then, as the ship heeled far over, stop eating and stare fearfully at each other, knowing that if the flattop turned turtle, everyone on the galley deck had had it. Then the carrier would right herself, and the diners took up eating again—until the next roll.[251]

Of course, a lot of the food came back up, though not as much as some might believe. Most of these sailors had been at sea for months, often not touching land for weeks at a stretch. They were seasoned, and had gotten seasickness out of their systems. But already conditions were worse than anything most of them had endured and some of their stomachs just couldn't take it. *Yorktown*'s Herb Lapp never lost any of his meals, but the sailor soon got a headache that lasted for two days, even though he didn't normally suffer from that particular symptom of seasickness.[252]

Aboard *The Sullivans,* coxswain Jack Matthew slept like a baby, bothered not at all by any seasickness. He had had the watch before turning in; stationed on the ship's flying bridge, high up and exposed to the elements, he marveled at the waves the destroyer was smashing straight into. One moment he and his fellow watch stander were staring into the gloom, fighting to keep from being swept off the deck by the rain, blind to anything but a mountain of water looming out of the darkness ahead of them; the next came the crash of the wall of salt liquid, and *The Sullivans* stood at the very peak of the mountain. After his watch ended, he strapped himself into his bunk, and the rolling of the ship seemed as if it were the rocking of a cradle. A few minutes later he was out like a light.[253]

Others slept less well, both then and during the day after coming off watch. Aboard the destroyer escort *Tabberer,* assigned to the replenishment group, sailors had to take hitches in the chains that held up their bunks so instead of lying flat each bunk formed a V with the neighboring bulkhead; that was the only way the occupant could stay in it.[254] *Essex*-class carriers, dwarfing the destroyer escorts, had a different problem. Each *Essex* consisted of three main sections—fore, middle, and aft—joined by expansion plates. Gene Bullard, a sailor of the gunnery department, stationed aboard one of these carriers, had an expansion plate directly over his bunk, and all night, as his ship battled the waves, he lay awake and watched it. Fleet carriers, like many other large ships, were prone to hogging. This is the opposite of sagging, a condition in which the forward and after sections droop. Each time the ship hit a wave, Bullard would take a deep breath as he saw the expansion plate slide apart in its struggle against the hogging; then the plate would move back together, and he would breath a sigh of relief. He got no sleep that night.[255]

Others' jobs kept them awake, and in the night they experienced things that told them that they were indeed facing something deadly. Ben Coulliard was a young sailor aboard *Yorktown* who had the midwatch, the dark hours just after midnight. The waves, whipped up by a wind that threatened to blow men on the weather decks overboard, were already bad, and the carrier, heading directly into them, was pitching ominously in the blackness. Coulliard's station was on the flight deck, but already it was a dangerous place to be. Whenever *Yorktown*'s bow pitched down into the trough, it would scoop up a huge sheet of water, thirty feet high, which would come hurtling up the long flight deck that stretched away into the night. And high in the rigging the deadly wind screamed eerily, giving the sailor chills. That high, keening sound was a warning: *Do not treat me lightly*, it seemed to tell Coulliard. Heeding the warning, he stayed safely inside the island.

Around two hours after midnight the officer of the deck approached him. "Coulliard," he asked routinely, "is everything secure on the flight deck?"

"I guess so, sir," replied Coulliard uncertainly. "I haven't been out there."

"What do you mean you haven't been out there?" snapped the officer. "That's your station, isn't it?"

"Yes, sir," answered Coulliard. "But if you go out there, you'll die."

As if on cue, *Yorktown* plunged into a trough, bow first. From outside, over the shrieking of the gale, Coulliard heard the deep thunder of the cascading water climbing the flight deck.

"You hear that sound?" he asked the officer. "That's water . . . and the wind. The next time the bow goes down, I'm gonna crack that hatch towards the fantail, and you look out there."

They didn't have long to wait. Soon the ship began plunging downward again, and again came the crash of the water.

When Coulliard estimated that the wave was even with the island, he cracked open the hatch, having to use all of his strength to do so against the malevolent winds. "You look through there," he told the OOD.

The officer looked.

"Oh, my God," he said. He turned, walked away, and didn't bother Coulliard again.[256]

Coulliard found the ordeal worse than combat. Another who shared that view was Herbert Hepworth, a coxswain on the light cruiser *Santa Fe*. For him things passed in a blur of wild pitching and rolling as the ten-thousand-ton warship struggled through the elements. At least, he reassured himself, *Santa Fe* was fully ballasted, unlike several destroyers in the task force. Her rolling was bad; theirs, Hepworth knew, would be worse.[257]

As the day wore on, the seas even got to the battleships, the heaviest, most stable vessels in the whole of the navy. At full load, USS *Washington* weighed in at forty-five thousand tons, exceeded only by the ships of the *South Dakota* and *Iowa* classes. Yet as the day wore on, the growing swell began using her for a toy.

If things had been too rough to fuel the day before, then today there was no chance at all. As to what passed for daylight grew, Jasper Acuff, in command of the replenishment group, called up McCain to tell him that trying to rig for over-the-stern refueling was out of the question. One oiler, *Mataco*, had even lost contact with the rest of the group. McCain agreed with Acuff's assessment; a few minutes later he ordered the thirstiest of the destroyers to get into the lee of the carriers and, shielded from the wind by their bulk, to make one last effort to fuel from the flattops.[258]

By now things were dire; more than a dozen tin cans were reporting fuel levels of less than 20 percent. Most of them had considerably less than that. But the carrier gambit failed, too. Less than an hour after McCain's fueling order, Rear Admiral Bogan in TG 38.2 reported that it was no good. And as the effort continued, people were getting hurt. One sailor crushed his toe when he dropped a five-inch shell on it; another crushed his finger when closing a hatch. Conditions would only get worse. As the watch changed throughout the fleet at 0800, Halsey stepped in, and for the second time in less than twenty-four hours, cancelled the refueling operation. The fleet's course remained due south, 180 degrees.[259]

During this last attempt to refuel, the idea, or rather the hope, was that the carriers, with their high freeboard, could protect their smaller companions. But as the storm came on in all of its fury, the carriers themselves became its prey. Bulkier than the other ships of the fleet, lacking the battleships' stout armor belts, and far higher out of the water than any other ship in the navy, the carriers were very susceptible to the rising seas and the winds that were howling at greater and still greater forces. As the fleet began to struggle back to its course to the south, the first crisis began.

Steaming southward into the storm's track, many ships of the task group found themselves among the nearest to the typhoon's center, and all the while the storm was coming closer. Among those in the most deadly position were the ships of Rear Admiral Montgomery's Task Group 38.1, with its three dozen warships centered around four aircraft carriers. Two of these, *Yorktown* and *Wasp*, were *Essex*-class fleet carriers; the other two were the light, *Independence*-class *Monterey* and *Cowpens*.[260]

Monterey had begun life as the cruiser *Dayton*. Laid down a few weeks after Pearl Harbor, she swiftly underwent an identity change as the navy's leadership and the White House realized that this was to be a carrier war. The *Essex*-class ships were already in the pipeline, but building and commissioning them would take time. Shipyards could make light carriers out of cruiser hulls quickly; so *Monterey* and her sisters were born. The change, however, had costs. The light carriers, with half the tonnage and two-thirds the power of the *Essex* flattops, tended to be top heavy even for carriers. Protecting the ship's bowels proved troublesome, with most of the ships receiving lighter Class B armor, and a few of them getting none at all, which increased the top-heaviness problem. The island structures common to most carriers threw the cruiser hulls out of balance; to solve this problem, the designers had to add a blister to the opposite side of each carrier's hull, filling it with eighty tons of concrete ballast, which put a drain on the ship's power and speed. Even so, the class wasn't too stable. *Monterey*, for instance, rolled lazily even in calm seas.[261]

Unlike some of the aerologists, Captain Ingersoll had smelled a typhoon the day before. He wasn't quite sure where it was—it may have been swirling somewhere off to the southeast, or maybe more to the south—but he still knew it was lurking out there. He was one of the carrier skippers who, on

Sunday evening, had given orders to secure for heavy weather. Using wire and manila, he tied down his planes on the hangar and flight decks "at every available point," as he later described it. He rigged palisades on the flight deck; he doubled the security watches to keep an eye on the hundreds of lines; and in addition to the watches, he ordered roving patrols to move about as best they could to check on aircraft security.[262]

Ingersoll's instincts were good. By seven o'clock Monday morning, his barometer was falling, and by the time the watch changed an hour later, he saw that the wind was beginning to back. About this time he received word to resume the fleet course of 180 degrees, which would put the wind on his quarter, the worst point for steaming when it came to *Monterey*'s quirky stability.[263]

Dutifully Ingersoll put the ship around onto a course to the south. Then right away things started happening. The howling winds and the ever-higher waves grabbed hold of the vessel and began to throw her into a rhythm of steady, precipitous rolls of between thirty and forty degrees. The inclinometer, which measured the rolling, began to swing metronomically back and forth as *Monterey* slipped down into troughs and then climbed back up onto the top of the following waves.

The hard ride nearly claimed the life of a future U.S. president. Lieutenant Gerald R. Ford, the ship's assistant navigation officer and one of *Monterey*'s plank owners, had had the midwatch, and he was just dozing off after dawn general quarters when he was again awakened by the alarm. Making his way to the catwalk surrounding *Monterey*'s island, he was starting to climb the ladder up to the bridge when the carrier heeled to the port. Suddenly Ford was down, sliding completely across the flight deck toward the far edge.

A two-inch lip of metal saved him. It ran along the rim of the flight deck, a small ridge designed to keep tools from skittered overboard. It wasn't enough to stop Ford, but it slowed him sufficiently to give the athletic officer time to roll onto the catwalk below and resume his trek toward the bridge, this time taking more care.[264]

On other ships, too, the eroding weather was becoming impossible to ignore. Aboard *Yorktown*, the navigation officer came out of the chart house after conferring with *Washington* by TBS. "According to their information," he stated to those in the wheelhouse, "this ship can safely take a 13 degree roll."

"Commander, that's fine," Quartermaster Don Ziglar responded. "We just passed 19." Rattled, the navigator went back into the chart house.[265]

Even aboard the heavy, stable *New Jersey*, people were getting anxious. Anthony Iacono, a young gun pointer of the Fourteenth Division, happened by an inclinometer whose face bore two ominous-looking red marks, one to either side. "What if we hit that red mark?" he asked a nearby sailor.

The answer was brief and not at all comforting. "We just flip over."[266]

That was unlikely on a monster such as *New Jersey*, but top-heavy *Monterey* actually ran that risk. Another, and greater, danger was that she would lose some of her topside planes. The fighters, bombers, and torpedo craft she carried were heavy beasts, and while Slim Ingersoll had done all he could to secure them, it still might not be enough. The wind was now shrieking at around fifty knots, with higher gusts. The sailors of the flight deck securing patrols couldn't possibly stand; instead they kept themselves steady by holding on to the island, watching their charges from a distance. The rain was blowing horizontally, and the wings of the secured aircraft struggled to lift their burdens into the pallid and streaming sky. All the while, *Monterey* kept up her wild rolling.

Casualty reports were beginning to trickle in from all over the fleet. Radars were beginning to crash; equipment was being blown off weather decks. *Wasp*'s lookouts spotted a life raft drifting by her, apparently with three sailors in it, but she could do nothing to help. A few minutes later came a TBS call from the fleet tug *Jicarilla*, a deep ocean brute designed to slug it out with the sea as no other ship in the fleet. Her main engine was failing, and she was losing power.[267] The escort carriers in the refueling group, meanwhile, were having trouble maneuvering; even flimsier than the *Independence*-class carriers, they were getting creamed. McCain, having given up hopes of refueling, ordered the jeep carriers to maneuver at discretion, as long as they kept together. Ingersoll, meanwhile, having neither asked for nor gotten permission to do likewise, grimly hung on to fleet course.[268]

About thirty minutes after coming to the southerly heading, *Monterey* reached the breaking point. A half hour of steady rolling had stretched the soaked manila beyond its endurance. The carrier reached maximum roll to one side and then swung like a pendulum to the other, a total swing of nearly seventy degrees. As the helpless securing detail looked on, the lines on four planes on the flight deck popped. The sudden shift of tensions onto the re-maining cables was too much, and the fittings on the planes themselves were ripped loose. Suddenly the planes were skidding across the deck and, an in-stant later, over the side.

The loss of the aircraft actually made the ship less top heavy, but Inger-soll wasn't thinking about that now. As the planes, now wreckage, drifted away sinking, he was still trying to maintain fleet course. He had decided not to call for help or permission to maneuver; with the fleet being blasted this way, he figured, Halsey would have to change course, and soon. Ingersoll didn't want to become a navigational hazard by breaking formation if he could possibly help it.

Twenty minutes elapsed and no word came. Then, a few minutes after nine, another hard roll pried loose three more flight deck planes, throwing In-gersoll's earlier decision into doubt. As they went, they smashed into the fragile safety nets, never designed to hold the planes' weight, shredding them instantly. Three twenty-millimeter guns snapped like matchsticks, and the landing signal officer's platform, from which the officer directed returning planes, was ripped away. Then planes, netting, and equipment splashed into the boiling water alongside the ship and were gone.[269]

But by then Ingersoll had bigger worries than that.

As the second group of flight deck airplanes burst loose, a single F6F Hellcat below on the hangar deck broke its own cables. *Monterey*'s rolling flung the ten-thousand-pound aircraft into its neighbor. Ingersoll decided that things were at last out of hand. The time had come for maneuver. Quickly he raised the task group commander on TBS. "Cannot hold present 180 degree course." he reported. "Am coming to 140 degrees at fifteen knots."

Ingersoll had ordered these planes degassed the night before, and the crews had dutifully suctioned as much of the high-octane aviation gasoline as they could from the belly tanks. The tanks on the Hellcats, though, were built in a way that kept the crews from being able to suck out the last few gallons from the after ends of the tanks. As *Monterey* kept rolling wildly, the loose Hellcat hit its tied-down neighbor squarely in its fuel tank, blasting it open. As hangar deck sailors scrambled to get things under control, the leaking avgas exploded.[270]

A sheet of flame swept outward, enveloping the central part of the hangar deck. The hatch to the firefighting station blew out, and the fire raced into the station, blanketing the fire sprinkler controls. It was one of the worst spots for *Monterey* to have been wounded; the sprinklers stayed dead, and the fire whipped out into the length and breadth of the whole hangar deck.[271]

Snapping helm orders, Ingersoll got off another TBS to Montgomery. "Present course 220 degrees," he spoke over the storm. "All planes on my hangar deck on fire." He had no time to say anything else.[272]

Unchecked, the fire kept licking outward. The explosion had blown apart a number of ventilation ducts on the port side of the hangar deck. These ducts normally fed air to the boiler and engine spaces, the ship's mechanical heart. Now breached, they fed dense smoke instead to the lungs of the sailors below. Within a couple of minutes, choking and coughing men had to evacuate most of the critical engineering spaces; only the after engine room was habitable.

Monterey began to lose steam.

As the boiler pressure dropped, the engines became anemic, and the pumps feeding the fire hoses faltered. By now the firefighting crews had begun spraying water on the spreading blaze, and the fire room crews, before leaving, had managed to cut in the sprinklers manually, but without power those sprinklers wouldn't last long. Cataracts of water from the firefighters' hoses soon began to pour down the damaged air shafts, making things below even worse.[273]

All the while, *Monterey* kept up her hard rolling, the firefighting crews staggering and desperately trying to keep on their feet as they shot streams of water and foam at the fire and the loose planes and equipment. Lights and electrical power were out on the deck, lurid flames illuminating the space in a ghastly way. One sailor slipped and shot straight over the side; another threw a fire hose into the water after him. The aim was good; the man in the water burst to the surface right next to the hose, grabbing it and climbing hand over hand back into the burning warship. "Just enough to cool him off after the heat of that damn fire," one of the firefighters grimly joked.[274]

Within fifteen minutes of the fire breaking out, Admiral Montgomery, the task group commander, dispatched a cruiser and a pair of destroyers to help *Monterey*. Montgomery doubted that the carrier's men could fight the fire in such conditions, suspecting that he would have to order Ingersoll and the crew to abandon ship. But Ingersoll wasn't ready to accept a death sentence for the ship without a fight. "Give us more time," the captain radioed Montgomery. "I think we can solve the problem."[275]

Despite his request, Ingersoll knew that the ship was in very great danger, and he put *Monterey* on a heading of 240 degrees, roughly west-southwest. This took the edge off the rolling, and the carrier began to ride somewhat more easily. But she still wasn't too steady. Worse, she was still low on power. The engine space crews had begun donning their respirators and going back down into the machinery rooms, but conditions there were bad. Scalding water, heated by the hangar deck flames, forced the crew in the number two fire room to douse their boilers and retreat, robbing *Monterey* of more power.[276]

The insatiable flames then found another ruptured supply duct, and down it they raced to the third deck. Another explosion there rocked the ship, blowing out the laundry space and a good many bulkheads. The fire also threatened to move upward: the terrific heat on the hangar deck was beginning to melt the beams that supported the flight deck above. The same heat threatened to cook off the ready service magazines on the flight deck, which would add to the chaos. Men were already dead; if twenty- and forty-millimeter rounds, to say nothing of five-inch shells, began to go off, they would have lots of company.

Sailors had already moved to the magazines, hosing them down and flooding them, and pilots were busy with gun crews jettisoning ammunition, but in two sectors there was no water pressure. Conditions below were taking their toll. Ingersoll had to do something, so fifteen minutes after the first explosion he hove to, putting *Monterey* at the mercy of a typhoon that knew neither mercy or pity, stopping his engines and diverting all his steam pressure to fighting the worsening blaze.[277]

The ploy worked. No longer fighting the elements, *Monterey* simply rode with them, rolling a mere eleven degrees, bobbing corklike on rising seas in winds gusting at nearly one hundred knots, more than a hundred miles an hour. Burned and choking sailors, three dead, many more seriously wounded, were dragged from the hangar deck, but others took their places, now attacking the fires and the melting, deadly aircraft and tractors with nearly a dozen high-pressure hoses. Avgas storage spaces were safe; Ingersoll made sure that they had been flooded with carbon dioxide. All of the hangar deck sprinklers were back online, and slowly the murderous heat began fading.

An hour after the initial explosion, with the cruiser *New Orleans* and two tin cans on the way toward the stricken carrier to render assistance, the fire was losing the battle. *Monterey*'s crew had beaten it back into the central part of the hangar deck, from whence it had first erupted. By 1030 the fires themselves were all out, though the wreckage of several airplanes, still nearly glowing with heat, jostled and shifted as the ship rolled. Ingersoll was getting his boilers back online, but he decided to stay hove-to in light of all the loose wreckage. All the while he'd been keeping an eye on the weather, and there was no longer the least bit of doubt. The wind had backed and was blowing ever more strongly, and the seas were growing steeper. *Monterey*, so far only on the fringes of the typhoon, was now being overtaken by the heart of the storm.[278]

Even though *Monterey* had taken a pounding, the typhoon had yet to unleash its full fury. It wouldn't make its closest approach to the fleet for another few hours. It didn't matter; *Monterey* wasn't the only ship in trouble. Even before her aircraft broke loose and burst into flames, other vessels were beginning to run into danger. The wind, as might some rabid animal, clawed at men and equipment. It tore the eyeglasses from the face of a quartermaster as he stepped through a hatch into the open air outside his carrier's pilothouse. It ripped loose a life raft from another warship; the raft careened

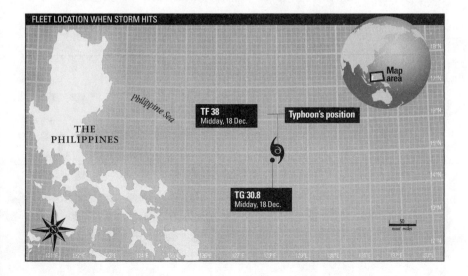

among the ships of the fleet, some lookouts spotting what they thought to be sailors aboard. And shortly before the *Monterey*'s blaze began, it conspired with the waves to take a man from the decks of the carrier *Independence*. Soon others, off balance and helpless, began to follow him.[279]

As the bad news continued to come in, McCain, who was exercising tactical command, asked his staff in frustration, "What's the fastest way out of here?" The problem was there was still no accurate fix. Halsey and Kosco estimated that the typhoon was moving westward, but no one was certain.[280] With Halsey having ordered the refueling attempt canceled, there was no reason to stay on the southerly course. McCain had ordered the fleet to come to a southwesterly heading, away from the storm's apparent track at a right angle, but this course had been murdering his task force. With *Monterey* in trouble, McCain tried a different approach, aiming the fleet southeast on a reciprocal heading to the typhoon, paralleling its path but going in the opposite direction in order to run out of the heavy weather more quickly, and, of course, to stay out of the dangerous semicircle.

It didn't work. Men continued to go overboard by ones and twos. The rolling was fantastic, produced by steeper, even more awesome waves. Men off watch lay strapped in their bunks as ships took rolls of thirty and forty degrees. Aboard the jeep carrier *Nehenta Bay*, Storekeeper Delos Smith and his shipmates were trying to follow a simple order: when the ship heeled to the port, the commanding officer told them, the men on the hangar deck were to run to the starboard to help offset the roll, and vice versa. The problem was that the rolls were so severe that Smith and the others could barely keep on their feet, much less run. Another carrier, *Langley*, was soon rolling regularly through thirty-five degrees.[281]

As the fleet changed direction, some ships now met the waves, taking them on their bows as best they could. The rolling had been fearsome, but the pitching, with the high waves breaking over flight decks and forecastles, was even more frightful. Aboard the fleet carrier *Lexington*, young Seaman Third Class Robert E. de Jong watched as the bow furrowed into a wave, throwing a wall of water up the flight deck almost as far as the island, much as Ben Coulliard had seen the night before. Aboard *Hancock*, the flying waters tore up some of the planes on the flight deck, even though many of them were parked aft of the island. Aboard the heavily pitching *Yorktown*, signalman Ed Joyeusaz decided to measure the height of these monstrous waves. Descending the island to the flight deck, he opened a hatch aft, which the island structure shielded from the wash of the wind and spray. Dropping to his hands and knees, he looked straight across the flight deck, which in calm seas stood sixty-five feet above the surface of the ocean. The waves Joyeusaz now saw towered at least twenty-five feet above that same deck. When one of them hit *Yorktown*, the ship would shudder all the way down her vast length, something that Joyeusaz never experienced before or after the storm.

Charlie Boyst, an aviation ordnance specialist aboard *Hancock*, experienced the same thing. As the ship crested—or rather, smashed through—one of these towering waves and then hurried down into the deep trough that followed, Boyst would very nearly be thrown from his bunk on gallery deck, just below *Hancock*'s flight deck. Boyst had faith in *Hancock*; he wasn't worried that she would break up. Strapped tightly into his bunk aboard *Lexington*, feeling her shake all around him as she slammed into wave after wave, Sal DeLuca was far less confident that his carrier would come through the storm. In his quarters aboard *Yorktown*, directly over the screws, Bishop Burmeister felt much the same way, though he wasn't sure if the end would come through capsize or instead a simple breakup.[282]

The top-heavy carriers were pitching and rolling madly, but they weren't alone. Cruisers, even heavy battleships with their stabilizing belts of thick, heavy armor, were having bad moments. *Marias*, an oiler laden with Navy Special, might just as well have been a cork on the water; now and then she would shake as her screws came out of the sea. Before long her skipper, like other COs, had ordered the crew into life jackets.[283]

As the storm came on, the task force battleships, each displacing at least forty thousand tons, became no more than the toys of a furious giant. Lieutenant Herbert J. "Scotty" Campbell was seated on a sofa in *Washington*'s chart house, checking the ship's position with a quartermaster, when one of the biggest waves he had ever seen came bursting out of the typhoon's heart and hit the great battlewagon. The unsecured sofa took to the air, along with the quartermaster and Campbell, flying across the chart house and smacking into the far bulkhead. Below, in the wardroom, other furniture tumbled the width of the compartment, eighty feet in all.[284]

Aboard *Iowa*, which sat lower in the water than the carriers did, Electrician's Mate Grier Sims hung on as the battleship swung through rolls of up to forty degrees, wondering whether she would ever come up out of whatever trough she was in or whether, instead, the gigantic waves would simply roll over her and bear her to the bottom of the Pacific. From his position on a twenty-millimeter antiaircraft gun on the second deck of *Iowa*'s sister *New Jersey*, Blackie Leonard watched the bow of his ship as it broke through the waves, then lurched down and hit hard, shaking all of her forty-five thousand tons. Through the driving rain and spray he could catch glimpses of other struggling vessels, mostly carriers. The destroyers, much smaller, were harder to see; they were often buried in troughs, with only their mast showing above the towering wave tops.[285]

Despite the fears that were beginning to spread, Leonard wasn't alone in wanting a view of the storm, especially since the spaces belowdecks were crowded with men, many of whom were seasick. Gordon McBride, for one, always found rough weather exciting to watch. As one of *Altamaha*'s helmsmen, he started out for the bridge, where he was sure he would be allowed to stay and see what was happening even though it wasn't his watch. But on the way, a friend of his, a gunner's mate, stopped him and asked for his help: he was having trouble securing some forty-millimeter shells that had gotten loose, so McBride went with him to the magazine.

While the two sailors were in the after elevator, *Altamaha* took a sudden steep roll as a wave swept her up, and then she heeled over in the other direction as she slid down the wave's opposite side. McBride's friend slipped and then hit the bulkhead. Equipment began tearing loose, and it was all McBride could do to get behind a beam, shielding himself from various flying objects.

The wind was now whipping water aboard, and it was spilling down into the after elevator. McBride couldn't get farther below, but another friend of his made it, only to find that five-inch shells, too, had broken loose in the magazine. Sailors got to work securing them before they could blow a hole in the ship. McBride began his climb back topside, but when he got to the mess hall, he learned that one deck above, on the hangar deck, a forklift had worked its way loose and was running amok. McBride then decided to stay where he was. He never made it to the bridge during the storm.

Aboard *Vincennes* in Task Group 38.2, things were much the same. Tiring of the rough-weather fare of coffee and sandwiches, eighteen-year-old James R. Thomas decided to brave the open deck and smoke a cigarette. As he stood near a pile of tied-down five-inch shell casings, a shipmate approached him to ask for a light. Suddenly *Vincennes* lurched, and the approaching sailor was airborne, flying straight toward the shells. Landing on his feet, he managed to grab a safety pipe before he hit the ungainly pile. Thomas, watching mutely, decided to scurry back belowdecks, but not before he caught sight of a nearby carrier. The massive ship's screws, when it crested, were clear of the water.[286]

Back aboard *Yorktown*, George Thompson, one of the carrier's plank owners, was in an ammunition handling room, working with a fellow sailor to secure five-inch rounds that had broken loose. The ship was rolling madly, and the heavy shells skittered back and forth over the deck. As they darted past, Thompson and the other sailor tried to grab and secure them. None went off, but in later days Thompson would try hard to forget the harrowing episode.[287]

As winds and seas increased, tossing the fleet madly, something, it seemed, had to give. Even as *Monterey* fought both water and fire, the escort carrier *Cape Esperance*, in the replenishment group, began slipping beyond the control of her crew. When McCain ordered a new fleet course of 140 degrees around 0930, the carrier's skipper, R. W. Bockius, tried to comply, but he couldn't. The pressure of the wind and sea on the hull was too much, and none of his engine and rudder commands could get the ship around. *Cape Esperance* began making regular rolls of thirty-six degrees, the strain on the cables holding her planes to the deck soon growing terrific. It was only a matter of time.[288]

Cowpens beat her to it. Steaming in the same task group as the embattled *Monterey*, the "Mighty Moo," as she was known, always listed a half dozen degrees starboard when she was fueled to capacity, as she was now. That list made her roll to starboard all the worse. The port rolls, too, were bad, but when *Cowpens* heeled over to starboard, the edge of her flight deck would go all the way down, touching solid green water again and again. During some of the most extreme rolls, Captain George DeBaun and the bridge crew, high on the island, could reach out from the bridge wing and touch the same green water. One sailor, Frank Grech, had already torn up his right side when a roll had thrown him onto the deck; another had his leg smashed when a roll tore loose an oil line coupling and threw it at him.[289]

Even as *Monterey*'s planes burst into flame, DeBaun had let his task group commander know that he was maneuvering independently in order to try to get the heavy rolls under control. The rudder was almost useless; De-Baun worked with starboard and port engines to try to control his ship. But it didn't help much. The seas were pounding a whaleboat to pulp. At first De-Baun ordered the men to secure it, but the job was too dangerous and the crew gave it up. Another wave hit the ship broadside; *Cowpens* rolled hard. DeBaun was suddenly off his feet and skidding wildly by the seat of his pants to the starboard bulkhead. Then another roll; the inclinometer swung against the stop at forty-five degrees.

At 1020 came still another murderous roll. This time the sea invaded the radio transmitter room, killing most of *Cowpens*'s communications, along with her radars. At the same time the whaleboat finally came tearing loose, flying into the maelstrom of wind and sea. On the flight deck a TBM torpedo plane, in a kind of forlorn triumph, broke free of its cables and rolled off the starboard edge into the expectant waters, accompanied by two jeeps, as if part of a suicide pact. Another plane on the hangar deck got free, prowling hungrily, daring the crew to secure it.[290]

The wind, still climbing, was now backing. The typhoon was upon *Cowpens*, and her battle for survival had started.

Blinded, deaf and dumb except for one VHF radio channel, her hangar deck crew making wild efforts to secure her loose aircraft, *Cowpens* heaved and lurched through the cyclone, her people unable to see even the burning *Monterey* not far from their ship. DeBaun had ordered every hand not on watch to strap himself into his bunk to avoid further injuries. Of course, if *Cowpens* rolled over, this would make the death toll a high one.

A half hour after the TBM went over the side, another series of violent rolls racked the carrier and, again on the flight deck, a Hellcat got loose, skid-ding toward the ocean. At the same time, two extraordinarily heavy air force bombs in the forward magazine leapt clear of their storage spaces. These were no five-inch shells, which would have been bad enough. Each one of these monsters weighed a full ton. They were the modern equivalent of loose cannon, rolling to and fro in the volatile magazine, smashing into things with such force that DeBaun could feel the vibrations all the way up in the island, seven decks above the munitions.

The Hellcat didn't make it into the sea. Things would have been better if it had, because as its belly went over the lip of the flight deck, the residual fuel in its tank caught fire.

As DeBaun called *Cowpens*'s crew away to fire quarters, volunteers ran for the magazine to get the bombs under control. Reports of gasoline fumes were coming up from the hangar deck, where the loose plane had obviously done some kind of damage.

DeBaun had to get the fire and the rolling under control. The burning Hellcat, a torch that could set alight the rest of the planes on the flight deck, was aft of the island, and the wind was blowing from its direction. Reluctantly, DeBaun stopped his port engine, letting *Cowpens* swing to the left and directly into the bansheelike winds.

On the one hand, this kept the flames from blowing forward; on the other, it put *Cowpens* on a course for the eye of the storm, around which stampeded its deadliest forces. Then, as DeBaun's crew fought against the jackal-like threats, he hove to.

The long turn to the north did shake loose the burning Hellcat, along with five other flight deck aircraft and *Cowpens*'s acting air officer, Lieutenant Commander Bob Price, who went flying overboard and was never seen again. Soon afterward another fire started near the number three stack, burning for several minutes before the crew put it out. On one of the hard rolls, the radar antenna ripped free of the mast, whipping across the flight deck into the churning ocean. DeBaun now got under way again, trying to dodge the worse of the storm, but the barometer kept going down even as the cyclone winds increased. At noon, the glass reached its lowest ebb, and the officer of the deck, Lieutenant Junior Grade C. C. McCulloch, made the final notation of his watch: "1200 estimate passed nearest storm center," he remarked, "distance 25 miles."[291]

Afterward, the range between *Cowpens* and the eye wall began opening, but that was scant comfort to the carrier's sailors. *Cowpens*, still without radar, was taking her cues from the destroyer *Halsey Powell*, trying to maneuver by radio so as to avoid hitting ships in her path. A half hour after noon, the winds were raging at well over a hundred knots, and not long thereafter they ripped a cup off the frantically spinning anemometer. The seas remained nightmarish, bashing at the after portside hangar deck curtain, tearing away the forward port sponson around three antiaircraft guns, pulling smokestacks away from the ship and dishing them in, wrecking another whaleboat as well as two gangways, and, with the wind's help, blasting another jeep and two tractors off the flight deck.

As *Cowpens* continued to take the brutal punishment, DeBaun got a report that a fleet tug was lumbering into her path, off her port bow. He went to emergency full on his engines, maneuvering hard to miss the vessel, as invisible to *Cowpens* as the *Flying Dutchman*; a breathless minute later came word that the ships would clear each other, and DeBaun slowed to two-thirds. Sometime during all the excitement—perhaps during the noon change of watch—the busy skipper overheard something that proved to him the resilience of his crew. Two teenage sailors showed up on the bridge to relieve the lookouts. One said lackadaisically to the man he was relieving, as if he had been through a dozen typhoons, "It's a stinker, ain't it?"[292]

While *Cowpens* battled the elements, jeep carrier *Cape Esperance* of the replenishment group had been struggling, half out of control, for nearly three hours with no amount of engine and rudder maneuvering enabling her to beat the storm. A half hour after Halsey and McCain ordered the fleet to its new southeast course, one of the planes on the flight deck skidded to starboard and tipped just over the side, gutting itself on the forward stack. Fire bloomed from the wreck, leaping as high as the bridge on the carrier's small island as other planes broke loose and tumbled toward the pyre. Captain Bockius had long since secured his forward lookouts and most other watches who would have been exposed to the typhoon's full brutality. Now, as the searing tongues came close to the carrier's nerve center, Bockius ordered everyone out of the area except for the bare bones, the handful of men absolutely needed to conn the reeling ship. Things looked bad for a few moments; then the typhoon itself solved the problem, dousing the fire three minutes after it started with rain and salt spray.[293]

That, however, wasn't the end. A minute after the fire went out, the storm hurled the gutted airplane from the stack into the water. It was soon followed by others, and within a half hour or so, the stream of flight deck planes going over the side was nearly constant. In the hour following noon, *Cape Esperance*'s barometer had dropped like a stone to the lowest point it would reach, and the waves became mountainous. She was far into the depths of the typhoon, and her crew could do nothing to halt the careening aircraft. Before it was all over, thirty-two planes had gone, eight others were wrecks, and a lone Hellcat had had its wings pulled off as if it were a housefly and the storm a malicious boy. Electrical fires began flaring on the madly tossing hangar deck, but the crew contained them before they got out of hand.

Miraculously, as *Cape Esperance* began to clear the typhoon, no sailors had joined the lost planes in the water and none had died, or even suffered critical injuries, aboard ship. A score of them, though, had had arms, legs, scalps, and faces bruised or torn open as the rolling threw them around. Throughout the ship, decks and bulkheads were warped by the stress, hatches were sprung, masts and booms were totaled or lost, and girders were bent.[294]

Shortly after noon, as *Cape Esperance* ran into the typhoon's heart, the light carrier *Altamaha* heard her put out an SOS. There was nothing *Altamaha*'s sailors could do; they didn't even know where *Cape Esperance* was, and anyway they had their own troubles.

Conditions on *Altamaha* had gone bad much earlier. At 0845, a mobile crane on the hangar deck tore loose and ran wild, smashing up three aircraft, and that was just the beginning. In the following ten minutes, severe rolling had dumped supplies and equipment on two hapless sailors and sent them to sick bay. One of the men had been in an elevator well when several barrels tumbled in, half crushing him. Meanwhile, the crew tried to secure the rampaging crane. It wasn't easy; by now the waves had the ship rolling past thirty degrees to each side, and the skipper, A. C. Olney, had begun maneuvering—or trying to—with his engines as well as the rudder. Then, just as the crew was locking the crane down, Olney lost his steering. Somehow the storm had contaminated the pilothouse's hydraulic lines with air.

There was only one thing to do—bleed the air from the lines. As the ship continued to roll violently, Olney shifted his steering control to the after steering station. *Altamaha* surged blindly ahead, visibility shrinking, as the task was completed. Ten minutes or so later, the pilothouse regained steering control.

Relief was short-lived. One minute later, *Altamaha* swung wildly to a southwest heading. Fleet course was southeast, but Olney could do nothing. Before long his task group began to come apart as ships battled in vain to hold to the prescribed course.

At 1050 the first airplane on the flight deck came loose. Eight minutes later a plane tumbled into the yawning forward elevator pit, and in a few more minutes the fire main blew in the after pit, beginning to flood the ship. To make things worse, *Altamaha* was being pooped; heavy seas were bursting repeatedly over her fantail, flinging tons of water into the pit. Soon the bulkheads began warping, and the sailors scrambled to shore them up as others formed a long bucket brigade, with several men teetering on the edge of the water-filled pit. As they worked, a second plane crashed down into the forward pit, and others, their propellers spinning as if their engines were running, flew off the sides of the flight deck.

Olney's people weren't able to get the flooding under control until the afternoon, by which time *Cape Esperance* was in trouble. But by then *Altamaha* had lost thirty-one planes, nearly half of her total number, over the side. Of the remaining thirty-three, more than a third were irreparably damaged. No other carrier lost more aircraft.[295]

The story on each embattled carrier was similar, but the details often differed. On *Monterey*, death and destruction came by fire; on *Altamaha*, the main factor was water. In all cases wind and waves were behind everything. On the *Independence*-class carrier *San Jacinto*, the culprit was a huge mass of junk.

The starboard rolls that had ripped planes loose on other carrier hangar decks did the same thing aboard *San Jacinto*. A sudden roll of forty-two degrees pulled loose a single plane, just as had happened on *Monterey*, and — just as on *Monterey* — the loose plane smashed into others, tearing them free as well. On *San Jacinto*, however, no fire resulted. Instead the planes, soon joined by spare engines, caromed along the deck, hitting bulkheads, ripping away air intakes, and destroying vent ducts. One of the planes, in an irony that *Monterey*'s crew might have appreciated, hit a remote control for the hangar deck sprinklers, which began dousing the whole fire-free deck with useless, slippery water. The water then rained through the broken ductwork into the spaces below, joining other water that had poured in through the deck's side doors and down the stacks during the severe rolling. The water flooded her engine rooms, one of her fire rooms, and other engineering spaces as well, playing havoc with her boilers.[296]

Then fires did start, small electrical fires in the fume-filled hangar deck, threatening to turn *San Jacinto* into another *Monterey*. There was no way for the sailors to venture out onto the unsteady hangar deck without being crushed, so Commander G. E. Schecter tried something radical. Grabbing a fire extinguisher, he climbed up a bulkhead and then crawled out along an overhead beam, dangling thirty feet over the deck to play the extinguisher on the blaze.[297]

Other sailors soon got into the deadly new circus act, grabbing lines and then swarming up the bulkheads and out onto the overhead. Tying themselves to the overhead, they lowered themselves to the deck and began working to secure the marauding wreckage and fight the sporadic electrical fires. Whenever the ship rolled, they would swing, pendulumlike, free of the deck. The conditions were still dicey, but at least the sailors could work. Still, they weren't able to secure everything until midafternoon, when *San Jacinto* began to clear the worst of the storm.[298]

Some men, like the youngsters DeBaun of *Cowpens* had overheard or like *San Jacinto*'s sailor-acrobats, faced their trials with bravado. Others were, justifiably, more fearful or, more likely, simply hid it less successfully; such a storm would inspire fear in most human beings. On the larger ships, the radios blared TBS chatter, including stark reports from men on the much smaller destroyers: "We're taking a 55! We're taking a 55!" one carrier sailor heard from a loudspeaker, and the terror in the voice on the other end of the radio was unmistakable. A fifty-five-degree roll in such weather would be hard to come back from. Aboard *New Jersey*, sometimes almost half buried by waves that warped the steel mounts of twenty-and-forty millimeter AA, as well as some ladders, Anthony Iacono was "plenty scared," at the ride he was getting, plummeting from the mountaintop of a wave one instant to the trough and rushing, submarinelike, below the wave the next. The cruiser *Oakland*, like most ships, was buttoned up tightly, all hatches secured, the men wearing life jackets and staying clear of the weather decks, but water still got below. In her CIC, Don Darnell was another sailor who overheard other ships' cries for help, which filled him with "a silent, sickening fear," as he later described it. As *Oakland* took her own heavy rolls, Darnell prayed under his breath. "Please, Almighty God," he said every time his vessel heeled, "don't let us go all the way over. . . ."[299]

Far above Iacono, in *New Jersey*'s crow's nest, perched Charles Edwin Eamigh, who had volunteered to serve as a lookout. At that distance from the ship's center of gravity, *New Jersey*'s insane motions were greatly magnified, and Eamigh found himself wheeling through the rain-filled air. He was the only living thing outside the buttoned-up hull; for two hours he peered through the water-choked atmosphere at the vessels below, including his own. In the vicious swirl of wind, rain, and sea, visibility in many spots was down to nothing, with sailors in pilothouses unable to see even their own ship's bows, but in the two hours Eamigh stood watch, he could make out the patch of water surrounding *New Jersey*. Exhilarated, Eamigh beheld the waves crashing high over the superdreadnought's main deck, making it shudder noticeably. Those waves were the reason for his lofty position; had it been any lower they would have been smothering him, and he wouldn't have been able to see. But here he had one of the best vantage points in the fleet. He could see another battleship steaming astern, perhaps *New Jersey*'s sister *Iowa*, as she grimly kept station. As ships fell out of formation, held prisoner in troughs or unable to fight the winds, some of them came quite close to Eamigh's own, and he hung on as the captain threw the massive warship into hard turns to keep the range open. Despite the danger, he loved every minute of it.[300]

In flag country below, Halsey took a different view, having the weight of the fleet on his shoulders. Now in the teeth of the storm, he knew that his efforts to dodge the typhoon had utterly failed. Reports of destruction, damage, men overboard, and ships out of control were streaming in from all over the fleet. Held captive by lines, airplanes on weather decks mindlessly tried to be true to their nature and take to the sky; cruisers and battleships reported their Kingfisher scout planes flying overboard. Carriers were hove-to, dead in the water, and other ships were scrambling to avoid running straight into them. Destroyers, out of control, were reported to be steaming far off course, sometimes straight for the typhoon's maleficent heart. Even battleships were so storm-tossed that those on nearby vessels could see their screws; on some occasions destroyers were rolling so hard that even their sonar bulbs, fair on their bottoms, were visible. Even USS *Massachusetts*, one of the fleet's heaviest and most powerful ships, had to lie to for a time, unable to hold herself to fleet course. Aboard *New Jersey* alone, the waves were now rising above the third superstructure; life rafts, twenty-millimeter guns, and everything else that wasn't welded down was being ripped from the decks by the water and thrown into the Philippine Sea; ladders and forty millimeter mounts, although staying put, were warped, the elements bending the steel as if it were putty.[301]

After the war, Halsey set down his own thoughts on the ferocity of the weather.

> No one who has not been through a typhoon can conceive its fury. The 70-foot seas smash you from all sides. The rain and the scud are blinding. They drive at you flat-out, and you can't tell the ocean from the air. At broad noon I couldn't see the bow of my ship, 350 feet from the bridge. The *New Jersey* once was hit by a five-inch shell without my feeling the impact; the *Missouri*, her sister, had a kamikaze crash on her main deck and repaired the only damage with a paintbrush; yet this typhoon tossed our enormous ship as if she were a canoe. Our chairs, tables, and all loose gear had to be double-lashed; we ourselves were buffeted from one bulkhead to another; we could not hear our own voices above the uproar.[302]

Now that he was in the maw of the beast, Halsey's only thought was of getting back out. His first objective was to avoid the cyclone's dangerous northern semicircle. In the Northern Hemisphere, this was the half of the storm in which its counterclockwise-spinning winds were moving in the same direction as the cyclone itself, usually its northern half, unless it recurved to the east or northeast. Most of his ships seemed to be somewhere to the south of the eye, which was moving roughly northwest, so a few minutes before noon Halsey contacted McCain and told him to put the wind on his task force's north quarter. This was when McCain ordered the fleet onto the reciprocal heading of 120 degrees. With luck the new heading would keep Halsey's fleet in the oddly named "safe" semicircle, while at the same time putting the typhoon behind it as quickly as possible.

Most of the harm to the fleet took place, it seems, before the typhoon's height. Perhaps the equipment that was going to come loose had already done so before Halsey's ships hit the worse of the storm. Halsey, or at least his staff, was getting running reports of damage and ships in distress, but for some reason, Halsey remained silent until after 1300, the peak of the storm, by which time most of the damage had already been done. It was nearly 1400, in fact, when at least some fleet barometers had begun rising at last, that Halsey sent a message to Nimitz, MacArthur, and King, notifying them that Third Fleet was in the midst of a typhoon. This, apparently, was the first use of that word in any fleet communication.[303]

For all of Halsey's colorful description of the typhoon in his autobiography, and for all of the pounding *New Jersey* and her crew had gone through, the flagship had gotten off lightly compared to the flattops and other task force vessels. *New Jersey*'s barometer never dropped below 29.23, considerably above the readings on some other ships, and for her the highest seas, which were not the highest the task force recorded, only lasted a couple of hours.[304] Despite all the slamming and shuddering, despite the waves that swept over her superstructures, *New Jersey* was a heavy and stable warship. For all his years on destroyers and carriers, Halsey had trouble imagining what must be happening aboard these lighter ships. Intellectually he could know, but he wasn't experiencing it for himself.[305] Thus, for a time, he failed to grasp the enormity of what was happening to his fleet.

After the crescendo of violence that struck most of the ships in the hours just after noon, the winds slowly began ebbing as barometers began to edge up. The heavy waves, flung out from the typhoon in all directions, took much longer to die down. Ships edged out of the worst of the storms by ones and twos, moving from torrential rain and spray to more manageable conditions either slowly or quite suddenly. Chaos, by definition, lacks pattern. By 1500, three o'clock in the afternoon, the winds buffeting *New Jersey*, never having reached eighty knots, had ebbed to the midfifties; an hour later they were twenty knots slower. They were blowing, too, from roughly southwest, telling the mariners plainly that they had passed the worse of the storm and were still moving away from the eye.

Halsey's thoughts now turned once more to the crucial need for refueling. The storm hadn't done away with that problem; quite the contrary. Having fought such fearsome weather, the thirsty destroyers would need oil in the worse possible way. But only a few hours of daylight remained; the fleet couldn't refuel in the dark and, anyway, the seas were still too rough by far. By around 1700, Halsey had set a new rendezvous for refueling the following morning: 12° N, 129° E, a hundred miles southeast of the fleet's current position.

While fairly well protected aboard his flagship, Halsey had already gotten several reports from around the fleet of men overboard. Communications were still spotty, with many ships having lost their radios, antennas, or masts. Halsey had to figure that he had not heard everything. An hour after setting the new rendezvous, he ordered McCain to put together a search of the area through which the fleet had just steamed, the region that the typhoon was now sluggishly leaving, in order to locate and rescue anyone who had been blown or tossed into the waters. It wouldn't be easy; the area was huge, visibility was bad, and night was coming on. But Halsey had given his orders.[306]

Meanwhile, the fleet commander's staff sat at the conference table in flag mess while Halsey, pale faced, flitted back and forth between his place at the table and his office nearby. Mick Carney was involved in making a list of ship damage and losses, and from time to time Halsey took a look at the list. Ships were reporting in, but with radios out all over the task force, the list couldn't be accurate. Hours ticked by slowly as more and more ships checked in, their messages sometimes relayed by vessels nearby.

Then, halfway through the midwatch, in the early morning hours of December 19, a TBS message arrived in flag plot. It was from the destroyer escort *Tabberer*. Her radios, too, were out; the message was being relayed by another ship. "Now engaged in picking up survivors of *Hull* (DD 350) in approximate latitude 13° 32' N longitude 128° 11' E. *Benham* also in vicinity. *Hull* capsized with little warning at about 1030."[307]

Until that moment, regardless of any fears that Halsey had had, his fleet was searching for individuals who had been blown from their ships. But this message changed everything. Now, for the first time, the fleet began to learn that the typhoon had sunk a warship. And perhaps it had taken others.

PART FIVE

Lost Boys

THREE MONTHS EARLIER, CAL CALHOUN, fresh from destroyer-minesweeper duty at Pearl, had stood on the bridge of his new command, putting her through her paces as she steamed out of Puget Sound, and he wasn't entirely pleased.

She was USS *Dewey*, Destroyer Squadron 1's flagship, a *Farragut*-class destroyer named for the renowned admiral of Manila Bay fame. At ten years of age she was in excellent shape. Her turbines thrummed as she knifed through the water, and the faint haze that streamed from her twin stacks told Calhoun that the boilers were both well crewed and efficient. For the most part he was satisfied; yet she still worried him.

The eight *Farragut*s were the first destroyers to come off the ways since the rash of World War I building had ended in 1921, and the first since the 1930 Treaty of London had put restrictions on tin can design. Like all warships, she was the result of compromises in armament, displacement, mission, and other variables, which in her case included diplomatic constraints imposed by the London agreement. She had been built with War Plan Orange in mind. Despite all the twists that had afterward happened in Orange and in the course of the actual war, in many respects she was now in the midst of carrying out her original goal of supporting a trans-Pacific advance; but she was still a compromise, as well as an innovative, though now aging, design.

First sketched out by Bethlehem Steel, she had been built in Maine by Bath Iron Works and launched just over a decade before. By 1944 she was heavier than she used to be, like a middle-aged person beginning to put on a bit of unhealthy weight. Though still called 1200-tonners, a reference to their original specifications, *Dewey* along with each of her sisters now displaced more than seventeen hundred tons at full load. In fact, she was quite top heavy. Jacks-of-all-trades, destroyers were always attracting more topside equipment, more guns, more torpedo tubes, more ammunition. The *Farragut*s, too, like subsequent vessels, had the additional weight of their gun directors, the heavy boxes that squatted atop their bridges, the nerve centers that controlled their batteries of five five-inch guns. The directors greatly increased those weapons' accuracy; they also raised the ships' centers of gravity.[308]

Actually, in warship design, the key to stability wasn't so much the center of gravity as a factor known as *metacentric height*, the amount by which a mathematical point called the metacenter exceeded the center of gravity. The greater this height the better, at least in terms of stability. When a ship is at rest, metacentric height is easy to calculate, provided the right data is available. With a ship under way in a moving element, on the other hand, and subject to roll, pitch, yaw, sway, surge, and heave, even a modern computer might have trouble calculating the rapid stability changes a ship undergoes.[309] Calhoun had no such computers, but he knew the basic formulas and, more important, he could tell from the way *Dewey* was handling that something was wrong.

She had done well as she steamed through Juan de Fuca Strait at flank speed, just out of refit at Bremerton and in need of a shakedown, and Calhoun, who had been aboard less than a week, wanted to see how she handled. As she moved into open sea, he barked a helm command from where he stood on the port bridge wing. "Right, ten degrees rudder!"

As the destroyer swept into the moderate turn, she heeled over to fifteen degrees with an awkward lurch, hanging there far too long. That was the first thing that told Calhoun, with his five years of destroyer experience, that *Dewey* had some kind of problem. Finishing up with his full-power trial, he began to put *Dewey* through a series of moderate and more daring turns at various speeds.

His instinct had been right; a pattern soon became clear. On turns the ship heeled considerably and then hung there, returning to even keel very slowly. It was a sign of poor stability.

Calhoun next conferred with his exec, a seasoned lieutenant commander named Frank Bampton, who had served aboard *Dewey* for nearly the whole of the war in the Pacific. *Dewey*, Bampton observed, had "always had a lazy roll," but this behavior was new. Calhoun didn't like it.

Far away from the tropics where Calhoun would soon be fighting, the Pacific Northwest showed its typical streak of fickleness in weather. A heavy fog began to drift in as *Dewey* continued her run, and Calhoun turned his ship back toward Puget Sound in the white gloom. Arriving back at Bremerton, he put in a phone call to his squadron commander, Captain Preston V. Mercer, whose flag was aboard *Dewey*. Telling Mercer what had happened, Calhoun invited him out for the next day's run, and Mercer accepted.

The following day was much the same. After another full-power trial, Calhoun brought the ship down to a top speed of twenty knots for safety's sake and began engine and rudder maneuvers. Again *Dewey* heeled to an excessive degree, hanging there for a while before sluggishly coming back to an even keel. Neither Calhoun nor Mercer liked it, and the squadron commander decided to mention the problem to the personnel at the shipyard.

The next day he did so, but he got no results. Nobody at the yard had any authority to conduct stability tests, he was told. Next Mercer contacted the Bureau of Ships (BuShips) directly to ask for the tests, but the people there cut him off. The navy needed every destroyer it could get in the western Pacific; the best the bureau could do was promise to run tests on the next *Farragut* to come in for overhaul. Unfortunately for Mercer and *Dewey*, that wasn't scheduled until the following spring.

There was nothing Calhoun or Mercer could do except to continue to prepare *Dewey* and the rest of DesRon 1 for sea. And Calhoun wasn't especially worried. The sluggish, lazy behavior of *Dewey* was a nuisance, but he didn't consider it actually dangerous, as long as he knew about it. Certainly, he wasn't worried about capsizing. BuShips, he figured, had the numbers and knew what it was doing.

Unknown to both Calhoun and Mercer, the shipyard actually had conducted an inclining experiment on another *Farragut*, USS *Aylwin*, just a few days before. The test, moreover, confirmed Calhoun's gut feelings: wartime modifications had changed *Aylwin*'s original specifications and stability characteristics rather considerably, compromising her stability. Presumably, the same was true of her sisters. Calhoun, new to *Dewey*, hadn't heard about the experiment, and BuShips, which had gotten the report on the test, hadn't

seen fit to tell Mercer about it. Had they known the results of that test, perhaps later events would have unfolded differently. As it was, the squadron put
to sea, shaping course for Pearl Harbor, and ultimately Ulithi, where it would
become the screen for Task Group 30.8.[310]

Only eight *Farragut*s were built before newer designs came out. The mid- to
late 1930s saw a procession of classes and ships; the *Porter*s, the *Somerse*s, the
*Mahan*s, *Dunlap*s and *Gridley*s, *Bagley*s and *Benham*s, and finally *Simse*s. In
1941, as war loomed, the first *Benson*s came off the ways, soon after the
Gleaves class made its debut. Then came the wartime *Fletcher*s, nearly two
hundred of them, the quintessential destroyers of the Second World War. By
1944 Third Fleet had dozens of them.[311]

Whatever its class, a destroyer is a big object, at least in human terms. A
Farragut stretched nearly 350 feet with a beam a tenth as great; a *Fletcher*'s
length was closer to 400. The power plant that drove a *Farragut*'s twelve hundred (or seventeen hundred) tons through the water could generate more
than forty thousand horsepower. In absolute terms this was far less than an
Iowa-class battleship or an *Essex*-class carrier, but it was still a massive
amount of energy. What was more, the thrust-to-weight ratio of a *Farragut*
was far higher than that of a battlewagon or flattop, allowing her to sprint at
speeds well in excess of thirty knots. And the *Fletcher*s had still more brawn,
sixty thousand horsepower in all, to drive their nominal weight of twenty-two
hundred tons. Nearly 10 percent of that weight was armament, everything
from five-inch dual-purpose guns to torpedo tubes with their long, deadly
fish and a variety of antiaircraft weaponry. Operation of these large, intricate
vessels required more than 150 men in the case of a *Farragut*, and nearly 300
when it came to a *Fletcher*. All in all, a destroyer was a formidable concentration of firepower.[312]

Yet, compared to capital ships such as battlewagons and even carriers, destroyers were almost miniscule. Even jeep carriers had displacements that
were half a dozen times that of the *Fletcher*-class ships, and Halsey's flagship
New Jersey was roughly twenty times *Fletcher*'s weight. Hence, the destroyers'
nickname of "small boys." Striking a fist against the side of a battleship where

the armor belt stretches is like hitting Mount Rushmore; with a destroyer, one can hear a faint echo beneath the thin skin, very tin canlike. Destroyers, too, hugged the water more closely than did capital ships. The flight decks of *Essex*-class carriers, to say nothing of the islands, jutted more than sixty feet out of the water, while destroyer weather decks were much lower. *Fletchers*, in particular, were very wet vessels; being flush-decked, lacking raised forecastles, they tended to ship lots of water over their bows in any type of rough weather. *Fletchers*, luckily, were assigned mostly to the Pacific, for duty in the heaving, wintry North Atlantic would have easily half drowned them.[313]

On the other hand, the *Fletchers* had weaknesses that the Pacific only magnified, the greatest being range. They had considerably more power than most of the older classes, but they carried less fuel, making them very short legged. When steaming on the world's largest ocean, their limited range was a problem for every ship that traveled with them. They had to refuel often, every three or four days when steaming at full power or in combat positions. This, in fact, was why TF 38 was in a desperate position in the early hours of December 18. The fleet carriers had depleted their ammunition supplies and had lost some pilots and planes, but their fuel bunkers were nowhere near empty. The cruisers and battleships, supporting and protecting the carriers, were in still better shape. The *Fletchers*, though, were in trouble as far as fuel went, and their need dictated fleet movements.[314]

Being so small, destroyers faced the biggest threats from weather and sea, and in the open ocean these threats, which every ship in the fleet faced, were of two major types. The first was that heavy pounding from, for instance, a typhoon would compromise the ship's structural soundness. Certainly men on larger ships had moments during the storm of December 18 when they wondered if their vessels were going to hold together, though in the end all of them did.[315]

The other threat was that the high winds, the towering seas, or some other conditions would degrade a destroyer's stability, making her prone to plunging or capsizing. These behaviors, in turn, would cause flooding, which would reduce the ship's buoyancy. What keeps a ship afloat is a physical law briefly stated as Archimedes' Principle: *A body partially or completely submerged in a fluid is buoyed up by a force equal to the weight of the fluid displaced by the body*. If water pours into a ship's hull, the ship retains the same volume, displacing no more of the ocean than it did before flooding, but it gains weight. Too much weight exceeds the buoyant force on the vessel; once that happens, down goes the ship.[316]

One of the variables that went into the stability factor on December 18 was the amount of fuel left in the destroyers. With bunkers nearly dry, a ship bobs on the water, with more freeboard at which the seas and winds could batter. Thus, the same condition that caused the empty *Fletcher*s to remain in the typhoon's path, desperately trying to replenish, also made them supremely vulnerable to the effects of that storm.

The *Farragut*-class ships, on the other hand, while sharing the same limitations that small size imposed, were fat with Navy Special on December 18. They steamed in the company of the fleet oilers, and they had left Ulithi more recently. Unlike the flush-decked *Fletcher*s, they had raised forecastles, which reduced the water they took over the bow. In general terms, then, they seemed better off than their modern sisters as the gales swept upon them. But still, in retrospect, there was that odd heeling that *Dewey* had experienced a couple of months earlier during her sea trials . . .

It was *Aylwin*, in fact, the *Farragut* whose inclining test had proved so disturbing back in September, that first got into trouble.

Lieutenant Commander Bill Rogers, *Aylwin*'s skipper, had smelled a typhoon as early as noon on the seventeenth, just about the time that the replenishment effort was coming apart. Like others, he had noted a sharply falling glass in the hours that followed. That evening, when his radio messenger gave him the news about the refueling rendezvous change and a report of a weather disturbance, even before giving his OOD the general order to rig for heavy weather, he'd told Erwin Jackson to strike her ready service ammunition below. This would lower the ship's center of gravity and make her more stable. It would also make her temporarily impotent in the face of a submarine attack, but, as Rogers had pointed out at the time, the whole fleet was with *Aylwin*, and anyway the worsening conditions strongly suggested that nobody was going to do any attacking in the near future.[317]

Soon after midnight, *Aylwin* and the replenishment task group were steaming through on-again, off-again squalls, with freshening gales blowing from north to northeast. The seas had been rougher than usual for twelve hours, and heavier still since around sunset. With the increasing pounding and the corrosive salt spray that mixed with the squalls' freshwater, the ships electrical system was in jeopardy. At 0245 it went out.

The interruption lasted only ten minutes, but that is a long time on a black and heaving sea on which other warships are moving. By the time Rogers's people got the power back on, *Aylwin* had dropped out of formation, and she didn't regain her place for another half hour.[318] The event was a harbinger.

By daybreak, some destroyer officers were already reporting hurricane conditions, even though Halsey, on massive *New Jersey*, didn't cancel refueling attempts until two hours later. By then, the small boys already knew they were in trouble. Aboard *Aylwin*, Rogers put together repair parties and stationed his electricians around the ship to handle any new damage to the electrical system. On other vessels, skippers took similar steps.[319]

Around 0800, the wind's force leapt up, and it became a roaring giant trying to throw *Aylwin* and the other ships off balance. Sometimes the winds and waves synchronized, swatting the ships around as if they were matchsticks; at other moments, the elements fought each other, with the vessels caught in the middle, maneuvering only with the greatest of difficulty. Slowly the task group formations began coming apart.

Aboard the *Fletcher*-class *Cushing*, Captain L. F. Volk had decided to ballast soon after the forenoon watch began, a bit after 0800. *Cushing*, like most of the *Fletchers*, was low on fuel and riding high. To make her more stable, Volk ordered some of her fuel tanks to be flooded with salt water. These tanks were specifically designed to do double duty as oil bunkers and ballasting tanks, but there was still a risk of contaminating the fuel, and if *Cushing* got a sudden chance to replenish, the saltwater ballast would be a hindrance, for pumping it back into the sea would take time. It was a judgment call: Volk decided to do it, and other *Fletcher*-class skippers decided to wait.

An hour and fifteen minutes later, *Cushing* secured ballasting, having pumped fifteen tons of water aboard. She was riding more easily but still not well, and other ships were also having trouble staying on course. The spray and driving rain, on top of the high walls of seawater, had reduced visibility to a half mile or less, an uncomfortably small margin for ships trying to hold formation. Suddenly, shortly before 1000, the lookouts sighted a jeep carrier—perhaps the out-of-control *Cape Esperance*, perhaps another—cutting across *Cushing*'s bow only eight hundred yards away. Backing down emergency full, Volk sounded three blasts of the ship's horn and threw his helm over hard, skirting the carrier. *Cushing* then labored to rejoin the formation.[320]

Monterey, meanwhile, was battling the fire on her hangar deck, and Admiral Alfred Montgomery designated several ships, including the tin cans *Brown*, *Haggard*, *McCord*, and *Twining*, to stand by her and then escort her to Ulithi. But the rolling was getting worse; some of the ships Montgomery sent to *Monterey* made it, but the destroyers failed. *Brown*, for one, was rolling so badly she could do almost nothing. *Haggard* was no better off. Montgomery finally ordered them back to their respective task groups.[321]

Conditions were getting still worse. *Swearer*, a destroyer escort even smaller than a *Farragut*-class can, lost her gyrocompass just as *Cushing* was trying to dodge her carrier, and soon lost contact with the replenishment group in which she was serving. *Crowley*, another destroyer escort in the refueling group, maintained contact with some of the other ships, but in such weather this could be dangerous. She couldn't hold station; sliding off the side of a wave as if she were falling down a mountain, she splashed into the trough at the bottom, and the seas took her for a ride on a course of their own choosing. Stuck in the trough, *Crowley* headed southwest while the rest of the formation struggled on a southeasterly course. Her glass had dropped nearly half an inch in an hour; the storm, for her, was approaching its height.

Then, barely five hundred yards away, a tanker appeared out of the maelstrom. As *Cushing* had done, *Crowley* backed down hard, but it was useless; she still lacked the power to turn. But the oiler, with her greater mass, managed to heave herself over onto a course paralleling the little escort, and the ships managed to keep their distance.[322]

Dewey, too, was in trouble. The weird rolling that Captain Calhoun had noticed off Bremerton now reasserted itself; by midmorning, the destroyer was regularly rolling ten degrees farther to starboard than she did to port, and the typhoon was still getting worse. Her visibility was down to three

hundred yards when a carrier came looming at her out of the storm on a collision course, the wind gusting past at nearly a hundred knots.

"Hard left rudder," ordered Calhoun. "Come to course 130 degrees."
Dewey swung round under the stern of the flattop, and through the spray
Calhoun read her name: MONTEREY.

The carrier safely behind, Calhoun now prepared to resume his proper
place in his formation. "Right full rudder, return to course 180 degrees," he
said. The helmsman spun the wheel over, but *Dewey* swung her head sluggishly.

"She's not answering, Cap'n," the quartermaster observed.

Calhoun decided to give the rudder some help with the engines. "Port
ahead full," he ordered.

It didn't do any good. *Dewey* continued to disobey helm and engine commands.

Calhoun was beginning to run out of options. "Left full rudder," he
snapped. "Port stop. Starboard ahead full!" He was now trying to turn *Dewey*
in the other direction, around to port, in a vast circle of nearly three hundred
degrees to get her back on the task unit's course.

The destroyer swung her head twenty degrees and then stopped. The sea
had her, and she was helpless.

Quickly, Calhoun got onto the TBS, giving *Dewey*'s voice call sign. "This
is Achilles," he reported. "I am out of control, crossing through the formation
from starboard to port. Keep clear!"

Dewey was totally blind. The men on the bridge could not even see their
own jackstaff on the stem of the ship, and the radar screen was fouled with
sea return. They could only hope that the other ships in the unit could somehow see *Dewey*.

Then a huge black hull was coming at *Dewey* out of the typhoon directly
ahead of her. As the destroyer hurtled down a mountainous wave at the
oiler, the other ship was lifted out of her way by the next wave. It had been
close. "I could have thrown a spud at her," Calhoun said to his assistant gunnery officer.

At last *Dewey* steamed clear of the formation. Calhoun, worried about
the ship's ominous rolling and at the prompting of his squadron commander,
began ballasting his port tanks. As he did, he heard over his TBS before it
went out that *Monaghan*, too, was out of control.[323]

⚓

"Unable to steer base course," the voice crackled over the TBS. "Cannot get out."[324]

The voice belonged to *Monaghan*'s skipper, Lieutenant Commander Bruce Garrett. Aboard *Aylwin*, Captain Acuff, the commander of the replenishment group, listened as Garrett announced *Monaghan*'s refusal to obey helm and engine commands. Aboard *Dewey*, the group's screen commander, Captain Mercer, also heard the transmission. It was about 0930.[325]

Mercer didn't know Garrett well. *Monaghan*'s skipper had assumed command barely a week earlier, and now he had the job of conning his ship through a typhoon. Mercer briefly considered advising Garrett on how to handle his trouble in getting on course, but then he decided against it. For all his newness to his command, Garrett presumably knew what he was doing, and he was more familiar with *Monaghan*'s current status than Mercer was.[326]

Acuff reached a different decision. "Use more speed," he told Garrett.

"Have tried as high as standard," Garrett replied. *Monaghan* was in exactly the same trouble that *Dewey* and others were having that morning.[327]

She'd come off the ways at Boston Navy Yard almost exactly ten years earlier, in January of '35. She had seen her share of foul weather, serving in the North Atlantic for quite some time before circumstances had brought her to the Pacific. She had been at Pearl Harbor when the Japanese came; as battleships died all around her, she rammed and sank a midget sub in the harbor. She had steamed with *Aylwin* to try to relieve Wake Island; she had been at Coral Sea, and at Midway she had screened *Enterprise*. Later had come the Aleutians and more cold, rough weather. After that, the tropics seemed to pose little challenge. Still, wear and tear happened, and by 1944, after fighting in the Gilberts and Marshalls, she returned to the West Coast for overhaul. In her design, her construction, and even her war record, she was a typical *Farragut*.

There was another way in which she was typical. Upon leaving Bremerton after her overhaul several weeks earlier, *Monaghan* had developed a strange, pronounced roll.[328]

By 0930, as Garrett's TBS message showed, *Monaghan* was already in trouble. Then, soon after his exchange with Acuff, Garrett got back on the radio. "I am unable to come to the base course," he repeated. "Have tried full speed but it will not work."[329]

After that there was nothing but silence.

Aboard *Monaghan*, the roar and shriek of the typhoon was enormous, as it was on every ship in the fleet. As the waves grew steeper and higher, *Monaghan* began the long, heavy rolling that some of the lighter carriers were experiencing, except that the destroyer's rolling was worse. This wasn't because *Monaghan* was running low on fuel. Her oil king, Water Tender Second Class Joe McCrane, had sounded her tanks around daybreak and found plenty of Navy Special aboard. The ship was simply unstable.

Around 1100, while trying to fight down his concern that on one of these long, hard rolls *Monaghan* would stay on her side without righting, McCrane got word to start ballasting some of the tanks with salt water. He quickly made his way to the shaft alley and opened the appropriate valves, but by then it was too late. The seas had grown rougher than ever before; the wind was smashing at the ship from the port beam, and *Monaghan* crept slowly, at almost a standstill, her forty-thousand-horsepower engines seemingly impotent.

It was impossible to survive on the ship's open decks, wind and wave swept. McCrane, along with a few dozen others, took refuge in the after head on the main deck as the ship kept heeling crazily. In the tight compartment, fear was beginning to spread. "Dear Lord, bring it back. Oh God! Bring it back!" a sailor sang out whenever the ship heeled over. "Don't let us drown now!" Then, when *Monaghan* righted, he would yell, "Thank you, dear Lord! Thank you!"

Beyond the sealed hatch, life rafts and other weather deck gear had long since been beaten to pieces or torn away from the ship; now the elements started to break *Monaghan* herself. Down in the guts of the ship, the engine and fire room overhead began to separate from the bulkheads as the typhoon's insensate fury increased. *Monaghan* was starting to come apart. Water was forcing its way in, probably through the vent shafts, perhaps even down the stacks on the most extreme rolls, and the fire and bilge pumps struggled to get it back out.

Then came the death blow. As *Monaghan* heeled far over, farther than she had yet gone, her generators and steering engine went out. The lights failed; radio, radar, telephones, everything electrical was suddenly dead.

Monaghan's crew grimly endeavored to cope. Deprived of communications, the steering engine room crew sent a runner up to the bridge to tell Garrett that the sailors would try to steer manually if he could give them a course. The engines still labored; but the odds were now heavily against the destroyer.

A few minutes later came another series of long, hard rolls, and then it finally happened. On the last one, *Monaghan* simply stayed on her beam-ends, refusing to right herself. Water poured down the stacks, into the super-structure, and through every opening in the hull it could find. *Monaghan* was downflooding, massive amounts of seawater stealing her buoyancy.

In the after head, the sailors knew she was done for. McCrane and dozens of others now wrestled open the port hatches—*Monaghan* lay on her starboard side—and climbed out onto the vertical after deck. The waves, in concert with a hundred-knot wind, clawed at them, grabbing them and hurl-ing them off the foundering ship. Gunner's Mate Joseph Guio, who hailed from Holliday's Cove, West Virginia, stood outside the hatch, refusing to leave, helping to pull his shipmates out of the compartment; others at the hatch helped him as long as they could. One minute Fireman First Class William Kramer was helping pull a friend through the hatch; the next he was spinning wildly through the water, tumbling away from the wreck. Popping to the surface, he spotted a life raft nearby. He seized it and held on.

McCrane, too, had been washed loose, and he went skittering along the superstructure, grabbing hold of a depth charge rack. He boosted himself up and walked along the torpedo tubes amidships; he was afraid to jump into the water, having seen others who'd tried that smashed to bits against the ship's hull. But then another wave hit him and washed him overboard, and he, too, was being pounded against the hull. Choking and splashing as if he were a puppy in the froth of oily sea, McCrane at last got a grip on himself and began to strike out away from the ship more calmly.

"Hey, Joe!" he suddenly heard from behind him. "Grab that raft back of you!"

It was Joe Guio, now naked and bleeding. McCrane spotted the raft and dragged himself aboard; it was the same one that Kramer managed to find. Be-fore long more than a dozen sailors were there. The wind kept catching at the flimsy life raft; as Kramer, McCrane, and the others tried to lock the bottom into position, it flipped over nearly a half dozen times, scattering the men as if they were ninepins. At last they accomplished their task and dragged them-selves aboard, hauling the injured Guio in after them. Nearby, the iron hull of their foundering vessel slowly turned turtle, trapping scores of their shipmates inside it, and began to sink toward the bottom of the Philippine Sea.[330]

Monaghan's battle had ended.

⚓

Even as *Monaghan* was losing her fight, her sister 1200-tonner USS *Hull* was in equally serious trouble.

Hull's skipper, Lieutenant Commander James A. Marks, had recently served aboard a *Fletcher*-class ship. Compared to the *Fletcher*, he found that *Hull* handled quite badly, and her stability was pretty bad, too. But just like Calhoun on *Dewey*, Marks had put *Hull* through full-power trials during which he'd thrown the rudder hard over and then quickly reversed it. Unlike Calhoun, Marks had noticed no particular problems, at least in the calm seas where the tests had gone on.

Still, on the seventeenth of December with the weather going to blazes, Marks decided not to take any chances. That evening he ordered his exec and his first lieutenant to stow below all loose topside gear and to inspect the ship for security, but unlike Bill Rogers on *Aylwin*, he decided to keep his ready ammunition above.

Hull had a rough night, like many of her near neighbors in the replenishment group. *Hull*, like *Monaghan*, was fairly well fueled, but this added little to her stability as she plowed through inky-black seas. The waves, growing heavier by the hour, broke indifferently over the destroyer's raised forecastle, with spray flying as high as the bridge. The water soon found its way into the radio shack, CIC, and other compartments, where many of the ship's electrical vitals were located.

By 1030, as *Dewey* was completing her wild ride through the formation, *Hull* was beginning the battle of her life. In CIC, seams were opening; electronic equipment was arcing as seawater found it, wild sparks leaping back and forth between cables. Soon *Hull*'s radar was out, leaving her effectively blind.

Right away Marks got onto the TBS and let his screen commander know what had happened. Then the TBS itself went out, and Marks and his men were alone.

Despite all the pounding, *Hull* had so far managed somehow to hold her place in the screen. Still, the weather was taking its toll. The ship's whaleboat was smashed to pieces and then pulled free of its davits. As the waves became mountains, they grabbed at *Hull*'s depth charges, which Marks had set on safe, and whisked several into the tempest. They also claimed some men from the fantail. The fire room intakes were beginning to suck down water, and one boiler flickered and died, robbing the ship of power. And by now each roll was worse than the last.

Pat Douhan, one of *Hull*'s ping jockeys—sonar men—had been on the bridge all night, watching as the superstructure shipped water. After going off watch at 0800, he'd gone below and tried to sleep, but a hard roll had thrown him out of his bunk. Unable to get any rest, he made his way to the ship's after deckhouse, where he found twenty or thirty sailors. Other groups were congregating in the forward parts of the ship, in the issuing room and near the wardroom door. The open decks had turned deadly, and the men not on watch, afraid to be far below, were sheltering themselves where they could.

Around 1130, hemmed in by towering waters, *Hull* lurched hard to the starboard. Lieutenant Junior Grade George Sharp, *Hull*'s engineering officer, thought that this lurch may have torn loose the bulkheads between some of the fuel tanks, allowing fuel oil to pour to the starboard. If so, he could do nothing about it. What he could try to deal with was the three feet of water now pooling in the engine spaces. As his men locked down a damaged boiler, Sharp ordered the bilge pumps started. The fire room pumps began working, but aft, in the engine rooms, the pumps couldn't get any suction. The water remained where it was, sloshing freely as the ship rolled, rushing to the lower side and cutting her stability further.

The next thing to go was power steering control, along with the engine telegraphs. By now Marks, and quite a few sailors, realized that *Hull* was in mortal danger. Marks had given up trying to hold his place in the screen, which he could no longer see anyway, and began trying to bring the ship to an easier-riding course. But as he tried to turn *Hull*, the sea grabbed her. Marks tried to take her back, using every combination of rudder and engine speeds he could think of, but nothing would work—and then the helm controls were gone, adding to the confusion and trouble.

Marks now ordered the crew to don life jackets. In the after deckhouse, some men prayed while others yelled for Marks to get the ship out of the storm somehow. It was a natural, human reaction: it was also a plea for a miracle. *Hull* was in irons, locked in a trough, out of control near the storm's center.

The rolls were fearsome. Marks had delayed ballasting since he was well fueled, and anyway, if he ballasted to port to offset the starboard heeling, he would have risked capsizing to port if the ship suddenly reversed course. Now it was too late to think about ballasting. Marks did consider jettisoning his torpedoes, which added a great deal to the destroyer's weight topside. As the banshee winds screamed in his rigging, he also considered cutting the guy wires that secured his forward smokestack to reduce his sail area and thus gain stability; the wind's force was so great that he feared that the whole bridge structure might be blown off the ship unless he did something. But it was too late for that measure as well. The wind was a monster, something insane from the wastes of the sea that was attacking relentlessly, blasting at more than 110 knots. No sailor could survive on the ship's open decks long enough to cut any lines.

A few moments later it no longer mattered whether sailors were outside or not. The rolling, already severe, grew worse. As the destroyer heeled over again, the junior officer of the deck, standing on the port side of the pilot-house, suddenly went flying through the air, crashing against the starboard bulkhead, which was hanging almost level with the ocean.

The roll continued, approaching, then passing, seventy degrees.

From below men began rushing to get out of the ship, clearing the engine room, bursting from passageways. On the bridge Marks stepped from the starboard wing into the sea as the ship fell onto her side. Meanwhile, in the after deckhouse, sailors were holding on to anything they could grab in order to keep their balance, including the port hatch, which was now directly above them, pointing up toward the black, roiling sky.

Pat Douhan was one of those holding on to the hatch, and he also had a foot jammed into a vent, which gave him some leverage, perhaps enough to force the hatch open; then he and the others could escape the deathtrap that *Hull* had become. But the wind was holding the hatch in place with its insubstantial fist, and his grasping shipmates weren't helping.

In an act that would often come back to haunt him, Douhan kicked his fellow sailors' hands away from the hatch. It was the only way he could get the thing open. Then, bracing himself on the vent, he heaved against the iron door, against the killing wind.

The hatch swung open. His shipmates began swarming past him.

As Douhan himself went through, the wind grabbed the hatch once more, slamming it furiously down on his back, as if the storm blamed him for the loss of its victims. But some of his shipmates fought the wind, pulling the hatch off him and clearing the way.

As he climbed out of the deckhouse into the typhoon, a thought came to him. His life jacket was on the bridge.

Then, nearby, tied to a gun, he spotted an old life jacket, one he believed a mother's prayers had put there for him. He got to it and managed to put it on. Then the sea took him, sweeping him forward. He grabbed a forty-millimeter mount amidships, but the sea broke his hold, and he was washed clear of the ship. He never saw *Hull* again.

But *Hull* wasn't finished with Douhan yet, and the typhoon had just started on him. As the destroyer went under, a giant suction began pulling him down. He wasn't the only one.

Ken Drummond, who during general quarters served as the captain's talker, repeating instructions to officers and departments as needed, hadn't worried too much about capsizing. In her decade of life, *Hull* had served in the rough waters of the Aleutians, and she had never experienced much trouble there. But as the ship was now pounded slowly to pieces and then finally rolled over with men scrambling onto her side and bottom, Drummond realized how terribly wrong he'd been.

Unlike Douhan, Drummond wasn't immediately washed clear of the wreck; he was in the long line of men clinging to her starboard side when she went down, and Drummond went with her, sliding inexorably into the depths of the Philippine Sea. On the surface the water was warm, supplying the heat that drove the murderous storm, but several feet below it turned cold and, as Drummond later described it, "blacker than hell."

As his ship pulled him down after her, the young man had time for two ghastly thoughts. His first was "This is the end." The next was "This is really going to upset my mother." The darkness of Davy Jones's locker closed in all around him.

Then the suction broke. Drummond had no idea how deep he was, but suddenly he was rocketing toward the surface, buoyed up by his kapok life jacket. He popped high out of the water, tumbling twenty feet into the air before falling back down onto the sea with a splash that was dwarfed by the waves.

He could see no one. He was utterly alone in the Pacific's vast reaches, adrift in the middle of a howling typhoon.[331]

"Dracula has lost control," the radiomen on the carrier *Wasp* overheard. "Commander Task Group 30.8 unable to control his group."

As the message from *Aylwin* indicated, the typhoon was slapping her around horribly. The message to *Wasp*, in fact, came in over a VHF circuit; *Aylwin*, her radio shack knee high in water, had lost her TBS and was using the battery-powered radio she had left to try to contact someone else—anyone else—in the fleet and have him relay her message to Slew McCain.

Aylwin had been rolling violently since 0930. Shortly before 1100 Bill Rogers shifted both sailors and fuel to the starboard to counteract the winds that were swinging to hit her on that side. If he hadn't, *Aylwin* might have gone down right then and there, for a few minutes later the ship rolled sickeningly to port. The inclinometer veered farther and farther over until it touched the seventy-degree mark. It hung there for five, ten, fifteen seconds; only then did it slowly reverse itself as the ship struggled back toward a more even keel.

The waves had grabbed *Aylwin* and flung her around to a westerly heading, putting the murderous winds more or less on her beam. After the deadly roll had abated, Rogers began struggling to come to a southeasterly course, which would put the wind on his stern. Trying everything he could with his rudder and engines, he dragged *Aylwin* slowly around, getting as far as 150 degrees. But in the battle with water clawing at every opening in the hull, raining in wherever it could, *Aylwin* took terrible punishment. Her balky steering control chose this moment to go out once more, and again the destroyer veered over to starboard. As the wind came onto her beam, she began another long, hard roll to port, and again the inclinometer hit seventy degrees. As everyone hung on for his life, objects rolled and flew down the decks, and the whaleboat tore free of its davits.

As *Aylwin* came out of the roll, Rogers again tried to get her to do his bidding, but with even less luck than before. Finally he lay to for a time, with the ship in a trough, rolling violently and getting a drenching from the waves that towered above her.

The engine room blowers were out. The boilers produced terrific heat, and not all of it got to the turbines; a lot of it warmed the fire and engine spaces to uncomfortable levels. Air-conditioning was a rarity in the fleet; boiler rooms usually had to make do with simple ventilation. But the water, pouring down the vent shafts, had burned out the fans during the heavy rolling, and now, as noon approached, the heat was increasing to stifling levels. But the boilers were *Aylwin*'s heart. If they stopped, the ship would lie helpless before the typhoon, and they needed sailors to run them. Sweat now poured from them as they struggled in the infernal conditions to keep *Aylwin* alive.

Meanwhile, Captain Acuff had retreated to CIC. The wheelhouse was no place for him to try to control his task group; he could barely hear, could barely be heard over the howl of the wind. In CIC things were a bit more muffled. But even when *Aylwin*'s radios worked, Acuff couldn't be sure if his ships were receiving his messages or, for that matter, if they could comply. So, as *Aylwin* rolled almost onto her beam-ends, he sent out his message to Mc-Cain, hoping it would arrive.

It did. McCain, hearing of *Aylwin*'s plight, ordered the senior officers in each composite unit of TG 30.8 to take command and to try to conform to TF 38's movements. In *Aylwin*'s engineering spaces, meanwhile, the thermometer registered 180 degrees, and the salt water roaring down through the intakes did nothing to cool things off. Instead the water flashed to steam as it hit the blisteringly hot machinery, filling the room with billowing clouds of moisture. Even though sailors worked in shifts of only a few minutes, having stripped off life jackets and shirts to try to cool off in the boiling heat, things were nearly intolerable, and several passed out and had to be dragged from the spaces. Some of them would have been better off if they *had* fainted. One was Machinist's Mate First Class Thomas Sarenski. Exhausted and possibly confused, he stumbled above decks to cool off—and the sea snatched him up.

A few minutes later a messenger clambered up to the bridge. "Captain," he cried, "Sarenski's washed overboard to port by that last wave. I saw him

swimming, but he drifted out of sight. He was trying to get to the engine room."
He began to plead for his shipmate. "Please turn around and pick him up, sir."

It was out of the question. Even if Rogers had had control of the ship, an
attempt to reverse course, even if possible, might be deadly. There was nothing the skipper could do.[332]

Heaving to, Rogers grabbed his talker's telephone and spoke to Lieutenant Elwood Rendahl, his chief engineer, who was battling the heat in the
machinery spaces to keep *Aylwin*'s fiery heart pumping out power. "El, how
is it going there?" he asked.

"Kinda hot, Cap'n," Rendahl said, "but we're ready to answer bells."

"I'll give it a few more tries, and if we can't change course I'll secure the
engines and abandon the spaces. We don't want to lose more men. And El,"
warned Rogers, "your chiefs can run it. Don't you stay down there too long.
Stand by in two minutes and when I ring it up, give me all you've got."

Yelling rudder and engine commands over the roar of the atmosphere,
Rogers tried yet again to bring *Aylwin* around. "Right full rudder! . . . All
ahead flank!"

For a moment the effort seemed to be working. "Head is swinging right,
sir!" the helmsman reported. Then the sea took her again. "Head is steady, sir!"

As Rogers wrestled the typhoon for the control of his ship, a sailor sang
out. "Man overboard! Man overboard port side!" George Howes, who'd earlier voiced his wish to experience a real typhoon, now appeared on the
bridge, making his way across the lurching deck to his skipper, grabbing his
arm, half sobbing. "Who is it?" asked Rogers. "It's not Rendahl?"

Howes nodded. "He stayed below too long. When he came out of the
hatch, he just sank down on deck," he explained. "Before we could get him
clear, the water took him over. He was exhausted, Captain, and there was
nothing we could do but see him drift away."

"God rest his soul," answered Rogers.

Aylwin, a toy of the weather, was completely incapable of conducting
a search. All she could do was to try to ride out the storm, which was still
growing in power. Unable to fight, Rogers had to heave to. "Secure all engines and abandon the engineering spaces," he ordered. With that, *Aylwin* offered herself to the typhoon; all her crew could do was to hang on and pray
for their lost shipmates and themselves.[333]

Dewey's mad gallop through the formation, meanwhile, hadn't ended her troubles. On the contrary, it seemed a ride into even worse danger. Like *Aylwin*, she was taking on water with every roll and intermittently losing steering control. By noon the crew had at least two bucket brigades going to try to deal with the flooding, one in the mess hall and another aft. In the steering control room, sailors were reduced to stuffing rags in the ventilators to try to squelch the deluge.

Unlike *Aylwin*, *Dewey* had a major problem with her port engine. Something was wrong with the lubricating oil suction. *Dewey* was wracked with the same insane rolling that was plaguing her sisters, and every time she went over to starboard past forty degrees, the oil supply to the engine just vanished. Cal Calhoun tried to keep the engine in play, but his engineers had to stop the port screw every time the suction went out; if they didn't, the turbines would seize. As Rogers had done, Calhoun shifted his fuel to port to try to counteract the starboard rolling, but still the wild motion continued.

As *Dewey*'s rolls approached and then passed sixty degrees, Calhoun recalled that her stability tests had established her maximum roll at around seventy degrees. He also knew that since those tests, she'd had a lot of top weight added. Now the memory of her strange behavior during her postrepair trials in September loomed up. As *Dewey*'s rolls began to edge even closer to the seventy-degree mark, Calhoun began praying. "Dear God," he said silently each time she went over, "please make her come back!"

All over the ship watertight doors were leaking, and the force of the waves during the rolling sprang at least two of them. One was the steering control room door, and as the sea came in, it blew out the steering motors. The half dozen sailors there were reduced to heaving the massive rudder to and fro by their raw muscle power. Water poured down into the engine spaces, clouding the deadly hot regions in steam; here, too, the blowers were dead and the temperature was around 160 degrees. Water rained onto the main electrical switchboard, located just below a hatch that now leaked like a sieve, and sparks leapt as circuits shorted out. Electrical fires were popping up all over the ship when, around 1130, the main board finally gave out. *Dewey* was suddenly without any electrical power.

In the bridge, the cacophony was monstrous, a combination of roaring seas, chaotic gales, and a horrid screeching from the ship's rigging, something Calhoun later described as "hell's chorus." When Calhoun's lookouts and signalmen turned out of the wind and looked toward him, he saw that their faces were bleeding from the wind and salt spray abrasion. Men were staggering and falling all over the ship, and on one roll Calhoun lost his own grip on a stanchion. Instantly he was airborne, flying toward a far bulkhead. His face hit, and he went out.

A minute or two later he came to, down on his hands and knees. "Call the doctor," he heard over the voice of the storm. "The captain's broken his nose!" His nose, in fact, wasn't broken, and he was soon functioning once more, though there was little he could do at this point; *Dewey* was without electricity and one engine, in irons, out of control, and out of contact with the rest of the fleet.

Things were now desperate, as if they had not been before. The starboard rolls, each one now lasting for up to a minute, were so steep that the starboard bridge wing torpedo director was fully submerged each time. Calhoun watched, incredulous, as his executive officer, Lieutenant Frank Bampton, used his helmet to bail water off the bridge. "Hell, Frank," he yelled, "you're going to have to bail the whole damned Pacific Ocean!"

Bampton kept bailing. "I've got to do something!" he screamed back.

The task group's screen commander, Captain Mercer, riding out the storm on the bridge with Calhoun, tried to keep up his own spirits, but he doubted his flagship would come through the typhoon. By now the rolls were beyond the range of the bridge inclinometer, which stopped at seventy-three degrees, and even that of the engine room instrument, which maxed at seventy-five. During one of them, while Calhoun and Mercer hung from a stanchion facing each other, the starboard pilothouse window directly below them, they had a remarkably calm conversation. "If we go over and end up in this sea," asked Mercer, "do you think you can make it?"

Calhoun, in his early thirties, was fit, and he had a wife and son to live for. "Yes," he replied. "I think I can."

Mercer disclosed that he himself was a poor swimmer. "I don't feel too badly about it," he said nevertheless. "I've had a good life and my insurance is all paid up," he continued with a smile. "But I feel sorry for all of these youngsters," he went on, "many of them married and with families. Their lives have hardly begun and a lot of them wouldn't make it."

"Well, Commodore," Calhoun responded, "I'm betting on the *Dewey*. I think she'll get us through."

"Skipper, I agree with you," Mercer said over the howling voice of the wind.

At the height of the storm Calhoun considered cutting away the ship's mast to try to get her center of gravity down. But he feared that, instead of breaking away cleanly, the mast would pendulum down; if it did, the crosstree might hull the ship at the fire room. Then, not too long afterward, he saw that one of the guy wires that held the forward stack in place had slackened, and the wind was jerking it heavily. Quickly, he warned the signal gang to watch out; then the guy wire snapped with a deafening crack, slashing against the port wing of the bridge.

With that, the forward stack tore loose, collapsing like a huge, heavy sock onto the ship's starboard side and knocking overboard the ship's whaleboat, which had miraculously stayed in place until now. The steam line to the ship's siren, now broken, added an ear-splitting shriek to the howl of the storm. But if it was a harbinger, it was a good one. Freed of the stack's sail area and of the topside weight of the whaleboat, the ship began to ride somewhat more easily.

The ship was in a bit better condition, then, around 1300, when her barometer dropped off the scale and the winds fell well below the 125 knots of before.

Dewey had reached the eye wall.[334]

The raging storm did not reserve its worst punches for the ships of the *Farragut* class. Many other small boys faced their own particular hells. The smallest, the destroyer escorts, also had terrible rides.

USS *Tabberer* was roughly the displacement of a *Farragut*, but she had a lighter superstructure and weapons, which lowered her center of gravity and actually helped her ride the storm better. But as a destroyer escort she had smaller dimensions and less than a third of the power. With the seas on her stern she rode wildly, her stern completely out of the sea and her bow underwater. The experience was one that her skipper, Commander Henry Lee Plage, likened to surfing on a three-hundred-foot surfboard, with *Tabberer* hurtling down each mountainous wave. The fact that Plage, a twenty-nine-year-old reservist with only a year and a half of sea duty, could barely see his own bow—when it was clear of the water—didn't help matters any.

Suddenly another destroyer escort (DE) of the screen lost control, and the wind flung her directly across *Tabberer*'s bow. Plage backed down as hard as he could; he knew that this might poop his own ship if a wave chose that moment to break over her stern, but if Plage didn't reverse his engines immediately, *Tabberer* was going to run the other ship down.

The two vessels cleared each other in the rolling cauldron of sea, but just then *Tabberer* slewed broadside to the wind, and now she began the deadly pattern of rolling that was claiming other ships in the fleet. Like others, she soon passed seventy degrees, mostly on the rolls to starboard.

As her bridge inclinometer swung far over, the young helmsman, struggling to hold the vessel on course, looked at it nervously. "I ain't never seen nuthin' like this, Cap'n!" he burst out.

"Nor have I, Scott," answered Plage, "Nor have I." He watched the bow as a huge wave half buried it and made a decision. "Change course to 090 degrees," he ordered. "I don't want us smashing into another ship."

Lieutenant Robert M. Surdam, Plage's exec, voiced a question that was likely on everyone's mind. "How in hell did we get into this mess, skipper?" he asked.

"I don't know how the fleet wandered into this storm," replied Plage, "but what bothers me is how we're going to get the hell out of it!"

Tabberer was three-quarters fueled, but this wasn't enough ballast for Plage, who quickly started filling his empty tanks with seawater. As other skippers were doing, he pumped fuel from starboard to port tanks. He knew full well that if *Tabberer* came fully about, all the weight to port would conspire with the wind to flip the ship over, but the current rolling was so bad that he decided he had no choice.

The rolling also broke loose some five-inch shells in the forward magazine. Plage hesitated to order anyone to go in there, since the heavy shells could easily crush a man. But if one went off, the entire magazine might blow and *Tabberer* could lose her whole bow. The dilemma was solved when Plage learned that two sailors, not waiting for orders, had dashed into the magazine and started locking down shells.[335]

Melvin R. Nawman was another DE whose ammunition got loose, freed by the same kind of near-horizontal rolling. Blistering seas ripped away floater nets, lifelines and rafts, stanchions, and depth charges. When a loaded ready magazine leapt clear of its rack, a terrified gunner's mate and a somewhat calmer bosun's mate juggled it lest it go off.

"Hang on," joked the bosun's mate. "Ain't you got no guts?"

"I got guts," the gunner's mate answered, trying to keep the rounds from exploding. "But I don't want to see'em."[336]

The *Fletcher*-class *Hickox* was nearly twice the size of the *Farragut*s and the little destroyer escorts, but unlike them she was quite low on oil, which made her ride high. She had little stability with her bunkers at roughly 15 percent. The previous afternoon she'd made desperate attempts to fuel. For nearly two hours she'd struggled to stay alongside *Atascosa* as her crew heaved aboard messengers, phone lines, and fuel hoses, but time after time they parted and broke. Once, on the second attempt, the fuel hose stayed put for seventeen minutes before one of the supporting lines gave way and the hose fell away from the ship; that was the longest drink that *Hickox* got by far, and it wasn't nearly enough. By evening, Captain J. V. Wesson began pumping ballast aboard, fearful of what the next day would bring.[337]

He was right to have been concerned. He was also right in his decision to ballast. The two hundred plus tons of seawater *Hickox* had in her tanks spelled the difference, in all likelihood, between surviving and sinking.

The damage she took was much the same as that of the other tin cans. As had happened with *Dewey* and *Tabberer*, she had to maneuver sharply to avoid hitting an out-of-control ship that blundered across her bow, and, also like *Dewey* and *Tabberer*, the elements seized the opportunity she offered them to take possession of her. Within minutes, *Hickox* was in irons, locked in a deep trough of the sea and unable to turn back onto fleet course. Water began to cascade over the yawing, rolling ship, scrabbling at every opening in the hull to find a way in. An hour after pitching into the trough, the pilothouse wheel control went out and the steering motor room crew had to take over. "Am on course 040 degrees—unable to turn," Wesson announced on TBS. "After-deckhouse is badly damaged," he added. Water was pouring in aft, threatening to drown the sailors who were trying to manhandle the rudder, half submerging them on every hard roll. *Hickox* soon lost power, and sailors formed a bucket brigade to try to reduce the flooding, while in the engine compartments the temperature rose to the same killing levels of heat that were threatening other destroyers. On the open decks, meanwhile, the sea pulled at fittings with nearly incomprehensible power, succeeding in ripping away two stanchions and then rushing triumphantly through the resulting holes and into the ship. Soon water completely filled the carpenter shop and the twenty-millimeter clipping compartment. In the steering motor room, the water was waist high.[338]

It is an irony of physics and marine engineering that the water that *Hickox* was taking did nothing to increase her stability. Quite the opposite, in fact. Loose water in the bilges or anywhere else in the ship not safely enclosed in full or nearly full tanks constantly shifted as the ship rolled and lurched through the ocean, always seeking the lowest point, its surface endlessly striving to find the horizontal. This deadly free-surface effect meant that when *Hickox* rolled starboard, the invading seawater would pour to the starboard and add to the roll, even though this same seawater, if it had been safely enclosed in a stationary fuel tank, would have stayed put and added to *Hickox*'s stability. The result was the same kind of seventy-degree rolling that the less well-designed *Farragut*s were enduring.[339]

In a last-ditch effort to empty the steering motor room, Wesson ordered the crew to open a watertight door in the after crew compartment to give the bucket brigade an egress. When the hatch opened, two feet of loose water poured into the crew quarters from the flooded steering compartment, easing the danger somewhat. Then someone managed to rig an emergency power line to a pump in the steering motor room, which added to *Hickox*'s defenses. But by now the ship was close to the eye wall. She, like *Dewey*, had entered the region that Raphael Semmes had described nearly a century earlier: the place where the seas, like a pack of mad dogs, rushed furiously at each other in the extremely low pressure, colliding to produce high, conical peaks that burst into the air. *Hickox* no longer simply rolled but heaved, pitched, and tossed in the grip of a giant. Without her hundreds of tons of saltwater ballast, she would have gone down. But somehow she contrived to hang on.[340]

Compared to her sister, *Fletcher*-class *Spence* had an easy ride of it. No careening warships crossed her path to make her resort to the deadly maneuvering that might have thrown her out of control. Instead she held grimly on to the fueling group's course.

Normally a part of Vice Admiral Ching Lee's support forces in TG 38.1, *Spence* was steaming with Acuff's replenishment group on the eighteenth. After nearly crashing into *New Jersey* the previous day, thus alerting Halsey to the threatening weather, she'd endeavored to fuel two more times from two different oilers with no success greater than that of *Hickox*. Because she and *Hickox* were so low on fuel—*Spence* was down to barely ten thousand gallons—the destroyers had been ordered to stay with the replenishment group in hopes that they could refuel around dawn.

It hadn't happened. During the lone fueling attempt on the morning of the eighteenth, broadside waves mercilessly slammed *Spence* around, bashing her into the side of the oiler from which she was trying to nurse. The collision threw men off their feet, injuring several of them. Then, as the storm hit full force, *Spence* was reduced to steaming on only one of her four boilers to try to conserve her fuel. That still gave her a fair amount of power, perhaps even more than *Nawman*'s or *Tabberer*'s full output. But *Spence* was twice as heavy, and worse, she was light in the water, with a large sail area at which the winds could batter.

Captain James P. Andrea hadn't ballasted. *Spence* needed fuel; she had to fuel in the next several hours, or else she'd be a write-off. If Andrea filled his tanks with seawater, which could be a slow process, he'd have to take time to pump it back out, which would give him a smaller window for taking on oil. Even at dawn on the eighteenth, *Spence* was riding well, which seemed to confirm his decision. As a compromise with the weather, though, he did re-distribute his remaining fuel oil, as skippers on other ships did.[341]

As the typhoon's full force began overtaking the fleet, *Spence* continued to ride well. Earlier in the morning in the wardroom, Lieutenant Junior Grade Alphonse S. Krauchunas, *Spence*'s supply officer, had listened as Andrea checked with his department heads and other officers about actual and potential problems to watch out for. Other than the low fuel and the single lit boiler, nothing struck him as unusual. Even when the winds and seas went from bad to much worse, the lieutenant still wasn't concerned.

Andrea had heard the frequent reports of "Man overboard!" blasting over the TBS often that morning, distorted by volume and static, and as a precaution he ordered off-duty sailors below and told everyone above decks to wear life jackets. But *Spence* kept her place in formation, the waves coming at her from almost dead aft, which minimized the bad rolling. Quartermaster Second Class Edward F. Traceski, on the bridge with Andrea during the forenoon watch, paid close attention to the pilothouse inclinometer as he kept the ship's log. The worst roll, he noted, was forty-three degrees. It was uncomfortable, but nowhere nearly as bad as what some of the other destroyers were experiencing (through Traceski couldn't have known that), and anyway, *Spence* was built to take it.[342]

And she did have to take *some* damage, of course. A ship can hardly sail into the midst of a typhoon without something giving way. It was a very bad day for whaleboats; like many others that day, *Spence*'s broke loose, and the sailors had to cut the lines it hung from before it could damage the ship. A single depth charge also worked free of its rack, which caused a justifiable scare, but it didn't go off. Then there was the water that *Spence* was shipping, no worse than any other destroyer and a lot better than some. Unlike *Hickox*, unlike *Dewey* and *Aylwin*, she maintained her pilothouse steering control. The minor flooding and mountainous waves, however, began worrying Andrea around midmorning, and a couple of hours before noon, at Captain Acuff's direction, he finally issued orders to ballast.

Belowdecks, Chief Water Tender James M. Felty and his people quickly got to work. Just a few minutes earlier they'd completed shifting *Spence*'s remaining fuel according to Andrea's orders; now they set about bringing seawater aboard. Felty tracked the ballasting progress as the sailors began filling four tanks. Forward, Chief Water Tender George W. Johnson worked on two tanks, while *Spence*'s oil king took care of two more aft. Between them, Felty and Johnson later estimated that *Spence* took aboard somewhere between sixteen thousand and eighteen thousand gallons of ballast over the next hour or so.

High over the main deck, in *Spence*'s main battery director, sat young Seaman First Class Edward Miller of Clark, New Jersey, with an officer and two other sailors. Miller's uncle had once served on the old *Arizona*, years before her death at Pearl Harbor. "If you ever go in the Navy," he'd once told young Miller, "get on a destroyer. That's the best duty." Miller followed his uncle's advice and found it correct, at least until the typhoon. The heavy, enclosed gun director where he was sitting, *Spence*'s fire control nerve center, was one of the highest points of the ship, atop the bridge and abaft the pilot-house, adding to the vessel's center of gravity and decreasing her stability. From there Miller watched the mountainous seas: hundred-knot winds blew the tops off the waves in massive showers of foam, making him think of a giant blowing the head from a brimming beer mug. The director was cramped, and it was almost impossible to get through the hatch while wearing a life jacket, so Miller and the others had taken theirs off before climbing in, leaving them within easy reach on the deck next to the hatch.[343]

Below, Lieutenant Krauchunas was also without his jacket, since he wasn't on an exposed deck. Instead he was in his stateroom, trying to get some rest. Suddenly *Spence*'s chief engineer rushed by, pausing to tell Krauchunas that water was dousing the ship's main electrical board. "You had better get topside, Al!" he warned the supply officer. "We're taking water down the stacks!"[344]

The problem was a variation of the one that *Dewey* and others were having. Water, pouring down the fire room ventilator shafts, was hitting the board, causing it to arc, smoke, and spit. Then, around 1100, *Spence* lost all electrical power.

Ten minutes earlier, Chief Machinist's Mate Henry J. Deeters, in charge of the after engine room, had tested his diesel generator, preparing for just this scenario, and it had worked properly. But then, when down-flooding water cut out Deeters's main generator, the diesel petulantly refused to cut in. Forward, the other engine room was having similar trouble with its own diesel. In the bowels of the ship, Felty got word to delay taking on ballast until he and his people could be equipped with flashlights.

It was about that time that the crew first began feeling the stirrings of fear. Krauchunas, heeding the chief engineer's warning, moved from his stateroom to the wardroom on the main deck, where he found *Spence*'s medical officer, Lieutenant Junior Grade C. C. Caffney, sitting in a chair and in very low spirits. Krauchunas had already seen groups of men hanging around the nearby radio shack passageway, which would provide a fairly easy way out of the ship if something bad happened. Farther below, sailors might become trapped. But still *Spence* fought well, even on her lone boiler and with no electrical power. At 1117 Andrea sent a routine-sounding TBS message. "My last position 7,000 yards north of Task Unit 30.8.4," he said, "course 220 degrees, formation speed."

But by then something was very wrong.

All along, *Spence*'s rolling had been slight, at least compared to other embattled destroyers. But a few minutes before Andrea's TBS message, *Spence*, the wind on her starboard quarter and the seas from dead aft, heeled far to port, hanging for a moment before she came back, and even so, she didn't come all the way back. Instead, she held a list to port.

By now *Spence* had nosed somewhat to the left of her proper course. Trying to correct, Andrea ordered the helm to go to hard right rudder. Then *Spence* rolled again, this time to nearly fifty degrees. And then, instead of coming back, she began to roll farther and farther, until she was on her beamends. She continued going over, her hull rolling clear of the water until she was fully capsized.

As *Spence* went over for the last time, Krauchunas leapt clear of the wardroom and into the neighboring passageway. From there he headed toward the main deck passageway, everything tilting crazily all around him, but when he got there he met a flood of black oil and seawater. Retreating, he stumbled to the radio shack companionway and dove through, the waters chasing along behind him. A moment later he was in the ocean and clear of the ship.

High up in the gun director, Ed Miller had a bird's-eye view of the end. He watched as a huge wave suddenly hit the destroyer broadside, knocking her into a trough. It was quickly followed by two others, each one rolling *Spence* hard, and on the last roll she simply kept going. Miller and the others could hear a din from below as every piece of loose gear on the ship careened over to port.

As the director smashed down into the water, its crew quickly cranked open the hatches lest they go to the bottom in the little steel box. Struggling out of the would-be coffin, Miller and the others found that their life jackets had been washed into the ocean. Then the water grabbed Miller, too, pulling him down—a long way down. When he came up, he found himself on *Spence*'s opposite side. He had gone completely under the sinking destroyer. Just a few feet away was a floating life jacket. He got to it and put it on fast.

There was oil everywhere, on the surface, in Miller's clothing, on the floating debris, but not as much as there might have been. *Spence*, after all, had been nearly empty of fuel, and the storm was quickly dispersing what oil there was, giving the sailors now thrashing next to the wreck a chance of survival. Had it been any worse, it could have killed dozens of men by getting into their lungs or their stomachs.

Miller had surfaced right next to the hull of his ship, and several of his crewmates were swimming nearby. Having been pulled under once, he wanted to avoid a repeat performance. "Let's get away from here!" he shouted to the others over the typhoon's roar. "We don't want to be by the ship when it goes down!" With that, the sailors began trying to swim clear of *Spence*.

Al Krauchunas was alongside the ship's hull, tossed there by the irresistible ocean and wind. From within the thin hull he could hear, faintly, terrible sounds: the screams of men who were now trapped in the upside-down vessel. George Johnson, who had still been trying to ballast *Spence*'s forward tank when she got into trouble, floated by the supply officer and passed to him one of the life jackets that were bobbing around. Then Krauchunas, too, struck out to pull himself away from the ship before she and the men trapped aboard her went down. Swimming with another shipmate, he spotted through the high, heaving seas a floater net with about twenty men clinging to it, and the two swimmers made for it.

Miller, meanwhile, had found a piece of timber that about eight sailors were clinging to. One of them had his arm through the smallest life ring that Miller had ever seen. Still, he managed to get his arm through the opposite side of the ring and held on. Then he realized that the ring must have been prescribed to someone by the ship's pharmacist's mate, as a relief from hemorrhoids. Suddenly, the timber crested. The typhoon's breath caught it, blowing it off the top of the wave, and Miller and the others went flying. Miller splashed into the water, and when he came up, he still had the ring. Nobody else was in sight, and even the piece of timber had vanished.

A few minutes later another sailor floated up to him. It was Steward's Mate First Class David Moore, an African American with nearly a decade of service under his belt. This was no time for segregation, and anyway Miller and Moore were shipmates. Before long they were joined by Larry Collier, a Kansas-born gunner's mate, who was now about as far from the Great Plains as he could possibly get. The three men hung on as the typhoon tried to beat them apart, floating ever more deeply into the storm.

They never saw *Spence* go down. They only heard the muffled sounds of her boilers as they exploded.[345]

Nobody in the fleet knew that *Spence* had capsized; the same went for *Hull* and *Monaghan*. Communications and radar contact were chancy at best; each vessel was largely on its own. Even if someone had known, there was nothing that anyone could have done. A rescue attempt in a typhoon would have been doomed to failure. The fleet couldn't even do much about individuals being washed from the decks of still-floating ships. Every vessel in the fleet was fighting to hold station in its respective formation, or to keep from smashing into neighboring ships, or simply to stay afloat. There are as many stories as there were sailors in Halsey's Third Fleet, as many sagas as there were ships.

Aboard the jeep carrier *Altamaha*, with planes flying mindlessly over the sides, the radar operators tracked the blips of two nearby destroyers, probably *Hull* and *Monaghan*. One by one they disappeared; the radarmen may have chalked up the loss of signal to the effects of the sea scatter or balky equipment.[346]

On the destroyer *Taussig*, ship's doctor George W. Blankenship, assisted by his pharmacist's mates, performed an emergency appendectomy on a sailor in the tiny sick bay. At the height of the typhoon, *Taussig* was rolling dreadfully, and as she smashed into wave after wave, some of her deck rivets came loose, drenching the makeshift operating room with seawater. Blankenship removed the near-to-bursting appendix and finished the surgery. "He'll be up in a week," Blankenship promised, and the patient fulfilled the prediction.[347]

From the flight deck of the escort carrier *Kwajalein*, sailors threw perfectly good airplanes into the seas in the hopes that, relieved of top weight, the ship would ride somewhat more easily.[348]

From the typhoon's malevolent eye tore USS *Dewey*, still rolling and heaving madly, her forward stack gone and her weather decks a shambles. "Thank God," exclaimed Captain Calhoun when his quartermaster told him that the barometer was beginning to rise. "We're going to make it!"[349]

On raged the typhoon, still seeking victims.

⚓

Pat Douhan burst to the surface of the Pacific, gasping for breath.

As he'd been sucked underwater after escaping the sinking *Hull*, he had thought for a moment that he was being pulled into the screws of a passing ship. The thought had thrown him into a panic, but there was nothing he could do. Then the pressure relented, and his life jacket pulled him back up.

But soon he was being sucked down from the surface once more, and this time he realized what was happening. It was a wave, one of the towering, mountainlike waves that had dwarfed his destroyer. Rolling over him, it had buried him and his life jacket dozens of feet down, beneath thousands of tons of dark-green seawater.

Douhan was a strong swimmer. When he figured out what was happening, he doubled himself up, curling into a ball, rolling with the wave instead of trying to fight it. The tactic worked; soon the wave had moved past and he was back on the surface, where rain and spray fought each other for the privilege of drowning him.

At first, Douhan had seen other sailors. At one point he even grabbed hold of one life raft that was lashed to another, but then a shocking sight had made him let go. The men inside were all dead; evidently they had smashed against the hull of the ship, or an underwater concussion had gotten them, for their heads had all burst open—like popcorn, he later recalled. After that, the waves had begun battering him, and then he found that he was alone.

He floated that way for hours, held up by only the old life jacket he'd chanced to find. As evening came on the weather began slackening, but the waves remained huge; as he traveled up one toward its high crest, he looked over and saw a sailor descending another. Then darkness fell, and again he was alone.

But he began to fear that he wasn't entirely alone.

The sea is home to many creatures, especially in the tropics. Some of these are quite inoffensive, even playful, such as the manta ray or dolphin. But afloat in the stormy, gathering darkness, Douhan was thinking about other kinds of creatures, about barracuda and sharks. He began praying hard.

The typhoon had moved off to the west somewhat, and the skies had cleared slightly. Off in the distance Douhan suddenly saw a searchlight. He had no way of knowing that just before nightfall Halsey had ordered a search for overboard sailors, but a search was a logical action, and the light at any rate meant a ship. But a strong current had Douhan, and he was drifting so fast that a few minutes later he could no longer see the searchlight. The night grew blacker still.

Then something hit him on the back of the neck.

Douhan froze, terrified that a shark had just bumped him. Then he turned and managed to make out that it was a broom, floating there beside him. A broom! It wouldn't take a great deal of weight, but it was something material, something manmade. He grabbed it in relief, and for the first time since *Hull*'s sinking, he could rest his legs, numbed with swimming.

Then around midnight he saw another light, a small one, nearby, and he yelled.

"Who is it?" came a reply.

"It's Pat!" he called.

A few minutes later, still holding on to his broom, he came up on a life raft, half awash, its bottom slats broken. Standing in it were about fifteen of his shipmates.

He had returned, at least partially, to civilization.[350]

The man that Pat Douhan saw sliding down the face of a wave as Douhan was climbing up one may have been Ken Drummond.

Like Douhan, Drummond had floated alone for most of the day as the elements beat at him savagely. Unlike Douhan, he'd had little luck in finding either shipmates or anything to hang on to. Soon after he cleared the foundering *Hull*, a high wave did fling him into a life raft, and there he found his shipmate Ray Schultze, but the rendezvous was short-lived. A few seconds later, the wind caught the raft and blew it into the air as if it were a cigarette paper. The two men went flying over the ocean, and a moment later the raft, and Schultze too, disappeared from Ken Drummond's sight.

After that Drummond's life became a struggle to stay afloat and alive. As wave after wave came at him, he soon learned the same trick that Douhan discovered. Whenever a wave hit him, he simply curled up in a ball rather than fighting. The kapok life jacket he wore, vestlike and sporting a collar, was the best thing he had going for him. Unlike the life belts that some other men had, his jacket gave him a lot of support. Once he came through a wave, the jacket always brought him back up. He would even be able to sleep in it, if nobody found him before dark. And, given the huge section of ocean that the fleet occupied and the abysmal conditions, it was likely that no one would.[351]

In fact, though he spent little time thinking about it, Drummond was facing several possible deaths.

Starvation was a distant enemy; a man in fit shape can last weeks without food, and many of the fish swimming in the ocean all around Drummond unseen were edible sources of protein, provided he could catch them.[352] But while Drummond had no way of doing so, it made little difference, for unless he was picked up within a few days at most, he wouldn't last long enough to die of starvation. There were more immediate threats.

For now, Drummond's life jacket, which was filled with kapok fiber, was doing an excellent job of keeping him floating along. The fiber comes from the seed pods of the tropical kapok tree; while unspinnable, it is both highly buoyant and highly water resistant, making it an excellent natural raw material for a floatation device. The standard-issue jacket that Drummond and others in the water were wearing wrapped over the back of his neck and reached down his chest, allowing him to rest and even doze off without fear of drowning. But the kapok fibers that were keeping him alive had one major weakness. They would become waterlogged in roughly forty-eight hours, losing their buoyancy. When that happened, Drummond would only be able to stay afloat by paddling constantly. When he ran out of energy, he would drown.[353]

Even before the life jacket failed, however, Drummond would be facing threats to his life. The greatest, both directly and indirectly, was lack of water. While a castaway can go for a relatively long time without food, the outer limits for survival without freshwater is a little over a week. Long before reaching that point, however, someone in Drummond's position would be tormented with thirst, likely giving in to the impulse to drink salt water. This would only speed dehydration, raising salt levels in the blood, forcing the body to suck its organs dry of water much more quickly to maintain the proper salt balance in the bloodstream. Robbed of its water, an increasingly salty brain will soon function erratically and then at last shut down.[354]

These events, collectively, are inevitable for someone in Ken Drummond's position. A less certain danger also exists, but unlike these more or less remote ones, it can strike at any moment, with the savagery of a mouthful of gleaming teeth.

Sharks come in hundreds of varieties. Only a few of them have been known to attack humans, and in the great scheme of things shark attacks on humans are rare. In the wake of his best-selling book and famous film *Jaws*, Peter Benchley, having given sharks such bad press, tried to educate the public, showing that his work had greatly exaggerated the danger that sharks pose to humans. But that could provide no comfort to Ken Drummond, floating in the Pacific thirty years beforehand.

Sharks are, in fact, perhaps the perfectly designed predators. They can not only sense blood or other human liquids and solids in what seem to be impossibly small amounts, but they can lock in on the location. At closer ranges the shark employs its eyes, which incorporate a low-light imaging system, as well as its lateral-line array, with which it senses movement nearby; discordant, chaotic movement, such as that of a fish in distress, is particularly easy to localize. At closer ranges still, special electroreceptors can even pick up on the electricity generated by the prey's muscle contractions. Finally, when the shark attacks, moving at speeds that can exceed that of destroyers, it tears into the prey with two hundred exceedingly sharp teeth arranged in the jaws somewhat like those of a ripsaw.[355]

Drummond likely knew few of these details, but he had the general picture. Nevertheless, the only thing for him to do was hope that the storm had driven the sharks deep, to keep swimming, and to try to find others with which to await rescue. As evening approached, he came across another lone swimmer, the first person he'd seen since Schultze disappeared with the life raft. It was Radioman First Class Bert Martin, and Drummond was glad to see him. But both men were rapidly tiring, and neither had been adrift in the Pacific before.

What they next tried to do was an exercise in bad judgment born of inexperience and exhaustion. In order to keep from being separated, they set about tying themselves together. In one sense it was a good idea. What weak light the typhoon let through the atmosphere was vanishing; the whitecaps were countless, and between them and the spume, a single bobbing head, even if not concealed in a trough, would have been hard to pick out. A group of people, even two men, stood a better chance of being spotted than one. But lashed together, Drummond and Martin would have less maneuverability.

The two men had their life jackets unbuttoned and were about to tie them to each other when a wave came hurtling at them out of the gloom. It tore the two of them apart, and luckily so: Drummond realized that if they had finished with their task, the wave would have pulled them both underwater, uncoordinated and thrashing, and in all likelihood drowned them. As it was, Drummond lost sight of Bert Martin, just as had happened with Ed Schultze.

The light soon fled. Drummond, alone once more, was fast running out of energy, and he had likely swallowed a good bit of seawater in the high, heaving seas. Then, as he drifted on the dark ocean, he saw something about ten feet away. It was a Model A Ford, shining and black, with a gleaming chrome radiator. More chrome graced the headlights and surrounded the windshield.

Drummond stared at the vision. "If I can just swim and get on that hood," he said to himself, "I can rest."

He never got on the hood, obviously. In fact, he didn't remember much at all after that, continuing to float blindly in the darkness. Evidently the current that had caught Douhan and enabled him to come upon the broken life raft had left Drummond behind, but he had no way of knowing that. By the time he saw his shiny black Model A, he was out of his head.

At first, then, he was oblivious to the large, rakish shape that moved toward him through the churning black waters. It was close to midnight; he'd been swimming through the typhoon and its aftermath for at least twelve hours. In all likelihood he was paddling in the spastic motions that signal distress to marine predators. The life jacket had rubbed the underside of his chin raw, and the salt spray had removed more of the remaining skin on his face; he was bleeding into the water. And now something was in the sea near him.

Then he saw the searchlight. The dark object was a ship.

Drummond jerked back to reality. The navy's kapok life jackets were equipped with both lights and whistles. The light on Drummond's had been ripped away at some point, but it still had its whistle, and now Drummond began blowing on it for all he was worth. High and keening it sounded over the winds, still at gale strength. But Drummond was still just one whitish dot on a pitch-black sea that was covered with white dots of foam.

The ship was drawing nearer. "There he is over there!" Drummond heard someone yell, and soon a line splashed into the water nearby. Drummond reached for it, but blowing the whistle had used up the last of his strength. His grip on the lifeline slackened, and it slipped through his hands. Then someone was diving into the water and paddling up to him, and the next thing he knew he was being pulled aboard ship.

It was a destroyer escort, a bit smaller than his own lost ship, and she was a shambles. Her mast was gone, her topside gear was missing or smashed, and she rolled crazily as the waves hit her, but she was afloat. And Drummond was still alive.

His rescuers asked him what ship he was from, and he told them. "*Hull*."

"Did you fall overboard?" they asked. So they didn't know.

"No," he answered. "It sunk."[356]

The DE that pulled Drummond aboard was in fact *Tabberer*, which had somehow come through the typhoon.

As the storm's trailing edge battered at her sometime around sunset, she was still without radar and radio, and her crew had no way of knowing that just a few miles away *Dewey* was also fighting the weather. Both ships had taken a pounding, their weather decks littered, paint blasted off their structure by the salt spray.

Then, in the dying light, *Dewey* suddenly burst out of the storm. One moment she was in a typhoon, with wind and spume lashing out at her; the next she was in a patch of clear ocean, her lookouts now able to see, though dense clouds still hung overhead and the mountainous swell continued to surge hard against her. A few thousand yards astern of her, *Tabberer* broke into the clearing.

Lieutenant Commander Plage, the reservist from Georgia Tech, spotted *Dewey* and blinkered a message to tell the destroyer of *Tabberer*'s radio outage. "I have just lost my mast," he signaled. In a spirit of levity at having brought his ship through, Cal Calhoun answered the message. "Cheer up," he blinkered back. "I have just lost my stack."

The clearing weather was brief; squalls and spray hit the ships intermittently as more destroyers began to emerge from the main typhoon. *Tabberer* and *Dewey* soon became separated, each trying to resume fleet course. *Tabberer* was making eight knots; *Dewey* could only make turns for three, slowly dragging herself away from the tail of the storm.[357]

As night came on, *Tabberer*'s worn-out crew was busy effecting repairs. Around 2150, Chief Radioman Ralph E. Tucker was on top of the bridge structure, jury-rigging an antenna near *Tabberer*'s stack, when something caught his eye.

"Man overboard!" he sang out. "Light off starboard beam!"

Plage immediately brought the DE about, and her big twenty-four- and thirty-six-inch searchlights began stabbing the roiling waters. At first he thought that the light Tucker had spotted was from a life jacket that had washed off a ship, but then he spotted the jacket. It had a man in it.

As the floating sailor waved at the ship, Plage, thinking that he must have been carried away from *Dewey*, steamed around and downwind of him, and then turned *Tabberer* and began to steam upwind toward him, as if approaching a mooring buoy. But then the wind grabbed *Tabberer*, slowing her and pushing her off her course. Plage couldn't get close to the sailor.

Plage then tried a different approach. Steaming back upwind of the sailor, he then put *Tabberer* broadside to the gale. At once it grabbed her, and she resumed the steep, dizzying rolls that she had been taking earlier on. But as Plage had expected, the winds also began to nudge her down toward the sailor.

As solid green water slapped over onto the dipping main deck, the deck gang, fighting for balance, rigged a lifeline and put a bight in it. As *Tabberer* loomed over the drifting sailor, they heaved him the line, and an officer shouted for him to grab hold of it. The ship rolled again as the deck gang hauled on the line; water again washed over the deck, and when it receded, the sailor was sprawled on the main deck.[358]

Aboard *Dewey*, Preston Mercer, the squadron commander, had left the bridge not long before. "Well, Skipper, we've weathered an experience which will become famous in history," he'd told Calhoun before going below.

"Everyone will want to hear about it. Tell them as well as you can what it was like, but don't expect anyone to believe you." At that moment, Calhoun didn't care if anyone would believe him or not.

Then eyes aboard *Dewey* spotted the loom of *Tabberer*'s searchlight, just as Douhan, still adrift, had. Lighting a ship that way in the blackness was a sure way to attract any submarines that might be cruising the area, hungry for targets. There had to be a reason for it, and Calhoun, having overheard bits of TBS chatter between *Tabberer* and another destroyer that included the word "survivors," indicated that *Tabberer* must have found someone in the water. Hoping to help, he ordered his vessel toward the light.

The turn brought the seas, still towering, fair onto the bow of the ship. Now *Dewey*'s problem wasn't rolling but pitching. As she crested each wave, the water broke far over her forecastle, drenching her all the way back to her bridge. Then, sliding down the face of the wave, she would slam into the base of the trough with a terrible wracking shudder.

Calhoun telephoned Mercer to explain the reason for the hard ride. As commanding officer, it was Calhoun's decision, but Mercer was a veteran destroyer man, and he recommended that Calhoun turn back to his previous course toward the fleet. *Dewey*, he pointed out, may have taken some structural damage during the typhoon; if it had, the brutal pitching and heaving might be endangering the destroyer. Calhoun heeded the recommendation. *Dewey* turned and began steaming away at her crawl of three knots.[359]

Aboard *Tabberer*, Plage had picked up more men in addition to Ken Drummond, ascertaining that the fleet had lost a destroyer and that there might be dozens, even hundreds, of men in the water. Angry that no other ships were coming to help him—he didn't know of *Dewey*'s condition—he could do nothing but continue to keep up the search on his own. Even another destroyer, *Benham*, steaming nearby, left the area around midnight, low on fuel and shaping course for the fleet. By then *Tabberer* had picked up nearly a dozen survivors from *Hull*. Any further rescue attempts, at least for the rest of the night, were going to be up to her.[360]

Plage quickly had to develop a sound rescue technique, along with some new ship-handling skills. Soon he and his crew had a system. Several strong swimmers, both sailors and officers, donned kapok life jackets of their own, to which heavy lifelines were tied. They, along with every other free man on the ship, acted as lookouts as *Tabberer* steamed along at ten knots, watching for feeble life jacket lights. In order to let the crew hear life jacket whistles more easily, Plage killed every ventilating blower on the ship's bridge structure to keep noise levels down. Still the voice of the sea tried to drown out everything else; as *Tabberer* pitched through the blackness, water, half luminescent, sheeted high over her bow, drenching everyone on the forward part of the weather decks, knocking down many.

Then, when someone spotted or heard a swimmer, the real fun began. Plage would light up the ship like a Christmas tree, inviting pot shots from any Japanese sub that happened to be in the area. Next, as he'd done during the first rescue maneuver, he would jockey *Tabberer* until she was about fifty yards to windward of the swimmer or swimmers; he'd then lay her broadside and, with the help of the wind, drift down on them. The breeze was so stiff that it didn't take long.

The deck gang would then size up the man to be rescued. If he looked strong enough and alert, the crew would throw him a line; otherwise, the strong, lifelined swimmers would dive into the sea and make their way out to him and pull him to the side of the ship, where two cargo nets had been rigged, the others having washed away in the storm. Two men waited on the nets to drag the survivors aboard.

Tabberer made her first rescues, and when her men could see or hear no one else, Plage began a systematic, expanding box search. Already he'd picked up men from a very large area, and as his search progressed the area grew exponentially larger. And, for the time being, *Tabberer* had to search it alone.[361]

When Halsey's people in *New Jersey*'s flag plot finally got word from *Tabberer* in the predawn hours of December 19 that she was retrieving survivors, it caused some consternation. It was the first word they'd gotten that a ship was definitely lost. And the fact that *Tabberer* was a DE also worried some of them. One of the smallest warships to be found in the fleet, likely heavily crewed by reservists, dismasted and with little assistance, wasn't their idea of the ideal search-and-rescue vessel. At least, Halsey's officers thought, she had a few destroyers somewhere nearby.[362]

Halsey had already ordered all of his ships to look out for survivors. But he was trying to get his strikes on Luzon back on schedule, and he wasn't willing to divert the whole fleet to help *Tabberer*. MacArthur was counting on him. Even more critical was the fact that his destroyers were still starving for fuel. They had stretched things as far as they could. If they couldn't fuel on the nineteenth, some would be dead in the water by sundown.[363]

In the night, the weather was clearing. This often occurs with tropical cyclones; they seem to serve as giant vacuum cleaners that, in their passing, suck all humidity out of the air, leaving crystalline skies. The waves, radiating outward from the typhoon, were still high but beginning to weaken with distance. As daybreak arrived, the task units and groups quickly arrayed themselves in fueling formations, and the fuel hoses snaked out over the water. At long last the desperate small boys began to suck in huge volumes of the oil that they needed to keep the fires on their boilers alight. The exercise took most of the day. Halsey, meanwhile, contacted MacArthur, telling the general that the fleet planned to respread its Big Blue Blanket over northern Luzon on the twenty-first of December.[364]

Miles away from the main task force, Pat Douhan and his dozen or so companions knew none of this. They had passed an uncomfortable night on their broken, awash raft. The seas were slowly calming, but they were still high for a small, leaky wooden contraption crowded with sailors. *Hull*'s galley had been secured two days earlier, when things had grown rough on the seventeenth of December, and most of her men had not eaten much after that. Douhan and his castaway band hadn't had a solid meal, then, in at least thirty-six hours, and they had no food on the raft. Nor did they have any fresh water.

Then, as light began to return on the morning of the nineteenth, they saw something they did have.

Swarming around their faltering raft was a horde of dorsal fins, the fins of twelve-foot sharks.[365]

Tabberer's crew, too, could sometimes see sharks as well, circling hungrily around the men they plucked from the water. Plage had men ready with rifles to start shooting and drive them away when needed.

After around three in the morning, the little ship found no one else until daybreak. But soon after that the procession of rescues resumed. From just after dawn until two hours before noon, her crew brought aboard men by ones and twos. One of the first to be rescued in the daylight was *Hull*'s skipper, Jim Marks.

Like nearly all of the other survivors, Marks was in bad shape, and *Tabberer*'s people had to drag him aboard. His eyes were black from the pummeling of the waves, and his face was covered by saltwater sores. At times he had been sure he was going to drown, but the seawater that he involuntarily swallowed had made him throw up and instinctively keep gasping for breath. In most of this, Marks was like any other survivor. In one way he was unique: as a skipper whose ship and men had gone down, he was haunted by the specter that perhaps he could have done something different, something that might have saved *Hull*.[366]

In the sea conditions that could tear men up in this fashion, not everyone *Tabberer* found was alive. Sometimes the life jackets they spotted were empty; on other occasions they were tied around corpses. Rescue swimmers could do nothing for the dead but to carry out an expedited burial at sea, since *Tabberer*, small and now overloaded with living survivors, wasn't equipped to handle remains. The swimmers would remove the victim's dog tags and then cut him free of his life jacket so he would sink, as a sailor read aloud a prayer. The life jacket, like all others, was brought aboard so *Tabberer* wouldn't need to investigate it again.[367]

The rescue swimmers, too, were in danger. A little while after noon, as the ship drifted down on an exhausted, listless survivor, lookouts spotted an eight-foot shark swimming just a few feet away from him while *Tabberer* was still at least sixty yards off. Crewmen cut loose with Springfield rifles and even submachine guns as the executive officer, Bob Surdam, dove jacketless into the water, striking out for the floating sailor. Grabbing him by the back of the jacket, Surdam began towing him back toward the ship, but in the still-choppy water, he soon began tiring, with thirty yards still to go. The shark, uninjured, had been driven off for a time by the gunfire. But soon it returned, circling twenty feet around the men. Torpedoman First Class Robert L. Catton, who was manning a cargo net, dove in and made his way out to the two swimmers, helping Surdam tow in his sailor. All of them got aboard safely.[368]

The sea, too, could be deadly, even without the aid of her denizens, as the typhoon had clearly shown, and the danger had not ended yet. Bosun's Mate First Class Louis A. Purvis was one of the tethered rescue swimmers, spending most of the nineteenth either in the water or about to be in it. At one point, as he was off the port side of the ship trying to rescue a weakened sailor, *Tabberer* took one of her hard rolls. Purvis had too much slack in his tether, and it caught on a sonar dome far beneath the ship's waterline. Purvis sank like a stone, and then he fought his way back to the surface. The next roll jerked him under again, and again he came back up. The third roll, drawn out and slow, pulled Purvis all the way under the hull, where he banged against the dome and realized at last what had happened. Running out of breath, he paused just long enough to work his way out of his jacket, and then he struck out for the surface, bursting into the air off *Tabberer*'s starboard side. As sailors on the port side were frantically watching the water, starboard lookouts spotted him, and his shipmates hauled him aboard.

It had been close, but Purvis recovered quickly. Unfazed by the mishap, he was back on rescue detail in an hour. "Dammit," he said of the episode, "I bet I'm the first sailor to be keelhauled in 200 years."[369]

The rolling, unavoidable as it was, nearly claimed others as well. On one occasion it nearly got a survivor and a rescuer at the same time, pulling them both under the ship just as they reached one of the cargo nets. A lieutenant dove in and helped both back up to the surface.[370]

Once the rescued sailors got aboard *Tabberer*, they received excellent treatment. The ship had often guarded carriers during flight operations, and she had already picked up around two dozen downed pilots, so her crew had a good routine for this sort of thing. The division's medical officer, Lieutenant Junior Grade Frank W. Cleary, also happened to be aboard for what was in fact his maiden voyage, a turn of luck that helped matters further. Those who were in comparatively good shape immediately hit the shower and then went to a compartment near sickbay. Those in worse condition were carried by stretcher to the wardroom, where they were stripped of their soaking clothes and then examined and treated by Cleary and two pharmacist's mates.[371]

In the middle of the rescue operation, Plage received a message from Halsey. *Tabberer*, along with all other ships with serious damage, was to proceed to a rendezvous nearly one hundred miles distant, and the vessels would then shape course for Ulithi.

Plage didn't like it. He was still picking people out of the water, and there was an excellent chance that he was going to locate some more. "Maybe I just didn't hear these orders," Bill McClain, a sailor whose general quarters station was in the radar shack, heard him say. An hour or so later, he reluctantly set course for the rendezvous point. But then *Tabberer* came across more men in the water, and Plage resumed his search.[372]

Two hours after receiving the rendezvous message, the DE pulled a group of seven men from the ocean. The senior one was Lieutenant Junior Grade George H. Sharp, whose father was a serving rear admiral in command of Nimitz's minesweepers. Sharp had just saved his men's lives. When they first saw *Tabberer* hours before, they had wanted to swim for her, but Sharp hadn't let them. Watching her, he'd realized her skipper was making an expanding box search, and that she would come to them by and by. As he predicted, *Tabberer* eventually came close enough to spot them, though if Sharp hadn't kept his men in a group, her lookouts would likely have missed them, since her closest approach to them was two miles away.[373]

Plage was now in violation of orders, but he was finding that the course to the rendezvous, which he could no longer make in time, was at least bringing *Tabberer* across more men needing rescue. Whenever he located someone, he would stay and search the area, which was making the ship run ever later. As the tropical sun began setting in what was now a clear sky, Plage was debating whether to contact Halsey to try to explain his actions and ask for more time when another message from the fleet commander came in. Halsey had authorized *Tabberer* to stay where she was and keep searching. When Plage told his crew of the message, the sailors, most of them thirty-six hours behind on their sleep, burst into cheers.[374]

Halsey was still focused on hitting Luzon the next morning, but he had also deployed the fleet in such a way as to allow as thorough a search as possible while en route to his jumping-off point, and around midday he'd detailed other ships to devote themselves to rescue endeavors.[375] But the fleet had been spread out over a large swatch of ocean at the time of the storm, and it was a huge area to have to search. It was now fully twenty-four hours after the storm; dusk had again fallen, and still men were drifting on the face of the Philippine Sea, facing a second night in the water.

The night before, Joseph McCrane's group from *Monaghan* had almost been rescued. The drifting sailors had seen the lights of a ship, quite possibly the lit-up *Tabberer,* and they shouted and waved in the darkness. It hadn't helped, and the ship steamed on without seeing or hearing them. Joseph Guio, who had earlier probably saved McCrane's life by pointing the raft out to him, was next to McCrane. McCrane was trying to keep him warm when Guio spoke up. "Joe," Guio asked, "can you see anything?"

McCrane thought Guio was asking about the passing vessel, and he told the ailing gunner's mate that he could make it out.

"I can't see a thing," Guio replied. Then, perhaps sensing his death approaching, he thanked the sailors who had pulled him out of the water, and he thanked McCrane especially for trying to warm him up. Then he lay his head on McCrane's shoulder and dozed off. A half hour later, McCrane began to suspect something was wrong and tried to wake Guio, but by then he was gone.

The sailors held on to their shipmate for twenty more minutes. Then, as they recited the Lord's Prayer, they lowered Guio over the raft's gunwales and into the sea.[376]

Guio was only the first. The group had a few supplies, including a supply of fresh water, but it wasn't very much for all of the sailors, and it caused as many problems as it solved. As McCrane shared around biscuits and opened a can of Spam, sharks began nosing around the raft. During the nineteenth the sailors ate scant meals of a biscuit and a cup of water each.[377]

Krauchunas's floater net was better equipped, at first, than McCrane's raft, with two food kits, a medical kit, flares, flashlights, and dye markers. But when the typhoon left them, it took with it the medical kit and both of the food kits. Then, during the night of the eighteenth, the flares, too, washed away. It did leave behind, though, the most crucial items, two five-gallon kegs of fresh water. This let Krauchunas give the men a drink every two or three hours. They needed it: December 19 brought clear skies. At first, after the nightmare of the previous day, this seemed a blessing, but as the sun rose higher the heat began to come on, and so did sunburn.

That morning the group had its own near rescue, which came in the form of two planes. Since the flares were now gone, Krauchunas used one of the dye markers, which he'd stuffed in his pocket for safekeeping, but the planes never spotted it.

The day grew still warmer. The water, which Krauchunas handed out as freely as he could, did nothing to help the men who had ingested large gulps of ocean.

Small amounts of seawater, especially mixed with fresh, can actually help stave off the specter of dehydration, but in larger doses the salts merely speed the process along. The first signs of dehydration include headache, dizziness, and problems with vision; later, as Ken Drummond had learned when he spotted his Model A, the victim begins to hallucinate, and later still he often loses the will to live. Two of the men on the floater net, Lieutenant Junior Grade John Whalen and Seaman First Class James Patrick Hester, were in especially bad shape. They had been going downhill for much of the nineteenth, and the second night adrift proved too much for them. A few hours after midnight, Whalen slipped off the net. Hester followed a few minutes later. They were never seen again.[378]

On McCrane's raft, things were similar, but worse. They saw planes too, including, maddeningly, a TBF Avenger that flew directly overhead without spotting them. The skies may have been clear, but the chop and the whitecaps made them hard to see from the air. Then, with nightfall, came death. Ben Holland, a cook with a bad gash on the back of his head, finally succumbed to his injuries, and another sailor, driven berserk by thirst, began gulping seawater despite his shipmates' efforts to stop him and died a short time later. A third man leapt out of the raft and began swimming around it. Before long he was lost to view in the darkness.[379]

Less than an hour after the deaths of Whalen and Hester, the remnants of the floater net group spotted a ship, a destroyer escort, closing them in the darkness. By 0400 they were aboard USS *Swearer*, which, along with USS *Brown*, was escorting the jeep carrier *Rudyerd Bay* to relieve *Tabberer* and expand the search-and-rescue attempt. Halsey was at last sending reinforcements.

The number of survivors was dwindling. Then the night of the nineteenth ended and the twentieth dawned, another clear, hot day in the tropics.

Tabberer's search during the night of the nineteenth was negative. Plage had spoken with "Blackjack" (Halsey's voice call) via TBS late the previous evening, filling the admiral in on the little ship's work of the day. "Well done!" Halsey had answered, and reaffirmed his orders for *Tabberer* to keep up her efforts until she was relieved. But she found no one else that night. The only rescue in the hours of darkness had come soon after sunset, when a man with enough lung power to make himself heard had drawn their attention. He was the forty-first she had saved. After that, nothing.[380]

As the sun came up on the twentieth, *Tabberer* could see other ships nearby, engaged in picking up castaways. A couple of hours later *Rudyerd Bay* arrived and relieved the DE, and *Tabberer*, still with full power available despite the pounding she'd taken, set course for Ulithi and moved into a fifteen-knot lope. But two hours after that her lookouts once again spotted a raft, and she headed toward it. Within ten minutes, her crew brought ten more survivors aboard, these belonging to *Spence*, raising the number she'd rescued to more than fifty.

The newcomers reported that several men from the raft had swum off in the night, as had Whalen and Hester in Krauchunas's group. Plage began searching again, letting *Rudyerd Bay* know what had happened. The carrier set out toward *Tabberer*; by the time she arrived, the DE had picked up four more *Spence* men. With *Rudyerd Bay* now taking over the search, Plage again made for Ulithi. *Tabberer*'s role in the tale was finally complete. She had rescued fifty-five sailors.[381]

Many others, of course, were still adrift, now forty-eight hours after the typhoon, and the lapse of time was taking its toll. Ed Miller, Larry Collier, and the veteran seafarer David Moore from *Spence* had held on gamely so far. The day before they'd spotted a Catalina flying in the distance and waved frantically at it, but it had been too far away. To quell the heat and their growing thirst, each of them would occasionally slip out of his jacket and dive far below the surface, where the water was cooler. They couldn't drink it, of course, but they could rinse their mouths out without too much trouble. Unlike some others, they never saw any sharks.

By the twentieth, though, these measures were wearing thin. Daylight found them half delirious, fantasizing about what they'd like to be eating. One of them described, in great detail, his desire for a jug of milk and a half dozen ice-cold chocolate éclairs. As the day went on, it got worse.

Finally Larry Collier spoke up. "Hey, Ed, you know what?" he asked in a conspiratorial tone of voice. "The *Spence* didn't go down. I found it last night while you guys were sleeping. It's right over there. You know what?" he repeated. "I went over there and I swam down and I went in one of the scuttlebutts and I got a nice drink of water."

Collier was very convincing, and Miller didn't need much persuasion. The two men had begun to swim over to the spot that Collier had indicated when Moore piped up.

"Hey, there ain't nothing over there." he told them. "Now stay here. You guys stay here. Don't worry," he assured them. "They're looking for us. They're looking for us." He may well have saved their lives with his authority and his words.

But it was hard to keep up hope. By afternoon, with the sun beating down, Miller was nearing the end of his rope along with the others. "I don't know if they're ever gonna find us or not."

Then they saw the planes, two of them in the distance, and what appeared to be sticks floating on the horizon: the hulls and superstructures of ships.

One of the planes flew closer. By now the men were waving their T-shirts, frantically trying to draw its attention, but then the plane began moving away. "Aw, great!" Miller swore. "They'll never find us now!" But then the plane circled back around what turned out to be a carrier, turned again, and this time came flying right over the sailors' heads, and as it did it dropped a green smoke bomb. They'd been spotted. Now they watched as the ships turned in their direction.

Within a half hour a DE had steamed up to them, a cargo net over her side. Again, it was *Swearer*. "Over there!" Miller yelled. "Let's get over there and get on that!" Swimming to the net, he grabbed hold of it, but he couldn't pull himself up. Some men from *Swearer* dove into the water to help pull

Miller and his shipmates aboard, as crew members from *Tabberer* had done during its search-and-rescue duty.

Once the men were on deck, *Swearer*'s people tore off the *Spence* sailors' uniforms, sodden and filthy with oil. By now there was a shortage of bunks, but *Swearer*'s crew quickly made room for the newcomers. An officer gave up his stateroom for Miller. A medic visited him there and gave him some water and medicinal brandy, followed by a shot of morphine. With that, Miller was gone until the following morning.[382]

Two hours later the sun set. Miller and his companions were safe, but there were still men adrift, now beginning their third night on the ocean.

Some of Douhan's companions had been drinking seawater, and all were in rough shape. The sharks had been at them, too. On December 21, the men had been hallucinating about going to the galley to get sandwiches, and one of them, in the manner of Ken Drummond, thought that he saw his grandfather serving 7UP from a Model T Ford parked in a meadow. A shark went after a sailor who'd gotten off the raft to go in search of a sandwich, tearing his arm up. Adrenaline kicked in, and the men snapped back to reality. But the basic conditions that had caused the delusions had changed not at all: heat, hunger, and, of course, thirst.

Now, in the darkness, one of the sailors suddenly thought that he saw a ship nearby, and he let everyone know. Did he? Douhan later thought so, and at the time everyone else seemed pretty sure. They were all about to start yelling, but then they noticed one other thing, a strange, distinctive odor.

Some of the men had at times gone ashore on islands that had been held by the Japanese, and they swore that the scent of a Japanese body differed from that of a Caucasian. And now in the night, what they were smelling on the ocean that was empty of everything but the raft and the shadowy vessel was that same Japanese scent.

Suddenly the sailors suspected that what they were seeing was a Japanese submarine that had surfaced to charge her batteries. And their yells died in their throats.

They would never know. Maybe it was a submarine. Some even thought that it had been a Japanese island. But whatever it was, it left them alone, and they returned the favor. The long night continued to pass.[383]

At that moment, meanwhile, McCain and Halsey were learning that the typhoon hadn't quite finished with TF 38.

A couple of weeks before the Leyte invasion, Halsey and Marc Mitscher had ridden the tails of another typhoon into striking range of the Ryukus, in the backyard of Japan's Home Islands. That storm had chewed up Japanese airfields, grounding planes and setting the stage for a day-long string of carrier plane attacks. The westward-moving typhoon had allowed Halsey's aircraft to sortie while Japanese pilots were still unable to take off. Halsey had dubbed the storm Task Force Zero.[384]

As Halsey and his staff put together a new strike plan, they were hoping for a similar performance. The storm that had ravaged Third Fleet hadn't curved north as Kosco had thought might happen, which meant it was dead on course for northern Luzon, Halsey's target. As his ships finished refueling, the task force set course for a position that would let it begin predawn air strikes on the twenty-first of December.[385]

But again the typhoon interfered with the strike. As the fleet replenished on the nineteenth, it at last began the northward curve that Kosco had predicted; by late afternoon it was moving almost directly due north. In the end it missed Luzon completely, leaving the Japanese airfields and Tokkō planes operational. At the same time, steaming closely in the wake of the storm, the carriers found the waters too choppy and the winds too high and chaotic for flight operations. Shortly after midnight on the twenty-first, Halsey gave up and canceled the Luzon air strikes.[386]

As the carriers turned away from the Philippines, Halsey added the final measure to the fleet's quest for survivors. Moving toward the area of the sinkings and more manageable weather, the entire fleet began a day-long surface and air search of a rectangular area hundreds of square miles in size. Destroyer divisions crisscrossed the region abreast, with doubled lookouts scanning the water, while CAP and other planes looked down from above. Describing the storm's aftermath in his autobiography several years later, Halsey called the efforts to recover survivors "the most exhaustive search in Navy history." If the efforts of the previous days didn't add up to that, the resources he committed on the twenty-first certainly tipped the scale. But by then, any survivors had had nearly three full days to weaken and to drift far from the point of a sinking, although the search area Halsey prescribed accounted for drifting. Whatever the reason, few survivors were rescued after daylight on December 20.[387]

Pat Douhan and the group on his life raft had been three nights and most of three days at sea with nothing in the way of supplies. Two sailors were dead; before letting the water have their bodies, the others had to strip one of them to provide clothes to another man who didn't have any. Some of the living were beginning to give up hope.

"Hey," spoke up one of them suddenly. "There are ships on the horizon!"

It was a particularly cruel hallucination. "Boy," thought Douhan, "you've gone off the deep end too." But the instinct to survive is strong, and he and the others dutifully rubbed saltwater crust from their caked eyes and looked where their fellow sailor thought he saw something. And they did, in fact, see ships on the horizon, hull down.

In a flash, everything turned around, and then, before long, two high-flying fighters came over. The men shouted and waved with whatever strength they had left, but it was a fresh disappointment; they feared that the planes were simply too high to see them.

But as they watched, the planes came back over them, this time waggling their wings. It was a message to the castaways floating below: the pilots had spotted them. Then came a familiar sight, a cloud of black smoke coming in their direction. They were destroyer men, and they knew what it was. A tin can was lighting off her boilers to make better speed as it steamed to pick them up.

Before long USS *Brown* arrived; she was one of the ships that Halsey had sent to relieve *Tabberer*, and she quickly set about getting the sailors aboard. Lines sang through the air for the men on the raft to catch. And then the sea pulled its last trick.

The sharks that had been lurking around the raft, occasionally snapping at an offered arm or leg, somehow sensed that they were about to lose the rest of their meal. Suddenly, they went into a frenzy; the waters came alive with flashing fins and dead, fishlike eyes staring above razor-sharp teeth. As some of *Brown*'s men pulled the raft alongside through the melee, others began firing rifles at the predators.

It worked. All of the remaining castaways made it aboard *Brown*, pulled up her side by the sailors.

Once on deck, *Hull*'s men felt that things had returned to normal, and they wanted to shift for themselves. When *Brown*'s men tried to help one, he shrugged them off. "Aw, we can walk!" he said, so the sailors let him go. He hit the deck instantly. The others reacted in much the same way. Having learned a painful lesson, they swallowed their pride and let *Brown*'s people take over.

In dealing with dehydration and serious hunger, one must go slowly. Giving the stomach too much food or water at once simply means that it will come right back up. Douhan and each of the others got, to begin with, a sip of water; then each got a sip of soup. But the very first thing each of them got was a sip of bourbon. *Brown*, as are all U.S. naval vessels, was a dry ship, but at times like this alcohol sometimes showed up. Douhan's sip burned him all the way down.

Brown, like the other rescue ships, gave the castaways treatment fit for a king. Her sailors gave up their bunks, and every man who had been rescued was assigned a sailor to sit by his bunk for the rest of the way to Ulithi and see to his needs. Recovery, after the rescue took time. Douhan hallucinated sometimes. Once he believed that he was on a Russian submarine, and he couldn't understand how a sailor talking with him knew English.[388]

Others, still on the sea, were also delirious. The sailors on Joe McCrane's raft, despite having a little water and food, had had a rough time as well, and dawn on the twenty-first saw them still adrift on the ocean. One of the men saw land and houses, and the others couldn't stop him as he leapt in the water and swam off toward the vision, never to return. And they had shark trouble as well. Once they spotted an onion, a juicy, savory onion, bobbing on the water near them, and they began paddling toward it. Then they spotted an eight-foot shark swimming around it, and they gave up their effort.

Then they, too, saw two fighters. The aircraft may even have been the same ones that had spotted the group of sailors from *Hull*. McCrane and his people watched, overjoyed, as markers dropped toward them from the

planes. Within an hour came what McCrane described as "the most wonder-
ful sight in the world, a tin can steaming right at us." She was, in fact, *Brown*,
fresh from picking up Douhan's group.

Again the destroyer threw them a line, and before long McCrane and the
others were safely aboard. There were six of them left, and they were the first
Monaghan sailors to be rescued. As things turned out, they were also the only
ones. All the rest of *Monaghan*'s crew, roughly 250 men less these six, had
died in the capsized destroyer or had later perished on the Philippine Sea.

Though McCrane and his group didn't know it, they, too, were harassed
by a shark as they were dragged aboard *Brown*. Their rescuers waited until
they got all the castaways onto the ship to share that bit of information with
them. With a solid deck under his feet at last, McCrane shrugged it off. "Well,"
he replied nonchalantly, "he's welcome to the rest of the Spam, anyway."[389]

McCrane's half dozen were the last sailors that *Brown* picked up, and among
the last that anyone rescued. They had drifted seventy-five miles from the site
of *Hull*'s sinking in their three days on the raft, and they were lucky that Halsey
had cast so wide a net. The fleet found very few sailors other than those rescued
by *Brown*, *Swearer*, and above all *Tabberer*. The total was something less than a
hundred men. Nearly ten times that number had gone down with their ships, or
washed overboard, or were crushed or burned to death, or simply lost at sea.[390]

By the next day, December 22, the battered fleet was on its way to Ulithi.
Behind it, the remains of the typhoon, embraced by a cold front north of
Luzon, swirled, sputtered, and died.

PART SIX

The Reckoning

THE FLEET, DISRUPTED AND BATTERED, continued to head toward Ulithi. Some of the ships were in worse shape than others. *Aylwin*, her engine spaces still partly flooded, was down to one generator and steaming at only six knots. Fleet tug *Jicarilla* was less fortunate; with three engines out, she was under tow, an embarrassing reversal of roles. And, of course, three ships weren't there at all.[391]

Given the low fuel levels and the *Farraguts*' stability problems, perhaps the losses were light, in a relative sense. But in absolute terms they were severe. In the Battle off Samar, Taffy 3 had lost five ships, only two more than Third Fleet did in the typhoon. During TF 38's strikes of December 14–16, only twenty-seven planes had died in combat; on the eighteenth, the light carrier *Altamaha* lost nearly twice that number all by herself. Fleetwide, the number of destroyed or hopelessly damaged aircraft numbered 146, only one fewer than Spruance's losses at the Battle of Midway and five times more than his combat losses at the Philippine Sea the previous summer. And the ships themselves had received greater or lesser levels of mauling.[392] Destruction on this scale raised difficult questions—questions that, quite correctly, had to be asked. The highest priority, though, was for the fleet to refit.

The bulk of the Fast Carrier Task Force arrived at Ulithi on Christmas Eve. Many of the rescued castaways went straight to the hospital ship *Solace*, where they received a moving Christmas present: as they came aboard, the nurses sang Christmas carols to welcome them. Irving Berlin's recent hit "White Christmas" was on the minds of more than one sailor at the atoll, where the temperatures at night were nearly ninety degrees. But a small welcome was on hand: Chester Nimitz, just promoted to the novel rank of Fleet Admiral, appeared on Christmas Day, bringing with him a fully decked Christmas tree for *New Jersey*'s wardroom.[393]

His trip to Ulithi allowed Nimitz to see for himself the wreckage the typhoon had produced. It was striking. Even the men who'd steamed through the cyclone had trouble comprehending it. When *New Jersey* spotted the heavily battered and nearly unrecognizable *Tabberer* steaming into the atoll, she blinkered a question. "What type of ship are you?"

The query must have seemed condescending. "Destroyer Escort," the smaller vessel curtly replied. "What type are you?"[394]

Tabberer got more recognition when, several days later, Halsey, Mick Carney, and several aides came aboard to pin Navy-Marine Corps medals on Lieutenant Surdam, Bosun Purvis, and others, and to give a furiously blushing Captain Plage a Legion of Merit. The moment was an emotional one. The heroic Surdam, overcome by memories of corpses and wounded, exhausted survivors, burst into tears. Halsey broke the tension by slapping Plage on the back and suggesting that everyone head to the wardroom for a "cup of joe."[395]

By this time, Halsey and his superiors had long since begun the investigation that quite naturally had to follow such a disaster. Admiral King had wasted no time in letting both Nimitz and Halsey know that he wanted an explanation of what had happened on December 18. "When convenient and not to interfere with major current operations," he had written them right after the storm, "I need to know the circumstances which caused operating units of Third Fleet to encounter typhoon which resulted in the loss and crippling of so many combatant ships." Halsey sent back a reply in which he generally blamed poor weather data and the fact that his small boys had been low on fuel. It was a refrain that he and his officers would utter frequently in coming days. He also sent a priority action dispatch to Nimitz on the twenty-first, even before getting the definite word on *Monaghan*. "My 202235 initiates investigation into causes foundering *Hull* and *Spence* as preliminary measure," he told Nimitz. Then he added a circumlocutory sentence that navy communications jargon did nothing to clarify. "Requested if practicable that CincPac initiate ultimate desired administrative measures employing personnel not attached to Task Force 38. Please advise."[396]

Halsey had to have figured that an external investigation was likely, perhaps inevitable, and his request for one seemed designed to show that he welcomed it. But even so, he apparently couldn't bring himself to use the phrase "court of inquiry," the standard means of investigating such matters, employing his wordy euphemism instead. Courts of inquiry were serious affairs. They could cripple or wreck careers. And they often led to full-blown courts-martial.

Nimitz's response to both King and Halsey was to order just such a court of inquiry. He had brought with him Vice Admiral John H. Hoover, who served as Commander Forward Areas, Central Pacific. On the day he arrived in Ulithi, Nimitz wrote a formal letter to Hoover about what the two men had no doubt already discussed on their journey. "A court of inquiry, consisting of yourself as president and of Vice Admiral George D. Murray, U.S. Navy, and Rear Admiral Glenn B. Davis, U.S. Navy," he informed Hoover in official prose, "is hereby ordered to convene on Board the U.S.S. *Cascade* at 10 o'clock a.m. on Tuesday, 26 December 1944." Nimitz was wasting no time. The fleet was here; Halsey and his people were available; recollections were fresh; and Nimitz and King wanted answers. The court, the newly minted fleet admiral ordered, was to inquire specifically into the circumstances surrounding the loss of *Spence*, *Hull*, and *Monaghan*, the extreme damage aboard *Monterey* and *Cowpens*, and the rest of the destruction that Halsey's ships had sustained.

Then came an ominous paragraph. In addition to compiling a factual record, Nimitz directed, "the court will further give its opinion as to whether any offenses have been committed or serious blame incurred, and, in case its opinion be that offenses have [been] committed or serious blame incurred, will specifically recommend that further proceedings be had."[397]

This inquiry, although called a "court," is not a trial as a civilian would understand it. The closest parallel, though an imperfect one, would be a grand jury. A court of inquiry is essentially a fact-finding proceeding, more inquisitorial than adversarial in nature, lacking a true prosecution and defense in the manner of American civil and criminal trials. There were, as yet, no defendants to prosecute. The court might name some parties defendants, but again, from a civilian perspective, this is a misnomer. A better phrase would be "party under investigation," since court of inquiry defendants had no official charges against them. For now there were only three admirals, none of whom reported to Halsey; a judge advocate, whose job it was to get the important facts out in front of the admirals; and whatever records and witnesses the judge advocate brought into the proceeding.

But depending on the court's findings and recommendations, things could take a more serious turn. The fleet had failed to carry out a major combat operation. It had suffered millions of dollars of damage. It had lost three ships outright. And the better part of a thousand men were dead. This sort of thing usually didn't happen unless someone had committed serious errors of judgment.

Nimitz wanted to know if such errors had occurred in this case. And he meant business. Section 734 of the procedural vade mecum *Naval Courts and Boards*, which he explicitly called to Hoover's attention, dealt with how a sailor could become an interested party or a defendant as the investigation progressed. At any time during the inquiry, stipulated this section, if evidence came to light that implicated a party "in such a way that an accusation against him may be implied," the court was to name him a defendant.[398]

Nimitz was formally telling Hoover, then, quite apart from any face-to-face and private conversations they had had, that while CincPac didn't yet know the full story of what had happened, he wanted it; if it led to accusations of wrongdoing, that was fine with him. In fact, given all the death and destruction, he probably even expected it.

The legal consequences were clear. If the court of inquiry made findings of culpability, as Nimitz had empowered it to do, and if Nimitz concurred in those findings, then he would almost certainly convene a full-blown court-martial.

And the leading candidate for that court-martial that Christmas, given his role as Commander, Third Fleet, was none other than William F. Halsey.

The court met, as ordered, the morning after Christmas, taking over the wardroom of the destroyer tender *Cascade*. The first hour was spent over paperwork, the officiants reading the orders from Nimitz, administering oaths to each other, deciding on the order of witnesses, and introducing yeomen and others who would serve as reporters and helpers. The court then notified Jim Marks that, in light of what was already commonly known (especially the glaring fact that he had lost his ship), he was an official defendant. Preston Mercer, whose squadron had included *Hull* and *Monaghan*, was not a defendant but an interested party, which was a notch down the ladder of official suspicion. None of this was surprising; officers who lost ships routinely faced inquiries, and Mercer and Marks were both present, which showed that they had received prior warning. Marks also had counsel present in the person of Captain Ira H. Nunn. In addition to commanding a destroyer squadron in the Fast Carrier Task Force—his performance at Leyte Gulf had won him the Navy Cross—Nunn was a Harvard Law School as well as a Naval Academy alumnus, and he would later serve as the navy's judge advocate general. For now, nothing was said of Admiral Halsey's status, though that might at any time change. Once these preliminaries were out of the way, the judge advocate got the investigation on its way.[399]

Just as a court of inquiry is markedly different from civilian proceedings, so, too, the office of judge advocate is an odd one from the civilian perspective. American courts are generally adversarial. The basic premise in their structure is that the truth is best discovered by having two parties—a plaintiff or prosecutor on one hand, a defendant on the other—engage in judicial combat. The judge or judges, meanwhile, serve as neutral arbiters, making sure the parties play by the rules, explaining what those rules mean, and in some cases deciding the outcome. Courts of inquiry bear some resemblance to this process, but on the whole they are inquisitorial, not adversarial. In an inquisitorial system, the court plays a much more active role in finding and questioning witnesses, not to mention digging up evidence. The office of judge advocate bears the imprint of this system. The officer who serves in that role is not only the court reporter and custodian of the evidence, but chief inquisitor as well. Even though the proceeding in *Cascade*'s wardroom was a fact-finding exercise, the judge advocate would be expected to make sure that all of the facts—especially the damning ones—came to the court's attention.[400]

Herbert K. Gates, the four-striper whom Nimitz had tapped to serve as judge advocate, specialized not in law but in mechanical and marine engineering. He was undoubtedly more comfortable as *Cascade*'s skipper than as an inquisitor, but this was to be a fact-finding proceeding, and rules of procedure and evidence were few when compared to a full-blown trial. Gates would have a long leash, and, unfettered by procedural red tape, he was free to bring in all sorts of information.[401]

Gates's first concern, and that of the admirals who constituted the court proper, was to hear from the fleet's senior commanders and their staffs before they departed Ulithi. Since the carriers had had to scrub the second round of air strikes, the task force would likely need to move out as soon as it could. The court thus wanted to hear from the brass while it was able to. It especially wanted to hear how a fleet that had a number of aerological officers attached to it had managed to steam straight into a typhoon, since one of their jobs was to prevent just such an occurrence.[402]

The first witness, then, was Rear Admiral Mick Carney, who'd been Halsey's chief of staff for the past year and a half. Carney, an aloof professional accomplished in the arts of antisubmarine warfare, had been yanked off the cruiser he had commanded to replace Miles Browning, a volatile, difficult officer. Disappointed at first, and believing Halsey's staff to be perhaps too enamored of their leader, by late 1944 Carney himself had become a Halsey convert. His job now was to give the court his commander's perspective on what had happened and on what had gone wrong.[403]

When Carney entered the wardroom and took his seat, Captain Gates began the ritual that he would eventually repeat for more than fifty other witnesses during the following week. "State your name, rank, and present station," he said formally.

"Robert B. Carney," the witness replied dutifully. "Rear admiral, U.S. Navy, chief of staff to Admiral Halsey, Commander Third Fleet, flag now being in U.S.S. *New Jersey*."

Then Gates got down to business, asking Carney to recount the fleet's movements of the seventeenth and eighteenth, along with "such events as you consider pertinent."

Carney spent some time discussing what had happened during the typhoon, mentioning among other things that some of the destroyers were down to a 15 percent fuel supply. Gates pursued this. "Was that a normal amount of fuel oil for destroyers to have before replenishing oil?" he asked.

"No," Carney answered. "The operations were extensive by the necessity for high speed run ins initially on the night of the 13th and by three consecutive days of carrier strikes." No doubt fleet records would back Carney up, but he undoubtedly welcomed the chance to tell the court that Halsey didn't normally play games with fuel levels. "The obligation of Task Force 38 was a heavy one," he added for good measure, "and those operations did not permit interim fueling or topping off."[404]

Because this was a fact-finding process, Nunn's cross-examination didn't resemble that of a regular criminal trial. In the latter proceeding, cross tends to focus on what the witness said during direct examination, to expose contradictions and weaknesses in his statements. Usually it is limited to issues that the witness discussed on direct. Here, however, defendants had much more latitude, and Marks and Nunn used it, as they would throughout the inquiry. Their first question was to show that Marks was simply doing his best to do his superiors' bidding. "What orders were given to the fueling groups," they began, "after the generalized fueling was abandoned on December 17th due to bad weather?"

"That would not be a matter for Commander Third Fleet to concern himself with," Carney responded. "The rendezvous was given to the force and group commanders and they would issue their own orders to meet that rendezvous." As an attempt to shield Halsey, the answer was only partly successful. The intermediate commanders, as he observed, had the task of getting their ships, units, and groups to the rendezvous, but Halsey was the one who set the time and place of that rendezvous.

Next Marks tried implicating the aerologists. "Admiral," Nunn asked, "did local observations prove helpful in determining the path of the storm?"

Carney's answer was perhaps nonresponsive. "It was not until the forenoon of the 18th," he said, "that we were able to determine the position, course and speed of the storm."

Marks, still trying to get an answer to his original question, shifted ground slightly. "Was that determination by local observation?"

"Yes." A noncommittal answer; Carney didn't state whether those observations were made by aerologists or others.

This evasion was subtle and probably unconscious, though with more rigorous questioning Marks probably could have pinned Carney down. But it wasn't to be. This was the end of the cross-examination, and the court dismissed the admiral. His testimony, however, had revealed a good bit about fleet movements and operations. Even weather information could be useful to Japanese forces. There was, too, a hint that some serious blame might attach to someone before the inquiry came to an end. So, for one or another of these reasons, the court decided after Carney's departure to brand the proceedings as secret.[405]

The court of inquiry would run for more than a week, eight days in all. But the highest-profile witnesses testified early on, and one of them, George Kosco, appeared before the panel of admirals on the first afternoon.

At Gates's prompting, Halsey's aerographer recounted a long story of his efforts to forecast the weather during the days after the Luzon air strikes. One of the most interesting things that came out of this narrative was how heavily Kosco had relied not on his own observations or those of others in the task force, but on reports from distant stations and weather centrals. "The first indication that I had that things were not normal in the area," he noted, "was the fact that on the morning of the 16th of December I received a routine coded weather report from Ulithi saying that the wind was west force 4, and that they had heavy rain and also a report that the wind from Guam was from east Southeast force 4, which would be an ideal situation for a tropical storm to form."

Kosco also premised his forecasts on historical data, another standard aerologist's tool. "There is only one typhoon normally for December," he asserted. "According to the record for the last fifty years, 75 percent of these storms pass off to the Northeast and about 25 percent pass off into the Philippines." To put this another way, Kosco had been playing the historical odds. All this was interesting, and even useful, but it suggested that the commander had placed a lot of faith in the work of others.

The court listened as Kosco described how he puzzled over the reports and deliberated with other fleet aerologists about whether, and where, a storm center might exist. During his narrative—one of the longest during the inquiry—Kosco sometimes sounded irresolute, vague, and uncertain in comparison to other witnesses. The testimony gives the impression of a nervous officer, competent but under stress from the knowledge that more than seven hundred fellow sailors had died in a storm and the navy wanted to know why, and at that moment it was asking him. "We listened to the TBS and we heard somebody saying it might be a good idea to go south. . . . About 2:30 in the morning I waked up and sort of thought something was wrong. . . . About 4:20 in the morning I took over the watch. No, it was before that when I took over the watch. . . . During the height of the storm a search plane out of Leyte—I am not certain Leyte, but I was told Leyte—came up to the fleet formation. . . . I have not made an exhaustive study of this typhoon, because I would have to get a lot of records from places like Guam, Leyte, and Ulithi. They are not available on board the flagship."[406]

One of the more confusing set of statements concerned the matter of when Kosco realized that he was dealing with a full-fledged typhoon. At one point, when discussing conditions on the morning of the eighteenth, he noted that "about 8 or 9 o'clock it became rather apparent it was not an ordinary tropical storm, but was starting to get into typhoon conditions." But several minutes later he suggested otherwise. "About 1300 on the 18th we sent out a typhoon warning," he stated. "Until that time we thought we were dealing with a tropical storm." He then tried to clarify things, to little avail. "By this report, I don't mean that we didn't know about it before 1300, but by 1300 it became apparent that the outside world and weather centrals should know that this intense storm was in this location."[407]

Clearly Kosco was nervous about being in the spotlight of an important proceeding, as most people would be. There had been little time for anyone to prepare testimony or to explain to witnesses what to expect. After his long, sometimes technical account, Kosco abruptly closed. "On the afternoon of the 17th planes from carriers and search planes flew over the area and reported bad weather, but found nothing to be greatly excited about," he stated. "As a matter of fact, maybe they should have been, and maybe they would have given us more advanced information. That's all I have."

But the court had more for Kosco. "Do you consider your sources of information for prophesying weather adequate?" an admiral asked him.

"Under normal conditions, yes," replied Kosco, keeping his wits. "Under abnormal conditions, I would say they fell short, and the condition in question was a very abnormal one." This last point was one he'd maintained throughout his narrative.

Given the aerologist's statements on when he'd known he was facing a typhoon, the court remained uncertain as to the timing of this fact, so it further pursued that line of questioning. "You first diagnosed this as a typhoon at about 1300 on the 18th?"

"No, about 8 o'clock on the morning of the 18th," Kosco answered. "But we were fighting the typhoon and before I sent a message to the other weather centrals, it was about 1300, although I had sent a message at 8:30, saying it was increasing in intensity, and sent a weather report to interested parties in the Southwest Pacific and the Philippines."

This answer confused things more than ever. The aggregate of Kosco's statements suggested that he had at least suspected the existence of a typhoon at eight in the morning but that he did not identify it as such in a communication until five hours later, but this interpretation is debatable. For whatever reason, the court decided not to badger him about it. That was the last question it put to him—for the time being. Kosco, no doubt to his great relief, stood and walked out of the wardroom.

It was bad luck, perhaps, that the witness who followed Kosco was Captain Stuart H. Ingersoll of *Monterey*, which had taken one of the worst maulings. Gates had had almost no time to conduct an investigation, and the court was bringing in people as it found them available. It wasn't yet done with Halsey and his staff, but now Ingersoll was here, and for a time the focus shifted from the typhoon's prediction to the damage that it had caused. Still, to Kosco's misfortune, the testimony turned to weather prediction as Nunn started questioning Ingersoll. "Do you have an aerologist on board?" he asked.

"I do, yes, sir," affirmed Ingersoll.

"Did he forecast the approach of the storm?"

"In my opinion, not very accurately," Ingersoll answered bluntly. "In his opinion, he did."[408]

As far as it went, this statement could be taken as either a partial justification of Kosco, in that he wasn't the only weatherman the typhoon had baffled, or a rather damning indictment of the fleet aerologists as a group. Unfortunately for Kosco, Ingersoll hadn't yet finished. These few weather questions constituted the whole of Nunn's cross, but after that Mercer spoke up.

"When did you appreciate that you were in a typhoon," he asked Ingersoll, "or that one was imminent?"

"We knew that a typhoon was somewhere around our area on the 17th," Ingersoll answered. This, even with an aerologist whom he thought to have done a bad job. Kosco hadn't realized he was dealing with a typhoon until the following day. "But the plot on the storm was certainly not very good," the witness continued. "I think even the aerologists are still in disagreement."[409]

While these last statements shifted the heat from Kosco, they redistributed it among the fleet meteorologists. The measures McCain and others had worked out to protect the task force from Tokkō attacks had been quite successful. If the aerologists had been able to let Halsey know that a typhoon was coming at him, might he have risked refueling closer to Philippine shores, within land-based air range, in order to have calmer seas?

The next several witnesses consisted of more skippers, squadron commanders, and captains and flag officers in charge of task units and groups. Gates asked many of them about the reports of their own aerologists, most of whom were conspicuously missing from the witness list. At face value, the line officers' consensus was, in effect, that Kosco's performance was typical for the fleet's weathermen. Captain George H. DeBaun of the carrier *Cowpens*, which had suffered damage similar to *Monterey*'s, likewise mirrored Ingersoll's statements. When Gates asked if the ship's aerologist had predicted the tempest, DeBaun answered no. "On the day before, he said that the disturbance was a very local one, very small area, and definitely did not consider it a typhoon," the captain explained. "About 7 o'clock on the morning of the 18th I again questioned him and he still was doubtful that it was a typhoon. He said it might possibly be a small one." Of course, such a thing is akin to a small atomic bomb, given a tropical cyclone's energy release.

But by the time of that prediction, DeBaun said in answer to questions from the court itself, it was clear to him, if not to the aerologist, what was coming. "The weather followed the book description of a typhoon," he declared. "We had swells, increasing winds, barometer dropped, all that. A very good example of what is written in Knight's *Seamanship*." Knight's was, and is, a mariner's bible. "There was no trouble realizing there was a typhoon," he continued, his criticism of his aerologist implicit in his blunt statement. "This was all evident to me from 8 o'clock in the morning."[410]

The following day, after Henry Plage briefly recounted *Tabberer*'s rescue operations, Captain Robert W. Bockius of the jeep carrier *Cape Esperance* echoed DeBaun. "During the storm I had the aerologist on the bridge and asked him when should this lighten up," he narrated. "He gave me to believe shortly or around noon. The weather of the day before was the result of passing through the cold front and conditions did not look so bad with cirrus clouds in the skies" — or so the forecaster thought. "Continued falling of the barometer," Bockius wryly observed, "was a surprise to the aerologist on its happening."[411]

Bockius's narrative was a fairly long one, and perhaps Gates overlooked this part of it. On the other hand, he may have heard it and wanted to emphasize it for the court's benefit. At any rate, as soon as Bockius had concluded, the judge advocate's first question was "Do you have an aerologist attached to your ship?" as if Bockius hadn't just been discussing him.

"Yes," Bockius affirmed for the record.

"Did you receive any warning at the time of the storm?" Gates continued.

"He gave prognostications in the regular manner at 1700 or 1800 of the 17th," Bockius reported. "He thought that there was a storm brewing but not of a proportion to worry us at all. He thought maximum winds in that storm would be 55 to 60 knots, which we had already encountered in a previous typhoon. He thought the storm would peter out around noon." The captain charitably refrained from adding the natural follow-up statement that must have been in every listener's mind: *He was wrong.* On the contrary, Bockius excused what had happened. "I can say," he pointed out to the court, "that he had difficulty on account of atmospheric conditions in getting his reports."[412] Despite this concession, the weight of his and others' testimony so far was that the aerologists, whatever the reason, had not done a good job.

Another matter that Gates brought before the admirals was the whole issue of ballasting. When Bockius was done, the judge advocate called Jasper Acuff, the commander of the oiler task group. "Did you make any recommendations or suggestions to the Commanding Officer of the *Aylwin* concerning the handling of ballast of his ship which might be of interest to the court?" he asked the captain.

"No," replied Acuff. "I did make certain recommendations to ships the night before that they partially ballast and make the fueling the next day, if still rough, in two parts in order that they might handle better alongside," he elaborated. Then he added, somewhat defensively, "The ships in my group were not low in fuel." Still, two of the ships that went down had been his.[413]

Captain Mercer, perhaps sensing weakness, asked a very pointed question of his superior officer. "Have you ever served in destroyers?"

"No," Acuff said shortly. That meant that he had no firsthand experience of destroyer handling. He had no way to judge how much buffeting they could take, whether fueled or not.[414]

"The destroyers *Hull*, *Monaghan*, and *Spence* were in your task group," one admiral stated. It wasn't a question.

"*Monaghan* and *Hull* were attached to my task group," Acuff confirmed, naming the two *Farragut*-class victims. "The *Spence*," he corrected, "had been left behind the night of the 17th."

"Did you receive any reports of circumstances of the loss of these vessels?"

"No, sir," Acuff responded.

"How do you account for that? They were in your task group."

"I cannot account for it," Acuff conceded, "unless visibility conditions were so bad that nobody knew of their loss."

"I mean afterwards, not at the time they were lost."

Acuff replied vaguely that he had had to ask Halsey for information on *Monaghan*, and that he had overheard radio traffic inquiring about *Spence*.

"Have you any idea," one of the court members asked, "as to why these destroyers sank?"

"No, sir," Acuff stated. "Unless they failed to ballast."[415]

The court may have faulted Acuff for not knowing whether the destroyers had ballasted, but nobody knew much about their final minutes. Even the survivors only had partial pictures. Commander Marks could tell a lot of *Hull*'s story, but most of the officers from the other two ships were gone. Reconstructing the three disasters and finding common threads would be a difficult business. To accomplish it, the court called a number of witnesses who were under no shadow at all. One of these was Captain William T. Kenny, commander of Destroyer Division 104.

Spence hadn't been part of DesDiv 104, but she had steamed in company with her sister ship *Hickox*, in which Kenny had his flag. *Hickox*'s performance, then, might offer some clues to *Spence*'s demise. In response to Gates's prompting, Kenny described what had happened before and during the storm, recounting a string of somber, worsening messages he had gotten and overheard from the stricken destroyer. "'Fuel on hand as of 0800 this morning, 15 percent,'" he quoted. "'Motor whaleboat carried away. One depth charge over side.' 1117, from *Spence* to Commander Task Unit 30.8.4, 'My last position 7,000 yards north of Task Unit 30.8.4. Course 220, formation speed.'" Kenny stopped reading. "That's all, sir."

Nunn then went into a line of questions, which Mercer continued, about *Hickox*'s ballasting. Kenny testified that the night of the seventeenth, the task unit commander had ordered *Hickox* and *Spence* to ballast to 50 percent of their capacity, but that *Hickox* had gone further and ballasted to 100 percent. Even so, not all fuel tanks were equipped to handle salt water; even a ship with 100 percent ballast might still have only 50 percent of its total liquid capacity aboard if it was low on fuel, as *Spence* had been. *Spence*, presumably half ballasted, had sunk; *Hickox* had not.

The court took an obvious interest in the subject of ballasting. "You had about half of your total supply of liquids?"

"That's right," answered Kenny.

"And you rolled 70 degrees?"

"Yes, sir." An extreme roll in any case, and especially for a ballasted vessel.

"Did you feel at any time that the ship was going to capsize?"

Kenny's response was a delicious understatement. "There were approximately two occasions when the issue was in doubt."

"If you had been ballasted to only 50 percent in accordance with instructions, do you feel that perhaps you would have gone over further?" Seventy degrees was already close to the edge; another twenty and *Hickox* would have been lying full on her side in the water. By "gone over further" the admiral essentially meant "capsized." Kenny was no doubt aware of this. "It is quite possible," he responded, but he stopped short of committing himself.[416]

Ballasting, like the aerological issue, would remain a concern of the court for the rest of the inquiry, and after Kenny had concluded, it summoned two more skippers for questioning on both of these subjects. One of them, Captain

Michael Kernodle of the carrier *San Jacinto*, described his ship's damage in short, clipped sentences. Then Gates brought him around to the subject of weather prediction. "Does your vessel have an aerologist assigned to it?" he asked in the usual manner.

"Yes."

"Was he able to predict the storm that you encountered?"

"Yes." Another strike against Kosco.

"Did you receive any warnings from any outside sources as to the approach of the storm?"

"Yes."

This was interesting. Most of the testimony so far, including that of the fleet aerologists, suggested that those reports had been rather deficient. Kernodle's next comments hurt Kosco further. "I received warnings continuously for 24 hours before I got into the storm, from my aerographer, from the action of the ship, and condition of the sea," he explained. "I was fully aware of the storm, and that it was going to be severe. In addition to that, I also heard reports from other vessels who were in desperate trouble, and I was not." His final sentence was especially damning. "I had all the warnings one could possibly have."[417]

All of these sources, his own observations and the local reports, were the same ones available to every fleet weatherman and to Halsey himself. The ramifications were self-evident, and Gates didn't pursue things. Neither did he put Kernodle on the spot by asking why he hadn't brought his suspicions of danger to the attention of higher authority. Instead he dismissed Kernodle, who perhaps, lacking the court's perspective, didn't realize that he had just dodged a bullet. Gates now had his attention fixed on calling the next witness: Captain Mercer, the interested party whose command included *Hull* and *Monaghan*.

The judge advocate let Mercer begin with a very long account of what had happened. The narrative provided a lot of helpful detail and not much controversy, although the captain did suggest that he'd seen something bad coming, if not in this typhoon, then at some point. "I would like to say a little about the stability characteristics of these ships," he ventured at one point. "When in the Navy Yard recently, there was the usual effort by various people to add lockers and various items topside, which I resisted vigorously."

Mercer had known of the problems the *Farragut*s had. "All commanding officers and men of the squadron who have been in the ships any length of time were very much aware of the lack of stability of these ships."[418]

So much for the vessels themselves; what about their skippers? Gates asked as much. "Will you please compare the experience, capabilities as observed by you of the commanding officers of the *Hull* and *Monaghan*, with the remaining commanding officers of your squadron?" he asked carefully. It was an ugly thing to have to consider the possible culpability of captains who had died with their crews, but Gates had to do it. Nimitz had ordered it. It was routine.

"The commanding officer of the *Monaghan* was in the squadron for such a very short time that I had practically no opportunity to make a sound estimate," answered Mercer with equal care. "He handled his ship well in formation, kept her on station in the screen, but that was the limit of my opportunity to observe him."

Mercer gave Marks similar treatment. "The commanding officer of the *Hull* has been separated from his squadron a great deal," he explained. "Likewise, when she was with us for a very short time, his ship was handled well, and I have no criticism whatever of his ability."

Gates had asked Mercer to compare those commanders with the other ones in his squadron. Now he asked another and broader question. "How does the service experience of the commanding officers of your squadron compare with that of the commanding officers of other squadrons?"

Here Mercer also had some protection. "The commanding officers of the ships of my squadron are the most junior in destroyers, being of the Naval Academy class of 1938," he pointed out. Neither he nor his captains could fairly be blamed for the fact that wartime required the rapid promotion of less-experienced officers. A member of the court wanted to make sure the record emphasized this. "I gather from your answer," he broke in, "that these destroyer commanders of the class of 1938 are the junior ones in the fleet. Is that correct?"

"That's right, sir," said Mercer. It was some degree of exoneration for Marks as well as for two spectral destroyer commanders who could no longer speak for themselves. Although, in a sense, Andrea and Garrett were on trial by a court beyond whose grasp they had traveled forever, the navy could still reach their reputations. But blaming the dead would be wrong, even dishonorable, if the evidence to justify such an action was lacking. And Marks, of course, very much alive, could fight back. On this somber note, the court adjourned for the day.[419]

The following morning—the 28th of December, the third day of the inquiry—attention returned to the living, particularly some more of the senior admirals and their staff. Once again, the questions could sometimes be hard. "Do you consider that your task group had ample information and warning concerning the storm of 18 December 1944?" Gates asked Captain John B. Moss, chief of staff to Rear Admiral Alfred E. Montgomery, whose task group included *Monterey*.[420]

"Yes, sir," Moss replied briefly.

Gates wanted more than this. "Did you at all times have a clear picture of the nature and movement of that storm?"

"Well," Moss replied, "we had available all information that was put out by the weather central and the opinion of the aerologist on the *Yorktown*. Both sources of information turned out to have shown the center of the storm where it actually was. In other words, the estimates were pretty accurate."

By now it was clear to those who had heard all of the testimony that the witnesses disagreed about whether there was adequate warning of the typhoon, and Gates wanted to investigate further. After prompting Moss to discuss damage to task group vessels, the judge advocate returned to this point. "What was your estimate of the location, course, and speed of the storm prior to the 18th?" he asked.

"The original estimate of the course and speed of the storm was in a northwesterly direction at a speed of 12 knots," Moss tried to explain. "It was evident after observing the barometer and force and direction of the wind that the storm center was not moving at this estimated speed."

"If you realized this at the time," prodded Gates, "did you make your ideas known to higher authorities?"

"No, sir," Moss said. This was an uncomfortable answer to give when someone asks an officer if he had bothered to bring an important matter to the attention of his superiors. "It was apparent from the changes in rendezvous that the location of the center, course, and speed of the storm was not definitely fixed in everyone's mind," he rambled, apparently contradicting his earlier words. "The fact that the rendezvous was changed," he continued, "suggested that Commander Third Fleet had later and better information than was available to Commander Task Group 38.1." It was the best Moss could do, and it wasn't too bad, at that.[421]

The next few witnesses did better. One was Frederick C. Sherman, commander of Task Group 38.3. Together with 38.2's Gerald F. Bogan, who followed him, Ted Sherman was among the most experienced mariners to be found in Third Fleet. That made him one of the most valuable witnesses, and without waiting for Gates to get started, the court itself began firing questions at him. "Did you have timely warning or know that a severe storm was approaching?"

"I wouldn't say that I did, no," replied Sherman. "The aerologist on my staff kept reporting a typhoon 500 miles to the northeast. That was on the 17th." But Sherman himself hadn't agreed with that assessment. "I put it to the southeast and much closer than 500 miles. Apparently this typhoon developed in that direction very rapidly and came upon the task force without very much warning."

A few minutes later, perhaps nudged by Moss's mention of the three successive rendezvous that Halsey had designated for fueling, the court brought them up. "In view of the fueling rendezvous set for the morning of the 18th, did you feel that the storm would strike your task group?"

"I was not particularly happy over the last rendezvous."

"Did you make your ideas known to higher authority?"

"No, sir." Perhaps this was easier to admit for an admiral than for a captain, given his greater experience and familiarity with what McCain and Halsey needed to know. On the other hand, maybe these considerations contributed to his failure to communicate his views rather than mitigating it. McCain and Halsey were, after all, presumably more available to task group commanders. But there was no point in belaboring matters. Sherman wasn't on trial. "Are there any observations that you'd like to make on this storm to assist the board in evaluating the proposition?" It was the court's routine final question, and most of the previous witnesses had had nothing to add. Sherman was different.

"Without meaning any particular criticism of our present-day aerologists," he remarked, "I'm inclined to think that they have been brought up
to depend on a lot of readings they get from other stations." Despite his attempt to be diplomatic, it was a strong comment, and the next ones were
even more so. "I think they are much weaker than older officers in judging
the weather by what they actually see. Whether anything can be done along
these lines to either encourage or instruct them to watch weather that is
then existing without waiting for reports from Pearl Harbor or other stations, I don't know. I think they should be taught to judge the weather by
what they actually see."[422]

Bogan agreed with Sherman and Moss on one notable point. "In view of
the fueling rendezvous finally set for the morning of the 18th," the court
asked him, "did you feel that the storm would strike your task group?"

Bogan replied that while he hadn't believed that he had solid enough information to pinpoint the typhoon precisely, he knew enough, in light of the
pattern of northwest curvature, to be worried. "I felt that any rendezvous not
further south was one in which we could be overtaken by the storm."

"Did you make your ideas known to higher authority?" asked the court.

This time Bogan's answer differed from those of the others. "Yes, sir."

This was a new development. "Please tell the court what it was."

"I sent a signal to Commander Task Force 38, information Commander
Third Fleet," answered Bogan, "stating that the *Lexington* weather estimate
and the Pearl Harbor just received indicated that improved conditions would
be found further to the southward." That had been, he said, on the seventeenth: a message to McCain and Halsey.

With that Gates summoned McCain himself. During his testimony, the
commander of the Fast Carrier Task Force was brief and often noncommittal, although willing to acknowledge the value of hindsight. When his fellow
admirals asked what his thoughts on the seventeenth had been, he was forthright. "I did not appreciate at that time the oncoming speed of the gathering
storm," he confessed. "Having some experience with disturbances in this area
I was at that time of the opinion that a movement of 100 or 200 miles would
perhaps put us in the clear." It hadn't, a fact that went without saying, but Mc-
Cain did mention something that few others had. "We had, of course, the
pressure of a commitment to strike Luzon," he reminded the court, "which I

believe was uppermost in my mind and I'm sure uppermost in the minds of my staff." In light of such a commitment, McCain needed not add, the fleet had had to take a certain amount of risk. One of the main issues for the court was how much of it had been acceptable.

With this in the record, the court's examination continued. "Was the rendezvous finally set for 0700 on the 18th of December satisfactory to you?" one of the admirals asked.

"At that time it was," answered McCain.

"I understand that in shifting these rendezvous, you were not consulted," someone—possibly Hoover—observed.

"I was not consulted at the time," McCain agreed. This likely didn't surprise anyone.

Then came one of the stock questions. "Have you anything to say about the adequacy of the weather service of the fleet?"

The wizened admiral invoked hindsight again. "Plenty to say after the fact." But he didn't elaborate other than to state that he agreed with the views that Halsey had already expressed in a fleet dispatch, which had included orders for units to investigate bad weather more thoroughly.

"There has been testimony that indications were plain to certain commanders that the storm was approaching and increasing in violence during the 17th and that perhaps aerographers in the fleet did not estimate on local conditions sufficiently, but relied mostly on reports from outside stations," one of the board members informed McCain. "What is your opinion of this?" It was a thorny question. McCain was Halsey's top officer, an experienced sailor, and he had just testified that at the time of the storm he had misjudged its speed; he'd implied, further, that at the time he'd found no fault with weather reports. Now the court was confronting him with the fact that other commanders had seen more clearly than he what was coming. Because testimony was secret, McCain might not have known of this until the court told him. Taken by surprise, he gave a brief, noncommittal answer. "I have no opinion on that." It was a down note, but the court let it go, and after another routine question or two, it finished with him.[423]

The court next heard briefly from one of McCain's staff people, who helped enlighten it on the fleet's movements as the rendezvous shifted. Then it moved on to the next witness, who duly entered the wardroom and took his place.

"State your name, rank, and present station," intoned Gates, just as he always did.

The witness spoke up. "William F. Halsey, admiral, U.S. Navy, Commander Third Fleet, U.S. Pacific Fleet."

"Admiral," one of the court members began, cutting to the heart of things, "did you consider that you had timely warning or did you know that a severe storm was approaching around the 16th and 17th of December?"

The response was classic Halsey. "I did not have timely warning," the crusty admiral said. "I'll put it another way. I had no warning."

Then the court sprang the same information on Halsey that it had on McCain. "There has been testimony from other commanders that the local conditions indicated the approach of the storm. Was this evident to you?"

Unlike McCain, Halsey showed no signs of being thrown off balance. "The local conditions commencing on the 17th were very bad," he admitted. "So bad that I ordered the destroyers that were alongside tankers and heavy ships to clear." In this way he suggested that he hadn't been napping. "A disturbance was indicated, but whether it was a severe storm or merely a local disturbance, there was no way of determining. We still thought"—a casual switch to a corporate plural, a natural reference to himself and his staff—"it was a storm that had curved away to the northward and eastward and we were determined to get away from it."

Halsey hadn't quite answered the question. In a sense he'd almost dismissed it as irrelevant. Rather than stating whether he'd seen the typhoon coming, as he now learned other commanders claimed to have done, he instead denied that such a fact could have been determined. But that, again, was like Halsey. Both that December and thereafter, the Bull tended to shade some of the more important facts about what had happened off the Philippines.[424]

"When fueling had to be stopped on the 17th of December due to increasing bad weather," one of the court members wanted to know, "what were your considerations?"

This was a softball. "The general picture was sour," said Halsey. "I had numerous destroyers that were very short of fuel on board. I was under obligation to make a strike on Luzon, but of course a strike could not be made until the fleet was fueled. I was also obligated to avoid by that time what I considered a storm the magnitude of which I did not know."

This is where a good, adversarial cross-examination could have clarified matters, for cross-examinations are only partly designed to catch witnesses in lies. They can also help to clarify witnesses' thoughts as well as their language. Halsey had been very busy, and he had likely had little time to reflect on what he would say in court. His comments, like those of the other witnesses, were largely extemporaneous, and, as such, not perfectly clear. If he hadn't known the storm's magnitude, for instance, then why did he feel the need to jeopardize combat operations to avoid it? On the other hand, if he did have reason to fear that he was running into a typhoon, why did he begin his testimony by denying that he had had any warning? This mystery remained unsolved, because the fleet commander then resumed his criticism of the weather facilities.

"I got but one report, as I remember, of a possible disturbance, and that came from the *Chandeleur*, and it was obtained by one of her planes," he continued. "The report was some 12 to 14 hours late in arriving, due to being a mere routine report and did not agree with aerologist's position, of what he termed at that time, a tropical disturbance."

"At what time did the storm considerations begin to govern the disposition and movement of the fleet," asked an admiral, who then added rather cuttingly, "if at all?"

"On the forenoon of the 18th it was very definitely apparent that we were very close to a violent disturbance of some kind, which I believed was a typhoon," Halsey said easily. He gave no indication that his assessment of the storm as a typhoon rested on the judgment of Kosco, any other aerologist, or anyone else but himself. "We were completely cornered and in the dangerous semicircle. The consideration then was to get out of the dangerous semicircle and get to a position where our destroyers could be fueled."

Under prompting, Halsey then led the court through his course and rendezvous changes, explaining his rationale for them and using the plural rather than the singular, though whom he intended to include by this wording—his staff, McCain, or the fleet as a whole—shifted as he went. "To my recollection we took a generally westerly course up to midnight," he described. "We had decided that we would go to the southward and westward for a fueling rendezvous. We later changed that to the northward and westward so that we would be in a better position to strike Luzon on time." He then reemphasized an earlier point that both he and McCain had made.

"That thought of striking Luzon was uppermost in our minds right up to the last minute."

While the board questioning Halsey was by no means composed of yes-men, the questions it put to Halsey were rather sympathetic to him. "What seemed to be wrong with the weather service in this case?" one of the admirals asked, inviting Halsey to discuss others' failings.

Halsey took the offered opportunity. "It was nonexistent," he said flatly. "That's the only way I can express it. After the horse was out of the stable we established a system so that such a thing couldn't happen again. Heretofore we had always received reports. This time there was only one report of a disturbance that came in." Again he mentioned the tardy communication from *Chandeleur*, probably not realizing that he, too, was revealing to the court how heavily the fleet had relied on reports and not direct observations. "It is the first time in the four months that I've been operating in this area that I haven't had reports to enable me to track a storm," he declared.

"You have stated that you felt the storm was curving to the northeast. Do you know the basis upon which this idea was formed?"

"I am no weather expert," Halsey disclaimed. He then proceeded, incongruously, to give his fellow admirals a lesson in the weather patterns over the western Pacific at the time of the storm, stressing that cyclones over the Philippine Sea tended to curve north and east. "There have been numerous storms during the four months that I have been operating in this area," he observed, "and without exception they have followed this general rule. In addition," he continued, "my aerologist informed me that in a study of past typhoons during the month of December, three out of four curved to the northward and eastward."

A few more questions ensued, mainly about subjects that Halsey had already covered. Halsey did talk briefly about destroyer stability—"I believe that some time before we got into the worst of this storm we sent out a general signal advising everybody to ballast down," he testified—and then he was almost finished. But just before he withdrew from the wardroom, Halsey told the court that he was an interested party. Technically he probably lacked the authority to give himself that designation, although he did have the right to ask the court to do it. But the court was agreeable, and it granted the fleet commander's request to be represented by counsel in his absence. With that, Halsey left.[425]

His departure portended a change of direction for the inquiry. The same day Halsey testified, Nimitz returned to Ulithi after a brief trip to see Douglas MacArthur. Halsey was waiting for Nimitz with a request. He wanted permission to make a long-deferred strike into the South China Sea in search of the Japanese survivors of the Leyte Gulf engagement. The kamikaze and the typhoon had made him wait long enough. Nimitz, who had firmly denied Halsey permission to head east of the Philippines, now gave his approval, but it was conditional. Task Force 38 had to finish its job in Luzon, safeguarding MacArthur's landings on Lingayen first.[426]

That meant another round of strikes on the Philippines, the one that the typhoon had delayed, and Halsey was anxious to get them out of the way. The fleet had put right much of its damage, and two days after facing his fellow admirals across the green table, Halsey and his ships steamed out of Ulithi.[427]

In the meantime, the court fit in a few more Third Fleet officers before their ships sortied. After Halsey concluded his testimony, the rest of the day was taken up mostly with skippers who described their commands' storm damage, along with an expert from Service Squadron Ten who discussed the technical aspects of destroyer stability characteristics and ballasting instructions.[428] This latter officer, Commander James M. Farrin, Jr., was an expert in naval hull construction. After hearing a lengthy review of the various forces that kept destroyer hulls afloat in rough weather, the admirals put to him one simple question. "Can you offer an opinion to the court as to what might have caused the loss of the three vessels in question?"

"In my opinion," Farrin stated, "the capsizing of these vessels was due to insufficient dynamic stability to absorb the combined effects of wind and sea." He had already observed that the *Farragut* class had less dynamic stability than the *Fletcher*s; here he observed that, in the case of the *Fletcher*-class *Spence*, failure to ballast likely played a big role in her sinking. "In the case of the *Hull* and the *Monaghan*, with their dynamic stability appreciably less than the *Spence*," he continued, "momentary synchronization of the encountered waves with the natural period of the ship," that is, its rhythm of rolling, determined by a number of variables, "would cause the amplitude of roll to build up quite rapidly." In other words, for *Hull* and *Monaghan*, Farrin believed that the chief culprit was the sea with its titanic waves, and not the wind.[429]

All of this was interesting and useful, but it was largely theoretical. On the following day, with the fleet preparing to weigh anchors, the court would change direction sharply. It would begin hearing from the men for whom destroyer stability had become more than a theory: the survivors of the three lost ships.

The fourth day began with the court adjourning to *Cascade*'s pilothouse, large and relatively calm while the ship was at anchor. There it met with a group of around sixty men, the remnant of the officers and crew of USS *Hull*. Now they themselves were the eye of a storm; all around them the service force sped to make repairs to the ships of the fleet while they were sidelined, held back for this proceeding.

Commander Marks, too, had had time, unlike most of the previous witnesses, and he'd used it to write down a statement of his command's final hours. Writing focuses one's thoughts, and during what must have been difficult days since the sinking, Marks had been able to pen a coherent, detailed account of what had occurred. He had no logs or other records from which to reconstruct things; *Hull*'s papers had gone to the bottom. His only resources were his own memory and those of his shipmates. His story, nevertheless, was thorough. Everyone in the pilothouse listened as he read the statement aloud.

In the first few minutes, Marks dealt with routine matters, describing *Hull*'s duties as a screening vessel for the oilers and her general movements on the seventeenth. But a sense of the inevitable hung over the narrative. Everyone knew what was coming, what had to come. Finally it did. "The next morning the sea remained quite rough. The sky was heavily overcast," Marks read. "Roughly according to my best recollection about 1100 the fueling unit's course was changed to a southeasterly heading, which I remember as 140 true." That sort of detail would be easy to check. "It was during the following period while the ship was proceeding to her new screening station that her capsizing and sinking occurred."

Marks then described the trouble in CIC, the seams that began parting and the electrical arcing brought about by the sea spray. He didn't linger, but instead moved on quickly to the issue of ballasting, which he knew from the prior testimony was of major concern to the court. According to the engineer officer's report, he recalled, *Hull* was more than 70 percent fueled, which, he pointed out, was "well above the required ballasting point." And that wasn't all. "In view of the fact that the ship was riding the seas satisfactorily at the time and that I estimated that we would be fueled on short notice as soon as the heavy weather abated," he explained, "I did not consider ballasting advisable."

Then Marks returned to the electronic problems, noting the intermittent failure of first the SG radar, then the TBS radio. He continued inexorably toward what was to come.

"At a time I estimate roughly around 1130," he said, "the seas became mountainous and the wind increased to hurricane proportions. At this point I wish to state," he emphasized, "that there had at no time been any storm warnings received from any source whatsoever, although we had been keeping careful watch for same." Then the more serious damage had started to happen. "The motor whaleboat was smashed in at the bow and finally was torn clear of the boat davits, falling into the sea. Several depth charges were torn loose from the K guns and were lost overboard."

The litany continued. "Several of the metal covers on ammunition ready boxes were ripped completely off of the boxes by the wind," Marks noted. "The bridge structure itself was under such great strain that I was greatly concerned that the structure itself or a portion thereof might be torn off the ship." Marks also told how he had first feared, then half hoped, that one or both of the destroyer's funnels would be pulled loose by the wind. "If one of the stacks had been torn or cut loose," he theorized, "it might have lowered the center of the wind pressure on the hull sufficiently to reduce the ship's rolling." That was exactly what had happened to *Dewey*. He mentioned that he had considered giving the wind a hand, "but at this point," he observed, "no man could have possibly existed in an exposed position topside long enough to do the job; he would have been quickly blown overboard."

Despite what Farrin had said the previous afternoon, Marks several times noted the wind's effect on the ship. The seas, he conceded, were gigantic and had contributed to his inability to control her heading. "It was apparent," he read, "that no matter what was done with the rudder and engines the ship was being blown bodily before the wind and sea." But for *Hull*, at least, Marks was clear that the great villain had been the enraged blasts of air, especially in the final few minutes. "By this time the ship took several rolls because of high velocity wind gusts," he testified. "I estimate the rolls to have been about 70 degrees." The end was clearly approaching, and Marks now digressed for a moment. "I wish to state that the performance of the duty by the officers and crew was at all times highly creditable previous to and subsequent to the loss of the ship. Orders were promptly and quietly carried out and there was no confusion."

His eulogy ended, he proceeded to the final act. "Shortly after twelve o'clock the ship withstood what I estimated to be the worst punishment any storm could offer." Again he emphasized the furious gales. "I have served in destroyers in some of the worst storms in the North Atlantic and believed that no winds could be worse than that I had just witnessed." Marks believed their velocity to be at least 110 knots, 126 miles per hour. It was this wind that had pushed *Hull* onto her starboard side in the water. That had been the end of her.[430]

Once Marks had finished, one of the admirals asked Marks two formal questions. "Is the narrative just read to the court a true statement of the loss of the United States ship *Hull*?"

"It is, sir," Marks answered.

"Have you any complaint to make against any of the surviving officers and crew of the said ship on that occasion?"

"I do not, sir." With those four words, Marks forever took upon himself the responsibility for any wrongful acts or omissions aboard *Hull* that might have contributed to her sinking.

Then the court spoke to the other survivors gathered in the pilothouse. "Have you any objections to make in regard to the narrative just read to the court, or anything to lay to the charge of any officer or man with regard to the loss of the United States ship *Hull*?"

It was another pro forma question, and while some people made comments, they mostly concerned minor subjects, such as exactly when the radar went out or what boilers were on line. Then a gunner's mate spoke up.

"The captain has stated that the ship had over 70 percent of fuel," he said. "We did have that until we lost power the first time. Then after that we started taking the wind on the port beam and the ship kept rolling to starboard." He was concerned about fuel loss and its effect on stability. "Every time the ship took a roll to starboard the fuel would pour out of the tanks. I believe that the forward fuel tanks were all empty and I believe that was what caused the loss of the ship. She was top-heavy."[431]

Next a chief radioman piped up. "This is not a correction to the statement," he began. "It's an addition, I might say. The captain said there was no storm warning. Well," he remarked, "I don't know that there was. The only thing that I know about that, I was on the decoding board and the previous night on the 8 to 12 some message about a storm had been broken down by the chief yeoman who told me about it the next morning just before breakfast."

This was hearsay, but evidentiary rules were of little concern to the court, and the radioman continued in a jumble, explaining how the ensign supervising him had remarked around that time that only a single message—one regarding fueling—would be of any interest to Marks. The radioman had given the captain the message without paying any attention to what it had said. "I end this statement by saying that I don't know whether it was a storm or not," he reiterated. "My reason for making this statement is because in a previous interview I had mentioned knowing of this message. That's all."[432]

The other comments were minor, but these two statements, each touching upon a running concern of the inquiry, made an impression. When the radioman had wrapped up, the court trooped back to the tender's wardroom, and Gates began examining Marks. Most of his questions were innocuous, eliciting further small details of the events leading up to the sinking, but then Gates got down to it.

"Following the reading of your narrative a member of your crew suggested there was a possibility that a weather report had been received the evening of 17 December," he noted. "Have you anything to say in regard to this?"

There was nothing to say, really, except to reiterate earlier statements, and that is what Marks did. "I know of no such report having been received." That was surely the case; the radioman's comments had been rather confusing, and even he had equivocated. If a storm warning had come in, someone would have remembered, and since it probably wouldn't have changed how Marks had handled his ship, he had no reason to lie about it.

Gates moved on to the second difficult question. "At the same time," he said, "another member of your crew indicated that he thought a large amount of fuel oil had been lost from the forward tanks. Have you anything to say in regard to this?"

This one was an easier question. "Yes," answered Marks. "The oil of which the man spoke I believe came from the fuel tank vents, which are very small pipes and could not possibly pass the quantity of oil in those tanks over a short period of time." The gunner's mate who'd commented on the fuel loss, explained Marks, hadn't specialized in fuel systems, and thus likely thought the spillage to be much greater than it actually was. "I'm sure in my own mind," he said, "that if any great amount of oil had flowed into the sea from those tanks my engineer officer would have informed me of it."[433]

That was the roughest ground Marks had to cover, but there were other important moments as well. During his statement he had discussed his attempts to keep station in the typhoon and his eventual abandonment of those efforts as he had realized that his ship was in danger. When Gates had finished examining him, the court took up this subject. "Had you not been trying to maneuver all forenoon, do you think you could have taken better care of your ship?"

"Yes, I do," said Marks unequivocally.

"When you found that you were in a typhoon," the court continued, "did you feel constrained to maneuver without regard to the safety of your ship?"

"When I felt like the ship was in a typhoon I felt no hesitancy whatsoever in leaving my station in the screen and handling my ship to save her," Marks answered easily. But his questioner was getting at something a bit different. "If you had decided to maneuver independently at let us say 8 o'-clock in the morning would your ship have behaved better and gotten along better?"

At eight o'clock in the morning things had been bad, but not terrible. After the testimony that the court had already heard, most of those in attendance were probably clear on that. Absent an emergency, Marks couldn't have simply left the screen and gone steaming off on his own, and both he and the admiral questioning him knew it. This wasn't about Marks's decisions, but about those of his superiors. Perhaps Marks sensed this; his answer suggests that he did.

"Yes," he replied. "If I could have steamed clear to the southward to get clear I am sure I might have avoided the storm center completely." This might or might not have been hindsight. Whether Marks had believed that on the morning of the eighteenth, he didn't say. But something else he didn't say—something he could never voice—was that the only way that could have happened would have been for Halsey to order the fleet to steam south much earlier than he did.[434]

Neither the court nor the judge advocate had been unduly tough on Marks. They had asked forthright questions about his ship handling and his decisions, but he answered them all both fully and with obvious competence. After he'd finished, Gates summoned other witnesses who had been aboard *Hull*. Her engineering officer, Lieutenant Junior Grade George Sharp, showed some continued signs of stress, as others had, being somewhat reticent and at times failing to understand questions, but the court took it easy on him and the others.[435] From the patterns of questions that Gates and the admirals were asking, it was becoming apparent that morning that they did not blame *Hull*'s people, or by extension *Spence*'s and *Monaghan*'s, for the loss of the vessels. Their interest lay elsewhere.

After finishing with the final *Hull* witness, Gates called Kosco again.

This time all the questions came from the admirals, and with a more detailed picture of things as developed by all the testimony that had come forth, they pulled no punches. "The court asked Admiral Halsey," one of the flag officers told Kosco, "whether he considered that he had timely warning or did he know that a severe storm was approaching around the 16th and 17th of December." Then the admiral read back Halsey's response accusingly. "He answered, 'I did not have timely warning. I will put it another way—I had no warning.'" The admiral concluded his reading and refocused on Kosco. "In view of the fact that you are the aerological officer for Admiral Halsey," he asked, "how do you account for this answer?"

Kosco had to say something. "I take it that the admiral means he had no warning that a severe storm was approaching, although he did have warning that there was a light, moderate storm in the area," he managed. Given the full context of Halsey's statement, which Kosco presumably didn't have, the aerologist's opinion was probably accurate. "On the morning of the 16th," Kosco continued, "I showed him the weather map and told him that it looked like a small storm was developing between Ulithi and Guam. I continued telling him that this storm wasn't indicated to be very much of a storm. On the 17th when we decided to knock off fueling operations, I framed a dispatch on the storm and also indicated to the admiral that a storm was somewhere to the east of us." Kosco was showing pretty credibly that Halsey knew, or should have known, that at least moderately bad weather was coming; but the aerologist still hadn't accounted for the fact that a tropical cyclone had caught Halsey unawares. "No typhoon warning was given at any time," he had to concede, though his phrasing left open the matter of whether he was admitting to a failure to give such a warning or pleading that no weather station had given *him* such a warning. "That is about all I can answer to that question, sir."

But his inquisitors had another. "The court asked Admiral Halsey what seemed to be wrong with the weather service in this case, and his answer was in part: 'It was nonexistent. That is the only way I can express it.'" Clearly, Halsey's blunt and memorable statements had impressed themselves on the admirals, as the fleet commander had doubtless intended. "What have you to say in regard to this answer?"

In reply, Kosco suggested that previous storms had formed so far away that Halsey had always had a few days' notice. "In this case," he claimed, "the storm formed almost on top of him, and he was the first one to report it, so that he didn't have the advance information that he had in other storms. That is the only plausible answer that I could give to that."

But the storm hadn't formed all that closely; and anyway there had been storm warnings, as the court now pointed out. "What weight did you give to Commander Task Group 38.2's report of approximately 1400 on 17 December with regard to the location of this storm and his recommendations regarding the direction in which clear weather could be found?" one of the admirals asked, referring to the report Bogan had forwarded just before Kosco received *Chandeleur*'s warning.

Here Kosco was on firmer ground. "As I recall it," he answered, "he did not give the location of the storm. He just said that if we headed south we should find clear weather." The staff carefully considered the course, Kosco stated, until it got a report from *Chandeleur* warning of the storm to the south. "A southerly course would've taken us right into the center of *Chandeleur*'s estimated position of the storm," he explained.[436]

There was no point in badgering him. Few lawyers were present; the gray arts of cross-examination were beyond the court's ken. Kosco was in a bad place, but after all he hadn't willed the typhoon or the sinkings. And when Gates brought in the reservist who served as *Chandeleur*'s aerologist, he confirmed that he had broadcast the storm center's location on December 17.

"Do your search planes ever transmit the weather direct to the fleet?" asked Gates. If they did, after all, it would save a lot of steps, bypassing *Chandeleur*, the Navy's weather centrals, and all the time for coding, routing, and sending.

"As far as I know, they never have," the lieutenant said. "The search planes which transmitted the weather to me on the 17th transmitted it only to me on the *Chandeleur* and to ComForward Area."

Gates had another idea. *Chandeleur* had addressed its weather report to Halsey as well as to the fleet weather centrals. Maybe others had gotten it too. "Would a dispatch that you sent on the forenoon of the 17th to ComThirdFleet be on such a circuit as to make it available to all ships of the Third Fleet?"

"I don't know," the lieutenant said. He then described the communication bottleneck that had helped slow down the message. But he had followed procedure, just as had everyone else.[437]

That afternoon the court heard from more products of these standard procedures, the half dozen bedraggled survivors of *Monaghan*. None of them was an officer; the senior was Joe McCrane. All of them had had rather myopic views of the events leading up to the sinking, not only because of their narrow duties and specialties, but because the ship's communications systems had gone out sometime before she went down.

This time there wasn't a need to adjourn to the pilothouse; the woefully small number of sailors could easily fit into the wardroom. The court listened as McCrane read a statement much briefer than Marks's; afterward it examined him and his shipmates. When asked if he had anything to add to his narrative, McCrane gave a reply that added strength to the notion that something had been wrong with *Farragut*-class stability. "Ever since we left Bremerton the ship seemed top-heavy," he reported. "I was on there for two years. Ever since we left Bremerton in October 1944, she seemed to roll worse than she ever did."[438]

The others could add little, but most of them agreed on some major points, the most important of which was that, as had been the case with *Hull*, and in contravention of Farrin's testimony, the wind had been a major force in *Monaghan*'s death. It had blown from her port. After several steep rolls to the starboard, she had gone over and stayed there. The stunned survivors, making their way to the life raft, recalled seeing no one but themselves make it into the water.[439]

If *Spence*'s story was sobering because of her survivors' accounts, the horrifying thing about *Monaghan*'s was that it was so empty of facts. The handful of survivors could tell the court little, except that communications had gone out and that the ship had rolled over. Humanity had been victimized; except for sparse accounts of trying to ballast and to control the ship from the steering room, there wasn't even any perceived effort to fight back, as had been the case with *Spence*. There must have been, of course, but none now living had seen it or could comment upon it. The sea had simply eaten the ship along with nearly all hands. The disaster had been so sudden, so thorough, that the navy didn't even know whom it had lost, or how it had lost them. Had men made it into the water, or had they gone down in the ship? The survivors were not able to say. They had seen no one else, but in the hell of spray, seeing anything would have been difficult. As for who had died, the court asked the *Monaghan* witnesses to try to remember any transfers to or from the ship in the days before the typhoon, in order to try to reconstruct the ship's roster. This, perhaps more than anything else, conveyed the sense of sudden and total destruction.

In the end the survivors could tell the court little, but it was clear, once they had done so, that *Monaghan*, too, had had major stability problems, and that she had been a disaster awaiting her cue.

When the court finished with *Monaghan*'s men, it adjourned for the day. Its last scrap of business was to hear from Ira Nunn, Marks's counsel, that the lawyer was to leave with the fleet the following day. When the court reconvened the next morning, based on what the admirals had heard, they notified Mercer that he was no longer an interested party. Thus freed, Mercer became, at Marks's request, Nunn's stand-in as counsel.

The court gave no formal reason for its decision about Mercer. Obviously what its members had heard so far had convinced them that nothing Mercer had done or failed to do had any relevance to the sinking of the destroyers, although they never said as much. But Marks remained a defendant. The record, now blurred by sixty years' dust, shows little, if anything, that would have kept him in the crosshairs, except for one little fact: he was, or had been, a commanding officer, legally charged with the safe operation of the ship and the welfare of her crew. The weight of these duties could not be removed easily, and the admirals knew it. So, whatever the record may have suggested to them so far, they left Marks's status unchanged.

Having heard from the remnants of the *Hull* and *Monaghan* crews, the court spent the morning of its fifth day examining the survivors of *Spence*. Her losses, while heavier than *Hull*'s, were not quite so bad as *Monaghan*'s. Al Krauchunas was the only surviving officer, and it thus fell to him to prepare the official statement, which he read in the pilothouse with his shipmates in attendance. But *Spence*'s capsizing had been rather sudden, and he had been belowdecks. A more valuable witness was Quartermaster Second Class Edward F. Traceski, a clearheaded sailor who had been on watch on the bridge when *Spence* went down. Once Krauchunas had read his statement and then, back in the wardroom, answered some questions, Gates called Traceski.

The sailor was a wealth of information about the details of *Spence*'s steaming, and he answered questions with precision. Krauchunas had testified that *Spence* had had a list to port of something like fifteen degrees, which nobody from the other ships had reported, and this drew the court's interest. (*Hull* and *Monaghan* had rolled over to starboard.) Krauchunas had also opined that *Spence* hadn't ballasted, so this was on the admirals' minds when Traceski came before them.[440]

"Was any order issued during the morning of the 18th to ballast ship?" one of them asked the sailor.

"There was, yes, sir," said Traceski. "Given by the captain."

"Do you know approximately what time?"

"Approximately 1030 in the morning."

"Ten thirty?"

"Ten thirty, yes, sir," Traceski confirmed. *Spence* had gone down, by his and others' reckoning, less than an hour later.

Gates took up this matter. "Was any report received that ballasting had been accomplished?"

"Not on the bridge," said Traceski. "There was no report given that I know of. Usually the reports came by the engine room telephone circuits and I was in the habit of answering all telephone calls and I had received no such report."

Gates also had Traceski go over wind and sea conditions at the moment *Spence* capsized. "What was the direction of the wind in relation to the ship at this time?"

"It appeared to come from the starboard quarter."

"What was the direction of the sea in relation to the ship at this time?"

"It seemed to be coming almost directly aft."

Here was the strongest refutation of Farrin's theory. This sea's direction, if Traceski was right, would have produced pitching, not rolling. It wasn't the likely culprit. On the other hand, the wind wasn't blowing directly from *Spence*'s starboard, but more from the four or five o'clock position. It was obviously a cause; but given the list Krauchunas and others described, something clearly had been wrong before then. The presence of an inherent stability problem was growing quite obvious.

Gates thus stayed with the ballasting issue as he called George W. Johnson, a chief water tender. Johnson, too, was knowledgeable, though unlike Traceski he hadn't been on watch at the time of the sinking. Still, he had followed some of the action before he became part of it when the ship went down.

"Can you tell the court at what time ballasting was started?" Gates asked.

Johnson's figure agreed with Traceski's. "Approximately 10 o'clock of the 18th." He also identified the tanks that had been ballasted.

"How much ballast would you say was on board?"

"Approximately 16,000 gallons." That was a fairly small amount, especially for a ship that was practically out of fuel. *Spence* could have held five times as much. "What is your estimation of the rate at which you can take on ballast?" Gates continued.

"I would say," replied Johnson, "we could take on 30,000 gallons of ballast in one and a half hours."[441]

It was beginning to look as if *Spence*'s captain had held out some hopes of being able to fuel until the weather went from dangerous to deadly, at which time the list and curious rolling had begun. Given the fuel emergency and the lack of a typhoon warning, that hadn't been unreasonable, although other captains might have made different decisions. But by then it had been too late to ballast in time.

Following witnesses verified most of these facts, and one of them, another chief water tender, pointed out that Captain Andrea had begun shifting *Spence*'s dwindling supplies of fuel oil to different tanks even before ballasting, presumably to increase her stability. The picture was clear: fighting the clock and slowly disappearing fuel, Andrea had been ambushed by a weather disaster with too little warning to get ready. Whether he should have been able to predict it himself was an issue neither Gates nor the court explored. But it was one that would no doubt live near the heart of the admirals' coming deliberations.[442]

With the task force's departure and the conclusion of the survivors' testimony, the investigative phase of the inquiry began to wind down. The afternoon of the thirtieth was taken up by the testimony of two officers from Fleet Air Wing One, to which belonged *Chandeleur*'s planes, together with that of Nimitz's own senior aerologist, Captain Wilbur M. Lockhart. The first two officers sketched out the details of how, in conformance with standing orders issued from the office of Admiral Hoover, the court's president, the air wing's pilots and crews were to make weather reports. As everyone else had done, they had gone by the book.[443]

Lockhart was a different matter. Pearl Harbor's weather central had played a role in the drama, but it was tangential. Lockhart, being a senior aerologist, was in a position to critique his juniors as well as the system of weather reporting in the Pacific, and he freely did both. Most of his concern lay with the latter. "Communications in the fleet are in my opinion still not adequate for handling weather," he declared under prompting from the court. "Various attempts have been and still are being made to improve them and to provide weather with priority and operational priority classification, that is"—he clarified—"to get weather messages from the bottom of the heap of messages in the communication center up to the top of the heap." But as recent events had shown, it still wasn't happening.

But Lockhart also had things to say about the fleet aerologists, things that echoed some others' testimony. "I do not believe that most forecasters in the fleet broke out a compass and lay down the possible positions that the typhoon might be in," he said. He recounted the same statistics that Kosco and others had: historically, three out of four storms in the area had curved north. But one out of four, he remarked, did not. "This possibility," he noted, "was apparently lost sight of completely."[444]

That should have been the coda to the court's investigation; it concerned what was perhaps the major running theme of the inquiry. In fact, it nearly was the last word, but not quite, even though the proceedings had three days left to run.

The following morning, a Sunday, the final day of the last full year of the war, the court met long enough to hear from another maritime engineering expert from Service Squadron Ten, who had carried out, on paper, further stability tests on *Spence*. He was the only witness that day, and timing suggests that he was an afterthought. James Farrin, three days earlier, had tended to stress the role the seas had played in turning the destroyers turtle, but the survivors' testimony hadn't completely borne out those statements. The new expert was here to shed more light on the sinkings, which he attempted to do by referring to inclining experiments on other ships, explaining graphs filled with mathematics, and making some educated guesses as to how much water had flowed into the bilges of *Spence*.[445]

Then the proceedings appeared to move toward a close. The recorders noted that neither the court nor anyone else wished to hear from more witnesses; with that, the inquiry, which had been rather flexible, and the gathering of evidence became a bit more by the book. Gates declined to make any summation—called, somewhat oddly by civil trial standards, an opening argument. This paved the way for Marks to read a brief statement. He submitted, in a few words, that his goal had been to keep his designated place in the screen as long as he safely could do so during "a tropical storm of unprecedented violence." Marks further explained that he had not felt "tactically free to leave the station" in order to combat the storm "until the situation had developed to a degree where danger to the ship could be anticipated." Marks asked the court, based on these facts, to note his blamelessness in its findings.

Marks and Nunn had doubtless done their best, but they had left open a gaping hole, both in language and argument. The crux was this: when could—and should—Marks have anticipated the danger he mentioned? In his statement he made no mention of the lack of warning about which the court had heard so much. This might have been a tactical decision rather than an oversight. While legal proceedings are a kind of combat, the two sailors may have thought it ungentlemanly as well as unwise to try to foist the responsibility on some of their fellow officers in the fleet, especially since one of them wore four stars. Anyway, given all the coverage of that topic, the court hardly needed reminding of the issue. For all that, Marks's statement raised the question of whether he acted soon enough. Even if he had—and little in the evidence suggests otherwise—it isn't the sort of question a defendant should put into the minds of his judges, especially just before they start to deliberate.

When Marks had had his say, eyes turned once more to Gates, who declined to make a closing argument. The court adjourned for the day.

The closing steps, it turned out, were premature. By the time they reconvened the following morning, having been out for nearly twenty-four hours, the admirals, or at least a couple of them, changed their minds. They wanted to hear more. Up until now Gates had been choosing most, perhaps all, of the witnesses, but now the court summoned some of its own, as it was entitled to do. The new voices had little to add to what had already been said; two discussed weather reporting procedures, and another supplied further details of one of *Monaghan*'s final messages. But the court seemed to want or need the new information, and that was what mattered. Then it adjourned again, this time for two days, to digest what it had heard and seen during the previous week. On Wednesday, January 3, it reconvened, this time to announce its findings.[446]

Genial John Hoover, who did much to shape these findings, was a tough customer. Although junior to Halsey, he'd been in naval aviation longer. He had served as exec on the old *Saratoga* a decade earlier, when Ernest J. King was her captain, later becoming her CO himself. He was one of the few who could hold up under King's treatment, which in itself says much about him, and his name had sometimes been mentioned in the list of those who could take over for Halsey or McCain as a fleet or task force commander. Halsey was being judged by someone who knew his business, as Nimitz had doubtless intended.[447]

And this was to be judgment, even if not in a legal sense. Halsey's professional reputation was on the line. Unofficially, Hoover was very critical of the Third Fleet commander. Halsey's losses had been serious. As the court assembled for the reading of its recommendations, the question was now whether this private opinion would carry over into the record.

Naval Courts and Boards makes a sharp distinction between a court of inquiry's finding of fact and its opinions and recommendations.[448] In the latter, the court would start assigning official blame. But the facts came first, and even here, the court's inclinations soon became obvious.

The court began by describing the fleet's task organization, its fuel state, the deteriorating weather, and the attempt to find an acceptable rendezvous. All of this seemed innocuous. Then the court slipped in a new fact. "During the storm, which lasted roughly throughout the daylight hours, no orders were issued to the fleet as a whole to disregard formation keeping and take best courses for speed and security," it stated. "In Task Group 30.8, where the principal damage occurred, vessels were maneuvering to maintain formation up to the times they were disabled or lost."

The implication was that Halsey should have issued such orders. Others, however, drew subtle criticism as well: further into the recounting of facts, the court noted that "various commanding officers in the fleet, some to the eastward of the fleet, evaluated the weather signs as indicating the approach of a tropical storm, but for one reason or another, made no report."

But then the court came back to Halsey. "For a period of nineteen hours," it noted, "a message from Commander Third Fleet, indicating the center of a storm of increasing intensity to be at 15 N. and 138 E. moving NNW at 12 to 15 knots was permitted to remain uncorrected even though the weather indications pointed to the fact that the storm was closer and getting closer to the fleet." Kosco had made corrections on his own map, the court pointed out, "but this correction was not relayed to the fleet."[449]

One may be tempted to dismiss these statements as merely part of an un-
biased factual record, but as any litigator well knows, factual records are
often highly selective. Many a case has been won or lost based on the version
of the facts that a judge or jury accepted. Here the admirals seemed to be including facts that reflected badly upon Halsey.

At the same time, the court was gentle with Kosco and the other fleet
aerologists. "All these officers have had at least two years experience in forecasting, although some may have had less than a year in forecasting in the
tropics." Kosco himself, the court stated, was rather more seasoned; still, it
noted, "he has been on his present station about one month."[450] Next came
a breakdown of major fleet damage by ship. Then came the opinions.

Right away the court started on Halsey. His initial fleet movements, it
found, were "logical," but given the bad weather on the seventeenth, he
should have ordered special weather flights as well as reports from his ships.
As to the reports that he did have, it said, "the large errors made in predicting the location and path of this storm are the responsibility of Commander
Third Fleet." Halsey, it further emphasized, "was at fault in not broadcasting
definitive danger warnings to all vessels early morning of December 18 in
order that preparations might be made as practicable and that inexperienced
commanding officers might have sooner realized the seriousness of their situations." Of course, the commander has the ultimate responsibility for the
conduct of his people, but here, within the space of two or three paragraphs,
the court handed off the whole weather reporting trouble to Halsey rather
than to Kosco, and then it defended others by noting their lack of experience.
"Instructions to vessels and subordinate commanders," it continued in this
vein, "should have been given in the early stages of the storm as to the relative importance of stationkeeping compared to security."[451]

When the court turned its attention fully to Kosco, it made clear what it
had already hinted at. Given the weather reports that Kosco had had on the
seventeenth, it declared, his initial advice to Halsey had indeed been sound.
"In view of the conflicting reports," it went on, Kosco "gave Commander
Third Fleet his best information on the position of the storm and advised him
correctly as to the best course to steer to get in the safe semicircle of the
storm which was then in progress." After all this, Kosco drew only a brief rebuke, further softened by a typical naval use of the passive voice: "Too much

reliance was placed in the analysis broadcast from the Fleet Weather Central, Pearl Harbor."[452]

In recounting the damage to various vessels, the court exonerated the crews of those ships, using again and again variations of the ritual phrase "no blame attaches to any officer or man ... for loss of life, damage to ship, loss of aircraft and damage thereto." The court largely extended these comments to the complements of *Spence*, *Hull*, and *Monaghan*. The loss of the two *Farragut*s it attributed, not surprisingly, "to insufficient dynamic stability to absorb the combined effects of wind and sea." In *Spence*'s case, the court found, the problem hadn't been any inherent instability but rather the high winds, the low fuel, the absence of ballast, and the free water in the ship's bilges, among other things, all of the factors that witnesses had discussed. The upshot was that the skippers of *Hull* and *Monaghan* — Marks and the dead Bruce Garrett — had incurred, stated the court, no "serious blame" for the loss of their ships. Commander Andrea, the captain of *Spence*, was another matter. The sparse evidence of *Spence*'s final hours tended to show that he had failed to ballast in time and to button up his ship as tightly as possible, but given how little was known, the court did not blame him in so many words.

Still, the court did have something to say about all three of the captains. They had, it declared, "failed to realize sufficiently in advance of the fact, the necessity for them to give up the attempt to maintain position in their disposition and to give all their attention to saving their ships." Even this hand slap, however, it softened. "In extenuation," it continued, "it can be said that the good judgment for such decisions will, in many cases, require more experience than had the commanding officers of those ships."[453]

Then, in the final paragraphs of its opinion, the court returned to Halsey. It was inevitable. The admirals had already, expressly or otherwise, absolved everyone else in the drama of "serious blame," and someone had to bear that blame, or so it would seem. This was where the court now headed.

> The preponderance of responsibility ... falls on Commander Third Fleet, Admiral William F. Halsey, U.S. Navy. And analyzing the mistakes, errors and faults ... the court classifies them as errors in judgment under stress of war operations and not as offenses.... The court

fully realizes that a certain degree of blame attaches to those in command in all disasters, unless they are manifestly "Acts of God." The
extent of blame as it applies to Commander Third Fleet or others, is
impractical to assess.[454]

In the end, then, the court straddled the question. On the one hand,
Halsey was responsible, even for his subordinates' failure to realize the danger. On the other, the court mentioned "Acts of God," and a typhoon certainly
counts as one of those. Did Third Fleet's losses number among them as well?
The admirals didn't actually say. They left it hazy, and so avoided the question
of Halsey's blameworthiness. That was probably the most charitable thing that
they could have done.[455]

The court also enumerated its recommendations, but these were relatively brief and predictable. It suggested, among other things, measures to
improve weather reporting in the Philippine Sea and more training for
aerologists there; a BuShips investigation into destroyer design characteristics with an eye to stability; steps to make sure that ship captains would
know fully about the stability quirks of their ships as well as the dangers of
typhoons in the western Pacific; and some modifications to light carrier
hangar decks to assist in damage control. The final recommendation doubtless came as a relief to the *Hull*'s skipper: the court submitted "that no further proceedings be had in the case of Lieutenant Commander James A.
Marks, U.S. Navy."[456]

For all the reassurance the living may have felt, they probably knew that the
court of inquiry, which adjourned on January 3, did not have the final word.
It wasn't technically subject to reversal, since it hadn't rendered a judgment
that anyone could appeal. Neither Halsey, nor Kosco, nor Marks, nor anyone
else for that matter, had been legally acquitted; nor had they been charged.
In Fifth Amendment terms, no jeopardy had attached. They could still be
blamed, even punished. What had occurred during the last week of December was merely a process of getting the relevant facts to Admirals Nimitz and
King, whose ships, planes, and men had been lost in the storm. Nimitz was

Halsey's friend, but he was also Halsey's commander. And Nimitz reported to King, the man who shaved with a blowtorch. King, for his part, had to account to the White House.

The record of the inquiry thus began its long trip east, to Pearl Harbor and Washington. Meanwhile, the only thing the officers of the fleet could do was to wait — and vent their feelings on their intractable Japanese enemy.

Epilogue

Chester Nimitz had graduated from the Naval Academy in 1905, the year after Bill Halsey, whom he'd gotten to know as a midshipman. Unlike Halsey, who'd been in the bottom third of his class, Nimitz stood seventh in a class of more than one hundred, and in his first years as an officer he turned in an outstanding performance. He spent these years in the Philippines, first on a battleship, next commanding a gunboat on which one of his officers was John S. McCain of the class of 1906. Then, at the almost unheard-of age of twenty-two, he'd been given command of one of the navy's first-ever destroyers, 450-ton *Decatur*. His classmate Ray Spruance got his first destroyer command at age twenty-six, and Halsey got his at age thirty.

In the spring of 1908, on a run from Saigon to Manila, *Decatur* steamed into a tropical cyclone—"my first, and I hope it may be my last, real live typhoon," Ensign Nimitz told his grandfather shortly after the fact. "Although my ship behaved remarkably well, for one of its size, we spent three very uncomfortable days. The ship rolled 50 degrees continually, and when the sea was ahead or astern I thought she would surely break in the middle, as a former destroyer, British, once did in a heavy sea."

Although Nimitz brought his ship through the storm, reaching Manila only a few hours late, not many weeks afterward he blemished his sterling record. On July 7, 1908, as he steamed into Batangas Harbor south of Manila Bay, he neglected to take bearings, navigating by estimating instead. He realized his mistake only when his leadsman sang out. "We're not moving, sir!" shouted the sailor. Nimitz had grounded his ship. The result was no mere court of inquiry, but a full-blown court-martial.

The court handled the ensign lightly, reducing the charge from "culpable inefficiency in the performance of duty" to the less catastrophic "neglect of duty," found him guilty, and sentenced him to nothing more than a reprimand. He lost his command, of course, but other than that his career was intact. The court probably took several items into account: Nimitz's youth, his previously spotless record, and a lack of sound information, for charts of Batangas weren't very good. Whatever the reason, Nimitz survived the ordeal.[457]

Now, nearly thirty-seven years later, Nimitz found himself having to judge other officers' actions in circumstances that had to remind him of his early days in the service. The fact that two of those he was judging were friends he'd known and served with for close to four decades added a complication, but in the little world of the professional navy, all the senior officers tended to know each other, and well. There was no help for it. Anyway, Nimitz's wasn't the last word. King, a man hard on subordinates, would review his conclusions, and King would ultimately pass the matter on to the secretary of the navy, James Forrestal. He could theoretically reject the reports of the admirals and reach his own conclusions, and he could very well mention the affair to the president.

A few days after the court finished its work, Nimitz had the transcript and the digest of the record. He also took the opportunity to interview Marks himself. He asked *Hull*'s last skipper tough, blunt questions, although he wasn't unpleasant about it: after all, he himself had conned a ship through a typhoon, and he had been on the carpet too. He was simply trying to find out, from the horse's mouth, what had happened. Of particular interest to him was whether Marks had seen a storm coming. "On the 17th," he asked the commander, "did you have any indications that storm weather was approaching?"

"Yes, sir," Marks answered, "the seas were very rough, choppy. That's the reason we had to give up fueling. The sky was overcast."

"The barometer was falling?" Nimitz persisted.

"Yes, sir."

"The wind direction changing?"

"I couldn't say positively about the wind on the 17th," replied Marks. "It was a circular storm," he added unnecessarily.

"What I am getting at," Nimitz explained, "is whether in the *Hull* there was any attempt made to forecast the storm or to forecast in the same manner the sailors used to do before they had radar and radio weather forecasting."

"Yes, sir, I knew we were in for a storm," reaffirmed Marks. "That is the reason I had the ship well secured."

Nimitz kept pushing Marks to clarify exactly when he'd known what was coming; now and then he showed just a touch of impatience. Near the end of the interview he reiterated what was obviously bothering him. "I get the impression that with all of the new instruments we have on the ships," he said, "that we can't rely too much on instruments and that we don't use the old time-honored things that were taught us by our predecessors for forecasting weather." By paying attention both to wind direction and the barometer, the fleet admiral pointed out, sailors could plot the typhoon's center.[458]

Nimitz continued to ponder these thoughts as he put together his comments on the court of inquiry's findings. He worked quickly; Third Fleet, after all, was still in a typhoon area. In late January, just before moving his headquarters from Pearl Harbor to Guam and only a couple of weeks after getting the court's record, he was done.

In contrast to the court's hundreds of pages of records, Nimitz's memorandum was only two pages long, and at the start of them he got right to the point. "The proceedings, findings, opinions, and recommendations of the court of inquiry in the attached case are approved," he declared in the opening sentence. But other sentences followed. "The evidence brought forward by the court," he observed, "indicates that the preponderance of responsibility for the storm damage and losses suffered by the Third Fleet attaches to Commander, Third Fleet, Admiral William F. Halsey, U.S. Navy. However," he went on to state immediately, "the convening authority"—that is, Nimitz himself—"is of the firm opinion that no question of negligence is involved, but rather, that the mistakes made were errors in judgment committed under stress of war operations and stemming from a commendable desire to meet military commitments." Nimitz ended his opening remarks with words that were of utmost importance to Halsey and Marks: "No further action is contemplated or recommended." There would be no courts-martial, unless King overrode Nimitz.

Then Nimitz moved on to his own recommendations, which included such things as an increase in the number of weather stations and the establishment of weather reconnaissance flights, design improvements in the ventilating systems of light carriers that would prevent the sort of flooding of engineering spaces that had happened aboard *Monterey* and *San Jacinto*, and a BuShips investigation into destroyer stability characteristics. But first on the list was the concern that he had expressed to Jim Marks. "It is the intention of the convening authority," he declared, "to see that all flag and commanding officers of the United States Pacific Fleet are impressed with the necessity of understanding the laws of storms and of giving full consideration to adverse weather conditions when occurring." In a similar vein he critiqued the current state of weather prediction resources in the Pacific. "The aerological officers assigned to the principal task force commander in the Third and Fifth Fleets," he stated, "should have training and experience commensurate with the importance of their assignments. To this end," he continued, "it is recommended that the Bureau of Naval Personnel be directed to make available a greater number of older and more experienced aerological officers to the higher commands of the fleet." Thus Nimitz, likely recalling his own early career, dealt with George Kosco and the other fleet aerologists. There was nothing wrong with them; they were simply too junior. Having finished his own observations, Nimitz packed them off, with the courts' records, to Ernest J. King.[459]

A month later—just over two months after the typhoon hit Third Fleet—King announced his decision to James Forrestal. As Nimitz had done, King kept his comments to two brief pages. "I concur in the opinion of Commander-in-Chief United States Pacific Fleet," he informed Forrestal, "that, although the preponderance of responsibility for the storm damage and losses suffered attaches to Commander Third Fleet, there is no question of negligence involved." Halsey had cleared another one of his hurdles. But King did make a few changes in what Nimitz had said. Cominch-CNO could be ruthless, and he thought, correspondingly, that Nimitz was sometimes too soft on subordinates. In this instance King thought that Nimitz's characterization of Halsey's mistakes as resulting from "a commendable desire to meet military commitments" was too solicitous of the Third Fleet commander. Likewise, he wanted at least a suggestion that someone, either Halsey or his weather forecasters, had gotten things wrong in the fleet, when it came to aerology. King thus revised Nimitz's statements accordingly: "The mistakes made," he wrote, "were errors in judgment resulting from insufficient information, committed under stress of war operations, and stemmed from the firm determination to meet military commitments."[460]

That, as it turned out, was largely the end of the matter. Over the next several months, BuShips conducted inclining and stability tests on two of the remaining *Farraguts*, including *Aylwin*, and reported—over the objections of Cal Calhoun and other 1200-tonner skippers—that the ships were sufficiently stable, although shortly after the end of the war, the bureau at last changed its tune. Weather services in the Pacific were upgraded; the navy established several new weather stations in the central Pacific, reaching northward from the

Caroline Islands toward Japan, regions where typhoons were born and where the Fast Carrier Task Force might be expected to operate as it drove closer to Japanese waters. The first months of 1945 also saw the creation of a new fleet weather central on Leyte, which later moved to Manila, and another one, not coincidentally, on Guam, where Nimitz set up his advanced headquarters late in January.[461]

Once he had established himself at Guam, Nimitz made good his promise to make sure that his officers got the word on knowing about and being prepared for bad weather. On the fifteenth of February he distributed a Pacific Fleet confidential letter sketching out for his subordinates what had happened in the typhoon and giving a basic comparative analysis of fuel, ballasting, free surface, and other conditions aboard the three lost destroyers. His main thrust in this letter, however, was to stress the need for commanders, both skippers and flag officers, to pay more attention to signs of approaching bad weather and to take early precautions.

Here, too, he empathized with the mariners whom the typhoon had assailed. "In the light of hindsight it is easy to see how any of several measures might have prevented this catastrophe, but it was far less easy a problem at the time for men who were out there under the heaviest of conflicting responsibilities," he wrote. "The important thing is for it never to happen again." To that end, Nimitz offered his analysis, together with some strong admonitions. These later remarks showed that he was still very concerned, as he'd said to Jim Marks a month earlier, that sailors were so wrapped up in technology that they weren't using their own observations of the sea and the sky. "A hundred years ago, a ship's survival depended almost solely on the competence of her master and on his constant alertness to every hint of change in the weather," pointed out the fleet admiral. "Ceaseless vigilance in watching and interpreting signs, plus a philosophy of taking no risk in which there was little to gain and much to be lost, was what enabled him to survive."

Then Nimitz became even more blunt.

> Seamen of the present day should be better at forecasting weather at sea, independently of the radio, than were their predecessors. The general laws of storms and the weather expectancy for all months of the year in all parts of the world are now more thoroughly understood,

more completely catalogued, and more readily available in various publications. An intensive study of typhoons and Western Pacific weather was made over a period of many years by Father Depperman at the Manila observatory, and his conclusions have been embodied in the material available to all aerologists. What Knight and Bowditch have to say on the subject is exactly as true during this war as it was in time of peace or before the days of radio. Familiarity with these authorities is something no captain or navigator can do without. The monthly pilot charts, issued to all ships, give excellent information as to the probable incidence and movements of typhoons. Stress on the foregoing is no belittlement of our aerological centers and weather broadcasts. But just as a navigator is held culpable if he neglects "Log, Lead, and Lookout" through blind faith in his radio fixes, so is the seaman culpable who regards personal weather estimates as obsolete and assumes that if no radio storm warning has been received, then all is well, and no local weather signs need cause him concern.

It is possible that too much reliance is being placed on outside sources for warnings of dangerous weather, and on the ability of our splendid ships to come through anything that wind and wave can do. If this be so, there is need for a revival of the age-old habits of self-reliance and caution in regard to the hazard from storms, and for officers in all echelons of command to take their personal responsibilities in this respect more seriously.

After further analysis, Nimitz ended with a final pointed warning.

In conclusion, both seniors and juniors must realize that in bad weather, as in most other situations, safety and fatal hazard are not separated by any sharp boundary line, but shade gradually from one into the other. There is no little red light which is going to flash on and inform commanding officers or higher commanders that from then on there is extreme danger from the weather, and that measures for ships' safety must now take precedence over further efforts to keep up with the formation or to execute the assigned task. This time will always be a matter of personal judgment. Naturally no commander is going to cut thin the margin between staying afloat and foundering, but he may nevertheless unwittingly pass the danger point even though no ship is yet in extremis. Ships that keep on going as long as the severity of wind and sea has not yet come close to capsizing them or breaking them in two, may nevertheless become helpless to avoid these catastrophes later if things get worse. By then they may be unable to steer any heading but in the trough of the sea, or may have their steering control, lighting, communications, and main propulsion disabled, or may be helpless to secure things on deck or to jettison topside weights.

"The time for taking all measures for a ship's safety is while still able to do so," Nimitz wound up the letter. "Nothing is more dangerous than for a seaman to be grudging in taking precautions lest they turn out to have been unnecessary. Safety at sea for a thousand years has depended on exactly the opposite philosophy."[462]

With that, and with the beefing up of weather facilities, Nimitz had done a great deal to make sure, as he'd written, that this sort of disaster wouldn't happen again on his watch. Perhaps, given that he was busy overseeing a huge, bloody theater of the biggest war in history, it was all he could practically do. But he found himself revisiting the problem when, four months after he'd circulated this letter, Admiral Halsey led the Fast Carrier Task Force squarely into another typhoon.

When Third Fleet departed Ulithi at the end of December, Halsey swung it around the northern tip of Luzon, battering Japanese airbases on Formosa to keep them from resupplying the Philippines. Then he traveled back south to the area where the fleet had done battle with the typhoon. He was in the same reach of ocean where *Spence*, *Hull*, and *Monaghan* and their men had gone down. But Halsey was concentrating not on drowned friends but living and dangerous enemies, blanketing the Luzon airfields once more. Then, rounding north again, Third Fleet went marauding into the South China Sea following a second strike on Formosa.[463]

What Halsey really wanted was capital ships; somewhere in range, he believed, were the carriers *Ise* and *Hyugo*, and perhaps even the giant battlewagon *Yamato*, all of which had escaped him at the Battle of Leyte Gulf in October. During the rest of January, he hit Cam Rahn Bay in French Indochina — Vietnam — and later attacked the harbors of Hainan and Hong Kong.

The strikes against French Indochina on the twelfth day of the month were particularly devastating. Third Fleet sank nearly fifty Japanese ships, a dozen of them tankers. Only fifteen were combatants, and all of them small; Japan's capital ships had retreated far to the south, to Lingga Roads. Halsey thus never got his revenge for being decoyed at Leyte. Still, the war was approaching the point at which the tankers were becoming the key targets. Halsey was at last astride Japan's supply lines from the Indies, and her strangulation was now starting. The flow of conventional and Tokkō planes to Luzon came to an end.[464]

By the end of the month, with MacArthur's forces solidly ashore on Luzon and Japanese airpower over the Philippines interdicted, Halsey's job in the Philippines arena was done, and the fleet returned to Ulithi. "I am so proud of you that no words can express my feelings," the admiral signaled his sailors. "We have driven the enemy off the sea and back to his inner defenses. Superlatively well done. Halsey." With that he surrendered command of the fleet to Ray Spruance, who would take on those inner defenses.[465]

During the months that Halsey and McCain had been assaulting the Philippines, Spruance and his staff had been planning for the next step. King had wanted that step to be Formosa; Nimitz and Spruance had held out for Iwo Jima and then Okinawa. Iwo Jima, a barren pile of volcano ash halfway between Ulithi to the south and Tokyo to the north, served Japan as an early warning point for the new B-29 raids from Saipan. In American hands, however, it could be an emergency landing base for those same B-29s, as well as an unsinkable aircraft carrier that could remove some of the operational pressure from the Fast Carrier Task Force. With Iwo Jima secured, Nimitz's forces could move on to Okinawa, a much larger island in the Ryukyu chain, just to the south of Japan's Home Islands. From there the navy could complete its interdiction of supplies from the Indies, and the army, if necessary, could launch its invasion of Japan proper. Neither Nimitz nor Spruance thought that in the face of the mounting blockade this last step would be necessary. In the end they convinced King, and King convinced the Joint Chiefs of Staff, that Iwo Jima and Okinawa were the right targets.[466]

The Iwo Jima campaign began in mid-February, after two weeks of fleet downtime. The island proved a tough nut to crack; honeycombed with fortifications protected from bombing and shelling by thick volcanic rock, it resisted for more than a month, and seven thousand Americans died in taking it. Then, in mid-March, the assault on Okinawa began, and it was even worse. The large, green island, owned by Japan since the late nineteenth century, was within easy striking distance of airbases on Formosa, Kyushu, and elsewhere, more than a hundred in all, from which the navy expected to see as many as three thousand planes flying at it, a lot of them Tokkō craft.[467]

To complicate matters further, Spruance had a bigger job than Bill Halsey had had in the Philippines. Under Spruance, the fleet—redesignated the Fifth after the change of command—consisted not merely of the Fast Carrier Task Force under Mitscher, but also of the amphibious assault force with its Marine divisions, gunfire support forces, minesweeper forces, a British carrier task force, and, of course, the logistics group.[468]

The intensity of the Iwo Jima and Okinawa campaigns, and the escalating carnage wrought by Tokkō planes off Okinawa, took a huge toll on Spruance's staff, and by the end of May the frail Marc Mitscher weighed less than a hundred pounds. Spruance himself, a highly fit man who was accustomed to and even welcomed physical hardship, appeared to be in better shape than his staff. His physician never noted any signs of fatigue in Spruance, not even a need for so much as an aspirin. But Spruance, too, was feeling the strain after three months. "No one," he admitted to his wife many years later, "knew of the butterflies in my stomach." Normally stoic and unflappable to the point of earning the nickname "ice water admiral" in the press (a sobriquet he dismissed as "much hooey"), he once flew into a fury when he read a poorly worded dispatch from a senior subordinate, nearly ordering the man relieved before getting himself under control.[469]

Halsey and his staff, meanwhile, were busy planning for post-Okinawa campaigns, especially the invasion of Kyushu, to take place in November, and the conquest of the main island of Honshu, scheduled for March of 1946. But when Halsey paid a visit to Nimitz on Guam in the last days of April, the fleet admiral told him to relieve Spruance ahead of schedule a month later, even if Okinawa was still unsecured. The Fifth Fleet commander and staff needed some rest. Halsey, delighted to be getting back into battery, soon set out from Guam in his new flagship, the *Iowa*-class *Missouri*; *New Jersey* was refitting.

Spruance would have preferred to hang on until the Okinawa campaign was over, but his staff members were very worn down, and for their sakes he was prepared for Halsey to take command. *Missouri* arrived off Okinawa shortly after dawn on May 26, and after conferences between the two old friends, Halsey relieved Spruance less than forty-eight hours later. With Halsey came George Kosco, along with the rest of the staff.[470]

Despite the court of inquiry's recommendations, George Kosco, in his midthirties, was still to be the fleet's senior aerologist. New weather stations were operating, including the new Fleet Weather Central on Guam, but fleet weather communications were still slow, and the navy hadn't yet established long-range weather reconnaissance flights. Because of all of this, and despite the tragedy of December, many weather-related factors were the same as they had been when Halsey had last had command.[471]

A few days after Halsey relieved Spruance, on the first day of June, various fleet weather centrals began reporting a tropical disturbance in the Philippine Sea. It was the beginning of an eerie, déjà vu pattern. In mid-December, Halsey's task force had been west of Luzon, threatened by Tokkō attacks. In early June, it was to the southwest of Okinawa, where the kamikaze presence was even greater. In each case, Halsey got reports of a storm, but those reports were spotty, and he and Kosco had to make guesses about its position and track. In each case, moreover, Halsey was leery about moving west, which would expose the task force to attacks from Japanese planes.

But there were also differences. The biggest, perhaps, was that this new typhoon, smaller, faster moving, and more vicious than December's tropical cyclone, was in the process of recurving, changing its direction from the usual west and north track to a northeasterly heading. December's storm had threatened Halsey's forces from the southeast, threatening to push them toward Luzon; the June storm came at them from the southwest, giving him a chance to evade by heading into the open ocean. The recurvature, too, meant that this typhoon's dangerous semicircle was its southern and not its northern half, the exact opposite of December's typhoon. That was bad luck for Halsey, for if he chose to dodge the typhoon by heading eastward, away from

Okinawa and into the Pacific, he would be on the storm's bad side. Of course, if he dodged quickly enough, he'd miss the storm altogether.

All of these variables, however, were in flux during the first few days of June. Aboard *Missouri*, George Kosco noted the initial weather reports on the first day of the month, but those reports were of a disturbance and not a typhoon. His main concern that day was about the weather for the second and third, since the plan was for the task force to carry out air strikes at that time. The disturbance, whatever it was, was still too far away to pose any immediate threat.[472]

But the picture changed during the next few days. Reports of a tropical storm kept coming in from various sources, among them intercepted Japanese transmissions. They were all vague and contradictory; it was the old problem of too few direct observations.

On the morning of June 4, Kosco received a typhoon warning from Nimitz's Guam headquarters predicting that the storm was moving toward Okinawa. Kosco thought that the report was wrong. For one thing, the recurvature to the northeast the message suggested didn't fit the historical picture of area typhoons. (Neither had the movements of the December typhoon, but either Kosco forgot that or else he figured that the historical data was still generally the safest bet.) Meeting with Halsey and other staff members that morning, Kosco mentioned this CincPac report, but he also told Halsey of his belief that it was erroneous. Kosco recommended that the task force maintain its position and await more concrete reports.

Kosco's recommendation provoked some discussion in the staff meeting. In his usual fashion, Halsey listened to what everyone had to say, and then he announced his decision. "You are probably right, but I can't take a chance," he told Kosco, probably remembering what had happened half a year earlier. He wanted to move while he could. "If I should be forced to go westward," he explained, "I would be in shallow waters with no room to maneuver in and be in range of Japanese aircraft from China. If possible," he concluded, "I would like to be south of the typhoon."[473]

Before the morning was out, the task force was steaming slightly south of east, clearing Okinawa and the reported typhoon. At least it had just refueled, a welcome difference from December 18, and Halsey had also directed various ships in the area to make regular weather reports. But Kosco was still skeptical. His skepticism increased that afternoon when he intercepted another CincPac dispatch that reported not one, but two different storms in the area, one moving north and the other north-northeast. To Kosco, who believed that only one storm was riding the waters, the message showed the unreliability of the weather reporting system.[474]

At about the same time Kosco was reading the weather report, the transport ship USS *Ancon*, some two hundred miles west of *Missouri*, picked up something on her powerful SP radar. It was the typhoon that stations had been reporting for days. Obeying Halsey's orders, *Ancon* tracked the typhoon and radioed in a report of her contact, and then she continued on her way to the Philippines, having received no orders to the contrary.

Ancon's radar showed the typhoon to be much closer to the fleet than Kosco had suspected; it had indeed recurved and was pointing directly at the Fast Carrier Task Force and the replenishment group, which were only a hundred miles from it. To make matters worse, Halsey didn't receive *Ancon*'s dispatch until nearly midnight, several hours after she'd sent it. By that time the fast-moving storm was nearly upon him. Recent history was repeating itself.[475]

Halsey and the rest of the staff knew that the typhoon was bearing down on them, but *Ancon*'s dispatch was already old. They didn't know the storm's exact track. The dilemma, however, was simple: should they try to dodge it to the southeast, or to the northwest?

For most of the fourth, Halsey's ships had been moving east, unknowingly into the crosshairs. Farther eastward lay the freedom of the open Pacific, but also the risk of the dangerous semicircle. Westward lay the safe semicircle, along with the danger posed by the Japanese air umbrella.

Halsey discussed things hurriedly with his staff, and he also put in a call to McCain on the carrier *Shangri-La*. McCain suggested that the fleet hold its present course, 110 degrees, just south of east. Kosco, fearing that the fleet was moving straight for the dangerous semicircle, suggested a northwesterly course of three hundred degrees, almost exactly the opposite direction the fleet had been steaming for hours.[476]

McCain had tactical command of the task force, but Halsey never shirked at putting in his two cents' worth. Shortly after midnight, Halsey sided with

Kosco and recommended that McCain swing to a heading of three hundred and that the replenishment group do the same. McCain complied, reluctantly; it was a roll of the dice, and everyone knew it. "Someday," observed Mick Carney sardonically, "we are going to maneuver blindly right into a typhoon."[477]

Two hours later, that was exactly what happened.

At that point in the Okinawa campaign, the various task groups of the Fast Carrier Task Force were widely dispersed. The only two groups that Halsey and McCain had in company were TG 38.4, in which both of these admirals steamed, and TG 38.1, which was about fifteen miles to the south as the typhoon struck. Task Group 30.8, the replenishment group, was slightly farther south. The typhoon was so small and unstable that the fifteen miles made a difference; TG 38.4 escaped almost unscathed, while the storm vented its full fury on the other two groups.[478]

The best that can be said of this second typhoon is that it claimed no ships. Most of the vessels were fueled, and few of the inherently unstable *Farragut*s remained. But one of them, *Aylwin*, had the bad luck of getting caught in the path of the cyclone. Running squarely into the southern, dangerous semicircle, Bill Rogers and his crew again experienced the terrible rolling that threw the unstable destroyer hard onto her side, this time in the middle of a tropical night. Again the towering waves hurtled at her from the heart of the storm, working hard with the wind to heel the ship onto her beam-ends.

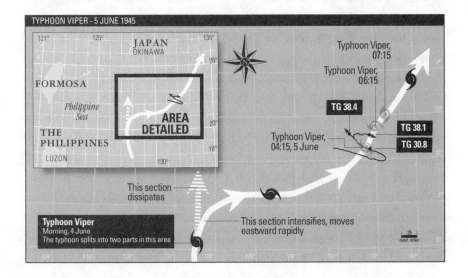

But *Aylwin* was a survivor, and once again she came through the typhoon, venturing into the maelstrom-like eye along with the rest of the replenishment group. There, jostled by the violent conical waves, nearly fifty warships struggled to keep from slamming into each other. Above them the deceptively peaceful stars gazed down while the hundred-plus-knot winds of the eye wall circled the ships like a mad pack of wolves, waiting for the inevitable moment when they would attack the vessels again.[479]

One of the destroyer escorts, *Conklin*, also had a close call, probably closer than any of her sisters experienced in the December typhoon. As she struggled against the elements, a huge, black wall hurtled towards her, nearly swamping her as it hit her full force. Suddenly she was seventy-five degrees on her starboard side, the wave flooding her engine spaces and radio rooms and washing the officer of the deck and the talker off the bridge. The talker landed on *Conklin*'s fantail just as the same wave lifted another man from the quarterdeck. Though he and the OOD were lost, *Conklin* herself survived.[480]

The open bridges of the DEs made for wild rides. Lieutenant Junior Grade J. A. Buehler of the *Evarts*-class *Mitchell* had arrived on the flying bridge at four in the morning to relieve the OOD to be greeted by the worst wind he'd ever experienced. Blowing from astern, it nearly threw him forcibly onto the bridge as he came through the hatch. Clad only in foul weather gear, Buehler made his way to the officer he was relieving. "For God's sake, send up my life belt!" he screamed into the man's ear. That was nearly the only thing anyone on the bridge heard for nearly another hour. Fighing the gale, which carried the overpowering diesel exhaust directly onto the bridge, all Buehler and the others could do was to hang on.

At one point Buehler did hear that a TBS message had ordered all the ships in his group to turn on their running lights, and the beleagured OOD passed the order on to the helmsman. But when the masthead light came on it caught the lieutenant by surprise, creating an eerie glow forward of the bridge. For a moment he thought that a canister of ammunition had exploded. He needed a moment to realize that the effect was caused by the near-zero visibility that the typhoon had imposed.

On *Mitchell* struggled, into the eye and then back into a region of the storm that made her roll more than ever, unseen vessels around her tracked only by radar and closing to as little as four hundred yards. Below in the after motor room, Harlan Dible actually had a fairly smooth ride for part of the time. The sailor had slung a hammock between two stanchions directly over the motor, and as the typhoon raged in the darkness he dozed fitfully. The hammock was largely immune to *Mitchell*'s rolling, but Dible held onto its sides anyway. The swaying motion actually helped lull him, but then the ship took a roll that went much farther than the others. Dible opened his eyes and looked below him. Instead of seeing the motor that he was expecting, he saw the bulkhead with its equipment racks. *Mitchell* was lying practically on her side. Even though she righted herself and came through the typhoon with no deaths or serious damage, that remained one of the worst moments of the war for him.[481]

Two jeep carriers of the replenishment group, *Salamaua* and *Windham Bay*, weren't as lucky as *Mitchell*. No fires started, but their planes did burst free of their lines, as so many had in December. As the seas stripped away a boom and a gun mount, while simultaneously twisting the forward part of *Salamaua*'s flight deck, a torpedo plane further aft on that deck rolled free of its fastenings and careened into others, wrecking them all and killing a sailor. *Windham Bay* had planes break free on both hangar and flight decks, and she shipped huge volumes of water into one of her elevator wells. The damage, on the whole, was less than that of December, but it was still bad, and it was of much the same type.[482]

If TG 30.8 had stayed on its original east-southeast heading, it would have cleared the typhoon completely, but the turn to the northeast in the early hours of June 5 sealed its fate. Task Group 30.1, now under the command of Rear Admiral Jocko Clark, was to the north of the replenishment group and thus closer to the track of the storm, but even it could have gotten clear with a little maneuvering. Clark had disliked the fleet's turn to the northwest from the moment it happened. But, as many commanders had in December, he'd kept his mouth shut in the belief that Halsey and McCain presumably had better information than he did. In fact, though he likely didn't know it at the time, if Halsey and McCain had turned northwest a few hours earlier, they could have cleared the safe semicircle; it was the reversal an hour and a half after midnight that kept the task groups in the bull's-eye.[483]

Even so, Clark had another chance for escape. An hour after the northwest turn, he could see the nightmare on his radars as it approached, still sixty miles in the distance, but even so he maintained course. Not long afterward one of his destroyers lost steering control, and Clark slowed his task group to keep her in company, even as the typhoon moved closer.

Then, shortly after 0400, as the seas wildly churned and the wind beat at his task group, Clark could keep silent no longer, and he contacted McCain. "I can get clear of the center of the storm quickly by steering 120 degrees," he informed the task force commander, increasing his ships' speed even as he fired off the message. "Please advise."

"We have nothing on our scope to indicate storm center," answered McCain, steaming to Clark's north in Task Group 38.4, as was Halsey.

"We very definitely have," emphasized Clark. "We have had one for one and a half hours."[484]

McCain got back to Clark within fifteen minutes and asked him for data on the storm's location, but as fate would have it, that was all the time they had left, and it may have made little difference anyway, given the warships' speeds. Five minutes later McCain gave Clark permission to maneuver at his discretion. But it was too late.

Clark's task group included four carriers. Two of them, *Hornet* and *Bennington*, were *Essex*-class ships. The other two were the light carriers *Belleau Wood* and the hapless *San Jacinto*, which the December typhoon had so badly abused. But this time *San Jacinto* got off lightly. Michael H. Kernodle, still in command, had read Nimitz's typhoon letter quite carefully, and this time he tried different tactics than he had six months earlier. In December he'd kept the terrific seas on his beam and his ship had rolled badly, shaking off her planes as a dog shakes off water after a hated bath. This time, as the storm peaked shortly before dawn, Kernodle kept the seas on his bow, and *San Jacinto* "rode beautifully," as he later declared. In December, the ship lost eight planes; on June 5 she lost only two, and those were duds incapable of flight anyway. Kernodle had placed them forward on the flight deck to serve as windbreakers.[485]

The fleet carriers, on the other hand, which had escaped serious damage six months before, found that it was their turn on June 5. Captain James B. Sykes of *Bennington* had, like Kernodle, thoroughly briefed himself on the contents of Nimitz's letter. On the fourth, when it became clear that the storm was approaching, he set Typhoon Condition Two, a state of readiness designed specifically for the contingency. Throughout the ship, department heads met with their people to make sure they were doing everything necessary to rig for heavy weather. Later, four and a half hours after midnight on the fifth, Sykes sounded general quarters and went to Typhoon Condition One as conditions began to go bad. The big ship, with the wind on her beam, rolled moderately and pitched very little. But something strange was starting to happen.

The rain and spray cut visibility from *Bennington*'s island down to nearly nothing; only occasionally could the pilothouse crew see the carrier's bow. As somewhere above, unseen, the sun presumably rose, the sailors caught a glimpse of the forward antenna mast; it was tilting over. Then rain and spray closed in again.

Three minutes later came another brief clearing, and the pilothouse crew looked again toward the bow. The mast had disappeared and now the sailors could see why: the flight deck itself was collapsing. The whole forward section, especially the corners, were being driven down by the incessantly pounding seas, which were folding the planking like a series of matchsticks.[486]

Hornet, skippered by typhoon veteran Austin K. Doyle, took the same kind of damage. Doyle, like Kernodle, was more concerned with the seas than the winds, working hard to keep *Hornet*'s bow to the former and letting the latter do what they wanted. In this attitude *Hornet* rode well, losing only two planes when a 130-knot gust blew a torpedo craft on top of a fighter. But *Hornet*'s flight deck, like *Bennington*'s, crumpled as seas crashed into it repeatedly. As in *Bennington*'s case, *Hornet*'s flight deck damage wasn't due to the pitching, which was slight, but simply to the headlong seas. The ship rode so well, in fact, that neither Doyle nor anyone else knew exactly when the deck began to collapse. At 0500 it was in good shape; by 0600 twenty-five feet had sagged onto the forecastle.[487]

The worst damage, though, was reserved for the cruiser *Pittsburgh*. A newcomer to the task force, she'd been in the Pacific for only three months when she found herself in the maw of the new typhoon. The previous December, the bow frames of the light cruiser *Miami* had buckled as the ship splashed headlong into the seas, but this was just one among many notations of damage that the Court of Inquiry had recorded. *Pittsburgh* was a newer ship, a heavy cruiser of a different class, and on June 5 nobody aboard her was likely thinking about *Miami*. But soon *Pittsburgh*'s men had their own troubles, similar to but far worse than the other ship.[488]

Sometime after the hypothetical dawn, shortly before 0630, *Pittsburgh* was taking a serious pounding, and her captain, John Gingrich, responded by setting Condition Zebra, a high-integrity status in which the ship buttoned herself up tightly both inside and out. His timing was exquisite. A few minutes later, Gingrich's first lieutenant showed up on the bridge. "There's a buckle in the second deck about frame 26," he reported, referring to a spot on the cruiser's bow roughly a hundred feet abaft the stem. Gingrich had barely had time to take this in when a massive sea hit *Pittsburgh*, lifting the whole bow section upward; then another wave hurled itself at the cruiser, sweeping under her and heaving her up. With that the whole bow, 104 feet of it, dropped and broke free, drifting ahead of the rest of the vessel. Nobody was in that section, but this reprieve from disaster lasted just a few moments. Then the bow became a potential missile that the seas could fling at the ship.

Gingrich immediately got on the TBS to Admiral Clark. "Our bow has broken off," he reported, already making decisions. "We are having to come around." *Pittsburgh* was already down at the head by six feet and flooding. As repair crews dashed forward to seal the hatch to the missing bow section and shore up the bulkhead that now stood between them and the sea, Gingrich backed the ship down. Running *Pittsburgh* stern first in waves like these might poop her, or worse, damage her screws, shafts, or rudder control, but the alternative was to risk a deadly collision with the bow and a collapse of the bulkhead under the sea's nearly incomprehensible pressure.

Gingrich's gamble paid off. Backing down hard and spewing oil from her ruptured fuel bunkers, *Pittsburgh* swung her head and cleared the dangerous wedge of metal, turning slowly inside it as Gingrich put the wind and seas first to his stern, and then, as waves broke over her from aft, onto her starboard beam. That set *Pittsburgh* to rolling, but only about twenty degrees, and it greatly eased the seas' pressure on the weak bulkhead.[489]

Just aft of that bulkhead, a nineteen-man repair party struggled to put heavy shoring timbers in place. Just behind them, and all over the ship, hatches were dogged down; if the bulkhead gave way, the whole party was dead. None of its members had any way to escape. "Come on boys," yelled a sailor as the men worked frantically, "it's curtains if we don't get this job done!"

They did it. *Pittsburgh* survived and made port. So, too, did her bow. Late that afternoon, with the typhoon having moved on and left the damaged and bruised task groups bobbing behind it, the fleet tug *Munsee* reported in. "Have sighted the suburb of *Pittsburgh* and taken it in tow," read the dispatch. The bow, nicknamed "McKeesport," which was in fact a Pittsburgh community, safely completed its journey to Guam, arriving on the eleventh, only a day behind the rest of the ship. None of *Pittsburgh*'s officers or men had been injured.

Preston Mercer, who had commanded the squadron of *Farragut*s in the December typhoon, also rode out the June storm. But by this time he had moved on to command DesRon 54, attached to Task Group 38.4, which got off quite lightly. As it so happened, during the Korean conflict Mercer would find himself the skipper of *Pittsburgh*—and of her bow.[490]

Cal Calhoun and *Dewey*, however, missed the second storm, being detailed to ferry vessels between the Ryukyus and Ulithi, and luckily so, for Mercer turned out to have been right on the night of December 18 when he advised Calhoun to turn out of the pounding sea. *Dewey* had been alongside a tender on and off ever since then to correct serious hull damage. Had Calhoun gone to *Tabberer*'s aid, the three sunken destroyers might have gained some company in Davy Jones's locker, although no one will ever know for sure. But a little over a week after the June 5 typhoon, when the task groups arrived at their new base at Leyte Gulf, where the story had begun so many months earlier, Mercer happened upon *Dewey*'s skipper. "He did it again!" were his first words to Calhoun.[491]

That was probably Nimitz's reaction as well, and likely King's too. Six sailors were dead and four more were badly injured; seventy-five planes had been lost or destroyed, with nearly another seventy needing major repair; and more than a half dozen ships had been seriously mauled. It was not the disaster of six months before, but it was still a mess. And it was precisely the sort of event that CincPac had tried to ensure would never happen again.[492]

Not seventy-two hours went by after the typhoon, then, before Nimitz convened a new court of inquiry, this one to meet on Guam, near his own headquarters. The cast was much the same: Genial John Hoover would again be its president, and Vice Admiral George D. Murray, who had been on the previous court, would serve on this one too. Ira Nunn, who'd represented Marks in December, would now serve as judge advocate. And Nimitz again empowered the court to give an opinion on whether anyone had committed offenses.[493]

On June 15 the new court met, and it, too, ran for eight days, the same length of time as the earlier one. Many of the witnesses were the same, among them Kernodle, Carney, McCain, Kosco, and, of course, Halsey. This time, though, the questioning was sometimes more pointed. On many occasions the admirals at the green table asked skippers bluntly about whether they were acquainted with Nimitz's typhoon letter. While the answer was routinely a very emphatic yes, skippers still put forth reasons why they delayed independent maneuvering, and those reasons weren't without merit. They were best stated by Captain Doyle of *Hornet*, who'd also conned his carrier though the December typhoon. "We were getting into something where we had to extricate ourselves as a group rather then by any individual action," he tried to explain of the turn to the northwest.[494]

The court took it remarkably easy on Halsey when the fleet commander testified. Halsey probably knew even before the typhoon was over that he would face a new inquiry, and as the seas began calming he'd angrily signaled Nimitz about the continued state of sluggish communications and spotty, contradictory weather reports. Once the court swore him in, he continued the attack on these systems, not so much testifying as complaining. "It is not necessary for me to tell you gentlemen what typhoons in their formation are—that their movement is very unpredictable and that they are very prima donnish in their actions," he said bluntly. The early reports placed the storm well to the west; the *Ancon* dispatch, he explained, had come as a nasty surprise, putting as it did the fleet in the target area. In the face of the risk of being overtaken by the dangerous semicircle, he stated with no apology, he had decided to advise McCain to cut across the front of the storm by heading northwest.

Then he renewed the attack. "As the responsible commander in the combat zone I believe that I am fully entitled to have every bit of information that can be made available about storms," he fumed. After all, he observed, aerologists in the Atlantic could track hurricanes with high-altitude weather flights. "I believe we have the facilities in this area to have given me this information," he argued. "I did not get it. B-29s can travel up to high altitudes," he pointed out. "They have all the equipment. They could be placed over any suspected typhoon and the typhoon can be tracked. Had I had any knowledge beforehand of the track of this typhoon such as I now possess it would have been the easiest matter in the world to have employed it away ahead of the storm."

Then he moved on to the message log jam.

> I was without such knowledge, from my own point of view, the point of view of my staff, of any specific knowledge of this storm, until I got the report from the *Ancon*. This report was delivered to me four and a half hours after the time of its file. We had another report from the *Ancon* which gave an erroneous report of the storm center, which we received some nine hours after it was filed. We had a report from the southwest Pacific area twenty-seven odd hours late. It is imperative that communications in regard to storms must be immediate. We are not telling the Japs anything when we tell them a typhoon is coming because they have nothing out there they can use it for. I believe it absolutely imperative that these messages come under plain English on operational priority and if necessary on a special circuit. I will let the communicators handle that because it is out of my province and knowledge. But it is not out of my province that they must be immediate.[495]

McCain took a different approach. Questioned more closely than Halsey, he simply stated that he had preferred the easterly course, which he still thought would have taken the fleet clear of the storm, but that he'd deferred to Halsey. But it had been McCain's decision about the independent maneuvering of his task groups. Jocko Clark, who commanded the group that took the worst pounding, highlighted this in a question. "We would like to know why you did not release Task Group 38.1 at 0420 when you were advised, 'I can get clear of the center of the storm quickest by heading 120 degrees. Please advise,'" the task group commander asked his superior.

"I debated that question for twenty minutes to find out if I knew something that Admiral Clark did not know," answered McCain. "I did know that course 120 degrees would buck heavy seas," he added, "but on finding that Admiral Clark did know this I told him to use his own judgment. If twenty minutes delay made any difference," he concluded, "I'm sorry."[496]

Kosco drew some of the closest questioning of all. He agreed with Halsey about the confusing nature of the weather reports during the first days of June. The report from *Ancon*, he stated, was "the only one that was of any value" in fixing the storm's true position. With the receipt of that message, Kosco explained, he'd believed that the fleet was in the face of the dangerous semicircle. "All rules and all precautionary measures," he stated, implicitly referring to Nimitz's typhoon letter, "indicated that we should make every effort to get into the safe semi-circle. At that moment," he confessed, "I recommended to the admiral to come to course 300 degrees until the weather cleared."[497]

And so went the proceedings, with its usual moments of drama, uncertainty, and confusion, the court trying to piece together the story of what really had happened. Then, after the last witness departed, Nunn arose to make an argument unlike anything that Gates had said in January or December.

> I believe it is my duty as judge advocate to advise the court officially in matters of law if there appears to be any doubt on questions of law. Whether or not the matter which I will discuss is doubtful, I don't know, but it is very important, in my opinion. It is my opinion that the testimony that this court has heard contains sufficient material to make out a prima facie case of culpable inefficiency in the performance of duty on the part of the Commander Third Fleet. It is a type of thing which is made punishable by paragraph 9 of the 5th Article for the Government of the Navy, and is treated briefly in Section 67 of *Naval Courts and Boards*. It is also my opinion that the record discloses that an act or omission by the Commander Third Fleet was the proximate cause of the disaster. In examining the facts and in employing the usual legalistic methods of fixing liability as between two persons or in finding a liability to the public on the part of any public servant, the law of causation indicates that the proximate, or legal, cause of damage to the Third Fleet on June fifth, was the turning of the Fleet to course 300° at about 0130 on June fifth. Any other inefficiencies either subsequent or previous to that moment, any other

pieces of negligence either previous or subsequent to that event, may be contributory causes, but the outstanding and proximate cause, the legal cause, of the disaster was that change in course at a time when the officer who caused that change to be made had in his possession, or in the exercise of reasonable care should have had in his possession, sufficient information which if properly and promptly evaluated would have shown the danger involved.[498]

With that the court began to prepare its statement of findings.

The paragraph to which Nunn was referring was akin to a catch-all provision in the navy's governing articles. Formally entitled "Neglect of Orders," the offense applied to anyone in the navy who proved to be "negligent or careless in obeying orders, or culpably inefficient in the performance of duty." Nunn had focused on the paragraph's latter portion, which centered on the words "culpable inefficiency," as Nunn had pointed out. *Naval Courts and Boards*, glossing the phrase, defined "inefficiency" as "want of power or energy sufficient for the desired effect; inefficacy; incapacity." But the critical word was "culpable," which meant "deserving of blame or censure." To put this another way, culpable inefficiency, as Nunn had just pointed out to the court, was an offense that called for court-martial. It was, in fact, the very same charge on which Ensign Nimitz had been tried after grounding USS *Decatur* in 1908.[499]

John Hoover had lost patience with Halsey. Whatever shortcomings remained with communications and the weather service, the final responsibility lies with the commander. Despite Nimitz's pointed warning of February, Halsey had repeated, to an almost eerie degree, the events of December barely a week after resuming command of the fleet. Personally, Hoover wanted to see Halsey court-martialed.[500]

But Halsey was famous and powerful, and whatever his shortcomings, he had worked tirelessly from the first day of the war to beat the Japanese down. That counted for something. So Hoover and the other top admirals tried to find the right balance, and the day after Nunn's statement, they announced what it was.

While not recommending any courts-martial, the court came down hard on Bill Halsey, and to a lesser degree on other commanders. Explicitly noting the similarity between the June and December typhoons, Hoover and his associates found that "the evident meaning and plain intent" of Nimitz's typhoon letter "was not fully understood or followed by responsible commanders in the Third Fleet." The court further declared, in keeping with Nunn's argument, that the key moment came "when the fleet course was changed from 110 degrees to 300 degrees by Commander Task Force 38 on instructions of Commander Third Fleet, in an attempt to cross ahead of the storm into the left semi-circle. . . . This change to 300 degrees was extremely ill-advised considering the known location of the storm center. . . ." Hoover and his fellows also criticized Nimitz's staff for problems in the communications and aerological divisions, but then it returned to Halsey as well as McCain. In the end it absolved everyone of serious blame except for them; Admirals Clark and D. B. Beary, the commanders of the two task groups that the typhoon overtook, shared blame to a lesser degree. The latter two, the court found, should be admonished by Nimitz; but Halsey and McCain deserved different treatment. "The court recommends," read the opinion, "that serious consideration be given to assigning Admiral William F. Halsey, Junior, U.S. Navy, and Vice Admiral John S. Mc-Cain, U.S. Navy, to other duty."[501]

It was up to Nimitz, of course, as it had been before, to accept or reject these conclusions. The following month he rendered his own judgment, concurring that the main responsibility for the storm damage rested with Halsey and McCain, with Beary and Clark to a lesser degree, and with himself along with his staff. Nimitz did note, however, that while the Pacific weather reporting system was patterned after the Atlantic system, the Pacific problem "is very much more difficult in that extensive communication systems connecting reliable observing stations are not available for rapid dissemination of weather information from areas that affect direction of movement of storms in the western Pacific, such as Siberia and North China. On the contrary," he continued, "currently available continental information is generally unreliable, considerably delayed, and often misleading." Nimitz pointed out that he had discussed these problems with King in the past. It was partly for these reasons that Nimitz disapproved the court's finding that Halsey, McCain, Beary, and Clark were deserving of blame, as well as its recommendation of admonishing and reassigning the officers. "Admiral William F. Halsey, Junior, U.S. Navy," CincPac declared, "has rendered invaluable service to his country. His skill and determination have been demonstrated time and again in combat with the enemy." The three subordinate admirals, Nimitz went on, "have likewise, during their present assignments, rendered services of great value in prosecuting the war against our enemies." Because of these factors, Nimitz concluded, he would not censure the officers, let alone court-martial anyone.[502]

The affair reached King's desk by the end of the month. Some sources say that Secretary of the Navy Forrestal, taking an interest in it, wanted to retire Halsey. But in the end King, rather sourly, concurred with Nimitz. "The record shows conclusively that there was ineptness in obtaining, disseminating, and acting upon meteorological data," he stated, which had led the fleet into the storm. "The gravity of the occurrence is accentuated by the fact that the senior officers concerned were also involved in a similar, and poorly handled, situation during the typhoon of December 1944." King admitted that the difficulties in getting good weather reports that Nimitz described made things tricky in the Pacific; nevertheless, he stated, "responsible officers on each occasion had sufficient information to enable them to avoid the worst part of the storm area had they reacted to the situation as it developed with the weatherwise skill to be expected of professional officers."

Then, having spoken so bluntly, King backed off, though he remained rather surly. "Notwithstanding the above, I recommend that no individual disciplinary measures be taken," he declared, for the same reasons that Nimitz had given.[503]

By then, however, King had already taken steps to express his displeasure. In mid-July McCain had received word that he was to be relieved the following month, after which he would become the deputy head of the Veterans Administration. It was a hard blow. The turn to three hundred degrees had been Halsey's idea, and McCain had disliked it. But King apparently decided that someone's head had to roll, and Halsey was too popular. Because of McCain's position, then, and despite his invaluable Tokkō defense tactics, he was the man King chose to pay for the mistakes that many people had made.[504]

The news hit McCain hard. Always frail, he seemed to shrink even further at this turn of events. Some believed that McCain may even have suffered a heart attack during his final weeks at sea but kept quiet about it. But whether or not it was true, McCain was dead by mid-September, surviving only long enough to return to the United States following Japan's surrender. "He knew his number was up," Mick Carney decided, "but he wouldn't lie down and die until he got home."[505]

Halsey lived considerably longer, surviving his friend by nearly fifteen years. Late in 1945, he was awarded a fifth star, joining Nimitz, King, and de facto chairman of the Joint Chiefs of Staff William D. Leahy in the rank of Fleet Admiral. It was an accolade Ray Spruance never received. In the short run, Halsey continued to maintain that he had lacked enough information to enable him to escape the typhoons; in the long run, though he remained perhaps the most popular admiral in the history of the United States Navy, he found himself often defending, sometimes quite angrily, the actions he'd taken in the Battle of Leyte Gulf. About the courts of inquiry following the typhoons, he tended to remain silent.[506]

George Kosco, too, had a long career after the war, becoming a well-known aerologist in naval circles. More than twenty years after the fact, he penned his memoir of the two deadly typhoons. To keep them straight, he gave them names. The practice of naming tropical cyclones didn't begin until after the war, and Kosco's designations were never official. Nevertheless, they became well-known titles and, except for Halsey's Task Force Zero and the original Divine Wind of the year 1281, they were probably the first two typhoons to have even unofficial titles. Both of them Kosco named after poisonous, dangerous serpents, due to their winds' coiling patterns. The June 1945 storm he called Viper. The first, more catastrophic typhoon he named Cobra.

The sailors who had steamed with Kosco and Halsey into the jaws of these tropical cyclones and survived the ordeals remembered them with a vividness that was frightening to the point of inspiring nightmares, well into ripe old age.

All this, however, even McCain's impending death, lay in the future. For now, Third Fleet had a war to fight and to finish. By the end of June, Okinawa was largely secure. On the first day of July, the fleet under the command of Admiral Bill Halsey weighed anchor at Leyte Gulf and steamed north, toward the Japanese Home Islands.

Behind it, deceptively calm, lay the the tropical reaches of the Pacific, the bones of three recently-sunken destroyers resting somewhere within it, biding its time with the patience of eons.

Author's Note

During World War II, William F. Halsey received a letter from an admirer who was angry at the "armchair admirals" who were always second-guessing America's top military and naval commanders. "I believe in this war we have more of these 'experts' than ever before," he wrote Halsey. "I am sure you fellows who are in the 'thick of things' must get a laugh out of some of these armchair gents."[507]

I am, quite obviously, one of those armchair admirals, having written this book in the comfort of my study at sixty years remove from the Philippines campaign and Typhoons Cobra and Viper. As such, I have tried to remember my place. I have little if any right to criticize decisions and actions taken by men who were feeling the pressures of combat and violent weather at sea, defending the United States at the risk, and often the cost, of their lives.

Such criticism hasn't been my intention. Anything of that sort in these pages merely reflects, I believe, concerns and comments of participants in these episodes, or else their superiors. The Pacific Fleet was a large organization in the final year of the war, and many viewpoints were to be found. What I have written simply recovers what people in the know thought at the time, and they often disagreed with each other, sometimes quite strongly.

I hope, then, that readers will take this book not as a condemnation of any member of the Third/Fifth Fleet or of any other part of the United States Navy. On the contrary: Americans should stand in awe of the fact that an organization consisting mainly of men who were neither professional warriors nor professional mariners steamed forth to form, with their ships, one of the greatest fleets in history. That people of later generations can at leisure suggest how that fleet's sailors might have done things differently should be seen as a tribute to greatness, which is what I have tried to write here. In the past few years, I have interviewed dozens of graying, elderly men for this project in person or by telephone, listening to their jokes, their anecdotes, their sober stories of their friends' deaths in the war and being under their enemy's guns, their hilarious accounts about life aboard ship, and, of course, their battles with a sea and sky whipped by a typhoon into frenzy. Usually, when I expressed my admiration of what they had done, they shrugged it off, remarking that they hadn't done anything special. "It was just a job," they would say, or "We only did what we had to do." Never in my years as a historian have I been more aware of men's heroism than in those moments.

Whatever value this book has is due to these men, and to the many other people who helped me complete it. My first thanks go to the veterans who graciously allowed me to talk and correspond with them: Walter J. Barry; Ralph J. Baum; Don Beaty; Howard A. Becker; William Cal Bengston; Charlie Boyst; Ervin Eugene Bullard; Bishop Burmeister; Cal Calhoun; Ben Coulliard; Leo J. Cox; George Culpepper; Don Darnell; Robert E. de Jong; Sal DeLuca; Harlan Dible; Pat Douhan; Ben Doyle; Ken Drummond; Charles Edwin Eamigh; Walter "Walt" Ellis; Stan Franklin; Bill Hanger; Ralph Hanson; Robert Harp; Herbert H. Hepworth; Joe Hoyer; Arthur "Art" J. Hussey, Sr.; Anthony Iacono; Edward J. Joyeusaz; Fred Keller; Albert J. Konan; Herb Lapp; Oneil "Blackie" Leonard; Sheldon Levin; Jack M. Matthew; Robert G. McAlpine; Gordon McBride; Bill Mc-Clain; David Mincey; Cloud Morgan; William Murphy; Howard Nations; Wiley S. Obenshain, Jr.; Mark Pence; Bill Pondel; Thomas M. Reavley; Grier L. Sims; Delos W. Smith; James R. Thomas; Lewis Thomas; George Thompson; Stewart Wasoba; and Don Ziglar. I am also grateful to the friends and family members of these and other veterans who shared their materials and their memories with me, and who helped me to locate men who steamed with Halsey.

My next thanks go to the readers and researchers I have leaned upon during this project, especially during the final weeks of writing when, as I nursed a broken elbow (my writing arm, of course), my leaning was some-times quite literal: Vicki Arnold; Eriko Baxter; David Bushey; Olivia Bushey; Phillip Bushey; the honorable Saxby Chambliss; Patsy White Cotten; Dave Hayden; Cary Knapp; Jason Levitt; Lieutenant Commander Buckner F. Melton, Sr., USNR (Ret.); Mrs. Buckner F. Melton, Sr.; Sarah Rice; Bill Stembridge; Edna Williamson; and of the Naval Historical Center, Dr. Bob Schneller and his fellow staff members. Special thanks are due to Dr. R. Kirby Godsey, chancellor and former president of Mercer University, and Dr. Horace Fleming, Mercer's provost, whose generous support allowed this book to come into being; Cathy Hayden; Leigh Singleton; David Edward Nelson; and to my agent, Ed Knappmann, who found it a home.

No acknowledgments of mine are complete without the name of Dr. Carol K. Melton of Macon State College.

Notes

I have occasionally altered spelling, punctuation, and capitalization in primary source quotations for the sake of standardization and readability. While I have not changed the substance of any of the quotations, readers should consult those sources directly for the most accurate renderings.

1   B. H. Liddell Hart, *History of the Second World War* (New York: Perigree, 1982), pp. 225–26.

2   Samuel Eliot Morison, *History of United States Naval Operations in World War II*, vol. 12, *Leyte* (Boston: Little, Brown, 1958), p. 90; Francis E. McMurtrie, ed., *Jane's Fighting Ships 1944/5* (New York: Arco, 1971), pp. 460–61.

3   Theodore Roscoe, *United States Destroyer Operations in World War II* (Annapolis, MD: U.S. Naval Institute, 1953), p. xvii.

4   Roscoe, *Destroyer Operations*, chs. 1–2.

5   McMurtrie, *Jane's Fighting Ships*, pp. 461–85.

6   On Japanese expansionism in the generation prior to the war, see Paul Kennedy, *The Rise and Fall of the Great Powers: Economic Change and Military Conflict from 1500 to 2000* (New York: Random House, 1987), pp. 298–303; Carol Willcox Melton, *Between War and Peace: Woodrow Wilson and the American Expeditionary Force in Siberia, 1918–1921* (Macon, GA: Mercer University Press, 2001), pp. 3–8, 54–55.

7   Walter A. McDougall, *Let the Sea Make a Noise: Four Hundred Years of Cataclysm, Conquest, War and Folly in the North Pacific* (New York: Avon Books, 1993), pp. 18–19; Ellen Churchill Semple, *American History and Its Geographic Conditions* (Boston: Houghton, Mifflin, 1903), ch. 19.

8   On American strategy to defeat Japan, and naval theory generally, see Edward S. Miller, *War Plan Orange: The U.S. Strategy to Defeat Japan, 1897–1945* (Annapolis, MD: Naval Institute Press, 1991); Ronald H. Spector, *Eagle Against the Sun: The American War with Japan* (New York: The Free Press, 1985); Julian S. Corbett, *Some Principles of Maritime Strategy* (London: Longmans, Green, 1911); Alfred Thayer Mahan, *The Influence of Sea Power Upon History, 1660–1783* (Boston: Little, Brown, 1890).

9   E. B. Potter, *Nimitz* (Annapolis, MD: Naval Institute Press, 1976), p. 319.

10 Thomas J. Cutler, *The Battle of Leyte Gulf 23–26 October 1944* (New York: HarperCollins, 1994), p. 19.

11 William F. Halsey and J. Bryan III, *Admiral Halsey's Story* (Washington, DC: Zenger Publishing, repr. 1980), p. 81; E. B. Potter, *Bull Halsey* (Annapolis, MD: Naval Institute Press, 1985), p. 13.

12 Walter J. Barry, interview by the author, tape recording, January 9, 2006; Don Beaty, interview by the author, tape recording, November 2, 2003.

13 Oniel "Blackie" Leonard, interview by the author, tape recording, January 9, 2006.

14 Anthony Iacono, interview by the author, tape recording, August 5, 2005. This doubtless took place on the same occasion as the episode Halsey himself referred to in his autobiography. Halsey and Bryan, *Admiral Halsey's Story*, p. 225.

15 Potter, *Bull Halsey*, p. 179.

16 Potter, *Bull Halsey*, p. 346.

17 Potter, *Bull Halsey*, p. 218.

18 Potter, *Bull Halsey*, p. 266.

19 Rear Admiral Frank Jack Fletcher, commanding Task Force 17, was the senior American naval officer present at Midway, but after his flagship, aircraft carrier *Yorktown*, was knocked out of action, Fletcher surrendered operational command to Spruance. Thomas B. Buell, *The Quiet Warrior: A Biography of Admiral Raymond A. Spruance* (Boston: Little, Brown, 1974), pp. 120–21, 139.

20 Potter, *Bull Halsey*, p. 160.

21 Cutler, *Battle of Leyte Gulf*, pp. 119–20.

22 Potter, *Nimitz*, p. 239; Potter, *Bull Halsey*, pp. 268, 275.

23 Morison, *History of United States Naval Operations*, 12:12; Cutler, *Battle of Leyte Gulf*, p. 115.

24 Potter, *Nimitz*, p. 298.

25 Buell, *Quiet Warrior*, pp. 257–58, 265.

26 William Manchester, *American Caesar: Douglas MacArthur 1880–1964* (Boston: Little, Brown, 1978), p. 166.

27 Manchester, *American Caesar*, p. 280.

28 John Gunther, *The Riddle of MacArthur* (New York: Harper, 1951), pp. 41–42; Buell, *Quiet Warrior*, pp. 207–8.

29 Manchester, *American Caesar*, p. 245.

30 Manchester, *American Caesar*, pp. 270–71.

31 Manchester, *American Caesar*, p. 368.

32 Manchester, *American Caesar*, p. 369.

33 Manchester, *American Caesar*, p. 370.

34 Potter, *Nimitz*, pp. 321–23.

35 Potter, *Bull Halsey*, p. 279; Cutler, *Battle of Leyte Gulf*, p. 60.

36 Cutler, *Battle of Leyte Gulf*, pp. 66–69.

37 Potter, *Bull Halsey*, p. 286.

38 Potter, *Bull Halsey*, p. 279.

39 Potter, *Bull Halsey*, p. 287.

40 For the role of *Darter* and *Dace*, see Clay Blair, Jr., *Silent Victory: The U.S. Submarine War Against Japan* (Philadelphia: Lippincott, 1975), pp. 751–58. For a critical treatment of the battle as a whole, see H. P. Wilmott, *The Battle of Leyte Gulf: The Last Fleet Action* (Bloomington: Indiana University Press,

2005), ch. 6.

41 Cutler, *Battle of Leyte Gulf*, p. 119; Morison, *History of United States Naval Operations,* 12:175.

42 Cutler, *Battle of Leyte Gulf*, p. 121.

43 Cutler, *Battle of Leyte Gulf*, pp. 148, 152–53; Akira Yoshimura, *Build the Mushashi! The Birth and Death of the World's Greatest Battleship*, trans. Vincent Murphy (Tokyo: Kodansha International, 1991), pp. 159–71; Morison, *History of United States Naval Operations*, 12:176.

44 Cutler, *Battle of Leyte Gulf*, p. 146.

45 Morison, *History of United States Naval Operations*, 12:185–87.

46 Cutler, *Battle of Leyte Gulf*, p. 150; Morison, *History of United States Naval Operations*, 12:187–89.

47 Cutler, *Battle of Leyte Gulf*, pp. 160–61.

48 Cutler, *Battle of Leyte Gulf*, p. 260; Morison, *History of United States Naval Operations*, 12:319.

49 Potter, *Bull Halsey*, p. 296.

50 Morison, *History of United States Naval Operations*, 12:189–90, 195.

51 Potter, *Nimitz*, pp. 735–36.

52 Cutler, *Battle of Leyte Gulf*, pp. 207–08.

53 Cutler, *Battle of Leyte Gulf*, pp. 210–11.

54 Theodore Taylor, *The Magnificent Mitscher* (New York: Norton, 1954), sec. 3.

55 Taylor, *Mitscher*, pp. 260–62; Cutler, *Battle of Leyte Gulf*, pp. 212–13.

56 Cutler, *Battle of Leyte Gulf*, pp. 226–27; Morison, *History of United States Naval Operations*, 12: ch. 12; Roscoe, *Destroyer Operations*, pp. 424–37. For the saga of Taffy 3's heroic battle, see James D. Hornfischer, *The Last Stand of the Tin Can Sailors: The Extraordinary World War II Story of the U.S. Navy's Finest Hour* (New York: Bantam, 2004).

57 Potter, *Nimitz*, pp. 338–41; Potter, *Bull Halsey*, pp. 302–04; Halsey and Bryan, *Admiral Halsey's Story*, pp. 220–21.

58 Potter, *Bull Halsey*, pp. 222–24.

59 Potter, *Bull Halsey*, p. 226. After the war, Halsey bristled whenever historians or other officers took issue with his decisions, engaging in blunt correspondence on the subject with, among others, Admiral King (Potter, *Bull Halsey*, pp. 371–72); Halsey's future, and generally sympathetic, biographer (Halsey to E. B. Potter, 27 July 1959, Halsey Papers, Military File, Library of Congress; Fleet Admiral Halsey's Comments on Chapter 39 [*The Battle of Leyte Gulf*] of Prof. E. B. Potter's New Book, Halsey Papers, Military File, Library of Congress); and "a son-of-a-bitch named Morison" (Halsey to Robert B. Carney, 10 November 1958, Halsey Papers, Military File, Library of Congress), all of whom were critical of his Leyte Gulf choices. While maintaining decorum in public, Halsey took a different tone in private, once telling former staff officers that he wanted to get Admiral Morison's "cajones in a vise and set up on them" (Halsey to Ralph E. Wilson and H. D. Moulton, 14 November 1958, Halsey Papers, Military File, Library of Congress; Potter,

Bull Halsey, p. 379.)

60 Buell, *Quiet Warrior*, p. 231–32.

61 Cf. Manchester, *American Caesar*, pp. 277–79.

62 David E. Fisher, *The Scariest Place on Earth: Eye to Eye with Hurricanes* (New York: Random House, 1994), pp. 41–45.

63 *Webster's Collegiate Dictionary* (11th ed.), s.v. "hurricane." Throughout the Caribbean one finds many tribal variations of the word. See *Oxford English Dictionary*, 2nd ed., s.v. "hurricane."

64 William J. Kotsch and Richard Henderson, *Heavy Weather Guide*, 2nd ed. (Annapolis, MD: Naval Institute Press, 1984), p. 167; *Oxford English Dictionary*, 2nd ed., s.v. "typhoon."

65 Ivan Ray Tannehill, *Hurricanes: Their Nature and History* (Princeton, NJ: Princeton University Press, 1938), p. 3.

66 *Oxford English Dictionary*, 2nd ed., s.v. "typhoon"; Tannehill, *Hurricanes*, p. 1; See Henry Piddington, *The Sailor's Horn-Book For the Law Of Storms* (London: John Wiley, 1848), bk. 8.

67 Kotsch and Henderson, *Heavy Weather Guide*, pp. 91, 95.

68 Fisher, *Scariest Place on Earth*, pp. 58–59.

69 Jeffrey Rosenfeld, *Eye of the Storm: Inside the World's Deadliest Hurricanes, Tornadoes, and Blizzards* (New York: Plenum Trade, 1999), p. 244; Kotsch and Henderson, *Heavy Weather Guide*, pp. 95, 102.

70 Rosenfeld, *Eye of the Storm*, pp. 117, 118–39.

71 Rosenfeld, *Eye of the Storm*, pp. 2, 117.

72 Kotsch and Henderson, *Heavy Weather Guide*, p. 66.

73 Fisher, *Scariest Place on Earth*, p. x.

74 Rosenfeld, *Eye of the Storm*, pp. 223–26; Kotsch and Henderson, *Heavy Weather Guide*, pp. xiii, 113.

75 Rosenfeld, *Eye of the Storm*, pp. 225, 234; Pete Davies, *Devil's Music: In the Eye of a Hurricane* (London: Michael Joseph, 2000), p. 273.

76 Fisher, *Scariest Place on Earth*, pp. 98–99. For an account of the notorious Galveston hurricane, see, for example, Erik Larson, *Isaac's Storm: A Man, a Time, and the Deadliest Hurricane in History* (New York: Crown Publishers, 1999); Patricia Bellis Bixel and Elizabeth Hayes Turner, *Galveston and the 1900 Storm: Catastrophe and Catalyst* (Austin: University of Texas Press, 2000); Bob Sheets and Jack Williams, *Hurricane Watch: Forecasting the Deadliest Storms on Earth* (New York: Vintage, 2001), ch. 3.

77 Davies, *Devil's Music*, pp. 6–7, 274. For the official categorization of Katrina, see http://www.nhc.noaa.gov/archive/2005/pub/al122005.public_b.026.shtml? (last visited October 9, 2006).

78 Davies, *Devil's Music*, p. 15.

79 Kotsch and Henderson, *Heavy Weather Guide*, p. 114.

80 Fisher, *Scariest Place on Earth*, pp. 44–46.

81 Kotsch and Henderson, *Heavy Weather Guide*, pp. 113–15.

82 Kotsch and Henderson, *Heavy Weather Guide*, p. 15.

83 Davies, *Devil's Music*, pp. 11, 14.

84 Joseph Conrad, "Typhoon," in *The Portable Conrad*, ed. Morton Dauwen Zabel, rev. ed. (New York: Penguin, 1975), p. 267.

85 Kotsch and Henderson, *Heavy Weather Guide*, p. 117.

86 Kotsch and Henderson, *Heavy Weather Guide*, pp. 116–18; Fisher, *Scariest Place on Earth*, pp. 97–98.

87 Lewis A. Kimberly, "Samoa and the Hurricane of March, 1889," in *Papers of the Military Historical Society of Massachusetts*, vol. 12, *Naval Actions and History 1799–1898* (Boston: Griffith-Stillings Press, 1902), pp. 305, 314.

88 Raphael Semmes, *Memoirs of Service Afloat During the War between the States* (Baton Rouge: Louisiana State University Press, 1996), pp. 475–76.

89 Rosenfeld, *Eye of the Storm*, pp. 234–35.

90 Fisher, *Scariest Place on Earth*, pp. 46–47; Harold C. Syrett, ed., Alexander Hamilton to the *Royal Danish American Gazette*, 6 Sept. 1772, in *The Papers of Alexander*, ed. Harold C. Syrett (New York: Columbia University Press, 1961), 1:35.

91 Paul M. Kennedy, *The Samoan Tangle: A Study in Anglo-German-American Relations 1878–1900* (New York: Barnes and Noble Books, 1974), pp. 8–9, 12–14. For a general account of the Samoan typhoon, see Edwin P. Hoyt, *The Typhoon That Stopped a War* (New York: David McKay, 1968).

92 Kennedy, *Samoan Tangle*, pp. 6–8; Lewis A. Kimberly, "Samoa and the Hurricane," p. 321; T. D. Taylor, *New Zealand's Naval Story: Naval Policy and Practice, Naval Occasions, Visiting Warships* (Wellington, New Zealand: A. H. & A. W. Reed, 1948), pp. 204–05; Kotsch and Henderson, *Heavy Weather Guide*, pp. 96–97.

93 Kimberly, "Samoa and the Hurricane," p. 313.

94 Kimberly, "Samoa and the Hurricane," pp. 313, 329, 336, 343.

95 Kimberly, "Samoa and the Hurricane," pp. 346–47.

96 Kimberly, "Samoa and the Hurricane," p. 343.

97 Kimberly, "Samoa and the Hurricane," p. 343.

98 Kimberly, "Samoa and the Hurricane," p. 322.

99 Kimberly, "Samoa and the Hurricane," pp. 325–26.

100 Kimberly, "Samoa and the Hurricane," p. 327.

101 Taylor, *New Zealand's Naval Story*, pp. 205–06; Kimberly, "Samoa and the Hurricane," pp. 328–31.

102 Taylor, *New Zealand's Naval Story*, pp. 205–06.

103 Taylor, *New Zealand's Naval Story*, pp. 203–04; Kimberly, "Samoa and the Hurricane," pp. 336, 343–44, 350–51, 355–57; J.A.C. Gray, *Amerika Samoa: A History of American Samoa and Its United States Naval Administration* (Annapolis: Unitied States Naval Institute, 1960) p. 91; Kennedy, *Samoan Tangle*, pp. 86; *Dictionary of American Naval Fighting Ships 5* (Washington: Naval History Division, Department of the Navy, 1970) (hereafter DANFS) 5:96.

[104] Cf. Samuel Flagg Bemis, *A Diplomatic History of the United States,* rev. ed. (New York: Henry Holt, 1947), p. 457.

[105] See, generally, Harold A. Winters, *Battling the Elements: Weather and Terrain in the Conduct of War* (Baltimore, MD: Johns Hopkins University Press, 1998).

[106] Kotsch and Henderson, *Heavy Weather Guide*, pp. 94–100.

[107] Kotsch and Henderson, *Heavy Weather Guide*, pp. 94–100; William C. Redfield, "Remarks on the Prevailing Storms of the Atlantic Coast," *American Journal of Science and Arts* 20 (1831): 17–51.

[108] Tannehill, *Hurricanes*, pp. 5–8; see, generally, Donald Robert Whitnah, *A History of the United States Weather Bureau* (Urbana: University of Illinois Press, 1961).

[109] Rosenfeld, *Eye of the Storm*, pp. 230–32.

[110] Rosenfeld, *Eye of the Storm*, pp. 96–97; John Keegan, *The First World War* (New York: Knopf, 1999), pp. 197–99.

[111] Rosenfeld, *Eye of the Storm*, pp. 97–102.

[112] Rosenfeld, *Eye of the Storm*, pp. 97, 108–14. The rise of aviation, naval and otherwise, increased both the need for and the ability to collect upper-atmosphere weather data. See Sheets and Williams, *Hurricane Watch*, chs. 3–4.

[113] Rosenfeld, *Eye of the Storm*, pp. 112–14. For the growth of the navy's weather system, see *World War II Administrative History, Bureau of Aeronautics*, vol. 15, *Aerology* (Washington, DC: U.S. Department of the Navy, 1957). These volumes are available at the Navy Department Library in Washington, DC.

[114] Rosenfeld, *Eye of the Storm*, p. 5; H. Arakawa, "The Weather and Great Historical Events in Japan," *Weather* (May 1960): 153–56; Richard Williams, "The Divine Wind," *Weatherwise* (October/November 1991): 11–14. This was, in fact, the second such storm. The first—possibly not a full-fledged typhoon—had struck with less fury but equally decisive results during Kublai's invasion of 1274. Williams, "Divine Wind," pp. 11–14; Arakawa, "Great Historical Events," pp. 155–56.

[115] Denis Warner and Peggy Warner, *The Sacred Warriors: Japan's Suicide Legions* (New York: Van Nostrand Reinhold, 1982), pp. 57–60, 85–88. On the symbolism of the cherry blossom in Japanese military culture, see Emiko Ohnuki-Tierney, *Kamikaze, Cherry Blossoms, and Nationalisms: The Militarization of Aesthetics and Japanese History* (Chicago: University of Chicago Press, 2002). In part three of her book, Ohnuki-Tierney deals specifically with the kamikaze squadrons.

[116] Raymond Lamont-Brown, *Kamikaze: Japan's Suicide Samurai* (London: Cassell, 1999), p. 52.

[117] Lamont-Brown, *Kamikaze*, p. 52; Warner and Warner, *Sacred Warriors*, pp. 90, 94, 103.

[118] Mordecai G. Sheftall, *Blossoms in the Wind: Human Legacies of the Kamikaze* (New York: NAL Caliber, 2005), p. 59n.

[119] Yamamoto Tsunetomo, *Hagakure: The Book of the Samurai*, trans. William

Scott Wilson (Tokyo: Kodansha International, 1979), p. 17.

[120] George Friedman and Meredith Friedman, *The Future of War: Power, Technology, and American World Dominance in the 21st Century* (New York: Crown Publishers, 1996), pp. 29, 209–10.

[121] See, for example, Sheftall, *Blossoms in the Wind*, pp. 34–35; Ryuji Nagatsuka, *I Was a Kamikaze* (New York: Macmillan, 1973), pp. 62–63.

[122] Friedman and Friedman, *Future of War*, pp. 29, 209–10.

[123] Nagatsuka, *I Was a Kamikaze*, p. 177.

[124] Cf. Arthur C. Clarke, *2001: A Space Odyssey* (New York: ROC, 1968), p. 93.

[125] Friedman and Friedman, *Future of War*, pp. 35, 184. During their discussion of the Tomahawk Land Attack Missile, the Friedmans define a cruise missile as "nothing but an unmanned plane on a one-way mission." (Friedman and Friedman, *Future of War*, p. 275.) This, of course, precisely describes the kamikaze aircraft, with the obvious difference that the latter is manned.

[126] Sheftall, *Blossoms in the Wind*, pp. 116–18.

[127] Rikihei Inoguchi and Tadashi Nakajima, *The Divine Wind: Japan's Kamikaze Force in World War II* (Annapolis, MD: Naval Institute Press, 1958), p. 12.

[128] Warner and Warner, *Sacred Warriors*, p. 89; Ohnuki-Tierny, *Kamikaze, Cherry Blossoms, and Nationalisms*, p. 166.

[129] Nagatsuka, *I Was a Kamikaze*, pp. 162–65.

[130] George Culpepper, interview by the author, tape recording, December 1, 2003.

[131] Stephen W. Roskill, *The War at Sea, 1939–1945*, 3 vols. (London: H. M. Stationery Office, 1954–1961). According to volume three, part two, p. 211, on October 21 HMAS *Australia* was attacked by a kamikaze. G. Hermon Gill, *The Royal Australian Navy, 1942–1945* (Canberra: Australian War Memorial, 1957–1968), p. 511, argues that "*Australia* was thus the first Allied ship to be hit by a suicide attack." Shinpū records do not substantiate these claims. See Inoguchi and Nakajima, *Divine Wind*, pp. 232–33.

[132] USS *Santee*, Action Report, Leyte, Philippines Operation, 5 November 1944, serial 0018, Record Group 38, Records of the Office of the Chief of Naval Operations (hereafter cited as Records of OCNO), National Archives and Records Administration, College Park, MD (hereafter cited as NARA II); Warner and Warner, *Sacred Warriors*, p. 103.

[133] USS *Santee*, Action Report, 5 November 1944; Nagatsuka, *I Was a Kamikaze*, p. 171.

[134] Warner and Warner, *Sacred Warriors*, p. 103.

[135] Morison, *History of United States Naval Operations*, 12:301–02.

[136] Morison, *History of United States Naval Operations*, 12:305.

[137] Friedman and Friedman, *Future of War*, p. 27.

[138] USS *Kitkun Bay*, Surface Action Report, Battle off Samar, 28 October 1944, serial 005, Record Group 38, Records of OCNO, NARA II.

[139] USS *Kalinin Bay*, Action Report, 25 October 1944—Engagement with Enemy Units East of Leyte, P.I., 30 October 1944, serial 094, Record Group 38, Records of OCNO, NARA II.

[140] USS *White Plains*, War Damage Report, 7 November 1944, serial 0131, Record Group 38, Records of OCNO, NARA II; USS *White Plains*, Action Report Damage, 25 October 1944, serial S-010, Record Group 38, Records of OCNO, NARA II.

[141] Morison, *History of United States Naval Operations*, 12:302; USS *Kitkun Bay*, Action Report, 28 October 1944; USS *Kalinin Bay*, Action Report, 25 October 1944—Engagement with Enemy Units East of Leyte, P.I., Supplement, 4 November 1944, serial 0102, Record Group 38, Records of OCNO, NARA II.

[142] Warner and Warner, *Sacred Warriors*, pp. 115–16.

[143] Warner and Warner, *Sacred Warriors*, p. 324; Inoguchi and Nakajima, *Divine Wind*, app. 1; *United States Naval Chronology, World War II, Prepared in the Naval History Division, Office of the Chief of Naval Operations, Navy Department* (Washington, DC: Government Printing Office, 1955), pp. 109–11.

[144] USS *White Plains*, Action Report, Attack on the Central Philippine Islands, 17 October–25 October 1944, 27 October 1944, serial 0011, Record Group 38, Records of OCNO, NARA II; Warner and Warner, *Sacred Warriors*, ch. 7.

[145] Warner and Warner, *Sacred Warriors*, pp. 114–15; Inoguchi and Nakajima, *Divine Wind*, p. 244.

[146] Halsey and Bryan, *Admiral Halsey's Story*, p. 232.

[147] Barry, interview.

[148] Robert G. McAlpine, interview by the author, tape recording, July 27, 2005; Ralph J. Baum, interview by the author, tape recording, January 9, 2006.

[149] David Mincey, interview by author, tape recording, December 1, 2003.

[150] Halsey and Bryan, *Admiral Halsey's Story*, p. 229; Morison, *History of United States Naval Operations*, 12:342.

[151] Potter, *Bull Halsey*, p. 329.

[152] Wayne P. Hughes, Jr., *Fleet Tactics: Theory and Practice* (Annapolis, MD: Naval Institute Press, 1986), pp. 227–31; Warner and Warner, *Sacred Warriors*, p. 168.

[153] Halsey and Bryan, *Admiral Halsey's Story*, p. 230.

[154] *United States Naval Chronology*, p. 111.

[155] Halsey and Bryan, *Admiral Halsey's Story*, p. 230; Potter, *Bull Halsey*, p. 310.

[156] USS *Santee*, Action Report, 5 November 1944.

[157] Samuel Eliot Morison, *History of United States Naval Operations in World War II*, vol. 13, *The Liberation of the Philippines: Luzon, Mindanao, the Visayas, 1944–45* (Edison, NJ: Castle Books, 2001), p. 58; Halsey and Bryan, *Admiral Halsey's Story*, p. 235.

[158] Halsey and Bryan, *Admiral Halsey's Story*, p. 233; Morison, *History of United States Naval Operations*, 13:58.

[159] Halsey and Bryan, *Admiral Halsey's Story*, p. 233; Morison, *History of United States Naval Operations*, 13:54–55.

[160] McAlpine, interview.

[161] Morison, *History of United States Naval Operations*, 13:58 n8; Halsey and Bryan, *Admiral Halsey's Story*, p. 233.

[162] Morison, *History of United States Naval Operations*, 12:424–29; Morison, *History of United States Naval Operations*, 13:53–54, app. 2. As the Pacific war evolved, the navy experimented with different formations, trying both dispersal and massing; the Japanese did the same. For the thinking behind these changes, see Hughes, *Fleet Tactics*, pp. 89–91, 103–04.

[163] Halsey and Bryan, *Admiral Halsey's Story*, p. 230.

[164] Halsey and Bryan, *Admiral Halsey's Story*, p. 233; Morison, *History of United States Naval Operations*, 13:54–55.

[165] Scott Huler, *Defining the Wind: The Beaufort Scale, and How a 19th-Century Admiral Turned Science into Poetry* (New York: Three Rivers Press, 2004), p. 78. See also Alfred Friendly, *Beaufort of the Admiralty: The Life of Sir Francis Beaufort 1774–1857* (New York: Random House, 1977).

[166] Thomas Wildenberg, *Gray Steel and Black Oil: Fast Tankers and Replenishment at Sea in the U.S. Navy, 1912–1995* (Annapolis, MD: Naval Institute Press, 1996), pp. 273–77; Daniel Yergin, *The Prize: The Epic Quest for Oil, Money, and Power* (New York: Simon & Schuster, 1991), pp. 155–56.

[167] *DANFS*, 2:117–18; Morison, *History of United States Naval Operations*, 13:318–19.

[168] See, generally, Edward S. Miller, *War Plan Orange: The U.S. Strategy to Defeat Japan, 1897–1945* (Annapolis, MD: Naval Institute Press, 1991); Alfred Thayer Mahan, *The Influence of Sea Power Upon History, 1660–1783* (Boston: Little, Brown, 1890), chs. 1, 8 ("Having therefore no foreign establishments, either colonial or military, the ships of war of the United States, in war, will be like land birds, unable to fly far from their own shores. To provide resting-places for them, where they can coal and repair, would be one of the first duties of a government proposing to itself the development of the power of the nation at sea."); Bernard Brodie, *Sea Power in the Machine Age* (Princeton, NJ: Princeton University Press, 1941), ch. 7.

[169] Herman Wouk, *War and Remembrance* (Boston: Little, Brown, 1978), pp. 960–61.

[170] Harold F. Williamson and others, *The American Petroleum Industry: The Age of Energy 1899–1959*, 2 vols. (Evanston, IL: Northwestern University Press, 1963), 2:749.

[171] Morison, *History of United States Naval Operations*, 13:318–19; Wildenberg, *Gray Steel and Black Oil*, ch. 17.

[172] Morison, *History of United States Naval Operations*, 12:51; Warner and Warner, *Sacred Warriors*, pp. 127–29.

[173] Morison, *History of United States Naval Operations*, 12:17–18.

[174] Morison, *History of United States Naval Operations*, 12:56; Commander Third Fleet Action Report, Operations, 1–29 December 1944, 10 January 1945, serial 0040, Record Group 38, Records of OCNO, NARA II; Commander Task Group Thirty Eight Point Two to Commander in Chief, United States Fleet, Action Report, 11 December–24 December 1944, Action against Luzon, 10 January 1945, serial 0044, Record Group 38, Records of OCNO, NARA II.

[175] Commander Task Group Thirty Eight Point Two, Action Report, 11–24

December 1944; War Diary, Commander Task Group 30.8, 1–31 December 1944, Record Group 38, Records of OCNO, NARA II.

[176] Wildenberg, *Gray Steel and Black Oil*, pp. 172–73. On carrier attrition, see Hughes, *Fleet Tactics*, pp. 93–110.

[177] Deck Log, USS *Hancock*, 14 December 1944, Record Group 24, Bureau of Naval Personnel (hereafter cited as BuPers), NARA II.

[178] Commander Task Group 38.2, Action Report, 11–24 December 1944.

[179] Commander Task Group 38.2, Action Report, 11–24 December 1944.

[180] Commander Task Group 38.2, Action Report, 11–24 December 1944; Commander Third Fleet, Action Report, Operations, 1–29 December 1944.

[181] War Diary, Commander Task Force 38, 1–31 December 1944, serial 0865, Record Group 38, Records of OCNO, NARA II.

[182] Commander Task Group 38.2, Action Report, 11–24 December 1944; Deck Log, USS *Lexington*, 16 December 1944, Record Group 24, BuPers, NARA II; Deck Log, USS *Hancock*, 14 December 1944.

[183] War Diary, Commander Task Force 38, 1–31 December 1944.

[184] Commander Third Fleet, Action Report, Typhoon in Philippine Sea, 17–22 December 1944, 25 December 1944, serial 00166, Record Group 38, Records of OCNO, NARA II.

[185] Record of the Court of Inquiry to Inquire into All the Circumstances Connected with the Loss of the USS *Hull* (DD350), USS *Monaghan* (DD354), and the USS *Spence* (DD512), and Damage Sustained by the USS *Monterey* (CVL 26) and the USS *Cowpens* (CVL 28) and Other Major Damage Sustained by Ships of the Third Fleet on 18 December 1944. Convened on Board the USS *Cascade*, US Pacific Fleet, 26 December 1944. Operational Archives Branch, Naval Historical Center, Microfilm Publication NRS 1978–43 (hereafter cited as Record of the Court of Inquiry 1944–45), p. 129.

[186] Record of the Court of Inquiry 1944–45, pp. 108, 130.

[187] Record of the Court of Inquiry 1944–45, p. 108.

[188] Record of the Court of Inquiry 1944–45, pp. 109–10.

[189] C. Raymond Calhoun, *Typhoon: The Other Enemy* (Annapolis, MD: Naval Institute Press, 1981), pp. 32–33; Deck Log, USS *Cushing*, 17 December 1944, Record Group 24, BuPers, NARA II.

[190] Record of the Court of Inquiry 1944–45, p. 37.

[191] Deck Log, USS *Hancock*, 17 December 1944; Commander Third Fleet, Action Report, Typhoon in Philippine Sea, 17–22 December 1944, p. 3.

[192] Deck Log, USS *Aylwin*, 18 December 1944, Record Group 24, BuPers, NARA II; Commander Third Fleet, Action Report, Typhoon in Philippine Sea, 17–22 December 1944, p. 3; War Diary, Commander Destroyer Squadron 53, 17 December 1944, Record Group 38, Records of OCNO, NARA II, p. 4; Record of the Court of Inquiry 1944–45, exhibit 10; Calhoun, *Typhoon*, pp. 30–32.

[193] Deck Log, USS *Nantahala*, 17 December 1944, Record Group 24, BuPers, NARA II; Deck Log, USS *Santa Fe*, 17 December 1944, Record Group 24,

BuPers, NARA II.

[194] Deck Log, USS *Boston*, 17 December 1944, Record Group 24, BuPers, NARA II; Deck Log, USS *Yorktown*, 17 December 1944, Record Group 24, BuPers, NARA II.

[195] Deck Log, USS *Anzio*, 17 December 1944, Record Group 24, BuPers, NARA II.

[196] Commander Third Fleet, Action Report, Typhoon in Philippine Sea, 17–22 December 1944, p. 4.

[197] Grier L. Sims, interview by the author, tape recording, July 27, 2005.

[198] Commander Third Fleet, Action Report, Typhoon in Philippine Sea, 17–22 December 1944, p. 4.

[199] Deck Log, USS *Nantahala*, 17 December 1944; Deck Log, USS *Atascosa*, 17 December 1944, Record Group 24, BuPers, NARA II; Deck Log, USS *Monongahela*, 17 December 1944, Record Group 24, BuPers, NARA II; Commander Third Fleet, Action Report, Typhoon in Philippine Sea, 17–22 December 1944, pp. 4–5.

[200] Deck Log, USS *Iowa*, 17 December 1944, Record Group 24, BuPers, NARA II.

[201] Deck Log, USS *Owen*, 17 December 1944, Record Group 24, BuPers, NARA II; Deck Log, USS *Essex*, 17 December 1944, Record Group 24, BuPers, NARA II.

[202] Captain George F. Kosco, Biographies Section, OI-300, NAVY, 5 August 1952, Record Group 24, BuPers, NARA II; Hans Christian Adamson and George F. Kosco, *Halsey's Typhoons* (New York: Crown Publishers, 1967), pp. 32–35; Record of the Court of Inquiry 1944–45, p. 11. See also Part 2, supra.

[203] Deck Log, USS *New Jersey*, 17 December 1944, Record Group 24, BuPers, NARA II; Adamson and Kosco, *Halsey's Typhoons*, p. 34; Commander Third Fleet, Action Report, Typhoon in Philippine Sea, 17–22 December 1944, pp. 3–4.

[204] Adamson and Kosco, *Halsey's Typhoons*, pp. 34–35; Record of the Court of Inquiry 1944–45, p. 77.

[205] Halsey and Bryan, *Admiral Halsey's Story*, p. 237; Record of the Court of Inquiry 1944–45, p. 13; Adamson and Kosco, *Halsey's Typhoons*, pp. 35–37.

[206] Adamson and Kosco, *Halsey's Typhoons*, pp. 35–38, 41, 43–45; Commander Third Fleet, Action Report, Typhoon in Philippine Sea, 17–22 December 1944, pp. 5, 7.

[207] Nathaniel Bowditch, *American Practical Navigator: An Epitome of Navigational and Nautical Astronomy* (Washington, DC: Government Printing Office, 1943), p. 289; Deck Log, USS *New Jersey*, 17 December 1944, Record Group 24, BuPers, NARA II; Austin M. Knight, *Modern Seamanship*, 10th ed. (New York: Van Nostrand, 1943), pp. 622–24.

[208] Commander Third Fleet, Action Report, Typhoon in Philippine Sea, 17–22 December 1944, p. 6; Record of the Court of Inquiry 1944–45, pp. 58, 69.

[209] Commander Third Fleet, Action Report, Typhoon in Philippine Sea, 17–22 December 1944, p. 6; Record of the Court of Inquiry 1944–45, pp. 53, 61, 127; Calhoun, *Typhoon*, p. 134.

210 Deck Log, USS *Atascosa*, 17 December 1944; Deck Log, USS *Nantahala*, 17 December 1944.

211 Calhoun, *Typhoon*, p. 36.

212 Wildenberg, *Gray Steel and Black Oil*, pp. 31–38.

213 Deck Log, USS *Atascosa*, 17 December 1944.

214 Commander Third Fleet, Action Report, Typhoon in Philippine Sea, 17–22 December 1944, p. 8; Adamson and Kosco, *Halsey's Typhoons*, pp. 40–41.

215 Adamson and Kosco, *Halsey's Typhoons*, pp. 40–41.

216 Adamson and Kosco, *Halsey's Typhoons*, p. 38; Record of the Court of Inquiry 1944–45, pp. 13–15, 22, 25, 35, 43, 56, 71, 80.

217 Don Ziglar, interview by the author, tape recording, October 11, 2003.

218 Record of the Court of Inquiry 1944–45, pp. 71, 108.

219 Kotsch and Henderson, *Heavy Weather Guide*, pp. 100–01, 163; Commander Third Fleet, Action Report, Typhoon in Philippine Sea, 17–22 December 1944, p. 7; Record of the Court of Inquiry 1944–45, pp. 5, 13–14, 76.

220 Deck Log, USS *New Jersey*, 17 December 1944; see *American Practical Navigator*, pp. 283–87.

221 Halsey and Bryan, *Admiral Halsey's Story*, p. 237; see Record of the Court of Inquiry 1944–45, pp. 13–14.

222 Commander Third Fleet, Action Report, Typhoon in Philippine Sea, 17–22 December 1944, pp. 8–9; Adamson and Kosco, *Halsey's Typhoons*, pp. 38–39; Halsey and Bryan, *Admiral Halsey's Story*, p. 237.

223 Commander Third Fleet, Action Report, Typhoon in Philippine Sea, 17–22 December 1944, p. 8: War Diary, Commander Destroyer Squadron 47, 17 December 1944, Record Group 38, Records of OCNO, NARA II; War Diary, Commander Destroyer Squadron 50, 17 December 1944, Record Group 38, Records of OCNO, NARA II.

224 Hughes, *Fleet Tactics*, pp. 148, 151, 176.

225 Record of the Court of Inquiry 1944–45, p. 12.

226 Morison, *History of United States Naval Operations*, 13:64; Deck Log, USS *New Jersey*, 17 December 1944. Admiral Nimitz raised the same concern in the weeks after the typhoon. See Epilogue, infra.

227 *American Practical Navigator*, pp. 286, 288.

228 Calhoun, *Typhoon*, p. 39.

229 Record of the Court of Inquiry 1944–45, p. 25.

230 Record of the Court of Inquiry 1944–45, p. 56.

231 Record of the Court of Inquiry 1944–45, p. 58.

232 Calhoun, *Typhoon*, pp. 39–40; Erwin S. Jackson, "Trapped in a Typhoon," *Naval History* (December 2004): 50ff.

233 Record of the Court of Inquiry 1944–45, pp. 19, 24, 35, 43.

234 Calhoun, *Typhoon*, pp. 38–39; Record of the Court of Inquiry 1944–45, pp. 45, 67.

[235] Commander Third Fleet, Action Report, Typhoon in Philippine Sea, 17–22 December 1944, pp. 8–9; Adamson and Kosco, *Halsey's Typhoons*, p. 41.

[236] Adamson and Kosco, *Halsey's Typhoons*, p. 41; Halsey and Bryan, *Admiral Halsey's Story*, p. 235.

[237] Adamson and Kosco, *Halsey's Typhoons*, pp. 41–42.

[238] Record of the Court of Inquiry 1944–45, p. 75; Adamson and Kosco, *Halsey's Typhoons*, pp. 41–42, 47.

[239] See, for example, *American Practical Navigator*, pp. 290–91.

[240] Deck Log, USS *New Jersey*, 18 December 1944; Calhoun, *Typhoon*, p. 176; see, for example, Deck Log, USS *Anzio*, 18 December 1944; Deck Log, USS *Cape Esperance*, 18 December 1944, Record Group 24, BuPers, NARA II; Deck Log, USS *Owen*, 18 December 1944; Deck Log, USS *Yorktown*, 18 December 1944.

[241] Deck Log, USS *Aylwin*, 18 December 1944; Adamson and Kosco, *Halsey's Typhoons*, pp. 49–50.

[242] Jackson, "Trapped in a Typhoon," pp. 50ff.

[243] Deck Log, USS *Aylwin*, 18 December 1944; Adamson and Kosco, *Halsey's Typhoons*, pp. 49–50.

[244] Record of the Court of Inquiry 1944–45, pp. 13–14; Adamson and Kosco, *Halsey's Typhoons*, pp. 43–48.

[245] Commander Third Fleet, Action Report, Typhoon in Philippine Sea, 17–22 December 1944, p. 10; Adamson and Kosco, *Halsey's Typhoons*, p. 50; Record of the Court of Inquiry 1944–45, pp. 14–15.

[246] Record of the Court of Inquiry 1944–45, pp. 14–15; Commander Third Fleet, Action Report, Typhoon in Philippine Sea, 17–22 December 1944, pp. 10–11.

[247] Conrad, "Typhoon," p. 228.

[248] Deck Log, USS *Anzio*, 18 December 1944; Deck Log, USS *Boston*, 18 December 1944; Deck Log, USS *New Jersey*, 18 December 1944.

[249] Adamson and Kosco, *Halsey's Typhoons*, p. 51; Deck Log, USS *Cushing*, 17 December 1944.

[250] Deck Log, USS *McCord*, 18 December 1944, Record Group 24, BuPers, NARA II.

[251] Jack M. Matthew, interview by the author, tape recording, July 23, 2005; Delos W. Smith, interview by the author, tape recording, July 28, 2005; James R. Thomas, interview by the author, tape recording, January 9, 2006; Leo J. Cox, interview by the author, tape recording, July 23, 2005; Ziglar, interview.

[252] Leonard, interview; Herb Lapp, interview by the author, tape recording, October 9, 2003; Ivan Musicant, *Battleship at War: The Epic Story of the USS Washington* (New York: Avon, 1986), p. 299.

[253] Matthew, interview.

[254] Bill McClain, interview by the author, tape recording, July 28, 2005.

[255] Ervin Eugene Bullard, interview by the author, tape recording, October 9, 2003.

[256] Ben Coulliard, interview by the author, tape recording, October 11, 2003.

[257] Herbert H. Hepworth, interview by the author, tape recording, December 1, 2003.

258 Commander Third Fleet, Action Report, Typhoon in Philippine Sea, 17–22 December 1944, p. 11.

259 Commander Third Fleet, Action Report, Typhoon in Philippine Sea, 17–22 December 1944, p. 12.

260 Morison, *History of United States Naval Operations*, 13:315–16; Deck Log, USS *Cowpens*, 18 December 1944, Record Group 24, BuPers, NARA II; Deck Log, USS *Wasp*, 18 December 1944, Record Group 24, BuPers, NARA II; cf. Deck Log, USS *Iowa*, 18 December 1944; Deck Log, USS *Langley*, 18 December 1944, Record Group 24, BuPers, NARA II; Deck Log, USS *Atascosa*, 18 December 1944; Deck Log, USS *Nantahala*, 18 December 1944.

261 Norman Friedman, *U.S. Aircraft Carriers: An Illustrated Design History* (Annapolis, MD: Naval Institute Press, 1983), pp. 188–90, 394, 403; *DANFS*, 4:427; Record of the Court of Inquiry 1944–45, p. 22.

262 USS *Monterey*, Action Report, 22 December 1944, serial 0036, Record Group 38, Records of OCNO, NARA II; Record of the Court of Inquiry 1944–45, pp. 19, 22–23.

263 Record of the Court of Inquiry 1944–45, pp. 21–23; USS *Monterey*, Action Report; Deck Log, USS *Monterey*, 18 December 1944, Record Group 24, BuPers, NARA II.

264 Gerald R. Ford, *A Time to Heal: The Autobiography of Gerald R. Ford* (New York: Harper & Row, 1979), pp. 58–59; John G. Norris, "Former Naval Person Makes Good: Interview with Vice President Ford," *Seapower* (March 1974): p. 6.

265 Ziglar, interview.

266 Iacono, interview.

267 Commander Third Fleet, Action Report, Typhoon in Philippine Sea, 17–22 December 1944, p. 11.

268 Record of the Court of Inquiry 1944–45, p. 21; Commander Third Fleet, Action Report, Typhoon in Philippine Sea, 17–22 December 1944, p. 11.

269 Record of the Court of Inquiry 1944–45, pp. 18, 21.

270 USS *Monterey*, Action Report, 22 December 1944; Record of the Court of Inquiry 1944–45, pp. 19, 21.

271 USS *Monterey*, Action Report, 22 December 1944.

272 Adamson and Kosco, *Halsey's Typhoons*, p. 55.

273 USS *Monterey*, Action Report, 22 December 1944.

274 Adamson and Kosco, *Halsey's Typhoons*, p. 57.

275 Commander Third Fleet, Action Report, Typhoon in Philippine Sea, 17–22 December 1944, pp. 12–13; Ford, *A Time to Heal*, p. 59.

276 USS *Monterey*, Action Report, 22 December 1944.

277 Record of the Court of Inquiry 1944–45, pp. 18–20; USS *Monterey*, Action Report, 22 December 1944.

278 USS *Monterey*, Action Report, 22 December 1944.

[279] Ziglar, interview; Commander Third Fleet, Action Report, Typhoon in Philippine Sea, 17–22 December 1944, pp. 12–13.

[280] See Commander Third Fleet, Action Report, Typhoon in Philippine Sea, 17–22 December 1944, p. 13.

[281] Sal DeLuca, interview by the author, tape recording, April 7, 2006; Smith, interview; Commander Third Fleet, Action Report, Typhoon in Philippine Sea, 17–22 December 1944, p. 15.

[282] Robert E. de Jong, interview by the author, tape recording, July 23, 2005; Edward J. Joyeusaz, interview by the author, tape recording, October 11, 2003; Charlie Boyst, interview by the author, tape recording, October 10, 2003; Bishop Burmeister, interview by the author, tape recording, October 9, 2003; Joe Hoyer, interview by the author, tape recording, October 9, 2003.

[283] Mark Pence, interview by the author, tape recording, July 26, 2005.

[284] Musicant, *Battleship at War*, p. 299.

[285] Sims, interview; Leonard, interview.

[286] Gordon McBride, interview by the author, tape recording, July 25, 2005; Thomas, interview.

[287] George Thompson, interview by the author, tape recording, October 9, 2003.

[288] Commander Third Fleet, Action Report, Typhoon in Philippine Sea, 17–22 December 1944, pp. 13–14; Deck Log USS *Cape Esperance*, 18 December 1944; Calhoun, *Typhoon*, pp. 89–90.

[289] Adamson and Kosco, *Halsey's Typhoons*, pp. 71, 73, 74; Deck Log, USS *Cowpens*, 18 December 1944.

[290] Deck Log, USS *Cowpens*, 18 December 1944; Record of the Court of Inquiry 1944–45, pp. 23–24.

[291] Deck Log, USS *Cowpens*, 18 December 1944.

[292] Deck Log, USS *Cowpens*, 18 December 1944; Adamson and Kosco, *Halsey's Typhoons*, pp. 71–74.

[293] Calhoun, *Typhoon*, p. 90; Deck Log, USS *Cape Esperance*, 18 December 1944.

[294] Deck Log, USS *Cowpens*, 18 December 1944.

[295] Deck Log, USS *Altamaha*, 18 December 1944, Record Group 24, BuPers, NARA II; Calhoun, *Typhoon*, pp. 90–93.

[296] Deck Log, USS *San Jacinto*, 18 December 1944, Record Group 24, BuPers, NARA II.

[297] Calhoun, *Typhoon*, pp. 87–88.

[298] Calhoun, *Typhoon*, p. 89.

[299] Iacono interview and Ziglar interview. Don Darnell, *All Sailors, Now Hear This! Man Your Pens, Clean Up & Sweep Down Those WWII Memories Fore And Aft* (Lincoln, NE: D. G. Darnell, 1999), pp. 111–12.

[300] Charles Edwin Eamigh, interview by the author, tape recording, July 23, 2005.

[301] Cox, interview; Joyeusaz, interview; Iacono, interview; Deck Log, USS *Yorktown*, 18 December 1944; Commander Third Fleet, Action Report, Typhoon in Philippine Sea, 17–22 December 1944, pp. 14–16.

302 Halsey and Bryan, *Admiral Halsey's Story*, p. 239.

303 Commander Third Fleet, Action Report, Typhoon in Philippine Sea, 17–22 December 1944, p. 16; cf. Calhoun, *Typhoon*, p. 49.

304 Deck Log, USS *New Jersey*, 18 December 1944.

305 As Halsey himself later wrote in his autobiography, "What it was like on a destroyer one-twentieth the *New Jersey*'s size, I can only imagine." Halsey and Bryan, *Admiral Halsey's Story*, p. 239.

306 Commander Third Fleet, Action Report, Typhoon in Philippine Sea, 17–22 December 1944, p. 17.

307 USS *Tabberer* to CincPac, ComThirdFleet, CTG 30.7, no. 181545, 18 December 1944. Later testimony tended to establish that *Hull,* in fact, went down around noon. See Record of the Court of Inquiry 1944–45, exhibit 10; Record of the Court of Inquiry 1944–45, p. 155.

308 Norman Friedman, *U.S. Destroyers: An Illustrated Design History*, rev. ed. (Annapolis, MD: Naval Institute Press, 2004), pp. 80–83, 463; Calhoun, *Typhoon*, pp. 3–8.

309 Thomas C. Gillmer, *Modern Ship Design*, 2nd ed. (Annapolis, MD: Naval Institute Press, 1975), pp. 51–53, 235.

310 Calhoun, *Typhoon*, pp. 5–8.

311 Friedman, *U.S. Destroyers*, ch. 6; McMurtrie, *Jane's Fighting Ships*, p. 479; Morison, *History of United States Naval Operations*, 13:app. 2.

312 Friedman, *U.S. Destroyers*, pp. 463, 472; McMurtrie, *Jane's Fighting Ships*, p. 479.

313 Friedman, *U.S. Destroyers*, pp. 111, 118.

314 Friedman, *U.S. Destroyers*, p. 472; Commander Third Fleet, Action Report, Operations, 1–29 December 1944.

315 Gillmer, *Modern Ship Design*, p. 71; see Part 4, *supra*.

316 Gillmer, *Modern Ship Design*, p. 71.

317 Calhoun, *Typhoon*, p. 69; Jackson, "Trapped in a Typhoon," pp. 50ff; see pp. 113–16, *supra*.

318 Adamson and Kosco, *Halsey's Typhoons*, pp. 49–50; Deck Log, USS *Aylwin*, 18 December 1944.

319 Deck Log, USS *Aylwin*, 18 December 1944; Commander Third Fleet, Action Report, Typhoon in Philippine Sea, 17–22 December 1944, p. 10; War Diary, Destroyer Escort Division 72, 1–31 December 1944, Record Group 38, Records of OCNO, NARA II; Calhoun, *Typhoon*, p. 69.

320 Deck Log, USS *Cushing*, 18 December 1944.

321 Deck Log, USS *Brown*, 18 December 1944, Record Group 24, BuPers, NARA II; War Diary, Commander Destroyer Squadron 47, 17 December 1944, p. 11; Commander Destroyer Squadron 47, Action Report, 24 December 1944, serial 0108, Record Group 38, Records of OCNO, NARA II, p. 3.

322 Deck Log, USS *Swearer*, 18 December 1944, Record Group 24, BuPers, NARA II; Deck Log, USS *Crowley*, 18 December 1944, Record Group 24,

BuPers, NARA II.

323 Calhoun, *Typhoon*, pp. 55–57; Deck Log, USS *Dewey*, 18 December 1944, Record Group 24, BuPers, NARA II.

324 Adamson and Kosco, *Halsey's Typhoons*, p. 88.

325 Record of the Court of Inquiry 1944–45, pp. 38, 61; Adamson and Kosco, *Halsey's Typhoons*, p. 88.

326 Record of the Court of Inquiry 1944–45, p. 61.

327 Adamson and Kosco, *Halsey's Typhoons*, p. 88.

328 *DANFS*, 4:412–14; Record of the Court of Inquiry 1944–45, p. 11.

329 Adamson and Kosco, *Halsey's Typhoons*, p. 88.

330 Adamson and Kosco, *Halsey's Typhoons*, pp. 89–90; Record of the Court of Inquiry 1944–45, pp. 110–18; Record of the Court of Inquiry 1944–45, exhibit 12; Hanson W. Baldwin, "When the Third Fleet Met the Great Typhoon," *New York Times Magazine* (December 16, 1951): 18, 49; Robert Sinclair Parkin, *Blood on the Sea: American Destroyers Lost in World War II* (New York: Sarpedon, 1996), p. 279; Calhoun, *Typhoon*, p. 77.

331 Record of the Court of Inquiry 1944–45, exhibit 10; Adamson and Kosco, *Halsey's Typhoons*, pp. 79–82; Calhoun, *Typhoon*, pp. 71–75; Pat Douhan, interview by the author, tape recording, July 26, 2005; Ken Drummond, interview by the author, tape recording, July 23, 2004; Ken Drummond, "The Best Christmas Present Ever . . . ," http://www.usd230.k12.ks.us/PICTT/paraphernalia/donated/USSBrown.html (last visited October 6, 2006).

332 Deck Log, USS *Aylwin*, 18 December 1944; Adamson and Kosco, *Halsey's Typhoons*, pp. 58–64.

333 Jackson, "Trapped in a Typhoon," pp. 50ff.

334 Deck Log, USS *Dewey*, 18 December 1944; Calhoun, *Typhoon*, ch. 7.

335 Adamson and Kosco, *Halsey's Typhoons*, pp. 114–18; Owen Gualt, "The 'Tabby' & Typhoon Cobra," *Sea Classics* (January 1989): 20; Friedman, *U.S. Destroyers*, p. 481.

336 Adamson and Kosco, *Halsey's Typhoons*, pp. 66–68.

337 Deck Log, USS *Hickox*, 18 December 1944, Record Group 24, BuPers, NARA II.

338 Deck Log, USS *Hickox*, 18 December 1944; Adamson and Kosco, *Halsey's Typhoons*, p. 60; Calhoun, *Typhoon*, pp. 80–82; Record of the Court of Inquiry 1944–45, p. 158.

339 Gillmer, *Modern Ship Design*, pp. 73–74.

340 Adamson and Kosco, *Halsey's Typhoons*, pp. 94–96; Calhoun, *Typhoon*, pp. 80–82; Semmes, *Memoirs of Service Afloat*, pp. 475–77; Deck Log, USS *Hickox*, 18 December 1944.

341 Record of the Court of Inquiry 1944–45, p. 127; Record of the Court of Inquiry 1944–45, exhibit 13; Parkin, *Blood on the Sea*, p. 268.

342 Record of the Court of Inquiry 1944–45, pp. 121–24.

343 Edward Miller, interview by family members, October 31, 1985; Parkin, *Blood on the Sea*, pp. 268–69.

344 Parkin, *Blood on the Sea*, p. 270.
345 Record of the Court of Inquiry 1944–45, pp. 121–28, 156; Parkin, *Blood on the Sea*, pp. 269–71; Miller, interview.
346 Adamson and Kosco, *Halsey's Typhoons*, p. 79.
347 Adamson and Kosco, *Halsey's Typhoons*, pp. 104–08.
348 Adamson and Kosco, *Halsey's Typhoons*, pp. 94, 105–08.
349 Calhoun, *Typhoon*, p. 65.
350 Douhan, interview.
351 Drummond, interview; Drummond, "The Best Christmas Present Ever . . . ".
352 Kenneth Kamler, *Surviving the Extremes: A Doctor's Journey to the Limits of Human Endurance* (New York: St. Martin's, 2004), pp. 102–05.
353 Lewis L. Haynes, "Survivor of the Indianapolis," *Navy Medicine* 86, no. 4 (July/August 1995): 13–17.
354 Kamler, *Surviving the Extremes*, pp. 107–09, 131–32.
355 Kamler, *Surviving the Extremes*, pp. 99–100; David H. Evans and James B. Claiborne, eds., *The Physiology of Fishes*, 3rd ed. (Boca Raton, FL: CRC, Taylor & Francis, 2006), chs. 11–12.
356 Drummond, interview; Drummond, "The Best Christmas Present Ever . . . ".
357 Calhoun, *Typhoon*, pp. 66–67; Deck Log, USS *Dewey*, 18 December 1944; USS *Tabberer*, Action Report, 28 December 1944, serial 031, Record Group 38 Records of OCNO, NARA II. Calhoun points out a discrepancy in the two ships' records: According to *Tabberer*, the vessels remained in company for some hours while trying to rejoin the fleet, with *Dewey* standing radar guard for *Tabberer* and blinkering courses and speeds to it. According to *Dewey's* log and Calhoun's recollections, the ships were together for considerably less time, and *Tabberer* requested a course for Ulithi. He speculates that *Tabberer* later mistook another destroyer, possibly *Benham* or *Hickox*, for *Dewey*. See Calhoun, *Typhoon*, pp. 111–12; Deck Log, USS *Dewey*, 18 December 1944; USS *Tabberer*, Action Report, 28 December 1944.
358 Adamson and Kosco, *Halsey's Typhoons*, pp. 122–24; USS *Tabberer*, Action Report, 28 December 1944.
359 Calhoun, *Typhoon*, pp. 67–68.
360 USS *Tabberer*, Action Report, 28 December 1944.
361 USS *Tabberer*, Action Report, 28 December 1944; Adamson and Kosco, *Halsey's Typhoons*, ch. 5; Calhoun, *Typhoon*, ch. 11.
362 Adamson and Kosco, *Halsey's Typhoons*, p. 121.
363 Commander Third Fleet, Action Report, Typhoon in Philippine Sea, 17–22 December 1944, p. 17.
364 Commander Third Fleet, Action Report, Typhoon in Philippine Sea, 17–22 December 1944, p. 19.
365 Douhan, interview.
366 USS *Tabberer*, Action Report, 28 December 1944; Calhoun, *Typhoon*, pp. 107, 116.
367 Adamson and Kosco, *Halsey's Typhoons*, p. 128.

[368] USS *Tabberer*, Action Report, 28 December 1944; Calhoun, *Typhoon*, pp. 114–15.

[369] Adamson and Kosco, *Halsey's Typhoons*, pp. 128–29; USS *Tabberer*, Action Report, 28 December 1944.

[370] Adamson and Kosco, *Halsey's Typhoons*, p. 129.

[371] Adamson and Kosco, *Halsey's Typhoons*, p. 124.

[372] Commander Third Fleet, Action Report, Typhoon in Philippine Sea, 17–22 December 1944, p. 19; USS *Tabberer*, Action Report, 28 December 1944; McClain, interview.

[373] Adamson and Kosco, *Halsey's Typhoons*, p. 133; USS *Tabberer*, Action Report, 28 December 1944.

[374] USS *Tabberer*, Action Report, 28 December 1944.

[375] Commander Third Fleet, Action Report, Typhoon in Philippine Sea, 17–22 December 1944, pp. 19–20.

[376] Record of the Court of Inquiry 1944–45, exhibit 12; Calhoun, *Typhoon*, pp. 77–78; Parkin, *Blood on the Sea*, pp. 278–79.

[377] Record of the Court of Inquiry 1944–45, exhibit 12.

[378] Kamler, *Surviving the Extremes*, pp. 131–32.

[379] Calhoun, *Typhoon*, p. 117.

[380] USS *Tabberer*, Action Report, 28 December 1944. The context of these statements shows Halsey's TBS conversation with *Tabberer* to have occurred on the night of December 19. Halsey's chronology, which appears in his own action report, has it taking place twenty-four hours later, but by that time *Tabberer* had left the area. Adjacent items in Halsey's chronology also appear to be misdated.

[381] USS *Tabberer*, Action Report, 28 December 1944.

[382] Miller, interview; Parkin, *Blood on the Sea*, p. 270; Deck Log, USS *Swearer*, 20 December 1944.

[383] Douhan, interview.

[384] Halsey and Bryan, *Admiral Halsey's Story*, pp. 204–05.

[385] Adamson and Kosco, *Halsey's Typhoons*, front end papers; Typhoon Track Chart, Record Group 38, World War II Action and Operational Reports, Third Fleet, 22 November 1944–24 January 1945, Box 40, NARA II.

[386] War Diary, Commander Task Force 38, 1–31 December 1944.

[387] Halsey and Bryan, *Admiral Halsey's Story*, p. 240; Deck Log, USS *Essex*, 17 December 1944; Action Report, Commander Third Fleet, Typhoon in the Philippine Sea, 17–22 December 1944.

[388] Douhan, interview.

[389] Record of the Court of Inquiry 1944–45, exhibits 12, 14, 19; Douhan, interview; Calhoun, *Typhoon*, p. 117; Parkin, *Blood on the Sea*, p. 279.

[390] Record of the Court of Inquiry 1944–45, exhibit 14.

[391] Adamson and Kosco, *Halsey's Typhoons*, p. 65; Commander Third Fleet Action Report, Operations, 1–29 December 1944.

[392] Commander Third Fleet, Action Report, Operations, 1–29 December 1944; Record of the Court of Inquiry 1944–45, p. 148; Spector, *Eagle Against the Sun*, p. 310.

[393] Miller, interview; Douhan, interview; Potter, *Bull Halsey*, pp. 322–23.

[394] Adamson and Kosco, *Halsey's Typhoons*, p. 142; Potter, *Nimitz*, pp. 349–50.

[395] Adamson and Kosco, *Halsey's Typhoons*, pp. 143–44.

[396] Thomas B. Buell, *Master of Sea Power: A Biography of Ernest J. King* (Boston: Little, Brown, 1980), p. 464; ComThirdFleet to CincPac, no. 202332, 21 December 1944.

[397] Record of the Court of Inquiry 1944–45, app.

[398] United States Navy Department, *Naval Courts and Boards, 1937* (Washington, DC: Government Printing Office, 1944), sec. 734.

[399] Record of the Court of Inquiry 1944–45, p. 1; Arlington National Cemetery Web Site, Ira Hudson Nunn, http://www.arlingtoncemetery.net/ihnunn.htm (last visited October 6, 2006).

[400] United States Navy Department, *Naval Courts and Boards*, sec. 732.

[401] Calhoun, *Typhoon*, p. 123.

[402] Record of the Court of Inquiry 1944–45, p. 1.

[403] Potter, *Bull Halsey*, pp. 244–47.

[404] Record of the Court of Inquiry 1944–45, p. 4.

[405] Record of the Court of Inquiry 1944–45, p. 6.

[406] Record of the Court of Inquiry 1944–45, pp. 13–16.

[407] Record of the Court of Inquiry 1944–45, pp. 15–16.

[408] Record of the Court of Inquiry 1944–45, p. 22.

[409] Record of the Court of Inquiry 1944–45, pp. 22–23.

[410] Record of the Court of Inquiry 1944–45, p. 25; cf. Knight, *Modern Seamanship*, ch. 20.

[411] Record of the Court of Inquiry 1944–45, pp. 27–30, 33.

[412] Record of the Court of Inquiry 1944–45, p. 35.

[413] Record of the Court of Inquiry 1944–45, p. 39.

[414] Record of the Court of Inquiry 1944–45, p. 40.

[415] Record of the Court of Inquiry 1944–45, pp. 40–41.

[416] Record of the Court of Inquiry 1944–45, pp. 47–51.

[417] Record of the Court of Inquiry 1944–45, p. 56.

[418] Record of the Court of Inquiry 1944–45, p. 60.

[419] Record of the Court of Inquiry 1944–45, pp. 62–64.

[420] Morison, *History of United States Naval Operations*, 13:315.

[421] Record of the Court of Inquiry 1944–45, p. 67.

[422] Record of the Court of Inquiry 1944–45, pp. 68–69.

[423] Record of the Court of Inquiry 1944–45, pp. 72–73.

[424] See, for example, Halsey and Bryan, *Admiral Halsey's Story*, pp. 220–21, in

which Halsey apparently embellished the story of the CincPac communicator who chose "the world wonders" as padding for Nimitz's message to Halsey during the Battle of Leyte Gulf. (Cf. Potter, *Nimitz*, p. 351.) While Halsey briefly mentions the typhoon in his memoirs, he omits any mention of the court of inquiry. See Halsey and Bryan, *Admiral Halsey's Story*, pp. 236–41.

[425] Record of the Court of Inquiry 1944–45, pp. 74–78; United States Navy Department, *Naval Courts and Boards*, sec. 734(c), p. 357.

[426] Morison, *History of United States Naval Operations*, 13:87.

[427] Potter, *Nimitz*, p. 351; Morison, *History of United States Naval Operations*, 13:87–92.

[428] Record of the Court of Inquiry 1944–45, pp. 78–93.

[429] Record of the Court of Inquiry 1944–45, pp. 83, 85.

[430] Record of the Court of Inquiry 1944–45, exhibit 10–4 pp. 1–4.

[431] Record of the Court of Inquiry 1944–45, p. 95.

[432] Record of the Court of Inquiry 1944–45, p. 96.

[433] Record of the Court of Inquiry 1944–45, p. 98.

[434] Record of the Court of Inquiry 1944–45, p. 100.

[435] Record of the Court of Inquiry 1944–45, p. 107.

[436] Record of the Court of Inquiry 1944–45, pp. 107–08.

[437] Record of the Court of Inquiry 1944–45, pp. 108–09.

[438] Record of the Court of Inquiry 1944–45, exhibit 13; Record of the Court of Inquiry 1944–45, p. 110.

[439] Record of the Court of Inquiry 1944–45, pp. 112–18.

[440] The questioning of Traceski was somewhat rambling and disorganized. For purposes of clarity the quotations from his testimony appearing here, while accurate, have been slightly reordered.

[441] Record of the Court of Inquiry 1944–45, pp. 120, 125–27.

[442] Record of the Court of Inquiry 1944–45, p. 127.

[443] Record of the Court of Inquiry 1944–45, pp. 129–32.

[444] Record of the Court of Inquiry 1944–45, p. 134.

[445] Record of the Court of Inquiry 1944–45, pp. 136–40.

[446] Record of the Court of Inquiry 1944–45, pp. 140–45; Record of the Court of Inquiry 1944–45, app. C.

[447] Buell, *Master of Sea Power*, pp. 70–72, 102, 353, 464.

[448] United States Navy Department, *Naval Courts and Boards*, sec. 720, p. 347.

[449] Record of the Court of Inquiry 1944–45, pp. 146–51.

[450] Record of the Court of Inquiry 1944–45, p. 152.

[451] Record of the Court of Inquiry 1944–45, p. 160.

[452] Record of the Court of Inquiry 1944–45, p. 161.

[453] Record of the Court of Inquiry 1944–45, pp. 164–66.

[454] Record of the Court of Inquiry 1944–45, p. 166.

[455] Record of the Court of Inquiry 1944–45, app.

456 Record of the Court of Inquiry 1944–45, pp. 166–67.

457 Potter, *Nimitz*, pp. 54–62.

458 Commander James Alexander Marks, USN, Answers to Questions by CincPac on Sinking of USS *Hull* in Pacific Typhoon, 9 January 1945, film no. PRO 40.

459 Record of the Court of Inquiry 1944–45, app.

460 Record of the Court of Inquiry 1944–45, app.; see Buell, *Master of Sea Power*, p. 464.

461 *World War II Administrative History*, 15:73–74; Potter, *Nimitz*, pp. 353–54.

462 Record of the Court of Inquiry 1944–45, app.

463 Morison, *History of United States Naval Operations*, 13:87–92; Potter, *Bull Halsey*, p. 325.

464 Morison, *History of United States Naval Operations*, 13:165–70.

465 Morison, *History of United States Naval Operations*, 13:183.

466 Potter, *Nimitz*, pp. 312–27; Buell, *Quiet Warrior*, pp. 305–10.

467 Morison, *History of United States Naval Operations*, 14:89.

468 Morison, *History of United States Naval Operations*, 14:app. 1.

469 Buell, *Quiet Warrior*, pp. 336, 361–63.

470 Potter, *Bull Halsey*, pp. 332–34.

471 Adamson and Kosco, *Halsey's Typhoons*, pp. 169–70.

472 Record of Proceedings of a Court of Inquiry Convened at Headquarters of the Commander, Marianas, by Order of the Commander in Chief, United States Pacific Fleet and Pacific Ocean Areas to Inquire into the Circumstances Connected with the Damage Sustained by Ships of the Third Fleet in a Typhoon or Storm on or about 4 June 1945, off Okinawa, CINCPAC Box No. S-5072 1945 Box 45, Record Group 38, Office of the Chief of Naval Operations, National Archives, College Park Branch, College Park, MD (hereafter cited as Record of the Court of Inquiry 1945), 60–73; Adamson and Kosco, *Halsey's Typhoons*, p. 171.

473 Adamson and Kosco, *Halsey's Typhoons*, pp. 173–74.

474 Record of the Court of Inquiry 1945, facts; Record of the Court of Inquiry 1945, pp. 62–63.

475 Adamson and Kosco, *Halsey's Typhoons*, pp. 174–77; Record of the Court of Inquiry 1945, p. 61; Record of the Court of Inquiry 1945, facts.

476 Record of the Court of Inquiry 1945, facts; Record of the Court of Inquiry 1945, pp. 53–54, 62–63.

477 Adamson and Kosco, *Halsey's Typhoons*, p. 178.

478 Record of the Court of Inquiry 1945, facts.

479 Calhoun, *Typhoon*, p. 197.

480 Adamson and Kosco, *Halsey's Typhoons*, pp. 180–81; *DANFS*, 2:165.

481 J. A. Buehler, "Typhoon," http://www.ussmitchell.com/TYPHOON.htm (last visited October 7, 2006); Harlan Dible, interview by family members, tape recording, February 4, 2003.

482 Adamson and Kosco, *Halsey's Typhoons*, pp. 180–81.

483 Samuel Eliot Morison, *History of Unitied States Naval Operations in World War II*, vol. *History of Unitied States naval Operations in World War II*, vol. 15, *Victory in the Pacific* (Edison, NJ.: Castle Books, 2001), pp. 299–301; Record of the Court of Inquiry 1945, facts.

484 Morison, *History of United States Naval Operations*, 15:299–300; Record of the Court of Inquiry 1945, p. 44.

485 Morison, *History of United States Naval Operations*, 15:382–83; Record of the Court of Inquiry 1944–45, n.p.; Record of the Court of Inquiry 1945, pp. 85–86.

486 Record of the Court of Inquiry 1945, pp. 83–84; Record of the Court of Inquiry 1945, exhibit 31.

487 Record of the Court of Inquiry 1945, pp. 79–82; Record of the Court of Inquiry 1945, exhibit 30.

488 Record of the Court of Inquiry 1944–45, p. 159; *DANFS*, 4:346–47; *DANFS*, 5:322–23.

489 Record of the Court of Inquiry 1945, pp. 10–11, 110; Adamson and Kosco, *Halsey's Typhoons*, p. 188.

490 Adamson and Kosco, *Halsey's Typhoons*, p. 188; Morison, *History of United States Naval Operations*, 15:304–05; *DANFS*, 5:322.

491 Morison, *History of United States Naval Operations*, 15:307; Calhoun, *Typhoon*, pp. 190–97; *DANFS*, 5:322.

492 Morison, *History of United States Naval Operations*, 15:307; Record of the Court of Inquiry 1945, facts.

493 Record of the Court of Inquiry 1945, n.p.

494 Record of the Court of Inquiry 1945, p. 81.

495 Record of the Court of Inquiry 1945, pp. 48–49.

496 Record of the Court of Inquiry 1945, pp. 53–55.

497 Record of the Court of Inquiry 1945, pp. 61–63.

498 Record of the Court of Inquiry 1945, p. 114.

499 United States Navy Department, *Naval Courts and Boards*, sec. 67, pp. 41–42; United States Navy Department, *Naval Courts and Boards*, sec. 67, pp. 457–58.

500 Buell, *Master of Sea Power*, p. 464.

501 Record of the Court of Inquiry 1945, pp. 125–28. The question of relieving senior naval officers in the face of serious incidents is a delicate one. For the legal aspects, see, for example, Roger D. Scott, "Kimmel, Short, McVay: Case Studies in Executive Authority, Law and the Individual Rights of Military Commanders," *Military Law Review* 156 (June 1998): 52.

502 Record of the Court of Inquiry 1945, app.

503 Record of the Court of Inquiry 1945, app.; Potter, *Nimitz*, p. 337; Buell, *Master of Sea Power*, p. 464; Potter, *Bull Halsey*, p. 340; Morison, *History of United States Naval Operations*, 15:308.

504 Potter, *Bull Halsey*, pp. 342–43; Buell, *Master of Sea Power*, pp. 464–65.

[505] Potter, *Bull Halsey*, p. 360.

[506] Potter, *Bull Halsey*, ch. 22; William F. Halsey to E. B. Potter, 27 July 1959, Halsey Papers, Military File, Manuscript Room, Library of Congress; Fleet Admiral Halsey's Comments on Chapter 39 (The Battle of Leyte Gulf) of Prof. E. B. Potter's New Book, Halsey Papers, Military File, Manuscript Room, Library of Congress; William F. Halsey to Robert B. Carney, 10 November 1958, Halsey Papers, Military File, Manuscript Room, Library of Congress; William F. Halsey to Ralph E. Wilson and H. D. Moulton, 14 November 1958, Halsey Papers, Military File, Manuscript Room, Library of Congress; Halsey and Bryan, *Admiral Halsey's Story*, pp. 236–41, 254.

[507] Tom J. Brislin to William F. Halsey, n.d., Halsey Papers, General Correspondence, Manuscript Room, Library of Congress.

Glossary

AA	Anti-aircraft. Surface-based weapons fire of various types directed against enemy air threats.
Avgas	Aviation gasoline; fuel for aircraft.
BatDiv	Battleship Division. A small administrative grouping of battleships.
BB	Battleship.
BuShips	Bureau of Ships. The naval bureau responsible for vessel procurement, engineering, construction, repair, and similar functions.
CA	Heavy Cruiser.
CAP	Combat Air Patrol. A defensive fighter patrol tasked to protect naval vessels or other assets.
CarDiv	Carrier Division. A small administrative grouping of aircraft carriers.
CIC	Combat Information Center. A section of a warship dedicated to the processing of tactical information from electronic and other sources.
CinCPac	Commander-in-Chief, Pacific Fleet.
CinCPOA	Commander-in-Chief, Pacific Ocean Areas.
CL	Light Cruiser.
CNO	Chief of Naval Operations.
CO	Commanding Officer (of a warship or other post).
Cominch	Commander-in-Chief, United States Fleet
CortDiv	Escort Division. An administrative grouping of destroyer escorts.
CruDiv	Cruiser Division. A small administrative grouping of cruisers.
CV	Fleet Aircraft Carrier.
CVE	Escort Aircraft Carrier.
CVL	Light Aircraft Carrier.
DD	Destroyer.

DE	Destroyer Escort.
DesDiv	Destroyer Division. An administrative grouping of destroyers within a destroyer squadron.
DesRon	Destroyer Squadron. An administrative grouping of destroyers.
Exec	Executive Officer. *See* XO.
LORAN	LOng RAnge Navigation. A radio-based navigation system.
Navy Special	A fuel oil for ships.
OOD	Officer of the Deck. An officer who, during his watch, has responsibility for the navigation and safety of the ship.
OTC	Officer in Tactical Command.
RADM	Rear Admiral.
Shinpū	A more accurate and elegant rendering of "kamikaze."
TBF	A type of American carrier-based torpedo plane.
TBM	A type of American carrier-based torpedo plane.
TBS	Talk Between Ships. A local radio circuit used for communications within a fleet or one of its components.
TF	Task Force. A naval unit, consisting of many different types of warship, established for a particular purpose or mission.
TG	Task Group. A subdivision of a fleet or task force.
Tokkō	"Special attack unit," an abbreviated version of the official designation of the kamikaze units.
TU	Task Unit. A subdivision of a task group.
VADM	Vice Admiral.
XO	Executive Officer. Second in command of a warship or other post.

Suggested Reading

Remarkably little has been written about the typhoons that struck Admiral Halsey's fleet in the final year of the Second World War; these events, after all, burned themselves indelibly into the memories of thousands of sailors, amatuer and professional alike. The only explanation can be that, as monumental as these episodes were, they were just two among many epochal events of the war. Only in such a setting as this worldwide conflagration could the disasters that befell Halsey's fleet pale into the commonplace. Had Typhoon Cobra struck the navy in peacetime, without distractions and the cloak of military censorship, its impact on the nation's imagination would have been greater, and the same is true of Viper's attack.

As it is, only two books have been published before now on the subject, and both are required reading for anyone who wishes to learn something of these typhoons. Like many of the works listed below on the Philippines campaign, they were written by men who played roles in the drama. The first, Hans Christian Adamson and George F. Kosco, *Halsey's Typhoons* (New York: Crown Publishers, 1967), was coauthored by the aerographer who was at the heart of the December battle between man and the elements. The second, C. Raymond Calhoun, *Typhoon: The Other Enemy* (Annapolis, MD: Naval Institute Press, 1981), is a memoir of the captain of the *Farragut*-class destroyer *Dewey*, sister ship to *Hull* and *Monaghan*. Both books contain primary material that is unavailable anywhere else.

Beyond these two books, relatively little exists apart from occasional journal articles, sporadic newspaper accounts, reminiscences in privately published ships' histories, mostly of small circulation, and, of course, the voluminous but unpublished records to be found in the National Archives, the Naval Historical Center, and other repositories. The first of two major exceptions is Herman Wouk's Pulitzer Prize–winning *The Caine Mutiny* (Garden City, NY: Doubleday, 1951). A Pacific war veteran, Wouk knew whereof he wrote. Although it is a work of fiction, the typhoon episode, during which the mutiny occurs and which is based heavily on Cobra, would in itself qualify this book as one of the finest seafaring novels ever written.

The second exception is more general. The best account to place Typhoons Cobra and Viper in the bigger picture of the Pacific war is Samuel Eliot Morison's *History of United States Naval Operations in World War II*, 15 vols. (Boston: Little, Brown, 1947–1962). Morison's volumes, too, are required reading for the student of Third Fleet's Philippines campaign.

As for the Battle of Leyte Gulf, several good accounts are available besides Morison's treatment. As the largest naval battle in history, as well as one of the most controversial, it has spawned a wealth of popular and scholarly narratives. A few of these are Thomas J. Cutler, *The Battle of Leyte Gulf* (New York: HarperCollins, 1994); H. P. Wilmott, *The Battle of Leyte Gulf: The Last Fleet Action* (Bloomington: Indiana University Press, 2005); Kenneth Friedman, *Afternoon of the Rising Sun: The Battle of Leyte Gulf* (Novato, CA: Presidio, 2001); and Carl Solberg, *Decision and Dissent: With Halsey at Leyte Gulf* (Annapolis, MD: Naval Institute Press, 1995).

The kamikaze phenomenon has also received considerable treatment, although the paucity of the Japanese sources in English due to wartime destruction or lack of translation has been a running problem for Western researchers. Firsthand accounts include Rikihei Inoguchi and Tadashi Nakajima, *The Divine Wind: Japan's Kamikaze Force in World War II* (Annapolis, MD: Naval Institute Press, 1958); Ryuji Nagatsuka, *I Was a Kamikaze* (New York: Macmillan, 1972); and Albert Axell and Hideaki Kase, *Kamikaze: Japan's Suicide Gods* (London: Longman, 2002). More recent and quite insightful is Mordecai G. Sheftall, *Blossoms in the Wind: Human Legacies of the Kamikaze* (New York: NAL Caliber, 2005), which draws heavily on interviews with surviving Tokkō officers. An interesting secondary work is Emiko Ohnuki-Tierney, *Kamikaze, Cherry Blossoms, and Nationalisms: The Militarization of Aesthetics and Japanese History* (Chicago: University of Chicago Press, 2002). Other sources include Raymond Lamont-Brown, *Kamikaze: Japan's Suicide Samurai* (London: Cassell, 1999); Bernard Millot, *Divine Thunder: The Life and Death of the Kamikazes* (New York: McCall, 1971); and Denis Warner and Peggy Warner, *The Sacred Warriors: Japan's Suicide Legions* (New York: Van Nostrand Reinhold, 1982).

William F. Halsey, of course, figures in all of these stories. One of America's most popular fighting men, both during the war and thereafter, Halsey nevertheless remains controversial, despite his successes in the Doolittle raid and at Guadalcanal, because of the Battle of Leyte Gulf and the two typhoons. Written by Halsey and J. Bryan III, *Admiral Halsey's Story* (Washington, DC:

Zenger Publishing, repr. 1980) is Halsey's popular postwar autobiography, in which he sets forth his Leyte arguments and his account of Cobra; conspicuously absent, however, is any mention of the court of inquiry that followed the typhoon. Several biographies of Halsey also appeared beginning early in the postwar period, but most of them are brief and uncritical. By far the best is E. B. Potter's more recent *Bull Halsey* (Annapolis, MD: Naval Institute Press, 1985). Potter, too, qualifies as something of a primary source, since he corresponded with Halsey concerning his own Leyte Gulf scholarship.

Other important information about Third/Fifth Fleet operations and the Philippines campaign appears in the biographies of other major participants. E. B. Potter's *Nimitz* (Annapolis, MD: Naval Institute Press, 1976) is a key work that details much of CincPac's oversight of Halsey's campaign; here, too, we have a primary source with material not to be found elsewhere, for Potter and Nimitz were both scholarly collaborators and friends. Thomas B. Buell has written two important but more tangential biographies: *The Quiet Warrior: A Biography of Admiral Raymond A. Spruance* (Boston: Little, Brown, 1974), which presents Spruance as an interesting contrast to Halsey, and *Master of Sea Power: A Biography of Ernest J. King* (Boston: Little, Brown, 1980), which, like *The Quiet Warrior*, is a definitive work. Admiral McCain, unfortunately, has found no biographer, but Theodore Taylor has profiled his counterpart in *The Magnificent Mitscher* (New York: Norton, 1954).

While it is true that, in the words of one Third Fleet veteran, "men make the ship," the ships, too, are important. Among the many works to have appeared since the war on the warships of the Pacific fleet, two of the more relevant and useful when it comes to exploring Typhoon Cobra are Norman Friedman, *U.S. Aircraft Carriers: An Illustrated Design History* (Annapolis, MD: Naval Institute Press, 1983), and Norman Friedman, *U.S. Destroyers: An Illustrated Design History*, rev. ed. (Annapolis, MD: Naval Institute Press, 2004). The statistics and photographs of all of the Third Fleet ship types, of course, can be found in *Jane's Fighting Ships 1944/5* (New York: Arco, 1971; originally published 1947), and brief individual ship histories appear in *Dictionary of American Naval Fighting Ships* (Washington, DC: Naval History Division, Department of the Navy, 1959–1991), which is also available online at the Naval Historical Center Web site (http://www.history.navy.mil/danfs/index.html). Another useful Web site for warship details is the Naval Vessel Register (http://www.nvr.navy.mil). For those wishing to examine a more technical discussion of warship design, see Thomas C. Gillmer and Bruce Johnson, *Introduction to Naval Architecture*, rev. ed. (Annapolis, MD: Naval Institute Press, 1982) and Robert B. Zubaly, *Applied Naval Architecture*, 2nd ed. (Centreville, MD: Cornell Maritime Press, 1996).

Much has been written about the strategy and tactics of the Pacific war, and we have many histories of combat, but the less flashy role of logistics is just as crucial. For this story, see Duncan S. Ballantine, *U.S. Naval Logistics in the Second World War* (Newport, RI: Naval War College Press, 1998), and Worrall Reed Carter, *Beans, Bullets, and Black Oil; The Story of Fleet Logistics Afloat in the Pacific During World War II* (Washington, DC: Government Printing Office, 1953). On the specific subject of at-sea refueling, see Thomas Wildenberg, *Gray Steel and Black Oil: Fast Tankers and Replenishment at Sea in the U.S. Navy, 1912–1992* (Annapolis, MD: Naval Institute Press, 1996).

If knowledge of ship design and logistics are necessary for the naval officer, knowledge of weather is crucial for every mariner. For those wishing a practical background that was available to sailors in 1944, the appropriate editions of the old standards, Nathaniel Bowditch's *American Practical Navigator: An Epitome of Navigational and Nautical Astronomy* (Washington, DC: Government Printing Office, 1943) and Austin M. Knight, *Modern Seamanship*, 10th ed. (New York: Van Nostrand, 1943), are still to be found, though they have, of course, been superceded by their later versions. A fairly recent title, still good but dated in some areas, is William J. Kotsch and Richard Henderson, *Heavy Weather Guide*, 2nd ed. (Annapolis, MD: Naval Institute Press, 1984). For a historical overview of the impact of weather on military operations, see Harold A. Winters, *Battling the Elements: Weather and Terrain in the Conduct of War* (Baltimore, MD: Johns Hopkins University Press, 1998).

The events of the last year or two, especially the effective destruction of a major American city by a hurricane, have focused national attention on tropical cyclones as never before. For further popular reading on this subject, see Pete Davies, *Devil's Music: In the Eye of a Hurricane* (London: Michael Joseph, 2000); Kerry Emanuel, *Divine Wind: The History and Science of Hurricanes* (New York: Oxford University Press, 2005); David E. Fisher, *The Scariest Place on Earth: Eye to Eye with Hurricanes* (New York: Random House, 1994); David Longshore, *Encyclopedia of Hurricanes, Typhoons, and Cyclones* (New York: Checkmark Books, 2000); Jeffrey Rosenfeld, *Eye of the*

Storm: Inside the World's Deadliest Hurricanes, Tornadoes, and Blizzards (New York: Plenum Trade, 1999); and Bob Sheets, *Hurricane Watch: Forecasting the Deadliest Storms on Earth* (New York: Vintage, 2001).

This list of readings would not be complete, of course, without a reference to Joseph Conrad's "Typhoon," published among other places in *Typhoon and Other Stories* (London: W. Heinemann, 1921). Along with Wouk's narrative in *The Caine Mutiny*, this quintessential sea tale gives as realistic and gripping an account of steaming through a tropical cyclone as to be found anywhere.

Index

About the Author

Buckner F. Melton, Jr., holds a doctorate in history from Duke University and a law degree from the University of North Carolina at Chapel Hill. He specializes in areas of national security history, including impeachment, treason, and constitutional war powers. His book *The First Impeachment: The Constitution's Framers and the Case of Senator William Blount* received national attention during the impeachment proceedings against President William J. Clinton. During the impeachment Melton served as an advisor to several members of Congress and as a commentator for National Public Radio, *NewsHour* with Jim Lehrer, and MSNBC. He is also the author of *Aaron Burr: Conspiracy to Treason* and *A Hanging Offense: The Strange Affair of the Warship Somers*. He currently serves as Distinguished Writer-in-Residence and University Press Fellow at Mercer University in Macon, Georgia.